# SECOND WAVE INTERTEXTUALITY
# AND THE HEBREW BIBLE

# RESOURCES FOR BIBLICAL STUDY

*Editor*
Hyun Chul Paul Kim, Old Testament/Hebrew Bible

Number 93

# SECOND WAVE INTERTEXTUALITY AND THE HEBREW BIBLE

*Edited by*

Marianne Grohmann and Hyun Chul Paul Kim

# SBL PRESS
Atlanta

Copyright © 2019 by Society of Biblical Literature

All rights reserved. No part of this work may be reproduced or transmitted in any form or by any means, electronic or mechanical, including photocopying and recording, or by means of any information storage or retrieval system, except as may be expressly permitted by the 1976 Copyright Act or in writing from the publisher. Requests for permission should be addressed in writing to the Rights and Permissions Office, SBL Press, 825 Houston Mill Road, Atlanta, GA 30329 USA.

Library of Congress Cataloging-in-Publication Data

Names: Grohmann, Marianne, 1969– editor.
Title: Second wave intertextuality and the Hebrew Bible / edited by Marianne Grohmann and Hyun Chul Paul Kim.
Description: Atlanta : SBL Press, 2019. | Series: Resources for biblical study ; Number 93 | Includes bibliographical references and index.
Identifiers: LCCN 2019000483 (print) | LCCN 2019009014 (ebook) | ISBN 9780884143659 (ebk.) | ISBN 9781628372427 (pbk. : alk. paper) | ISBN 9780884143642 (hbk. : alk. paper)
Subjects: LCSH: Bible. Old Testament—Criticism, interpretation, etc. | Intertextuality in the Bible.
Classification: LCC BS1171.3 (ebook) | LCC BS1171.3 .S38 2019 (print) | DDC 221.6—dc23
LC record available at https://lccn.loc.gov/2019000483

Printed on acid-free paper.

# Contents

Abbreviations ..................................................................................................ix

Introduction
    Marianne Grohmann and Hyun Chul Paul Kim ...................................1

## Part 1: Inner-Biblical Intertextuality

Eve, Abraham, and the Ethics of (Dis)Obedience: An Intertextual
Reading of Genesis 3 and 22 in Ancient Israel's Ethical Discourse
    J. Todd Hibbard ........................................................................................23

The Literary-Historical Dimensions of Intertextuality in Exodus–
Numbers
    Marvin A. Sweeney ..................................................................................41

Hidden in Plain Sight: Intertextuality and Judges 19
    Kirsten H. Gardner .................................................................................53

Ancestral Voices and Disavowal: Poetic Innovation and Intertextuality
in the Eighth-Century Prophets
    Francis Landy..........................................................................................73

Bloodshed and Hate: The Judgment Oracle in Ezek 22:6–12 and the
Legal Discourse in Lev 19:11–18
    Klaus-Peter Adam ...................................................................................91

Anthology as Intertext: Ambiguity and Generative Interpretation in
Qoheleth
    Hans Decker..........................................................................................113

Prophetic and Proverbial Justice: Amos, Proverbs, and
    Intertextuality
    Timothy J. Sandoval ............................................................................131

Genres, Intertextuality, Bible Software, and Speech Acts
    Tim Finlay ..............................................................................................153

Part 2: Postbiblical Intertextuality

Mikhail M. Bakhtin and Dialogical Approaches to Biblical
    Interpretation
    Patricia K. Tull ......................................................................................175

Between Abandoned House and Museum: Intertextual Reading
    of the Hebrew Bible as Embracing "Abjection"
    Soo J. Kim..............................................................................................191

Intertextuality in the Dead Sea Scrolls
    Lawrence H. Schiffman ......................................................................211

Intertextuality and Canonical Criticism: Lamentations 3:25–33
    in an Intertextual Network
    Marianne Grohmann............................................................................225

Who Is Solomon? Intertextual Readings of King Solomon in
    Reception History
    Susanne Gillmayr-Bucher ..................................................................241

Writing FanFic: Intertextuality in Isaiah and Christopher
    Columbus's *Libro de las Profecías*
    Steed Vernyl Davidson ........................................................................261

Dietrich Bonhoeffer, Dongju Yun, and the Legacies of Jeremiah
    and the Suffering Servant
    Hyun Chul Paul Kim ............................................................................289

Interpreting the Bible in the Age of #BlackLivesMatter:
    The Gideon Story and Scholarly Commitments
    Valerie Bridgeman................................................................................311

Bibliography ....................................................................................... 327
Contributors ...................................................................................... 365

Index of Ancient Sources .................................................................. 367
Index of Modern Authors ................................................................. 382

# Abbreviations

| | |
|---|---|
| AB | Anchor Bible |
| ABS | Archaeology and Biblical Studies |
| AIL | Ancient Israel and Its Literature |
| ANEM | Ancient Near East Monographs |
| *ANQ* | *Andover Newton Quarterly* |
| *A.J.* | Josephus, *Jewish Antiquities* |
| AOTC | Abingdon Old Testament Commentaries |
| *ArsArt* | *Ars Artium* |
| ASCE | *The Annual of the Society of Christian Ethics* |
| *AsJT* | *Asia Journal of Theology* |
| ASV | American Standard Version |
| ATD | Das Alte Testament Deutsch |
| AYBRL | Anchor Yale Bible Reference Library |
| *B. Qam.* | Baba Qamma |
| *BArts* | *Bible in the Arts* |
| BETL | Bibliotheca Ephemeridum Theologicarum Lovaniensium |
| BHS | *Biblia Hebraica Stuttgartensia* |
| BHWJ | Bericht der Hochschule für die Wissenschaft des Judentums |
| *Bib* | *Biblica* |
| *BibInt* | *Biblical Interpretation* |
| BibInt | Biblical Interpretation Series |
| BibOr | Biblica et Orientalia |
| BibRab | Bibliotheca Rabbinica |
| BibSem | The Biblical Seminar |
| BJS | Brown Judaic Studies |
| BJSUCSD | Biblical and Judaic Studies from the University of California, San Diego |
| BKAT | Biblischer Kommentar, Altes Testament |
| BLS | Bible and Literature Series |

| | |
|---|---|
| BMI | The Bible and Its Modern Interpreters |
| BO | Bibliotheca Orientalis |
| BRLJ | Brill Reference Library of Judaism |
| BSB | Berean Study Bible |
| *BTB* | *Biblical Theology Bulletin* |
| BTSt | Biblisch-Theologische Studien |
| BZAW | Beihefte zur Zeitschrift für die alttestamentliche Wissenschaft |
| BZNW | Beihefte zur Zeitschrift für die neutestamentliche Wissenschaft |
| CB | The Church's Bible |
| CBET | Contributions to Biblical Exegesis and Theology |
| *CBQ* | *Catholic Biblical Quarterly* |
| CBQMS | Catholic Biblical Quarterly Monograph Series |
| CBS | Core Biblical Studies |
| CC | Continental Commentaries |
| *ChT* | *Christian Thought* |
| *CI* | *Critical Inquiry* |
| CJAS | Christianity and Judaism in Antiquity |
| ColQuin | Columbus Quincentenary Series |
| *Compar* | *The Comparitist* |
| Contra | Contraversions |
| CQS | Companion to the Qumran Scrolls |
| *CR* | *The Centennial Review* |
| CRÉJ | Collection de la Revue d'Études Juives |
| CRTP | Critical Readers in Theory and Practice |
| CSCO | Corpus Scriptorum Christianorum Orientalium |
| CSHB | Critical Studies in the Hebrew Bible |
| CSRL | Cambridge Studies in Russian Literature |
| *CurBR* | *Currents in Biblical Research* |
| *CurBS* | *Currents in Research: Biblical Studies* |
| *DBI* | Hayes, John, ed. *Dictionary of Biblical Interpretation*. 2 vols. Nashville: Abingdon, 1999. |
| DBW | Dietrich Bonhoeffer Works |
| *Di* | *Dialog* |
| DJD | Discoveries in the Judaean Desert |
| DLB | Dictionary of Literary Biography |
| *DSD* | *Dead Sea Discoveries* |

| | |
|---|---|
| *DSE* | Green, Joel B., ed. *Dictionary of Scripture and Ethics*. Grand Rapids: Baker Academic, 2011. |
| DSS | Dead Sea Scrolls |
| EANEC | Explorations in Ancient Near Eastern Civilizations |
| ECC | Eerdmans Critical Commentary |
| EKKNT | Evangelisch-katholischer Kommentar zum Neuen Testament |
| *EMMM* | Landes, Richard Allen, ed. *Encyclopedia of Millennialism and Millennial Movements*. New York: Routledge, 2000. |
| ESLL | *Educational Studies in Language and Literature* |
| ESV | English Standard Version |
| ETS | Erfurter theologische Studien |
| *EvT* | *Evangelische Theologie* |
| FAT | Forschungen zum Alten Testament |
| FB | Forschung zur Bibel |
| FCB | Feminist Companion to the Bible |
| FOTL | Forms of the Old Testament Literature |
| Git. | Gittin |
| *GKC* | Gesenius, Wilhelm. *Gesenius' Hebrew Grammar*. Edited by Emil Kautzsch. Translated by Arther E. Cowley. 2nd ed. Oxford: Clarendon, 1910. |
| GPBS | Global Perspectives on Biblical Scholarship |
| HAT | Handbuch zum Alten Testament |
| *HBAI* | *Hebrew Bible and Ancient Israel* |
| HBM | Hebrew Bible Monographs |
| HBS | Herders Biblische Studien |
| *HBT* | *Horizons in Biblical Theology* |
| Hermeneia | Hermeneia |
| HThKAT | Herders Theologischer Kommentar zum Alten Testament |
| HTR | *Harvard Theological Review* |
| HUCA | *Hebrew Union College Annual* |
| ICC | International Critical Commentary |
| *IDB* | Buttrick, George A. *The Interpreter's Dictionary of the Bible*. 4 vols. New York: Abingdon, 1962. |
| IEC | *The International Encyclopedia of Communication* |
| Int | *Interpretation* |
| IRT | Issues in Religion and Theology |
| ISBL | Indiana Studies in Biblical Literature |
| ISV | International Standard Version |

| | |
|---|---|
| JAAR | *Journal of the American Academy of Religion* |
| JAJSup | Journal of Ancient Judaism Supplements |
| JAOS | *Journal of the American Oriental Society* |
| JBL | *Journal of Biblical Literature* |
| JDS | Judean Desert Studies |
| JETS | *Journal of the Evangelical Theological Society* |
| JHS | *Journal of Hellenic Studies* |
| JJS | *Journal of Jewish Studies* |
| JKML | *Journal of Korean Modern Literature* |
| JKP | *Journal of Korean Poetics* |
| JPS | *The Holy Scriptures: Tanakh*. Jewish Publication Society, 1917. |
| JR | *Journal of Religion* |
| JRE | *Journal of Religious Ethics* |
| JS | Jüdische Studien |
| JSJSup | Supplements to the Journal for the Study of Judaism in the Persian, Hellenistic, and Roman Periods |
| JSNTSup | Journal for the Study of the New Testament Supplement Series |
| JSOT | *Journal for the Study of the Old Testament* |
| JSOTSup | Journal for the Study of the Old Testament Supplement Series |
| JTS | *Journal of Theological Studies* |
| Jub. | Jubilees |
| KJG | King James Version with Geneva Notes |
| KJV | King James Version |
| KPS | *Korean Poetics Studies* |
| KTC | *Korean Thought and Culture* |
| LALC | Latin American Literature and Culture |
| LB | Wischmeyer, Oda, ed. *Lexikon der Bibelhermeneutik: Begriffe—Methoden—Theorien—Konzepte*. Berlin: de Gruyter, 2009. |
| LD | Lectio Divina |
| LHBOTS | The Library of Hebrew Bible/Old Testament Studies |
| LNTS | The Library of New Testament Studies |
| LPT | The Library of Philosophy and Theology |
| LSAWS | Linguistic Studies in Ancient West Semitic |
| LSTS | The Library of Second Temple Studies |
| LXX | Septuagint |

| | |
|---|---|
| *Marc.* | Tertullian, *Adversus Marcionem* |
| *MJSS* | *Mediterranean Journal of Social Sciences* |
| *ModB* | *Modern Believing* |
| MT | Masoretic Text |
| *MTh* | *Modern Theology* |
| NA²⁸ | *Novum Testamentum Graece*, Nestle-Aland, 28th ed. |
| NAC | New American Commentary |
| *Nar.* | Narratologia |
| NASB | New American Standard Bible |
| NCI | The New Critical Idiom |
| *Neot* | *Neotestamentica* |
| NICOT | New International Commentary on the Old Testament |
| NIV | New International Version |
| *NLH* | *New Literary History* |
| NLT | New Living Translation |
| NRSV | New Revised Standard Version |
| NSKAT | Neuer Stuttgarter Kommentar, Altes Testament |
| NT | New Testament |
| NTSI | New Testament and the Scriptures of Israel |
| OBO | Orbis Biblicus et Orientalis |
| OBT | Overtures to Biblical Theology |
| *ODMC* | Chandler, Daniel, and Rod Munday, eds. *The Oxford Dictionary of Media and Communication*. Oxford: Oxford University Press, 2016. |
| *OEBB* | Coogan, Michael D., ed. *The Oxford Encyclopedia of Books in the Bible*. Oxford: Oxford University Press, 2011. |
| *OEBI* | McKenzie, Steven L., ed. *The Oxford Encyclopedia of Biblical Interpretation*. Oxford: Oxford University Press, 2013. |
| *OEBL* | Strawn, Brent A., ed. *The Oxford Encyclopedia of the Bible and Law*. Oxford: Oxford University Press, 2015. |
| OTL | Old Testament Library |
| OtSt | Oudtestamentische Studiën |
| PH | Poetik und Hermeneutik |
| *PL* | *Philosophy and Literature* |
| *PMLA* | *Proceedings of the Modern Language Association* |
| *Poet* | *Poetics* |
| *Proof* | *Prooftexts: A Journal of Jewish Literary History* |
| *PRR* | *The Presbyterian and Reformed Review* |
| *PRSt* | *Perspectives in Religious Studies* |

| | |
|---|---|
| *PT* | *Poetics Today* |
| PTSDSSP | Princeton Theological Seminary Dead Sea Scrolls Project |
| PTSMS | Princeton Theological Seminary Monograph Series |
| QD | Quaestiones Disputatae |
| *RB* | *Revue biblique* |
| Readings | Readings: A New Biblical Commentary |
| *ResQ* | *Restoration Quarterly* |
| *RevExp* | *Review and Expositor* |
| *RevQ* | *Revue de Qumran* |
| RQ | Römische Quartalschrift für christliche Altertumskunde und Kirchengeschichte |
| RRBS | Recent Research in Biblical Studies |
| RTT | Research in Text Theory |
| SAeth | Scriptores Aethiopici |
| SBAB | Stuttgarter biblische Aufsatzbände |
| SBLDS | Society of Biblical Literature Dissertation Series |
| SBLMS | Society of Biblical Literature Monograph Series |
| *SBLSP* | *Society of Biblical Literature Seminar Papers* |
| SBS | Stuttgarter Bibelstudien |
| SCP | Studies in Contemporary Philosophy |
| SD | Sammlung Dalp |
| SDSS | Studies in the Dead Sea Scrolls and Related Literature |
| *SEÅ* | *Svensk exegetisk årsbok* |
| *Semeia* | *Semeia* |
| SemeiaSt | Semeia Studies |
| SHCANE | Studies in the History and Culture of the Ancient Near East |
| Siphrut | Siphrut: Literature and Theology of the Hebrew Scriptures |
| SIS | Studies in Interactional Sociolinguistics |
| SJLA | Studies in Judaism in Late Antiquity |
| *SJOT* | *Scandinavian Journal of the Old Testament* |
| SOTSMS | Society for Old Testament Studies Monograph Series |
| SRLT | Studies in Russian Literature and Theory |
| SSEJC | Studies in Scripture in Early Judaism and Christianity |
| StBibLit | Studies in Biblical Literature (Lang) |
| STDJ | Studies on the Texts of the Desert of Judah |
| *Sty* | *Style* |
| StudBib | Studia Biblica |

| | |
|---|---|
| SubBi | Subsidia Biblica |
| SymS | Symposium Series |
| Shabb. | Shabbat |
| TBN | Themes in Biblical Narrative |
| *TDOT* | Botterweck, G. Johannes, Helmer Ringgren, and Heinz-Josef Fabry, eds. *Theological Dictionary of the Old Testament*. Translated by John T. Willis et al. 15 vols. Grand Rapids: Eerdmans, 1974–2006. |
| *Text* | *Textus* |
| THKNT | Theologischer Handkommentar zum Neuen Testament |
| *TLZ* | *Theologische Literaturzeitung* |
| TSAJ | Texte und Studien zum Antiken Judentum |
| UBS⁵ | *The Greek New Testament*, United Bible Societies, 5th ed. |
| UTB | Uni-Taschenbücher |
| UTPSS | University of Texas Press Slavic Series |
| *VEcc* | *Verbum et Ecclesia* |
| *VT* | *Vetus Testamentum* |
| VTSup | Supplements to Vetus Testamentum |
| *WBC* | Newsom, Carol, Sharon H. Ringe, and Jacqueline E. Lapsley, eds. *The Women's Bible Commentary*. 3rd ed. Louisville: Westminster John Knox, 2012. |
| WisC | Wisdom Commentary |
| WMANT | Wissenschaftliche Monographien zum Alten und Neuen Testament |
| *WTJ* | *Westminster Theological Journal* |
| *WW* | *Word and World* |
| ZAW | *Zeitschrift für die alttestamentliche Wissenschaft* |
| ZBK | Zürcher Bibelkommentare |
| ZLThK | *Zeitschrift für die gesammte lutherische Theologie und Kirche* |

# Introduction

*Marianne Grohmann and Hyun Chul Paul Kim*

*No text is an island.* Julia Kristeva's hermeneutical analysis has been foundational: "Any text is constructed as a mosaic of quotations; any text is the absorption and transformation of another."[1] At the same time, *nor is a reader an island, either.* Accordingly, we may add that any reader too is a byproduct of a mosaic of cultural traditions, social contexts, and ideological concepts. Put together, both texts and readers share intricate, interactive interconnections in the webs of mutual and multifaceted influences. Texts are constructed in dialogues with other texts, whether intentionally/ uniquely or unintentionally/universally. Readers, too, engage in understanding the texts in light of numerous other readers, be they ancient authors/readers, contemporary readers, and even future readers. How such is the case and what we the interpreters can make out of it have been groundbreaking and rewarding outcomes of the theory of intertextuality.

Intertextuality, in terms of its definition, methodology, and praxis, has been one of the newest and most significant topics in biblical scholarship in recent decades. Ever since its introduction into the fields of biblical studies some decades ago, many works have appeared that cover issues related to methods and interpretive applications of intertextuality. Now at the turn of this century, more and more scholarly works in biblical scholarship either explicitly or implicitly (as "inner-biblical exegesis or allusion") specify the method or issue of intertextuality. In numerous ways, the influence of intertextuality has been enormous in both quantity and quality. The term *intertextuality* is no longer a foreign term in biblical scholarship, and many works using this approach have been published as of late.

---

1. Julia Kristeva, *Desire in Language: A Semiotic Approach to Literature and Art*, ed. Leon S. Roudiez, trans. Thomas Gora, Alice Jardine, and Leon S. Roudiez (New York: Columbia University Press, 1980), 66.

Our aspiration in this volume is neither to narrow down to methodological theories nor to review thoroughly all related thinkers. This book is not intended to be a pioneering work, either, as many substantial works have been produced exponentially. Rather, the collected essays here engage diverse methods and cases of intertextuality that contain various genres and portions of the Hebrew Bible. It is hoped that these essays, as manifold samples, experiment new and expansive ways of intertextuality, showcasing how, why, and what intertextuality has been and thereby presenting possible potentials or directions toward the next stages of this theory and praxis—the second wave of intertextuality in biblical scholarship, so to speak. However, before presenting the essays, a brief review of intertextuality and biblical scholarship, especially in the Hebrew Bible, is in order. Albeit merely selectively, we will first go over influential works on intertextuality in the fields of theory and then in the fields of biblical scholarship.

## 1. Hermeneutics

Before Kristeva, who coined the term *intertextuality*, there were many other theorists. Although the following retrospective genealogy of correlated thinkers is far too limited, it may be worthwhile to name many of them, which inherently displays a form of an intertextual web of the thinkers across generations and ages. Many works by philosophers and linguists have been influential for the birth of this theory, including Immanuel Kant, Karl Marx, G. W. F. Hegel, Jürgen Habermas, Theodor W. Adorno, Hans-Georg Gadamer, Jacques Derrida, Michel Foucault, Paul Ricœur, and Ferdinand de Saussure. Various philosophical and cultural movements—such as phenomenology, romanticism, existentialism, Marxism, deconstructionism, structuralism, poststructuralism, reader-response theory, and the like—have generated pertinent theorists, including Claude Lévi-Strauss, Jacques Lacan, I. A. Richards, Stanley Fish, Wolfgang Iser, Roman Jakobson, Roland Barthes, Michael Riffaterre, Jonathan Culler, and so on. Equally influential, if not more, is the Russian thinker Mikhail M. Bakhtin, whose trenchant work on dialogism Kristeva substantially gives credit.

Without belaboring all the details of these theorists, which are available in numerous publications, we will rehash key insights surrounding Kristeva's intertextuality, especially in hermeneutical dialogues with Bakhtin, Barthes, and Riffaterre. First of all, Bakhtin's dialogism is fundamental to

Kristeva's intertextuality. William Irwin captures the key methodological orientation that "language is dialogical, it always, despite the intentions of speakers and authors, expresses a plurality of meanings, as it is characterized by heteroglossia, a plurality of voices behind each word."[2] The plurality of voices, polyphony, causes hermeneutical doors to be wide open between the text and the reader. Reading, as well as interpreting, is not a one-directional phenomenon (from the text to the reader) but rather dual-directional or multidirectional phenomena reciprocally (between the text[s] and the reader[s]). Kristeva inherits such dialogical aspects with the theory of intertextuality as "permutation of texts." Intertextual dialogism challenges the rigid interpretive or conceptual singularity, as P. Prayer Elmo Raj analyzes: "Both Kristeva and Bakhtin emphasize the doubleness or the dialogic feature of words which interrogates the fundamentals of Western logic, unity and the Aristotelian logic and its propositions on singularity."[3]

On the one hand, Kristeva's intertextuality was embedded in the linguistic and philosophical reactions to structuralism, which tended to be bound by formal objectivity, into poststructuralism, which put equal or more weight on the free subjectivity of the reader. The objective author or authorizer has met multivalent strangers, as Mary Orr sums up Kristeva's theory of intertextuality, as "strangers to ourselves."[4] Intertextuality thus, as the permutation of texts, implies that "there can be no authoritative fixity for interactive, permutational (inter)text."[5] On the other hand, Kristeva's intertextuality equally owes its own theoretical transformation out of her sociopolitical context, when fixed authorities (of the author,

---

2. Cited from David I. Yoon, "The Ideological Inception of Intertextuality and Its Dissonance in Current Biblical Studies," *CurBR* 12 (2012): 62. See William Irwin, "Against Intertextuality," *PL* 28 (2004): 228.

3. P. Prayer Elmo Raj, "Text/Texts: Interrogating Julia Kristeva's Concept of Intertextuality," *ArsArt* 3 (2015): 79.

4. Mary Orr, *Intertextuality: Debates and Contexts* (Malden, MA: Blackwell, 2003), 32. Consider Raj, "Text/Texts," 80: "There is no independent meaning, no independent text and no independent interpretation. Singularity is illusory. The text would become texts to open up the dynamics of intertextuality within and outside the text."

5. Orr, *Intertextuality*, 28. See also Jonathan D. Culler, *The Pursuit of Signs: Semiotics, Literature, Deconstruction* (Ithaca, NY: Cornell University Press, 1981), 110: "What makes possible reading and writing is not a single anterior action which serves as origin and moment of plenitude but an open series of acts, both identifiable and lost, which work together to constitute something like a language: discursive possibilities, systems of convention, clichés and descriptive systems."

powers-that-be, capitalism, etc.) were challenged or even denied. David I. Yoon's emphasis on intertextuality amid the political realm, far more than linguistic or literary convention, is apt: "Intertextuality originated with a political agenda, as a reaction against the social and political milieu.... It is an attempt to take power away from the authority (author), and place it in the hands of the civilian (reader)."[6] Put simply, the reader is no longer an inferior slave to the authoritative text but rather an emancipated, empowered, and equal coproducer, deliverer, or even re-presenter.

Such a liberated role of the reader is augmented in the works of Barthes and Riffaterre, with the theories that put more emphasis on reader than text. Thus, for Barthes, "the death of the author" yields the authorial keys to the reader: "a text is made of multiple writings ... but there is one place where this multiplicity is focused and that place is the reader, not as was hitherto said, the author."[7] Accordingly, "it is language which speaks, not the author ... only language acts, 'performs', and not 'me.'"[8] Put another way, a text, once assembled and presented (e.g., published), has its own life. Orr captures Barthes's theory in one key term as "'dérive', usually translated as drift (as for ships off course, or continents).... The 'dérive' is lack of fixity and direction.... It is a move going directly against the flow."[9]

This multiplying, multidimensional drifting of a text and its meanings has induced the reader-response theory. Just as a text echoes other texts, a reader joins in a myriad of other readers of the text. Culler elucidates the insight suggested by Barthes: "Roland Barthes speaks of intertextual codes as a 'mirage of citations' likely to prove evasive and insubstantial as soon as one attempts to grasp them.... The I that approaches the text is itself already a plurality of other texts, of infinite or, more precisely, lost codes (whose origins are lost)."[10] The plurality of "I" as readers is further developed by Riffaterre: "Intertextual syllepsis claims verifiability by intersubjective response: a number of readers will join up the dots and find a similar resulting pattern of *expansion* of meanings."[11] This expansion of

---

6. Yoon, "Ideological Inception of Intertextuality," 67.

7. Roland Barthes, *Image, Music, Text*, trans. Stephen Heath (New York: Hill & Wang, 1977), 148.

8. Barthes, *Image, Music, Text*, 143.

9. Orr, *Intertextuality*, 35.

10. Culler, *Pursuit of Signs*, 102.

11. Orr, *Intertextuality*, 39 (emphasis original); see also Orr, *Intertextuality*, 40:

meanings leads to Riffaterre's essential axiom that "a poem says one thing and means another."[12]

These recaps and excerpts of key theorists of intertextuality are by no means exhaustive. Nevertheless, the notions of double, multiple dialogues leading to the permutation of texts—and thereby both challenging the author and freeing the reader—have been influential in the recent interpretive (r)evolution and transformation in the fields of biblical scholarship. Likewise, inasmuch as texts are distinguished from authors, so readers are not only emancipated from the authorial control of the texts but also invited into the ever-increasing dialogues with other readers and contexts (of past, present, and future). In her identification of three dimensions ("writing subject, addressee, and exterior texts") of intertextuality, Kristeva's two axes coincide with such divergent yet correlated interactions: "horizontal axis" (subject–addressee; i.e., author–reader) and "vertical axis" (text–context).[13]

However, despite the immense contributions or potentials of intertextuality, theorists and biblical scholars alike have encountered and wrestled with evident questions or limitations of intertextuality in method and praxis. Culler's characterization of intertextuality thus poses questions as to how much and how far we should investigate or rely on the issues of "sources" or "influences": "The study of intertextuality is thus not the investigation of sources and influences as traditionally conceived; it casts its net wider to include anonymous discursive practices, codes whose origins are lost, that make possible the signifying practices of later texts."[14] The hermeneutical problem concerning the control of the codes from the lost origins is further complicated with the consequences of multidimensionality: "Intertextuality does not seem to be simply a continuum on a single dimension and there does not seem to be a consensus about what dimensions we should be looking for. Intertextuality is not a feature of the text alone but of the 'contract' which reading it forges between its author(s) and reader(s)."[15]

---

"Unlike the monolingual Barthes, their bi- or trilingualism opens the 'inter-' and 'text' of intertextuality to properly translinguistic applications and dimensions."

12. Michael Riffaterre, *Semiotics of Poetry* (Bloomington: Indiana University Press, 1978), 1.

13. Kristeva, *Desire in Language*, 66.

14. Culler, *Pursuit of Signs*, 103.

15. Daniel Chandler, "Intertextuality," *Semiotics for Beginners* (London: Routledge, 2004), http://visual-memory.co.uk/daniel/Documents/S4B/.

We should thus recall certain caveats stated by the theorists. For instance, intertextual permutation does not de facto indicate limitless, infinite expansions: "Kristevan intertextuality is therefore not a mosaic, or a limitless web of deferred meanings, but a logical relationship of 'X and/or not X', an 'an(d)other.'"[16] Nor does it defy logic or principle, especially that which is confined or controlled by "language," as Culler points out in his critical appraisal of Riffaterre: "To discover the true meaning of a poem, one must interpret it in accordance with the principles by which it was constructed."[17]

It is no coincidence, therefore, that similar questions have arisen in biblical scholarship. What are certain measures, guidelines, or agreements concerning the issues of sources, influences, or directions? How much control should there be to identify cases of intertextuality? Where does the power lie: in the author, text, or reader? These debates have generated comparable questions: for example, diachronic versus synchronic, citation versus allusion, and author/text-oriented versus reader-oriented.[18] Our essays will present examples of these debates and questions in a variety of

---

16. Orr, *Intertextuality*, 32. "Dialogism is not 'freedom to say everything,'... Rather, it implies a categorical tearing from the norm and a relationship of nonexclusive opposites" (Kristeva, *Desire in Language*, 71).

17. Culler, *Pursuit of Signs*, 98.

18. For reviews and methods on intertextuality in biblical scholarship, see Lyle Eslinger, "Inner-Biblical Exegesis and Inner-Biblical Allusion: The Question of Category," *VT* 42 (1992): 47–58; Benjamin D. Sommer, "Exegesis, Allusion and Intertextuality in the Hebrew Bible: A Response to Lyle Eslinger," *VT* 46 (1996): 479–89; George Aichele and Gary A. Phillips, "Introduction: Exegesis, Eisegesis, Intergesis," *Semeia* 69–70 (1995): 7–18; Patricia K. Tull, "Rhetorical Criticism and Intertextuality," in *To Each Its Own Meaning: An Introduction to Biblical Criticisms and Their Application*, ed. Steven L. McKenzie and Stephen R. Haynes, rev. ed. (Louisville: Westminster John Knox, 1999), 156–80; Tull, "Intertextuality and the Hebrew Scriptures," *CurBS* 8 (2000): 59–83; Karl W. Weyde, "Inner-Biblical Interpretation: Methodological Reflections on the Relationship between Texts in the Hebrew Bible," *SEÅ* 70 (2005): 287–300; Geoffrey D. Miller, "Intertextuality in Old Testament Research," *CurBR* 9 (2010): 283–309; Yair Zakovitch, "Inner-Biblical Interpretation," in *Reading Genesis: Ten Methods*, ed. Ronald Hendel (New York: Cambridge University Press, 2010), 92–118; Yoon, "Ideological Inception of Intertextuality," 58–76; David M. Carr, "The Many Uses of Intertextuality in Biblical Studies: Actual and Potential," in *Congress Volume: Helsinki 2010*, ed. Martti Nissinen, VTSup 148 (Leiden: Brill, 2012), 505–35; Russell L. Meek, "Intertextuality, Inner-Biblical Exegesis, and Inner-Biblical Allusion: The Ethics of a Methodology," *Bib* 95 (2014): 280–91.

approaches. Before presenting these essays, a brief review of intertextuality and its impacts in biblical scholarship should be in order.

## 2. Biblical Scholarship

When it comes to the method and praxis in biblical scholarship, intertextuality is both new and old. It is new insofar as its hermeneutical assumptions are concerned, especially thanks to the emphasis on the interdependence and interconnectedness of texts. Yet, at the same time, it is old, as the applications of intertextuality (in the sense of inner-biblical exegesis) have been demonstrated not only throughout the patristic and medieval commentaries but also within the Hebrew Bible itself; indeed "there is nothing new under the sun" (Eccl 1:9 NRSV)! Before we can talk about authorship or plagiarism, the preserved Hebrew Bible displays ample evidences that the biblical authors and scribal communities have always quoted and alluded to one another.

Whether in conversation with—or inspired by—the theory of intertextuality, Michael Fishbane is one of the founding figures in biblical scholarship. As Kristeva duly gives credit to Bakhtin, so also Fishbane expresses owing the inspiration of this methodology to his predecessors, such as Martin Buber and Nahum M. Sarna.[19] His magnum opus starts with the premise that biblical texts did not originate merely from mechanical copying and transmitting of inherited traditions but also through scribal annotations, editions, reaffirmations, and even reinterpretations over long historical and complex processes—between "traditum" (the received text) and "traditio" (the scribal exegetical annotations).[20] In one respect, such insights stand in line with the millennia-old traditions of midrash.[21] Accordingly, Fishbane's work helps juxtapose key aspects of midrash with the key features of "inner-biblical exegesis" on the con-

---

19. "It was from [Nahum M. Sarna] that I first learned of the phenomenon of 'Inner Biblical Exegesis', and the term, which he used in his own excellent study of Psalm 89" (Michael Fishbane, *Biblical Interpretation in Ancient Israel* [Oxford: Clarendon, 1985], viii).

20. Fishbane, *Biblical Interpretation*, 12, 42.

21. See Jacob Neusner, *What Is Midrash?* (Philadelphia: Fortress, 1987), 16: "Since all Midrash begins in Scripture, we start with an account of what all later exegetes in Judaism learned *through* Scripture about correct interpretation *of* Scripture" (emphasis original). See also Gerhard Langer, *Midrasch*, JS 1; UTB 4675 (Tübingen: Mohr Siebeck, 2016).

tinuous line. Age-old midrashic traditions of Judaism have met their counterpart (or successor, or branch) in the theory of intertextuality of the modern era. In another perspective, Fishbane's systematic categories of inner-biblical exegesis coincide with comparable observations and analyses of redaction criticism. But, whereas redaction criticism tends to focus on disjoints of texts, inner-biblical exegesis pays attention to how a text conjoins with another. Over the course of years, redaction criticism and inner-biblical exegesis have constructively influenced each other with regard to methodological orientation and interpretive applications, as can be found in recent scholarship on the Pentateuch and prophetic literature.[22]

Hence, various methods in biblical scholarship have become more and more in *dialogue* with one another. The significance of intertextual or inner-biblical interconnections have earned a greater respect by scholars, thanks to the importance of reading the biblical texts in the present form as a canon.[23] For instance, as James A. Sanders elucidates, adaptations of biblical texts in Qumran scrolls, as well as numerous Second Temple literature, have provided additional clues for biblical authorship and readership vis-à-vis canonical processes.[24] Jewish exegesis traditions have become instrumental intertextual assets and templates for understanding the biblical texts in dialogue with rabbinic literature and postmodern readers, as expounded in the works by Daniel Boyarin.[25] Odil Hannes Steck has shown a model example of how redaction criticism and intertextuality can

---

22. Consider Jan C. Gertz et al., eds., *The Formation of the Pentateuch: Bridging the Academic Cultures of Europe, Israel, and North America*, FAT 111 (Tübingen: Mohr Siebeck, 2016).

23. Brevard S. Childs, *Introduction to the Old Testament as Scripture* (Minneapolis: Fortress, 1979); James Muilenburg, "Form Criticism and Beyond," *JBL* 88 (1969): 1–18; Rolf P. Knierim, "Criticism of Literary Features, Form, Tradition, and Redaction," in *The Hebrew Bible and Its Modern Interpreters*, ed. Douglas A. Knight and Gene M. Tucker, BMI 1 (Chico, CA: Scholars Press, 1985), 123–65; Erich Zenger, ed., *Die Tora als Kanon für Juden und Christen*, HBS 10 (Freiburg im Breisgau: Herder, 1996); and Georg Steins, *Kanonisch-intertextuelle Studien zum Alten Testament*, SBAB 48 (Stuttgart: Katholisches Bibelwerk, 2009).

24. James A. Sanders, *From Sacred Story to Sacred Text* (Philadelphia: Fortress, 1987).

25. Daniel Boyarin, *Intertextuality and the Reading of Midrash*, ISBL (Bloomington: Indiana University Press, 1994).

converge together toward a synthesis of both diachronic and synchronic exegetical analyses.[26]

These pioneering approaches have been influential for manifold successive explorations of intertextuality in a variety of fields.[27] For instance, in Isaiah scholarship of the last several decades, the concerted efforts of scholarly examinations on the internal connections of key words, phrases, and themes have inspired the "unity" movement.[28] Rather than dissecting differences in the so-called Proto-, Deutero-, and Trito-Isaiah, intertextual studies have helped discover and correlate countless explicit and indirect catchwords (*Stichwörter*) as signposts or markers that occur throughout the whole book of Isaiah. Scholars have thus begun to appreciate reading the prophetic book with continuity, inasmuch as discontinuity, as to how the so-called three Isaiahs would have related to one another both redactionally and in their final form.[29]

Intertextual readings have been expanded to observe interconnections not only in diachronic and synchronic dimensions but also in micro- and macrolevels. Scholars have started to inquire about the placement and

---

26. Odil Hannes Steck, *Studien zu Tritojesaja*, BZAW 203 (Berlin: de Gruyter, 1991).

27. See Danna Nolan Fewell, ed., *Reading between Texts: Intertextuality and the Hebrew Bible* (Louisville: Westminster John Knox, 1992); Barbara Green, *Mikhail Bakhtin and Biblical Scholarship: An Introduction*, SemeiaSt 38 (Atlanta: Society of Biblical Literature, 2000); and Richard B. Hays, Stefan Alkier, and Leroy A. Huizenga, eds., *Reading the Bible Intertextually* (Waco, TX: Baylor University Press, 2009).

28. Roy F. Melugin, "Isaiah 40–66 in Recent Research: The 'Unity' Movement," in *Recent Research on the Major Prophets*, ed. Alan J. Hauser, RRBS 1 (Sheffield: Sheffield Phoenix, 2008), 142–94.

29. Redactionally, on Deutero-Isaiah's editorial role for the book of Isaiah, see H. G. M. Williamson, *The Book Called Isaiah: Deutero-Isaiah's Role in Composition and Redaction* (Oxford: Clarendon, 1994); on Trito-Isaiah's final shaping, see Jacob Stromberg, *Isaiah after Exile: The Author of Third Isaiah as Reader and Redactor of the Book* (Oxford: Oxford University Press, 2011). Synchronically, for linguistic and literary connections, see Willem A. M. Beuken, "The Unity of the Book of Isaiah: Another Attempt at Bridging the Gorge between Its Two Main Parts," in *Reading from Right to Left: Essays on the Hebrew Bible in Honour of David J. A. Clines*, ed. J. Cheryl Exum and H. G. M. Williamson, JSOTSup 373 (London: Sheffield Academic, 2003), 50–60; for a thematic thread, see Roland E. Clements, "A Light to the Nations: A Central Theme of the Book of Isaiah," in *Forming Prophetic Literature: Essays on Isaiah and the Twelve in Honor of John D. W. Watts*, ed. James W. Watts and Paul R. House, JSOTSup 235 (Sheffield: Sheffield Academic, 1996), 57–69.

function not only between chapter 1 and chapter 2 of Genesis, but also between Genesis and Exodus, between Isaiah and Jeremiah, between Deuteronomy and Psalms, between Lamentations and the prophetic texts, between Job and Deutero-Isaiah, and so on.[30] Especially, on the macrolevel, diachronic and synchronic scholarships on the twelve prophetic books have concocted new observations as to how the twelve books may have been compiled together and what implications reading the Book of the Twelve as an editorial anthology (of twelve parts or sections, so to speak) can make.[31] Marvin A. Sweeney, among others, presented equally valuable insights on the importance of not only compositional but also thematic comparisons and contrasts, intertextually, between the MT and the LXX of the Book of the Twelve, as had been lucidly explicated on those between the MT and the LXX of the books of Jeremiah by Louis Stulman previously.[32] In addition to the books of Isaiah, Jeremiah, and the

---

30. On Genesis and Exodus, see Thomas B. Dozeman and Konrad Schmid, eds., *A Farewell to the Yahwist? The Composition of the Pentateuch in Recent European Interpretation*, SymS 34 (Atlanta: Society of Biblical Literature, 2006). On Isaiah and Jeremiah, see Reinhard G. Kratz, "Der Anfang des Zweiten Jesaja in Jes 40,1 f. und das Jeremiabuch," ZAW 106 (1994): 243–61; Benjamin D. Sommer, *A Prophet Reads Scripture: Allusion in Isaiah 40–66*, Contra (Stanford, CA: Stanford University Press, 1998); and Patricia Tull Willey, *Remember the Former Things: The Recollection of Previous Texts in Second Isaiah*, SBLDS 161 (Atlanta: Scholars Press, 1997). On Deuteronomy (Pentateuch) and Psalms (Psalter), see Patrick D. Miller, "Deuteronomy and Psalms: Evoking a Biblical Conversation," *JBL* 118 (1999): 3–18. On Lamentations and the prophetic texts, see Carleen Mandolfo, *Daughter Zion Talks Back to the Prophets*, SemeiaSt 58 (Atlanta: Society of Biblical Literature, 2007); and Mark J. Boda, Carol J. Dempsey, and LeAnn Snow Flesher, eds., *Daughter Zion: Her Portrait, Her Response*, AIL 13 (Atlanta: Society of Biblical Literature, 2012). On Job and Deutero-Isaiah, see Jiseong James Kwon, *Scribal Culture and Intertextuality: Literary and Historical Relationships between Job and Deutero-Isaiah*, FAT 2/85 (Tübingen: Mohr Siebeck, 2016); Alan Cooper, "The Suffering Servant and Job: A View from the Sixteenth Century," in *"As Those Who Are Taught": The Interpretation of Isaiah from the LXX to the SBL*, ed. Claire M. McGinnis and Patricia K. Tull, SymS 27 (Atlanta: Society of Biblical Literature, 2006), 189–200; and Katharine Dell and Will Kynes, eds., *Reading Job Intertextually*, LHBOTS 587 (London: T&T Clark, 2013).

31. James D. Nogalski, *Literary Precursors to the Book of the Twelve*, BZAW 217 (Berlin: de Gruyter, 1993).

32. Marvin A. Sweeney, *The Twelve Prophets*, 2 vols., BO (Collegeville, MN: Liturgical Press, 2000); Louis Stulman, *The Other Text of Jeremiah: A Reconstruction of the Hebrew Text Underlying the Greek Version of the Prose Sections of Jeremiah* (Lanham, MD: University Press of America, 1985).

Book of the Twelve, many of the Psalms scholars have also put a collaborative effort to observe the concatenated links within the Psalter, thereby comprehending the arrangement and interrelationship of the psalms in light of the overall shaping on the whole.[33] For example, while the holistic flow from lament to praise remains intact in its larger shape,[34] the intricate shifts and recurrences of lament psalms within the collection of predominantly hymnic psalms, or those of praise psalms amid lament psalms, are no longer seen to be haphazard editing but rather intentional arrangement with new interpretive ramifications.[35]

Beyond the intratextual links within the textual corpus and the intertextual correlations within and/or among the book(s), scholars have further worked on intertextuality in larger scopes as well. Thus, in the intertestamental relations, scholars have examined various ways the New Testament passages adopt and reapply the Hebrew Bible texts.[36] When it comes to the where, what, and how of the intertextual connections from the Hebrew Bible to the New Testament, the space does not permit reviewing the vast amount of works available (and this is a topic for another publication).[37] We have also noted how valuable the great volumes of midrashic texts and traditions can be in the intertextual studies of the canonized biblical books. By the same token, reception histories of the patristic exegetical texts, medieval documents, Renaissance paintings and frescoes, Reformation music, and so on have become legitimate ways to engage in intertextual dialogues.

---

33. Gerald H. Wilson, *The Editing of the Hebrew Psalter*, SBLDS 76 (Chico, CA: Scholars Press, 1985).

34. Claus Westermann, *Praise and Lament in the Psalms*, trans. K. R. Crim and R. N. Soulen (Atlanta: John Knox, 1981).

35. Nancy L. deClaissé-Walford, *Introduction to the Psalms: A Song from Ancient Israel* (St. Louis, MO: Chalice, 2004); deClaissé-Walford, ed., *The Shape and Shaping of the Book of Psalms: The Current State of Scholarship*, AIL 20 (Atlanta: SBL Press, 2014).

36. For example, see Craig A. Evans and James A. Sanders, *Luke and Scripture: The Function of Sacred Tradition in Luke–Acts* (Minneapolis: Fortress, 1993); Evans and Sanders, eds., *Paul and the Scriptures of Israel*, JSNTSup 83 (Sheffield: Sheffield Academic, 1993); Steve Moyise and Maarten J. J. Menken, eds., *Isaiah in the New Testament*, NTSI (London: T&T Clark, 2005); Hays, Alkier, and Huizenga, eds., *Reading the Bible Intertextually*; Craig A. Evans and Jeremiah J. Johnston, eds., *Searching the Scriptures: Studies in Context and Intertextuality*, LNTS 543; SSEJC 19 (London: T&T Clark, 2015).

37. For the impact of intertextuality on New Testament scholarship, among many others, see B. J. Oropeza and Steve Moyise, eds., *Exploring Intertextuality: Diverse Strategies for New Testament Interpretation of Texts* (Eugene, OR: Cascade, 2016).

Last, but not least, intertextuality as an interpretive correlation between text and context, or between (ancient) context and (contemporary) context, has come to the surface with many substantial contributions. In a way, this approach intertwines with reader-response criticism (the reader) and postcolonialism (the context). Tat-siong Benny Liew has demonstrated the interpretive importance of contextual correlations, which he terms "inter(con)textuality."[38] Accordingly, we can consider such inter-con-textual endeavors in tune with many thought-provoking interpretive works from the minoritized interpretive locations, which have brought forth indispensable contributions to biblical scholarship, including gender criticism, feminist/womanist reading, queer reading, disability criticism, Africana/African-American reading, Latino/a reading, Asian/Asian-American reading, Native-American reading, and so on.[39] In other words, intertextuality that incorporates contextuality has much to learn from these aforementioned interpretive works. Furthermore, out of the interrelations of contexts, scholars have also engaged in cross-cultural analyses of biblical texts via comparative studies, such as folklore, divination, art, literature, and film.[40] Indeed, just like postmodernism, the theory of intertextuality has branched out into numerous directions, applications, and reformulations in biblical scholarship.

When a house or a city gets extended and enlarged with so many evolving shapes, it becomes difficult to accurately identify it. Similarly, intertextuality as a biblical hermeneutical method or phenomenon has been expanded in such diversified and innovative ways that scholars share inherent problems concerning its (unique) values and (controllable) methods. At the outset, in this volume, we propose to subdivide intertextuality in two broad—yet interrelated—categories:

---

38. Tat-siong Benny Liew, *Politics of Parousia: Reading Mark Inter(con)textually*, BibInt 2 (Leiden: Brill, 1999).

39. Among countless works that have come out, see the volumes of collected essays in the Texts @ Contexts series, edited by Athalya Brenner-Idan, Archie C. C. Lee, and Gale A. Yee (Minneapolis: Fortress).

40. Archie C. C. Lee, "The Chinese Creation Myth of Nu Kua and the Biblical Narrative in Genesis 1–11," *BibInt* 2 (1994): 312–24; Samuel Cheon, "Filling the Gap in the Story of Lot's Wife (Genesis 19:1–29)," *AsJT* 15 (2001): 14–23; and Hyun Chul Paul Kim and M. Fulgence Nyengele, "Murder S/He Wrote? A Cultural and Psychological Reading of 2 Samuel 11–12," in *Pregnant Passion: Gender, Sex, and Violence in the Bible*, ed. Cheryl A. Kirk-Duggan, SemeiaSt 44 (Atlanta: Society of Biblical Literature, 2003), 95–116.

1. Inner-Biblical Intertextuality (within the canonical corpus of the Hebrew Bible)
2. Postbiblical Intertextuality (outside the Hebrew Bible)

These two divisions are arbitrary, as many aspects of one section/approach overlap with those of the other section/approach (in fact, postbiblical intertextuality inherently encompasses inner-biblical intertextuality). Nevertheless, we believe it to be worthwhile to make this general distinction. In terms of the features of inner-biblical exegesis, various attempts to identify the scopes, limits, and types of intertextuality have been made. Among many, Richard B. Hays proposed the following seven criteria: availability, volume, recurrence, thematic coherence, historical plausibility, history of interpretation, and satisfaction.[41] Benjamin D. Sommer suggested the following patterns of inner-biblical exegesis and allusion, notably (diachronic) directions from Jeremiah to Deutero-Isaiah: explicit citation, implicit reference, inclusion, exegesis, influence, revision, polemic, reversal, repredication, fulfillment of earlier prophecies, typological linkages, the split-up pattern, sound play, word play, word order, and so on.[42]

These various criteria and patterns are useful in the exegetical tasks. However, it still remains controversial as to how to distinguish between (verbatim) citation and (indirect) allusion. Whether quotations or allusions, inasmuch as identifying the interconnections and retrieving the literary directions are valid, so the interpreter can find it helpful to expound the unique authorial/redactional intention, historical contexts, and thematic implications of each text. In analogy, when we read the parallel texts among the New Testament Synoptic Gospels, analyzing the common and different materials among Matthew, Mark, and Luke can help illuminate not only the source and redactional routes but also what is unique in each book in terms of each's own authorship, worldview, and even theology. Comparisons, and contrasts, between two biblical texts thus have helped gain new insights that uniquely reside in each text.

What about the ample hermeneutical gaps between the text and the reader, between the text and the (ancient/modern) contexts?[43] Similar

---

41. Richard B. Hays, *Echoes of Scripture in the Letters of Paul* (New Haven: Yale University Press, 1989), 29–32.
42. Sommer, *Prophet Reads Scripture*, 6–72.
43. "Texts are instrumental not only in the construction of other texts but in the construction of experiences.... Intertextuality blurs the boundaries not only

problems remain as to how to establish the mutual connection, where the similarities and differences lie, and what implications such connections provide. These hermeneutical quests may go back to Krister Stendahl's call for biblical theology—and biblical hermeneutics—to be descriptive, and not prescriptive: to describe what "it meant" and not what "it means."[44] That which an interpreter finds to be "normative" (or "center" or *Mitte*) in the Hebrew Bible can thus be disputed by other texts, contexts, and concepts, as Walter Brueggemann's monumental tome attests ("core testimony," "countertestimony," "unsolicited testimony," and "embodied testimony").[45] What intertextuality can contribute here, too, may not be the rigid methodological rules per se. Rather, intertextuality that embraces the roles of readers and (contemporary) contexts can invite the potentials of dialogue, and debate, in multifaceted interchanges. While we value the text's descriptive roles, its prescriptive implications from the reader's vantage point can be reciprocally enriching, in which divergent or contending concepts stand in tension or dialogue with each other, as recently suggested in the post-Shoah Jewish biblical theology by Marvin Sweeney.[46]

## 3. Applications

The essays in this volume come out of the papers presented at the inaugural year of the Intertextuality and the Hebrew Bible consultation/section at the Annual Meeting of the Society of Biblical Literature (Atlanta, 2015), along with the papers invited afterwards with the similar approaches. When the section's name had to be formed, the leadership team had to deliberate whether to call it "Intertextuality *in* the Hebrew Bible" or "Intertextuality

---

between texts but between texts and the world of lived experience" (Chandler, "Intertextuality").

44. Krister Stendahl, "Biblical Theology, Contemporary," *IDB* 1:418–32; see also Ben C. Ollenburger, "What Krister Stendahl 'Meant': A Normative Critique of 'Descriptive Biblical Theology,'" *HBT* 8 (1986): 61–98. For distinguishing biblical theology from dogmatic theology, we should also trace back to Johann Philipp Gabler; see Rolf P. Knierim, *The Task of Old Testament Theology: Method and Cases* (Grand Rapids: Eerdmans, 1995), 495–56.

45. Walter Brueggemann, *Theology of the Old Testament: Testimony, Dispute, Advocacy* (Minneapolis: Fortress, 1997); see also Erhard S. Gerstenberger, *Theologies in the Old Testament*, trans. John Bowden (London: T&T Clark, 2002).

46. Marvin A. Sweeney, *Reading the Hebrew Bible after the Shoah: Engaging Holocaust Theology* (Minneapolis: Fortress, 2008).

*and* the Hebrew Bible." Although we chose the latter phrase, it is our hope that our intertextual works demonstrate interpretive engagements both within and outside the Hebrew Bible. Our main subject has to do with the texts of the Hebrew Bible first and foremost. At the same time, however, our intention is for our intertextual conversation partners not to be limited to the Hebrew Bible but to embrace dialogue partners with the variant manuscripts, Second Temple texts, and the New Testament, as well as subsequent literature, art, music, and so on.

Part 1, "Inner-Biblical Intertextuality," presents the essays that deal with strong cases of intertextual phenomena within the canonical corpus of the Hebrew Bible. In a way, these works tend to be more geared toward the author/text-oriented intertextual approaches. J. Todd Hibbard's "Eve, Abraham, and the Ethics of (Dis)Obedience: An Intertextual Reading of Genesis 3 and 22 in Ancient Israel's Ethical Discourse" explores the literary and thematic interconnections between Gen 3 and Gen 22 with regard to the ambiguous depictions on moral choice. More than verbal correlations, these two texts, when compared together, provoke a conceptual tension between disobedience (Gen 3) and obedience (Gen 22) toward the divine tests. Hibbard's intertextual (and intratextual) reading engages exegetical and theological dialogues of these two texts, resulting in new interpretive insights and in-depth ramifications on the issues of justice, theodicy, morality versus limitations of obedience, human choices, and so on.

Marvin A. Sweeney, in "The Literary-Historical Dimensions of Intertextuality in Exodus–Numbers," expounds intertextual readings of select legal materials in the Pentateuch. Juxtaposing intertextuality with the redactional strata, Sweeney delineates the transitioning processes and implications of the texts that concern the dedication of the firstborn, for example, Exod 22:28–29 and 23:14–19 as the basic E-stratum texts for the later J-stratum texts of Exod 13:1–16 and 34:10–27. These texts of the sanctification of the firstborns are developed into the motif of the Levites to replace the firstborns in, for example, Num 3:11–13, 40–43, 44–51 and 8:13–19—each text with its own inner-biblical exegetical themes and functions. Then, even larger intertextuality builds connections to 1 Sam 1–3, which describes the northern Israelite tradition of the firstborns, rather than the Levites, who should have assumed the role of the priests. This essay thus illustrates how the intertextual analyses of the redactional development can help understand both the contextual and conceptual processes of a threaded theme, such as that of the priesthood in the Pentateuch.

Kirsten H. Gardner's "Hidden in Plain Sight: Intertextuality and Judges 19" attempts an intertextual anatomy of Judg 19, with citations and allusions as thorough and extensive as one can make. Combining narrative criticism with intertextuality, Gardner examines a wide range of unique word combinations and phrases, especially those tied to the motif of violence. In tune with Fishbane's systematic categories, being more than haphazard echoes, Gardner's intertextual contacts are grouped by key thematic categories: the usurpation of the throne, hospitality and feasting vis-à-vis betrothal, the absence of divine intervention, the abandonment of the foreign wife/maid, and illicit worship practices. Such an intertextual study contributes to discovering thematic connections and tracing the leitmotifs, thereby helping comprehend the ways Judg 19 dialogues and develops its own unique messages.

Francis Landy, in "Ancestral Voices and Disavowal: Poetic Innovation and Intertextuality in the Eighth-Century Prophets," reevaluates key theoretical issues of Kristeva and Riffaterre, in concert with the literate society and authorship in the Israelite prophetic literature. Surveying select types of intertextuality, especially polyphony and sign systems, Landy investigates the books of Amos and Hosea with respect to the intertextual boundaries and tensions. This investigation creatively looks at the two books' intertextuality vis-à-vis key echoed Genesis texts and resultant implications. Another example explicates the intertextual connections between Micah and Isaiah, again exploring how the intertextual similarity generates thematic and interpretive differences.

Klaus-Peter Adam's "Bloodshed and Hate: The Judgment Oracle in Ezek 22:6–12 and the Legal Discourse in Lev 19:11–18" mediates the intertextual correspondences of lexicographic and thematic overlaps between the Holiness Code in Lev 19 and the Priestly undercurrents in Ezek 22, inspecting both similarities and differences. In addition to the compositional analyses of the two texts, this intertextual reading yields these additional thematic insights: Ezek 22 underscores the urban setting of the ruling elites, whereas Lev 19 bespeaks the rural setting of the lay community in kinship.

Hans Decker, in "Anthology as Intertext: Ambiguity and Generative Interpretation in Qoheleth," makes a nice complementary, comparative work with that of Gardner. If Gardner's intertextual study (on Judg 19) uses a telescope to observe as many celestial stars as one may find on the macrolevel, then Decker's intertextual study (on Eccl 10:5–11 and 7:1–3) adopts a microscope to investigate atomic molecules on the microlevel.

Thus, focusing on the minute intertextual correlations of a few verses in Qoheleth's anthology, Decker delineates how each saying in the anthology converses and conflicts with the adjacent sayings and, consequently, presents reinforcing and/or paradoxical counterarguments, thereby mirroring the very world and outlook with which Qoheleth must have been residing and wrestling.

Timothy J. Sandoval's "Prophetic and Proverbial Justice: Amos, Proverbs, and Intertextuality" contributes an intertextual perspective to the debate about the influence of wisdom books like Proverbs on Amos or vice versa. He further addresses the question raised by Samuel Terrien and Hans Walter Wolff, and more recently by John L. McLaughlin, as to whether Amos belonged to a wisdom school of sorts. The study follows Bakhtin, focusing on the dialogic relations and intertextual links between Amos and Proverbs, by drawing on several examples beyond the surface categories of source and influence.

Tim Finlay, in "Genres, Intertextuality, Bible Software, and Speech Acts," links considerations about genre and intertextuality with Bible software, vis-à-vis Aristotle's four causes with speech act theory. Finlay further gives some background information about tagging and empirical work for finding and classifying intertextuality beyond the Bible. These approaches and insights are exemplified by an intertextual reading of the Ruth story.

Part 2, "Postbiblical Intertextuality," features the essays that reach beyond the inner-biblical canonical corpora, such as extracanonical, postbiblical reception history as well as contemporary texts/contexts in hermeneutical dialogues. In a way, these works tend to be more geared toward the reader/context-oriented approaches. Patricia K. Tull's "Mikhail Bakhtin and Dialogical Approaches to Biblical Interpretation" recapitulates important concepts by Bakhtin concerning dialogism, polyphony, and intertextuality. Tull places particular emphasis on two aspects of Bakhtin's thinking for their importance to biblical studies. First, to challenge the overvaluation of originality, Bakhtin regards the dialogical nature of the Bible, lending shape to inner-biblical exegesis. Second, a dialogical approach to biblical texts and exegesis arranges theological and ethical claims in a pluralistic framework, as it pertains, for example, to the field of environmental ethics referencing Gen 1:26–28, Isa 40:12–31, and Ps 104.

Soo J. Kim, in "Between Abandoned House and Museum: Intertextual Reading of the Hebrew Bible as Embracing 'Abjection,'" marks two poles in the discussions about intertextuality. For her, the abandoned house of treasure is the place of experts and diachronic research, while the museum is the place where lay people are guided. Kim echoes voices about the concept of the "implied author" who can only be activated by readers. At the end of her paper she presents a reading of Jer 38:28 in an undergraduate class setting as illustration.

Lawrence H. Schiffman's "Intertextuality in the Dead Sea Scrolls" observes and expounds various cases of intertextuality, not only between the Dead Sea Scrolls and the Hebrew Bible, but also among the Dead Sea Scrolls manuscripts. Key analyses of select Qumran texts and the different types of intertextuality (e.g., 4QNum$^b$; 4QDeut$^n$; CD 10:14–17; 11QT 65:2–5; CD 10:17–19; CD 9:2–8; 1QapGen 19:14–20; 11QT 11–29; 1QS 10–11; CD 14:17–22; 1QS 7:7–16) present the Dead Sea Scrolls corpora as prime and prolific examples of intertextual echoes in the Hebrew Bible. These readings demonstrate the diverse yet logical ways in which the Qumran sectarians were likely the pioneers and prolific practitioners of intertextuality.

Marianne Grohmann, in "Intertextuality and Canonical Criticism: Lam 3:25–33 in an Intertextual Network," probes the methodological potentials of juxtaposing intertextuality and canonical criticism via reception history. Reassessing the similarities and differences in these methods, Grohmann engages bidirectional analyses, rather than one-way analysis, of the intertextual links for Lam 3:25–33. These links include select Hebrew Bible texts, New Testament texts, and rabbinic literature. The resultant insights demonstrate not only that the New Testament texts are firmly rooted in the textual and sociocultural traditions of the Hebrew Bible and rabbinic literature but also that these different texts represent different contextual and thematic voices that place text—and its unique (re)interpretation—in hermeneutical dialogues with other texts and traditions.

Susanne Gillmayr-Bucher's "Who Is Solomon? Intertextual Readings of King Solomon in Reception History" develops a methodological framework for analyzing the manifold history of interpretative, artistic, and literary adaptions of biblical figures. She combines aspects of intertextuality, interfigurality, and blending theory, developed by Gilles Fauconnier and Mark Turner. As an example, she traces the biblical King Solomon from inner-biblical exegesis to three poems from the eighteenth to twentieth centuries—by John Greenleaf Whittier, Heinrich Heine, and Matthias Hermann, respectively.

Steed Vernyl Davidson, in "Writing FanFic Intertextuality in Isaiah and Christopher Columbus's *Libro de las Profecías*," presents Christopher

Columbus as reader and interpreter of the Bible, especially of the book of Isaiah. Davidson defines intertextuality as "recycling" and "reuse of previous material" and follows four themes in Columbus's writing: global geography, the conversion of foreigner, the wealth of the nations, and the divine imperium.

Hyun Chul Paul Kim's "Dietrich Bonhoeffer, Dongju Yun, and the Legacies of Jeremiah and the Suffering Servant" follows traces of two biblical characters, the prophet Jeremiah and the Suffering Servant, in two distinct contexts in the early twentieth century: in the work of the German protestant theologian Dietrich Bonhoeffer and the Korean martyr Dongju Yun. Kim illustrates the intertextual relationships first between biblical verses of the books of Jeremiah and Isaiah and then in examples of poems by Dietrich Bonhoeffer and Dongju Yun.

Valerie Bridgeman, in "Interpreting the Bible in the Age of #BlackLivesMatter: The Gideon Story and Scholarly Commitments," expands the concept of intertextuality to black activism and scholarship. Referencing the story of Gideon as a starting point for current struggles for freedom, she also refers to Ps 137 in her quest to reveal the ways in which biblical texts speak into present-day violent events.

As these essays will present and probe, it remains a matter of choice how one considers whether intertextuality (as a mode of exegesis) is *science* or *art*.[47] It also remains a task to experiment and evolve through constant scrutiny and adjustment. Such tasks, however, have been marvelously exemplified in the very biblical texts, as the scriptural texts extend their own intertextual dialogues toward our/readers' own participation into those dialogues.[48] One certain thing remains that, to make an effective intertextual observation, one ought to read the Bible, as much as—if not more than—consulting the concordance or computer softwares. Such a task of finding the webs of intertextual connections both within and outside the Bible can be daunting. But, as the biblical texts themselves testify to the mutual dialogues, among the authors, traditions, themes, contexts,

---

47. "The weighing of such evidence (and hence the identification of allusions) is an art, not a science" (Sommer, *Prophet Reads Scripture*, 35).

48. "There is a constant interplay, an ongoing interchange, between everyday affairs and the word of God in the Torah—Scripture.... Midrash as the process of mediation between the Word of God in Scripture and the world in which we live and serve realizes the continuity, in the here and now, of the original revealed TorahTestament" (Neusner, *What Is Midrash?*, 103).

and lived worlds, so can our attuned listening to those echoes and humble observations of those connections be truly rewarding and inspiring. So, we invite all readers to these extended inner-biblical, intertextual, and inter-contextual dialogues.[49]

---

[49]. Special thanks to Marelize Bruner and Sarah Moon, faculty assistants and students at Methodist Theological School in Ohio, for creating the indexes of modern authors and ancient sources, respectively.

Part 1
Inner-Biblical Intertextuality

# Eve, Abraham, and the Ethics of (Dis)Obedience: An Intertextual Reading of Genesis 3 and 22 in Ancient Israel's Ethical Discourse

*J. Todd Hibbard*

As John Barton and others have shown, ancient Israel understood the basis of its ethical actions in several ways. In his most recent work on the topic, Barton notes that there were at least three different articulations of frameworks for ethical and moral action in Israel.[1] These included: (1) natural order, (2) obedience to the divine (a version of divine command theory), and (3) imitation of God. Of these, the second, obedience to the divine, is widely regarded (certainly among general readers) as the most common basis of ethical action in the Hebrew Bible. To be sure, there are several passages in the Hebrew Bible that demand human behaviors on this ground even if, as Barton notes, it is not as pervasive as is assumed.[2] Additionally, such a ground for moral action is not always presented without complications. To take just one broad example, one thinks of Jeremiah's complaint that he has urged moral choices only to conclude that YHWH has deceived him (Jer 20:7). So, while one may recognize that obedience to YHWH's declared will was clearly present in ancient Israel as a ground for moral action, one may also recognize that there is occasionally a certain ambivalence about this in our sources.

This brings us to the present study of Gen 3 and 22, both of which have been subject to innumerable individual analyses, but none that examines them jointly to my knowledge.[3] It is my argument that a com-

---

1. John Barton, *Ethics in Ancient Israel* (Oxford: Oxford University Press, 2014).
2. Barton, *Ethics in Ancient Israel*, 127–28.
3. Tryggve N. D. Mettinger notes the Abraham story in Gen 22 as a similar story, but he does not explore the similarities in detail; see Tryggve N. D. Mettinger, *The*

parative analysis of these two texts from the perspective of moral choice reveals an ambivalence about obedience to the divine as a foundation for human moral action.[4] The ambivalence becomes apparent on a close, critical reading that highlights elements of each that are at odds with each text's narrative conclusion. To anticipate the conclusions of this study: in Gen 3, the first human couple might be commended for partaking of the forbidden fruit, and in Gen 22, Abraham might reasonably be criticized for attempting to carry out YHWH's demand to slaughter his son. While these conclusions about each text individually are not unheard-of, the present study demonstrates how the two narratives contain similarities that put these conclusions in sharper relief. To demonstrate these interpretations, I offer a comparative analysis of the texts that demonstrates their thematic and narrative similarities. The point will be to show how each text's portrayal of the test in question expresses the ambivalence of the author(s) about obedience to the divine as a basis for ethical action.

My aim is not to provide a comprehensive analysis of these two complicated passages. Indeed, such an undertaking would require a lengthy monograph. Rather, my goal here is much more modest but, I think,

---

*Eden Narrative: A Literary and Religio-historical Study of Genesis 2–3* (Winona Lake, IN: Eisenbrauns, 2007), 49–55. One likely reason scholars have failed to examine the two texts simultaneously is undoubtedly because they are ascribed to two different authors according to the classical Documentary Hypothesis. Genesis 3 is regarded as a J text, while Gen 22 was usually attributed to E, though since the existence of the E document has been called into question there are certainly dissenters to that view (most of whom assign the chapter to J). The result of this source division is that the two texts are treated in isolation from each other. Those who take a more synchronic or final-form approach to Genesis might be regarded as more likely to explore thematic or theological associations between the two texts, but this has turned out rarely to be the case. Rather, among scholars writing from this perspective, each narrative's place in the book is treated in its location or larger unit.

4. Ethical thought in the Hebrew Bible is often associated with both the laws in the Pentateuch and the musings of the wisdom literature. Both of these collections provide insights into ancient Israel's ethical and moral formulations, but increasingly scholars are also turning to portions of the narrative literature for explorations of ethical and moral thinking. See, for example, Gordon J. Wenham, *Story as Torah: Reading Old Testament Narrative Ethically* (Edinburgh: T&T Clark, 2000); Eryl W. Davies, "Ethics of the Hebrew Bible: The Problem of Methodology," *Semeia* 66 (1995): 43–53; and John W. Rogerson, "Old Testament Ethics," in *Text in Context: Essays by Members of the Society for Old Testament Study*, ed. A. D. H. Mayes (Oxford: Oxford University Press, 2000), 116–37, esp. 125–27.

important: to examine these two passages *in light of each other* in order to ascertain each one's contribution to ancient Israel's ethical discourse. The study proceeds in two parts. In the first part, I offer an examination of thematic similarities that may be detected on an intertextual reading of the two passages. The second part builds on this examination and offers an analysis of obedience to YHWH's command as a basis for ethical or moral action.[5]

An observation about using the term *intertextual*: In recent years, the popularity of this mode of analysis is easily confirmed; the number of books and articles with the term in their title is so large that listing them all is impractical. Not all scholars have been pleased with this proliferation of so-called intertextual studies. Their displeasure generally is rooted in the criticism that the term is used too loosely and without precision, such that these studies lack methodological clarity. Additionally, because the term is used as an umbrella term that does not designate a methodology per se but rather identifies an orientation or disposition toward the text, it is often the case that scholars use the term to foreground different aspects of that orientation. So, let me stipulate at the outset what I do and do not mean by the term intertextual in the title of this essay. I use the term to identify a reading strategy in which these two texts are read in light of each other *intentionally*. That is not to say, however, that no warrant for doing so occurs in the texts themselves. Indeed, part of my argument relies on finding just such a warrant. However, I am not suggesting that in these two texts, Gen 3 and 22, the reader encounters quotations, allusions, or other verbal contacts that point to each other; neither am I suggesting that one text has influenced the composition of the other; finally, nor am I indicating that one text has absorbed the other.[6] Rather, in using the term intertextual, I am gesturing toward a way of reading and interpreting that recognizes common *thematic* and *narratological* features in these two

---

5. This ethical position is known in general philosophical discourse as divine command theory. The classic presentation of the dilemma of this position is offered by Socrates in *Euthyphro* (and is often referred to as the "Euthyphro dilemma"). I generally avoid using the language of divine command theory in this study, however, because it has traditionally not been used by biblical scholars who address this topic. See Bernhard Lang, "Three Philosophers in Paradise: Kant, Tillich, and Ricouer Interpret and Respond to Genesis 3," *SJOT* 28 (2014): 298–314.

6. For these notions of intertextuality, see Elaine Martin, "Intertextuality: An Introduction," *Compar* 35 (2011): 148–51.

texts. Some readers may object to using the term in this way. They may see my approach as straying too far from that which the term intertextuality customarily identifies, notwithstanding the term's varied meanings. This is a criticism which I accept. Nevertheless, I call this an intertextual study of Gen 3 and 22 because it seems like the most fitting, if problematic, term to label how I want to analyze this text. *Caveat lector.*

## Gen 3 and Gen 22: An Intertextual View

Let us begin by establishing the thematic and narrative similarities between the two passages. As outlined below, it is clear that there are correspondences between the two narratives that establish the basis of a comparative analysis of Gen 3 and 22.

| Gen 3 | Gen 22 |
|---|---|
| Directive ("Do not eat") | Directive ("Take your son") |
| Test (unstated but implied) | Test (stated: נסה) |
| Human act (*disobedience*) | Human act (*obedience*) |
| Threat of life or death (human couple) | Threat of life or death (Isaac) |
| Sacred location (Eden) | Sacred location (Mount Moriah) |

First, both texts are part of the limited number of texts in the Hebrew Bible depicting divine tests of human beings.[7] This idea or theme is generally, but not always, conveyed through the use of נסה. Indeed, Gen 22:1 uses this term: "After these things God tested [נסה] Abraham" (NRSV). Gen 3 lacks the specific terminology, but, as Tryggve N. D. Mettinger and Terje Stordalen have argued, it is best to view the passage as a narrative about testing.[8] Therefore, I conclude that both passages contribute to the

---

7. Other examples include the book of Job. Several other individual texts in the Hebrew Bible assert YHWH's ability and willingness to test human beings (Exod 15:25; 16:4; 20:20; Deut 8:2, 16; 13:4 [Eng. 13:3]; 33:8; Judg 2:22; 3:1, 4; Ps 26:2; Job 4:2).

8. Terje Stordalen in particular has argued that the plot of the story signals that testing is its primary theme. See Terje Stordalen, *Echoes of Eden: Genesis 2–3 and the Symbolism of the Eden Garden in Biblical Hebrew Literature*, CBET 25 (Leuven:

same thematic or theological conversation in ancient Israel and early Judaism, one that addresses an important aspect of the nature of human and divine interactions conceptualized as instances in which an individual's fidelity to God is tested.[9]

Second, both passages begin with a directive from YHWH. In Gen 22, this is voiced as a command, while in the case of Gen 3, there is knowledge of a previous prohibition:

> And the LORD God commanded the man, "You may freely eat of every tree of the garden; but of the tree of the knowledge of good and evil you shall not eat, for in the day that you eat of it you shall die." (Gen 2:16–17 NRSV)

> After these things God tested [נסה] Abraham. He said to him, "Abraham!" And he said, "Here I am." He said, "Take your son, your only son Isaac, whom you love, and go to the land of Moriah, and offer him there as a burnt offering on one of the mountains that I shall show you." (Gen 22:1–2 NRSV)

As is clear, the directive or prohibition is stated such that there can be no misunderstanding about what is required.[10] The reader is not provided with an explanation of why the suggestively labeled "tree of the knowledge of good and evil" is off limits nor why Abraham must sacrifice his son.[11]

---

Peeters, 2000), 27; and Mettinger, *Eden Narrative*, 23, 49–55. Mettinger notes that scholars have not paid attention to this as a "testing" narrative. He notes because the specific vocabulary does not appear, "one might therefore hesitate to speak of a test in the present text. The important thing, however, is not whether we have the precise terminology but whether the plot confronts us with what may be denoted as a test, and I believe this is precisely the case" (Mettinger, *Eden Narrative*, 23). See also Robert P. Gordon, "The Ethics of Eden: Truth-Telling in Genesis 2–3," in *Ethical and Unethical in the Old Testament: God and Humans in Dialogue*, ed. Katharine J. Dell, LHBOTS 528 (New York: T&T Clark, 2010), 30.

9. Jean Louis Ska, *The Exegesis of the Pentateuch: Exegetical Studies and Basic Questions*, FAT 66 (Tübingen: Mohr Siebeck, 2010), 97–110.

10. Ziony Zevit disputes the idea that there is a clear prohibition in Gen 2:17 based on the use of לא rather than אל but this is not persuasive; see Ziony Zevit, *What Really Happened in the Garden of Eden?* (New Haven: Yale University Press, 2013), 123–24. See *GKC* §107o.

11. The meaning and translation of the phrase "knowledge of good and evil" (הדעת טוב ורע) has been the subject of immense debate. For a recent overview of the matter, see John Day, *From Creation to Babel: Studies in Genesis 1–11*, LHBOTS 592

That God is commanding arbitrarily in each case is one reasonable conclusion; that God is acting against the protagonists' best interests is another. Nevertheless, in both cases, obedience to YHWH's directive defines the parameters of the test.

The threat of death represents another area of thematic similarity between the two passages, though the threat functions differently in each passage. In Gen 2, the stated penalty for consuming the fruit of the tree is death: "in the day that you eat of it [ביום אכלך] you shall die [מות תמות]" (2:17). Precisely what is in view here has been a subject of much debate, but the straightforward reading of the text indicates that the human(s) will physically die should he (they) consume fruit from the tree.[12] I base this conclusion on the fact that the other texts in which מות תמות occurs all portray instances of physical death.[13] I am also inclined to see the threat here as stipulating immediate death; otherwise, the chronological marker at the beginning of the sentence (ביום) would be meaningless. Additionally, it is not unreasonable to find here a threat of capital punishment, though other interpretations are also plausible. Even if one concludes that the death envisioned here is the lost chance at immortality, physical death is in view.[14]

There is more to this area of comparison. In the Gen 3 narrative, the human actors disobey the divine prohibition, but they do not die in any normal sense of the term. This incongruity has prompted all sorts of explanations.[15] I do not intend to survey them here; I only want to note that the couple does not die.[16] That is, the text includes the threat of death, but

---

(Edinburgh: T&T Clark, 2013), 41–44. In addition, see Michaela Bauks, "Erkenntnis und Leben in Gen 2–3: Zum Wandel eines ursprünglich weisheitlich geprägten Lebensgriffs," *ZAW* 127 (2015): 20–42. A novel interpretation informed by Mesopotamian ophiomancy has recently been put forward in Duane E. Smith, "The Divining Snake: Reading Genesis 3 in the Context of Mesopotamian Ophiomancy," *JBL* 134 (2015): 31–49.

12. A brief overview of the major lines of interpretation may be found in Day, *From Creation to Babel*, 38–41.

13. Besides Gen 2:17, see Gen 20:7; 1 Sam 14:44; 22:16; 1 Kgs 2:37, 42; 2 Kgs 1:4, 6, 16; Jer 26:8; and Ezek 3:18; 33:8, 14.

14. See Mettinger, *Eden Narrative*, 59.

15. Zevit, *What Really Happened*, 166–69. See also R. W. L. Moberly, "Did the Interpreters Get It Right? Genesis 2–3 Reconsidered," *JTS* 59 (2008): 22–40.

16. The fact that they do not die might be the rationale for the curses that follow in 3:14–19, since 2:17 does not anticipate these. At any rate, it seems unlikely that the

death does not actually occur. The same happens in Gen 22, albeit for different reasons. Here, Abraham is ordered to cause the death of his son, but God's agent (מלאך יהוה) halts the impending death (22:11–12). As in Gen 3, a threatened death fails to materialize. The fact that both texts mandate death and then fail to follow through is a noticeable point of similarity.

Finally, in both cases the test takes place in a sacred location. In Gen 3, the garden of God is the location in which the test takes place (Gen 2:8). In Gen 22, the action occurs on Moriah (Gen 22:2), a location elsewhere associated with the Jerusalem temple (2 Chr 3:1), the most sacred space in ancient Israel.[17] This serves to heighten the sacred quality of the test as well as the actions taken by the individuals involved. Sacred space is reserved for sacred acts.

In summary, there is sufficient evidence for interpreting Gen (2–)3 and 22 in light of each other. The thematic and narrative similarities between the two are clear, but the evidence does not give us good grounds for concluding how the commonalities came to be. Fortunately, that question, though interesting, remains ancillary to the issue I wish to pursue in the remainder of this article: what do the similarities reveal to us about how obedience to the divine was viewed by each text's author(s)? Additionally, what might we conclude about the contribution of these texts to the development of ancient Israel's ethical thought?

## Consideration of Obedience in Gen 3 and 22

As Barton noted several years ago, ethics is rarely dealt with in biblical studies, particularly if one means by that questions that normally arise in moral philosophy.[18] In his recent full-length treatment of ethics in

---

narrator intended to portray God as lying (though the ancient Near East abounds with portrayals of deities lying to human beings—see, e.g., Adapa). Bernard F. Batto has suggested that that narrator portrays YHWH simply as "innocently mistaken"; see Bernard F. Batto, *Slaying the Dragon: Mythmaking in the Biblical Tradition* (Louisville: Westminster John Knox, 1992), 61.

17. Wenham argues that Eden is also depicted as a temple; see Gordon J. Wenham, "Sanctuary Symbolism in the Garden of Eden Story," in *Proceedings of the Ninth World Congress of Jewish Studies, Division A: The Period of the Bible* (Jerusalem: Magnes, 1985), 19–25.

18. John Barton, *Understanding Old Testament Ethics: Approaches and Explorations* (Louisville: Westminster John Knox, 2002), 45–54. One recent attempt is that of Yoram Hazony, who attempts to read the Hebrew Bible as philosophical literature, an

ancient Israel, he notes that the model of obedience to the divine (ancient Israel's version of divine command theory) does appear in the Hebrew Bible, but he enumerates important ways in which the model "is frequently mitigated or even explicitly denied."[19] By this, he generally means that obedience to YHWH is given a rational basis; it is rarely the case that the biblical text simply demands obedience to a command from YHWH without offering a compelling reason. Such reasons include: ways in which the covenant makes obedience rational; how motive clauses added to laws attempt to persuade the reader of the law's correctness; the way in which laws present ideals rather than enforceable statutes; the Torah's uniqueness as an argument for the rationality of observing its laws; and, finally, the notice in Ezek 20:25 that YHWH required some laws that were not good, which on Barton's interpretation rules out divine command theory since it assumes that all laws are good.[20] Though not each of these arguments is equally convincing, Barton lays out a credible case for questioning the view that ancient Israel held the notion that blind obedience to YHWH was the ethical norm. In a recent article on moral discourse in the Old Testament, Joseph Ryan Kelly has taken a different approach to Barton's taxonomy of ethical models and demonstrated further the problems accompanying any attempt to evaluate obedience as a model for ethical thought in ancient Israel.[21] He draws a distinction between first- and second-order moral discourse and notes that in many cases, the language of obedience is a grammar for talking about ethics rather than an ethical foundation itself.

While both Barton and Kelly offer important considerations of how ancient Israel conceptualized and expressed its ethical commitments, I wish to add another angle to the discussion. I suggest that Gen 3 and 22

---

interpretive mode that includes room for a consideration of ethics. See Yoram Hazony, *The Philosophy of the Hebrew Scriptures* (Cambridge: Cambridge University Press, 2013). Alternatively, philosophers have long mined the biblical text in their work (e.g., Kierkegaard, Spinoza, etc.). One notable recent attempt in the area of theodicy that offers a reading of Gen 22 is Eleonore Stump, *Wandering in Darkness: Narrative and the Problem of Suffering* (Oxford: Oxford University Press, 2012), esp. 258–307; cf. Seizo Sekine, "Philosophical Interpretations of the Sacrifice of Isaac," in *Congress Volume: Ljubljana 2007*, ed. André Lemaire, VTSup 133 (Leiden: Brill, 2010), 339–66.

19. Barton, *Ethics in Ancient Israel*, 134.
20. Barton, *Ethics in Ancient Israel*, 134–56.
21. Joseph Ryan Kelly, "Orders of Discourse and the Function of Obedience in the Hebrew Bible," *JTS* 64 (2013): 1–24.

offer ambivalence about the "obedience to the divine" model by constructing scenarios in which obedience is deeply problematic. By problematizing the model, these narratives call it into question as a model for ethical behavior. In Gen 3, that knotty scenario is made apparent through the human couple's *disobedience*, while in Gen 22, the problem is made apparent through Abraham's *obedience*. The thematic similarities between these two narratives outlined earlier bring the disobedience/obedience contrast into sharper relief and provide a basis upon which to use these two narratives to speak to the same issue.

If these narratives are also statements of ambivalence about this model as a basis for ethical action, we should ask how these texts present such ambivalence. To insist that they are ambivalent makes room for the recognition that interpretations that condemn the first human couple in Gen 3 and laud Abraham in Gen 22 have warrant in the text while also recognizing that the obverse is true. That is, there is warrant in the relevant texts for commending Eve and condemning Abraham. How do the texts accomplish this? In the remainder of this study, I wish to focus on how the test in each case serves as an expression of ambivalence over the "obedience to the divine" model. In so doing, I will raise questions in both Gen 3 and 22 about the nature of the test, the basis of moral decision-making, the reward or punishment as incentive, and the portrayal of the divine.

In Kelly's article cited earlier, he notes that these and other episodes in Genesis do not "determine ethical principles for readers of the text to follow—readers neither avoid the fruit from trees in the midst of gardens nor offer their children as burnt offerings."[22] That is true. However, I do think the content of the tests can be probed in attempts to understand what the author(s) thought about obedience as a model. So, what do we learn in such an examination? In Gen 3, the couple is asked to forgo fruit which conveys certain benefits. Of course, the particularity of the test—consuming fruit from a tree—is simply the mechanism by which the author raises the discussion about choosing between two goods and the use of one's own judgment in making that choice. So, the content of the test pits obedience against such things as wisdom. In such a context, the first human couple's disobedience to the divine command is depicted as an assertion of their own autonomy and is based on their own assessment of the situation.[23] The

---

22. Kelly, "Orders of Discourse," 23.
23. Moberly, "Did the Interpreters Get It Right?," 22–40.

tree from which they partake—the suggestively labeled tree of knowledge of good and bad—is described in such a way that were they not to partake from it, one would not be mistaken in questioning their discretion. The serpent informs them when they eat from it their "eyes will be opened" (נפקחו עיניכם) and that they will be "like god(s)" (כאלהים), both of which are *affirmed* in the aftermath of their partaking (3:5; cf. 3:7, 22).[24] These assertions connote something attractive and desirable in the biblical tradition.[25] In particular, the phrase פקח עין, "to open the eyes," is always a *positive* image or metaphor in the Old Testament.[26] Additionally, the actual description of the tree highlights the benefits conferred by it. Genesis 3:6 reports:

> The woman saw that the tree was good for food [תרה האשה כי טוב העץ למאכל],
> that it was a delight to the eyes [וכי תאוה הוא לעינים],
> and that the tree was desirable for making one wise [ונחמד העץ להשכיל].[27]

The language used here is found in positive statements about wisdom and discernment in other texts in the Hebrew Bible, particularly in the wisdom literature.[28] Moreover, Gen 3:6 is nearly an exact match of the description of the other trees in the garden which are provided for the human couple's sustenance in Gen 2:9. The primary addition is that the forbidden tree is "desirable for making one wise"—a statement offered by the narrator and the veracity of which is never called into question.[29]

---

24. This is not meant to exonerate the serpent for its role in the human act of disobedience. As Gordon notes, the description of the serpent at the beginning of the scene as more crafty or cunning (ערום) than other animals "is not meant to be complimentary" ("Ethics of Eden," 16). Nevertheless, the serpent is correct on the facts as stated.

25. The phrase "you will be like god(s)" recalls the decision in Gen 1 to make humankind in the divine image. While these are not identical, they are similar.

26. In addition to this phrase's use in Gen 3:5, 7, see Isa 35:5; 42:7; Prov 20:13; Dan 9:13.

27. Unless otherwise indicated, all biblical translations are my own.

28. For example, שכל in the *hiphil* is found repeatedly in contexts in which it describes the positive quest for wisdom and discernment; cf. Deut 29:8 [Eng. 29:9]; Prov 1:3; 10:5, 19; 14:35; 15:24; 16:20, 23; 17:2, 8; 19:14; 21:11, 12, 16; Pss 2:10; 14:2; 32:8; 36:4 [Eng. 36:3]; 53:3 [Eng. 53:2]; 94:8; 119:99.

29. Joseph Blenkinsopp suggests that the woman may already have been aware of the benefits to be conferred by the tree; see Joseph Blenkinsopp, *Creation, Un-Creation, Re-Creation: A Discursive Commentary on Genesis 1–11* (London: T&T Clark, 2011), 76.

The attractive description of the forbidden tree—a description that matches what is elsewhere in the Hebrew Bible commended—suggests that the author is constructing a test the basis of which can be called into question. Simply put, how could the woman (and man) not be expected to partake of the fruit given the benefits it confers? From this perspective, disobedience to the divine is the ethical choice. Why should God withhold this from them? Here John Day's explanation likely explains the author's motivation:

> Indeed, in the light of the Old Testament as a whole, it is difficult to see why God should want humans to remain ignorant of the knowledge of good and evil for ever. The most likely explanation is that God disapproves of the first humans acquiring the knowledge of good and evil by the assertion [of] their human autonomy in disobedience to his explicit command.[30]

While this is the most likely explanation, this simply accentuates the problem that the tree is prohibited to the couple by God.

Some scholars mitigate this point by noting that the human couple's response to YHWH makes it clear that, whatever they gained through eating the fruit, it was not what they expected.[31] What did they come to know? As verse 7 makes clear, they understood that they were naked: "Then the eyes of both were opened, and they knew that they were naked" (NRSV). It must be pointed out, however, that this recognition of their physical state is a bodily recognition of their humanity.[32] As such, we might reasonably see here another element of the author's ambivalence about the model.

This brings us to a consideration of Eve in the narrative.[33] As Carol Meyers has recently asserted in *Rediscovering Eve: Ancient Israelite Women in Context*, "Eve is arguably the major character in the Eden story. She has a larger speaking role than her male counterpart. She is certainly the more

---

30. Day, *From Creation to Babel*, 44.
31. See, e.g., Gordon, "Ethics of Eden," 26.
32. This, too, may harken back to Gen 1:27, where humans are created in the image of God (see also 5:3 and 9:6). As many commentators have noted, צלם is often connected with the physical image of a deity; see Num 33:52; 2 Kgs 11:18; Ezek 7:20; 16:17; 23:14; Amos 5:26; 2 Chr 23:17.
33. Of course, the woman is not actually called "Eve" until Gen 3:20. I refer to her as Eve simply for the sake of convenience.

active character."[34] It is noteworthy that the serpent converses with the woman, not the man. Why is this so, given that she enters the story after the male character? Phyllis Trible notes, "If the serpent is 'more subtle' than its fellow creatures, the woman is more appealing than her husband. Throughout the myth, she is the more intelligent one, the more aggressive one, and the one with greater sensibilities."[35] Indeed, it is the woman who recognizes the benefits of the tree, not the man. While the serpent nudges her toward this recognition, she, through her own evaluation of the tree's qualities, decides to eat. Through her own agency, she makes a moral choice to seek what would enhance her own existence. That this choice puts her at odds with the divine prohibition raises more questions about the divine prohibition than her decision. To be sure, her act is disobedient and transgressive, but her choice is also moral. Successive centuries of interpreters have vilified her because she acted disobediently, but the morality of her choice must be acknowledged. Indeed, in my view, the narrative our author has created forces the reader to see her as both disobedient and moral.[36] Additionally, her act is courageous, since the threatened punishment for disregarding the prohibition is death (2:17).

Let us step back for a moment and ask: should Eve forgo the fruit? For those who would answer in the affirmative, there appear to be two reasons. First, YHWH has prohibited partaking of the fruit. Second, the penalty for consumption is death. Both of these are, in some sense, compelling. For those who answer in the negative, there appears to be only one reason: enhanced human existence marked by wisdom (the claim that she will not die is not really a reason to consume, only a recognition that the threatened penalty will not occur). Genesis 2:7 does state that the tree is good for food and a delight to the eyes, but as we noted above, these characteris-

---

34. Carol Meyers, *Rediscovering Eve: Ancient Israelite Women in Context* (Oxford: Oxford University Press, 2011), 59. Meyers goes on to call her the "protagonist" of the story.

35. Phyllis Trible, "Eve and Adam: Genesis 2–3 Reread," *ANQ* 13 (1973): 253. See also the comments of Susan Niditch: "She is no easy prey for a seducing demon, as later tradition represents her, but a conscious actor choosing knowledge." Susan Niditch, "Genesis," in *Women's Bible Commentary*, ed. Carol Newsom, Sharon H. Ringe, and Jacqueline E. Lapsley, 3rd ed. (Louisville: Westminster John Knox, 2012), 31.

36. In my view, the most trenchant feminist critiques of Gen 3 are those that focus on its later misogynistic interpretations rather than the narrative itself. For a brief overview, see Anne W. Stewart, "Eve and Her Interpreters," in Newsom, Ringe, and Lapsley, *Women's Bible Commentary*, 46–50.

tics apply to the nonforbidden trees as well. The only added quality—and, therefore, compelling reason—is the prospect that the fruit will make her wise. Note that I have not included the serpent's argument in Gen 3:5 here. While some might question this, I do so because the narrator's description of what convinces her in verse 6 does not replicate the serpent's rationale. In other words, the narrator does not simply say that she was convinced by the serpent. While the snake's claims undoubtedly are meant to play some role in how and why she decides as she does, it is noteworthy that the reasons stated by the narrator derive from her own assessment of the situation. So, what becomes the basis of her decision? She decides based on her own autonomous judgment, not the divine decree.

What makes this a narrative that displays ambivalence about the divine decree, that is, the content of the test? Her choice eventuates in humans who are like god(s) and fully cognizant of their own humanity, both of which suggest that she has chosen wisely. It is true that she suffers a penalty for her disobedient act (as do the man and serpent), but it seems to me that the benefits outweigh the penalties (Gen 3:16, 23). She is exonerated in some sense. This analysis also compels the concomitant conclusion that obedience to the divine—which would have caused her to forfeit these benefits—as a basis for moral action must be balanced against other competing rationales, in this case autonomous human judgment.

Finally, we need to consider YHWH in the text: What kind of deity makes available the possibility of enhanced human existence only to prohibit the woman and man from availing themselves of this enhancement? Additionally, the penalty or consequence (either is a possible reading) of eating the fruit is death, but that does not occur. At least, that is one way to interpret what YHWH has done in the text of Gen 3. It is true that the reader might interpret God's actions as *preventing* the couple's death, but if so, the text never states this. It might equally have been an empty threat. The serpent intimates as much (3:4–5). At any rate, the ambivalence over the obedience to the divine model to which I wish to draw attention is anchored in the choice YHWH creates for the couple. Is it really in their best interests to obey YHWH and forgo the fruit? Why would YHWH expect as much? It seems as if the test is really designed simply to gauge their willingness to abide by YHWH's dictates regardless of whether such decrees are in their best interests. Yes, they forfeited the possibility of immortality when YHWH expelled them from the garden, but such immortality would, apparently, have come at the cost of forfeited wisdom and recognition of their full humanity.

What about Gen 22? The text's positive understanding of Abraham's act is clear. For Abraham's willingness to kill his son, he is hailed as a God-fearer (22:12), a description that recalls Job (Job 1:1, 8; 2:3).[37] In something of an added postscript to the whole scene, the covenant promise is reiterated that Abraham's offspring shall be numerous, be successful, and carry residual benefit for other peoples (Gen 22:16–18; cf. 12:2; 13:16; 15:5).[38] This positive evaluation of Abraham in the narrative is elaborated in many ways in the postbiblical literature of Second Temple Judaism and early Christianity, but, interestingly, not in the Hebrew Bible itself.[39]

Given all this, how is the content of the test called into question? The obvious answer would be that ritual killing of children is condemned in the Hebrew Bible, so how could the reader be expected to take such a test seriously?[40] While there is merit to that line of questioning, I do not actually think it addresses the question in the best way. As with the consideration of the Gen 3 text, I think the best answer is one that looks at what the human protagonist—in this case Abraham—stands to gain or lose through his actions. If we ask, then, what Abraham stands to gain through his obedience, the answer appears to be: nothing. Moreover, unlike Gen 2–3, no penalty is stated for failure to comply. To put the matter differently: exactly what is being tested about Abraham? The answer must be his willingness to act as directed by God. Hence, Abraham obeys simply because he is told to perform the act, apparently in an effort to show his

---

37. This is one of many similarities between the two stories. See Ska, *Exegesis of the Pentateuch*, 111–39.

38. Most critical scholars argue that Gen 22:15–19 is a later addition to this chapter. See Claus Westermann, *Genesis 12–36*, trans. J. J. Scullion, CC (Minneapolis: Augsburg, 1985), 355.

39. See the thorough treatment of postbiblical elaboration of this tale in Jon D. Levenson, *The Death and Resurrection of the Beloved Son: The Transformation of Child Sacrifice in Judaism and Christianity* (New Haven: Yale University Press, 1993), especially chapters 14–16, as well as the essays in Edward Noort and Eibert J. C. Tigchelaar, eds., *The Sacrifice of Isaac: The Aqedah (Genesis 22) and Its Interpretations*, TBN 4 (Leiden: Brill, 2002). Important Second Temple elaborations include Jub. 17, 4 Macc 16, Heb 11, and Jas 2. I take the absence of any reference to this episode elsewhere in the Hebrew Bible as an important clue to its late date of composition.

40. Much has been written on the subject of child sacrifice in ancient Israel. Texts such as Exod 13:1; 22:28b, 29; and Mic 6:7 suggest its practice at some point, though eventually it was condemned. For an overview, see Heath D. Dewrell, *Child Sacrifice in Ancient Israel*, EANEC 5 (Winona Lake, IN: Eisenbrauns, 2017); and Levenson, *Death and Resurrection*, 3–17.

fidelity to God. However, unlike the Gen 3 text, we have a fuller portrait of Abraham, and that additional material adds considerably to how we should evaluate Abraham's actions.

In Gen 18:22–33, Abraham acts in ways that are dissimilar to his behavior in Gen 22 and which present a more pressing challenge to the Abraham of Gen 22.[41] In response to YHWH's expressed intention to destroy Sodom and Gomorrah, Abraham raises the issue of divine justice and questions whether YHWH will indeed act responsibly and justly. Abraham drives home the point with two pointed questions: "Will you indeed sweep away the righteous with the wicked (18:23)?" and "Shall not the judge of all the earth do justice (18:25)?" With these two questions, Abraham voices his own concern that divine justice must, at a minimum, protect the innocent. For God to sanction or promote the death of those undeserving of such a fate would call into question God's own reliability in maintaining justice. After all, it seems plausible that one could expect, Abraham seems to be saying, that God would meet if not exceed human standards of justice and fairness.[42] If YHWH could not be counted on to discriminate between the innocent and the wicked, allegiance to YHWH would seem risky at best and pointless at worst. The bargaining session that follows Abraham's questions takes the role of the innocent in a society one step further by arguing that their presence in the larger community possesses the capacity to stave off calamity. In other words, YHWH should view the presence of the innocent as not simply worthy of escaping death themselves, but also capable of saving even the wicked, given the right critical mass. The important point about this text from the perspective of this study is Abraham's insistence that YHWH's own sense of justice ought to prevent him from killing the innocent. In giving voice to this position, Abraham is forceful and bold with God—in other words, just what he is lacking in the Akedah narrative.[43]

Abraham's unwillingness to "push back" against the divine request in Gen 22 is quite startling in light of these two preceding narratives. Why,

---

41. Ronald Hendel stresses the different portrayals of Abraham in these two passages; see Ronald Hendel, *Remembering Abraham: Culture, Memory, and History in the Hebrew Bible* (New York: Oxford University Press, 2005), 37–41.

42. Joseph Blenkinsopp, "The Judge of All the Earth: Theodicy in the Midrash on Genesis 18:22–33," *JJS* 41 (1990): 3–12.

43. Nowhere is this more evident than when he states: "Far be it from you to do such a thing" (Gen 18:25 NRSV).

given his strong moral sensibility in chapter 18, does Abraham not interrogate the divine request? On what basis does he conclude that he should comply with God's demand? For readers of this narrative, it is frustrating that we have no access to Abraham's inner decision-making process as in Gen 3 with Eve. Rather, we are forced to intuit his decision-making process on the basis of his actions and his conversation with his son, Isaac. Unlike the Gen 3 text, we know of nothing specific that Abraham stands to gain by complying with the divine request. All we witness is Abraham's unquestioning obedience. If my contention is correct, however, that this narrative wishes to call into question this model as a basis for moral action, this fact might be part of the point. For his obedience, Abraham is praised (just as for their disobedience, the first couple is condemned), but other factors suggest the situation and, therefore, the moral considerations are more complex and complicated. Moreover, we noted earlier that Eve's act was based on her own autonomous judgment about what she stood to gain. Does Abraham exercise his own autonomous judgment or simply obey the divine? While it is more difficult to separate these two in Gen 22, it is hard to imagine that his own autonomous judgment would lead him to believe that this course of action—which will eventuate with him killing his son—is advisable.[44]

With Eve, we noted that though her action was transgressive and disobedient, it was nonetheless moral given what she stood to gain. In Abraham's case, we are forced to note something of the opposite: though his action is obedient, it is nonetheless immoral. Why? Because to follow through with it is to engage in activity that is condemned in the Hebrew Bible elsewhere. Moreover, just as Eve's choice bore some negative consequences, it also yielded benefits. In this case, Abraham's choice was commended by God (22:12), but it appears to have destroyed his relationship with Isaac.[45] First, as verse 19 makes clear, Abraham returns to his young men *alone*, despite the fact that he had informed them earlier that he *and* Isaac would return together. The language used by the author bespeaks an intentional contrast between verses 6 and 8 and verse 19:

---

44. It is sometimes claimed that Abraham knew God would not allow him to follow through with the act and kill Isaac. This cannot be the case, however. To be a test, Abraham must truly believe that he is going to kill Isaac. To claim otherwise would mean the episode is not really a test.

45. Mitchell J. Gauvin, "Can Isaac Forgive Abraham?," *JRE* 45 (2017): 83–103.

And the two of them walked along together [וילכו שניהם יחדו].
And they walked along together [וילכו יחדו].

The contrast could not be more evident. In the first case, it is Abraham and Isaac who comprise "the two of them" walking; that is precisely what is lacking in the second text, where "they" refers to Abraham and his men, but not Isaac. Moreover, Abraham and Isaac are never portrayed as interacting in Genesis again. The next time we see Isaac with his father is at his burial (25:9), and the text locates his residence not in Beersheba, Abraham's final home, but in Beer-lahai-roi with his brother Ishmael (24:62; 25:11). It appears that Abraham's act of faithfulness to God pushed his beloved son toward his half-brother and not his father (a clear intimation that Isaac is *not* his only son as 22:2 asserts). His obedience to God came at the cost of a relationship with his son, the son of promise. How ironic, then, that the episode in Gen 22 concludes with a reaffirmation of the covenant!

This brings us to a brief consideration of God in the narrative. The strongest argument in favor of seeing this test as providing a limitation to this ethical model is the author's portrayal of YHWH. In short, how could one expect to obey unquestioningly a deity who proposes such a "monstrous test"?[46] While it is true that the messenger of God intervenes to halt the killing, this in no way mitigates the horror of what God has required of Abraham (and Isaac!). While individuals and/or peoples often suffer as the objects of YHWH's wrath in the Old Testament, the suffering inflicted by this test on both father and son are nearly beyond comprehension. If one accepts the argument of this study, however, that is the point: the author has constructed a test that expresses the limits of unquestioning obedience. Such a test forces one to ask whether God has in mind the best interests of the one being tested.

## Conclusion

A close reading of each narrative reveals that they subvert an easy commendation of this ethic of obedience. While it is undeniably true that both Gen 3 and 22 valorize obedience to the divine directive and disapprove of

---

46. The phrase comes from James L. Crenshaw, *A Whirlpool of Torment: Israelite Traditions of God as an Oppressive Presence*, OBT 12 (Philadelphia: Fortress, 1984), 9–29.

disobedience, it is also the case that the details of each episode problematize the obedience to the divine and thereby suggest that there are, in fact, limits in the efficacy of the model. Should Eve (and Adam) be condemned for her (their) choice? Should Abraham be commended for his choice? While the explicit reading in the text suggests the answer is yes, other elements in each text raise the possibility that the authors thought otherwise.

I have argued that the narrative similarities between Gen 3 and 22 suggest that reading the two in light of each other and in light of similar questions shed light on both texts. In particular, my contention is that both texts provide a window into Israelite thought about the basis for ethical choices. While those choices are clearly not about eating fruit or killing children, these two narrative dilemmas offer windows into how these writers thought about the basis of ethical choices. The fact that each narrative presents a fanciful or absurd scenario serves to point to the deeper issue. Arguably, what is most alarming about each of the narratives when viewed together is the behavior of God. While the threatened deaths in both episodes are thwarted (presumably by God), the tests themselves—established by God—prove deeply problematic. What I have tried to show is that these two texts appear ambivalent about a deity who would create such tests.

# The Literary-Historical Dimensions of Intertextuality in Exodus–Numbers

*Marvin A. Sweeney*

1.

The exodus-wilderness narratives in the books of Exodus and Numbers are among the most important foundational narratives in the Hebrew Bible. They present an account of the formative experience of the nations of ancient Israel and Judah under the leadership of Moses, including the enslavement of Israel by the Egyptians, YHWH's confrontation with the Egyptian pharaoh, and the journey from Egypt through the wilderness to Mount Sinai and on to the borders of the promised land of Israel. In so doing, they also provide an etiological account of the origins and significance of the Israelite-Judean festival system, including especially the observance of Pesach, or Passover, as well as the festivals of Shavuot and Sukkot. With regard to Passover, the narrative includes the motifs of the blood of the Passover lamb, which serves as the main offering of the festival; the making of matzot, or unleavened bread, which is eaten during the festival; and the deliverance of the firstborn of Israel in contrast to the deaths of the firstborn of Egypt.

Although the roles of the Passover lamb and the matzot are clear in relation to Passover, the deliverance of the firstborn of Israel is not. The instruction account concerning the treatment of the firstborn in Exod 13:1–16 and the legal materials in Exod 34:19–20 are both J-stratum texts that call for the consecration or transference of the firstborn, including animals and humans, to YHWH.[1] Both appear to quote or presuppose

---

The initial draft of this paper was written during the term of my appointment as Visiting Scholar at Chang Jung Christian University, Tainan, Taiwan, June 8–28, 2015. I would like to thank Vice President Po Ho Huang, Dean Yatang Chuang, Professor

the earlier text from the Covenant Code in Exod 22:28–29, which calls upon the people of Israel to give their firstborn sons, cattle, and flocks to YHWH. Whereas the function of the firstborn animals is clear—namely, they are to be offered at the temple altar to YHWH on Passover—the function of the firstborn human males is not. They are to be redeemed, but the purpose for which they are to be redeemed is never stated. Hints as to the function of the firstborn males appear in three instances in the book of Numbers in which YHWH speaks to Moses about the consecration of the Levites (Num 3:11–13; 3:40–43, 44–51; and 8:13–19). Numbers 3:11–13 states:

> And YHWH spoke to Moses saying, "I indeed have taken the Levites from the midst of the Israelites in place of all the firstborn that break the womb from the Israelites, and the Levites shall be mine. For all the firstborn are mine. When I struck down all the firstborn in the land of Egypt, I consecrated for myself all the firstborn of Israel, including humans and animals. They shall be mine. I am YHWH."[2]

This quote and the others like it suggest that the original function of the firstborn was to serve in a priestly role alongside the sons of Aaron, but the text makes clear YHWH's intention to consecrate the Levites for this role in place of the firstborn. The book of Numbers is especially concerned with the consecration of the Levites for their sacred role. Other texts, such as 1 Sam 1–3, support this view, insofar as it portrays Samuel, the firstborn son of his mother Hannah and his Ephraimite father Elkanah, who is taken to the Shiloh sanctuary and raised to serve as a priest under the tutelage of Eli.

These considerations indicate that the role and function of the firstborn sons of Israel may well be clarified by intertextual study of the exodus–wilderness narratives. In order to proceed, we must first clarify what we mean by intertextual method and then apply it both to the study of the exodus–wilderness narrative both in relation to itself and in relation to other narratives. Such study demonstrates that the exodus–wilderness

---

Hye Kyung Park, and College of Theology Staff Member, Ms. Rita Li, for their collegiality and hospitality during my stay at CJCU.

1. Martin Noth, *A History of Pentateuchal Traditions* (Chico, CA: Scholars Press, 1981), 269, 271.

2. Unless otherwise stated, all biblical translations are my own.

narrative once understood the firstborn sons of Israel to serve together with the sons of Aaron as priests in Israel, but the Levites were later consecrated for this role in place of the firstborn of Israel.

2.

Intertextuality is the study of texts in relation to their literary contexts, including the citation of or allusion to other literary works, the placement and interpretation of a text in relation to its immediate literary context(s), and the interpretation of a text in relation to other literary compositions.

Current methodological overviews of intertextual interpretation indicate that it developed out of earlier diachronic or author-centered modes of exegesis, such as redaction criticism and inner-biblical exegesis, during the course of the twentieth century.[3] Such editing and citation was viewed as the product of later tradents or redactors of an earlier text who deliberately expanded and reworked earlier texts in an effort to reinterpret them to serve their own later interests.

Examples of such work from the latter twentieth century appear in efforts to define the various redactions of the Pentateuch from the early identification of the classical sources J, E, D, and P as conceived by Julius Wellhausen. Contemporary examples attempt to reconstruct the compositional history of the Pentateuch based on a later dating of the J material to the late monarchic or early exilic period and the earlier dating of selected P materials to the reign of King Hezekiah of Judah and his successors. Such work calls for the interpreter to reconstruct the authors of the texts and their particular viewpoints in relation to their posited historical contexts based on a combination of formal, lexical, and hermeneutical criteria.[4] In the case of the Pentateuch, such criteria would include: (1) the presence of a literary context in which one text would have access to another, such

---

3. Benjamin D. Sommer, *A Prophet Reads Scripture: Allusion in Isaiah 40–66*, Contra (Stanford, CA: Stanford University Press, 1998), 6–31; Patricia K. Tull, "Rhetorical Criticism and Intertextuality," in *To Each Its Own Meaning: An Introduction to Biblical Criticisms and Their Application*, ed. Steven L. McKenzie and Stephen R. Haynes, rev. ed. (Louisville: Westminster John Knox, 1999), 156–80; Carol A. Newsom, *The Book of Job: A Contest of Moral Imaginations* (Oxford: Oxford University Press, 2003), 3–31; Carleen R. Mandolfo, *Daughter Zion Talks Back to the Prophets*, SemeiaSt 58 (Atlanta: Society of Biblical Literature, 2007), 1–28.

4. Jeffrey Stackert, *Rewriting the Torah: Literary Revision in Deuteronomy and the Holiness Legislation*, FAT 52 (Tübingen: Mohr Siebeck, 2007), 18–29.

as Deuteronomy's rendition of events from the wilderness period in relation to those of Exodus–Numbers; (2) a lexical or motific correspondence between a posited later text and a posited earlier text, such as the development of the laws of the Holiness Code in Lev 17–26 or those of Deut 12–26 from the laws of the so-called Covenant Code of Exod 21–23; and (3) a hermeneutical perspective in one text that demonstrates an attempt to interpret another text in relation to concerns expressed in the first text, such as the presentation of events concerning the exodus from Egypt in Hos 12.

But current intertextual work is also rooted in contemporary synchronic models of literary criticism, particularly the recognition of the role played by readers in the construction and interpretation of a text. With the rise of reader-response criticism and the subsequent development of synchronic literary perspectives in biblical exegesis, interpreters have come to recognize the role that the reader plays in the construction of texts, whether biblical or not. Such work posits that texts are entities in and of themselves that stand independently of the author or authors who produced them and the historical contexts in which they worked.[5] With only the text as evidence, it is impossible to know the mind of the author, either on the part of the interpreter of the text or even of the author who wrote it. Interpreters construct an image of the author based upon their own subjective worldviews, which in turn influence their readings of texts and thereby give expression to their own concerns.

Wellhausen's identification of J as the earliest of the sources is a case in point.[6] He maintained that the anthropomorphic portrayal of YHWH and YHWH's relationship with human beings pointed to a primitive worldview that had to be assigned to the earliest periods of Israel's history. Given the state of the field of mythology at the time, Wellhausen followed most scholars who viewed mythological motifs as primitive expressions of a preliterate society. More recent study of mythology indicates that it continues to exist and function in relation to modern societies as well as ancient, as contemporary interests in Star Trek and superheroes would indicate.[7] Indeed,

---

5. John Barton, *Reading the Old Testament: Method in Biblical Study*, 2nd ed. (Louisville: Westminster John Knox, 1996), 140–236; Robert Morgan, *Biblical Interpretation* (Oxford: Oxford University Press, 1988), 203–68.

6. Julius Wellhausen, *Die Composition des Hexateuchs und der historischen Bücher des Alten Testaments* (Berlin: Georg Reimmer, 1889).

7. William E. Paden, *Religious Worlds: The Comparative Study of Religion* (Boston: Beacon, 1994).

Wellhausen's views were heavily influenced by the Protestant Christian interest in prophecy as an authentic and early example of human-divine interaction. Wellhausen sought to define such a face-to-face or prophetic model as the foundation for the composition of the Pentateuch. Priestly models of human interrelation with the divine were considered as later and less desirable or less authentic, both because they represented a more developed and literate society and because of Protestant Christianity's opposition to the Roman Catholic Church. But one must observe that the priesthood existed and functioned as the central religious institution of the nation throughout all stages of Israelite and Judean history, which raises questions concerning Wellhausen's decision to employ a prophetic model as the foundational feature for his earliest pentateuchal source.

Contemporary theorists, based especially in the work of Mikhail Bakhtin, posit that authors and interpreters draw upon the larger world of language and text which they inhabit, often subconsciously, so that it is impossible to know if an intertextual association is the deliberate work of an original author or the observation of a reader who reads her or his own ideas into the text at hand.[8] In such a view, texts do not necessarily convey the meanings intended by their authors, as it is impossible to know what an author intended, either by the interpreters or even by the author himself or herself. Meaning is thereby ascribed to texts by their readers, and the validity of the interpretation is decided by the numbers of other readers willing to accept it. So, we must ask if it is possible to account for such subjectivity in assessing potential intertextual relationships between and among texts.

Although the field is often polarized by author- and reader-centered theorists who deny the validity of the others' work, contemporary interpreters must recognize that textual interpretation calls for a synthesis of these views. Texts are indeed the products of authors who wrote them in specific historical contexts with a specific set of intentions that readers may or may not recognize and correctly reconstruct. At the same time, texts are read by readers who bring their own worldviews to bear in their interpretations—and therefore constructions—of the texts at hand. But the extent to which later readers correctly discern the presumed intentions of a text's author must be judged in relation to the criteria presented above.

---

8. Barbara Green, *Mikhail Bakhtin and Biblical Scholarship: An Introduction*, SemeiaSt 38 (Atlanta: Society of Biblical Literature, 2000).

In keeping with the concerns and goals of the new Society of Biblical Literature program unit on Intertextuality and the Hebrew Bible, this paper turns to the study of an important but not fully understood motif in the exodus-wilderness narratives: namely, the role and function of the redemption of the firstborn sons of Israel.

3.

We may begin by observing examples of the first type of intertextuality: the citation, expansion, and reworking of earlier texts. Exodus 13:1–16 presents a set of divine instructions concerning the significance of the redemption of the firstborn of Israel during the exodus.[9] Although Martin Noth considers it to be a D supplement to J in the pentateuchal text, the contemporary redating of J to the late-monarchic period enables us to conclude that it is a J-stratum text that has drawn on earlier D-stratum texts.[10] This text appears immediately following the notice that YHWH had brought out the Israelites from the land of Egypt in Exod 12:51 and prior to the account of Israel's journey from Egypt through the wilderness to the Red Sea in Exod 13:17–22. It is not unusual for instructional material concerning the observance of Passover to appear in the midst of the account of the exodus. Exodus 12:43–50 presents an account of YHWH's instructions concerning the treatment of the Passover offering in verses 43–49 followed by a notice of Israel's compliance with those instructions in verse 50. Exodus 12:1–28 likewise presents instruction concerning the preparation and eating of the Passover offering immediately following the account of YHWH's announcement of the tenth plague in Exod 11:1–10. Such features indicate that the exodus narrative is indeed an instruction account concerning the observance of Passover in ancient Israel and Judah that blends instruction together with the account of the event itself.[11]

---

9. Contra George W. Coats, *Exodus 1–18*, FOTL 2A (Grand Rapids: Eerdmans, 1999), 94–96, who considers Exod 13:1–16 as a "Story of Cultic Origins." See now, Thomas B. Dozeman, *Exodus*, ECC (Grand Rapids: Eerdmans, 2009), 286–98, who characterizes Exod 13:1–2 and 13:3–16 as divine or Mosaic instruction concerning the firstborn and the feast of unleavened bread and recognizes the agenda to substitute the Levites for the firstborn as priests in Israel.

10. Noth, *History of Pentateuchal Traditions*, 30 n. 106; see also 269. For a late-monarchic dating, see William H. C. Propp, *Exodus 1–18*, AB 3 (New Haven: Yale University Press, 2010), 373–80.

11. See Coats, *Exodus 1–18*, 3–20, who identifies the exodus narratives as a saga.

Exodus 13:1–2 begins with a report of YHWH's instruction, "And YHWH spoke to Moses saying, 'Consecrate to me every firstborn which opens every womb [כל־בכור פטר כל־רחם] among the sons of Israel, including human and animal. It is mine [לי הוא].'" Exodus 13:3–16 then follows with a report of Moses's instructions to the people to remember this day in verses 3aα⁵–5, to observe it by eating matzot for seven days, to explain it to their children in verses 6–8, to observe it by wearing tephillin as a sign upon their heads in verses 9–10, to set aside the firstborn animals for an offering and the firstborn sons for redemption, and to explain it to their children in verses 11–15. The concluding instruction is to wear the tephillin as a sign upon your hand in verse 16.

YHWH's instruction to consecrate the firstborn in verse 2 employs some of the same language that appears in the legal instruction concerning the treatment of the firstborn in Exod 34:19–20: "All that opens the womb is mine [כל־פטר רחם לי], as well as all your cattle that drop a male as a firstling, whether cattle or sheep. And the firstborn of an ass you shall redeem with a sheep, and if you do not redeem it, you shall break its neck. Every firstborn of your sons you shall redeem." Indeed, the phraseology of Exod 34:19–20 appears to be quite similar to that of Exod 13:2 insofar as it includes the instruction concerning treatment of the firstborn together with instruction concerning the observance of Passover and the other festivals in Exod 34:18–26. Indeed, the legal material in Exod 34:10–27 appears to be derived from earlier legal instruction in Deut 7:1–7, Exod 23:14–19, and Exod 22:28–29.[12] In the aftermath of the golden calf episode, Exod 34:1–28 presents YHWH's instructions to Moses to carve a new set of covenant tablets to replace the originals that were broken when Moses descended from Sinai to find Israel worshipping the golden calf. The new set of legal materials begins in Exod 34:10–16 with material derived from Deut 7:1–7 concerning the prohibition of intermarriage with the Canaanite nations so as to prevent them from leading Israel astray with their foreign gods. It continues in Exod 34:17 with a prohibition against the manufacture of molten gods to take account of the golden calf. It concludes with an expanded version of the legal instruction concerning observance of Passover and the other holidays from Exod 23:14–19, to

---

12. See Marvin A. Sweeney, "The Wilderness Traditions of the Pentateuch: A Reassessment of Their Function and Intent in Relation to Exodus 32–34," *SBLSP* (1989): 291–99.

which the statements concerning the treatment of the firstborn from Exod 22:28–29 have been added.

We may now turn to Exod 23:14–19 and 22:28–29. Both texts are part of the so-called Covenant Code, a northern Israelite law code that is cited by Amos 2:6–16. Although some contemporary scholars would date the Covenant Code to the period of the Babylonian exile in the sixth century BCE,[13] such a view is mistaken. The citations of the Covenant Code in Amos 2:6–16 indicate that the Covenant Code is known in Israel prior to the mid-eighth century BCE, when the prophet was active.[14] With the growing recognition that J must be dated to the late-monarchic period and that it functions as a redactional text that reworked an underlying E or northern Israelite narrative, the instructions concerning the sanctification of the firstborn in Exod 23:14–19 and Exod 22:28–29 then emerge as part of the underlying E-stratum text that serves as the basis for the references to the redemption of the firstborn in Exod 13:1–16 and 34:10–27.[15] Although the J-stratum texts in Exod 13:1–16 and 34:1–28 combined the concerns of the two E-stratum Covenant Code texts with the observance of Passover and the other holidays in Exod 23:14–19 and the sanctification of the firstborn in Exod 22:28–29, neither set of texts adds any clarity to understanding the function or purpose of the firstborn human beings. They are dedicated to YHWH, but for what purpose?

4.

We may now turn to the second type of intertextuality: the interrelationship between texts within their broader literary contexts. The above-noted texts in Num 3:11–13; 3:40–43, 44–51; and Num 8:13–19 each refer to YHWH's decision to take the Levites from Israel in place of the firstborn, the first issue of the tribes of Israel. All three of the texts are P-stratum texts

---

13. David P. Wright, *Inventing G-d's Law: How the Covenant Code of the Bible Used and Revised the Laws of Hammurabi* (Oxford: Oxford University Press, 2009); cf. John Van Seters, *A Law Book for the Diaspora: Revision in the Study of the Covenant Code* (Oxford: Oxford University Press, 2003).

14. Marvin A. Sweeney, *The Twelve Prophets*, vol. 1, BO (Collegeville, MN: Liturgical Press, 2000), 214–18.

15. See Tzemach L. Yoreh, *The First Book of G-d*, BZAW 402 (Berlin: de Gruyter, 2010); see now, Marvin A. Sweeney, *The Pentateuch*, CBS (Nashville: Abingdon, 2017).

that function as part of P's concluding narratives for the Sinai periscope in Num 1:1–10:10, but each also has a unique function.

The first in Num 3:11–13 simply states the principle that YHWH has decided to take the Levites in the place of the firstborn. This text appears as part of a sequence of statements by YHWH to Moses concerning the status of the Levites in the book of Numbers. Numbers 3:1–4 begins the text with an instance of the *toledoth* formula, "and these are the generations of Aaron and Moses on the day that YHWH spoke with Moses at Mount Sinai," which introduces the major structural components of the Pentateuch. In the present instance, Num 3:1–4 signals the narrative interest in the status of the priesthood, beginning with Aaron and his sons. Numbers 3:5–10 relates YHWH's statement to Moses that the latter is to bring near the tribe of Levi so that the Levites might serve Aaron and his sons in their priestly duties at the mishkan, or tabernacle. Numbers 3:11–13 then follows with its statement:

> And YHWH spoke to Moses saying, "I indeed have taken the Levites from the midst of the Israelites in place of all the firstborn that break the womb from the Israelites, and the Levites shall be mine. For all the firstborn are mine. When I struck down all the firstborn in the land of Egypt, I consecrated for myself all the firstborn of Israel, including humans and animals. They shall be mine. I am YHWH."

Numbers 3:11–13 clearly draws on the language concerning the firstborn that we have previously seen in the Covenant Code and the J-stratum texts, but the immediate text does not make clear the purpose or function of the firstborn—only that the Levites will replace them. But insofar as the prior text in Num 3:5–10 makes it clear that the Levites are to function as priestly assistants to the sons of Aaron, it would seem that the firstborn were understood to serve in a similar capacity.

Following a lengthy speech in Num 3:14–39 in which YHWH instructs Moses to take a census of the Levites, Num 3:40–43, 44–51 present two speeches by YHWH in which YHWH once again addresses the issue of the firstborn of Israel. The first in Num 3:40–43 presents YHWH's instructions to Moses to record all the firstborn of Israel, just as the prior speech instructed Moses to record the Levites. YHWH's speech in verses 40–43 continues as before with instructions to Moses to take the Levites in place of the firstborn. The second speech in Num 3:44–51 instructs Moses once again with the principle that he should take the Levites in place of the firstborn. But YHWH specifies the instruction by including the cattle of the Levites. Insofar as the firstborn in Israel outnumbered the Levites by 273, YHWH specifies that a redemption price be leveled on the excess numbers of firstborn at the rate of five shekels per head, for a total of 1365 shekels to be paid to Aaron and his sons for the redemption of the firstborn. Such a calculation thereby specifies the general statements in Exod 13:13 and 34:20 that the firstborn human beings are to be redeemed. Exodus 22:28–29, however, did not mention the redemption of the firstborn human beings.

The third and final text in the series is Num 8:13–19, which appears within a larger narrative in Num 8:5–22 in which Moses, Aaron, and the people of Israel comply with YHWH's instructions to Moses to consecrate the Levites as an elevation offering [תנופה] from the people of Israel for Aaron and his sons. A תנופה, or elevation offering, is a portion from the offerings of the people of Israel that is dedicated for the support of the priesthood, specifically the Aaronide priests (Exod 29:22–28; Lev 7:28–34; 8:22–29). Numbers 8:13–19 makes that role clear, and it specifies once again with language much like that of the earlier texts from Numbers that the Levites are taken by YHWH in place of the firstborn in Israel.

The three Numbers passages in 3:11–13; 3:40–43, 44–51; and 8:13–19 make it clear that YHWH's choice of the Levites in place of the firstborn of Israel was intended to provide Aaron and his sons with priestly assistance in their duties at the tabernacle and later at the temple. Such a role suggests that the firstborn once had an obligation to serve as priests alongside the sons of Aaron in the temples of Israel. It is also clear that such service could be redeemed by the payment of a specified price. Each text has a specific function. Numbers 3:11–13 states the principle, immediately following Num 3:5–10, which states that the Levites are to serve alongside Aaron and his sons in the tabernacle. Numbers 3:40–43, 44–51 specifies the redemption price to be paid on behalf of the excess firstborn sons to Aaron and his sons. Numbers 8:13–19 states that the Levites will function as a תנופה in place of the firstborn for Aaron and his sons.

## 5.

Finally, we may turn to the third type of intertextuality: the interrelationship between a text and the larger literary world beyond its immediate literary context. Although some might be inclined to see the role of the firstborn strictly as a monetary transaction to support the Levites, at least one text indicates that the firstborn sons did indeed serve as priests in the temples of early Israel. First Samuel 1–3 indicates that the priest and prophet, Samuel, was indeed a firstborn Ephraimite who following his birth was placed in the temple at Shiloh, where he was raised and educated to serve as a priest in ancient Israel.

First Samuel 1–3 illustrates the role of firstborn sons as priests in the early history of Israel.[16] Samuel's father is identified in 1 Sam 1:1 as Elkanah ben Jeruham ben Elihu ben Tohu ben Zuph of the tribe of Ephraim. He is from Ramathaim of the Zuphites in the territory of Benjamin. His mother is identified as Hannah, although her ancestry is not specified. Samuel is her firstborn son. Elkanah has a second wife as well named Peninnah. Although Hannah initially has no children, Peninnah has many. This issue leads to rivalry between the two women and narrative tension that provides the basis for plot development. When Hannah finally does give birth to Samuel, Hannah places him in the Shiloh temple where he will be raised by the high priest Eli to serve as a priest in Israel. The vision account in 1 Sam 3 in which YHWH summons the young Samuel apparently serves as his vocation account to serve both as a prophet and as a priest.

The portrayal of Samuel serving as a priest on the basis of his status as the firstborn son of Hannah and his Ephraimite father, Elkanah, is consistent with what we know about the priesthood in northern Israel. Figures such as the prophets Elijah and Elisha perform priestly functions. Elijah builds an altar for the observance of Sukkot in 1 Kgs 18, and Elisha performs music as part of his oracular performance in 2 Kgs 3. Neither is ever identified as a Levite or as a priest. Indeed, Jeroboam ben Nebat, the first king of northern Israel, is criticized for allowing non-Levites to serve as priests in 1 Kgs 12:25–33, and he officiates at the Beth El altar in 1 Kgs 13 when he has his confrontation with the man of G-d from Judah.[17] Northern Israel apparently did not rely on Levites to serve as priests in the manner of southern Judah. Firstborn sons apparently filled this role in northern Israel, at least to a certain extent.

---

16. See Marvin A. Sweeney, "Samuel's Institutional Identity in the Deuteronomistic History," in *Constructs of Prophets in the Former and Latter Prophets and Other Texts*, ed. Lester L. Grabbe and Martti Nissinen, ANEM 4 (Atlanta: Society of Biblical Literature, 2011), 165–74.

17. Marvin A. Sweeney, *1 and 2 Kings: A Commentary*, OTL (Louisville: Westminster John Knox, 2007), 172–82.

## 6.

In conclusion, this analysis points to a development in the conceptualization of the priesthood in the Pentateuch. Our intertextual considerations point to a process in which initial statements concerning the dedication of the firstborn sons of human beings and animals of the flock and herd in Exod 22:28–29 and the observance of Passover and the other festivals in Exod 23:14–19 stand as the basis of the evolution of ancient Israel's priesthood. Insofar as these texts derive from the Covenant Code, a ninth to eighth century E-stratum law code from the northern kingdom of Israel, they form the earliest basis for discerning the process of development. These texts are then revised and expanded in the J-stratum narrative of Exod 13:1–16 and the legal instruction of Exod 34:18–26. They conceptualize the dedication of the firstborn sons and animals of Israel to YHWH as part of the Passover narrative concerning the slaying of the firstborn of Egypt and their redemption of the firstborn of Israel as foundational components to the observance of Passover. Finally, the P-stratum texts in Num 3:11–13; 3:40–43, 44–51; and 8:13–19 point to further development in which the Levites will replace the firstborn sons of Israel as the priests who serve together with the sons of Aaron in the tabernacle or temple of Israel, according to Num 3:11–13. Numbers 3:40–43, 44–51 make it clear that the Levites will serve as a *těnûpâ* from among the tribes of Israel to support the work of the Aaronide priests. And Num 8:13–19 calculates the amount of funds necessary to pay for the full redemption of the firstborn of Israel to the Aaronide priests. Altogether, such an analysis points to the original obligation of the firstborn sons of Israel to serve together with the sons of Aaron as priests in the sanctuary of YHWH, based upon the model of Samuel, the prophet and priest, who was the firstborn son of his mother, Hannah, and her Ephraimite husband, Elkanah. Such considerations point to the motif of the slaying of the firstborn in the Passover narrative as an etiological account of how the firstborn came to serve in such a sacred role, certainly in the late-monarchic J-stratum text and potentially in the earlier E-stratum text of the Pentateuch from the ninth to eighth centuries BCE.

# Hidden in Plain Sight: Intertextuality and Judges 19

*Kirsten H. Gardner*

The text of Judg 19 includes literary representations of gang rape, murder, and presumed posthumous mutilation. These literary images are remarkable even within the literary landscape of a book whose narrated topics include political assassination (Judg 3), murder of enemy combatants (Judg 4–5), horrors of war crimes (Judg 9), and human sacrifice (Judg 11). All of these violent episodes appear to be eclipsed in the literary representation of the extraordinary act of a man forcibly delivering his wife to a raging mob to be gang raped onto near death, at which time he gathers her only to dismember her ravaged body in one final, grisly deed. One may reasonably argue that the literary portrait of violence described in chapter 19 causes readers to react to the narrated images rather than to discern the literary function and meaning of said images. Slavoj Žižek observed, "there is something inherently mystifying in a direct confrontation with [violence]: the overpowering horror of violent acts and empathy with the victims inexorably function as a lure which prevents us from thinking."[1] Žižek's observation may explain the treatment the chapter has received from biblical scholarship, which ranges from outright dismissal, labeling it a "literary creation," to dubbing it the *Text of Terror* par excellence, in which women are sacrificed in the service of male hospitality.[2] These pre-

---

This article is based on research originally conducted in support of a dissertation thesis. Kirsten H. Gardner, "Reading Judges 19: A Study of Narrated Apostasy and Literary Representations of Violence" (PhD diss., Fuller Theological Seminary, 2017). Some of these results were presented at the Annual Meeting of the Society of Biblical Literature, Boston, MA, 19 November 2017.

1. Slavoj Žižek, *Violence: Six Sideways Reflections* (New York: Picador, 2008), 4.
2. J. Cheryl Exum, *Fragmented Women: Feminist (Sub)Versions of Biblical Narra-*

vious analyses read the text as a self-contained narration, thereby severing it from the larger literary landscape in which it exists: namely, the book of Judges as well as the Old Testament canon.

Intertextuality recognizes that texts exist within literary and cultural landscapes, drawing from, interacting with, and corresponding to a library of other writings. It is an intrinsic characteristic of textuality to be inseparable from associations with other texts.[3] "Every text is constructed like a mosaic.... Every text is an absorption and a transformation of another text.'"[4] Within biblical scholarship, this attribute of textuality has been deployed to answer questions of dating, which caused Julia Kristeva rightly to bemoan that "intertextuality has often been understood in the banal sense of 'study of sources.'"[5] The current project does not intend to address source critical questions. While I acknowledge the literary growth of texts in general, and Judg 19 specifically, I will not attempt to address questions of dependency and dating. Working with the final form of the narrative, this essay combines tools from narrative criticism with those from intertextuality as it seeks to explore the literary significance of the represented violence of chapter 19 within the context of the Old Testament canon. Specifically, literary gaps,[6] lexical multivalence,[7] and

---

*tives* (Valley Forge, PA: Trinity Press International, 1993), 171; Phyllis Trible, *Texts of Terror: Literary-Feminist Readings of Biblical Narratives*, OBT 13 (Philadelphia: Fortress, 1984).

3. Patricia K. Tull, "Rhetorical Criticism and Intertextuality," in *To Each Its Own Meaning: An Introduction to Biblical Criticisms and Their Application*, ed. Steven L. McKenzie and Stephen R. Haynes, rev. ed. (Louisville: Westminster John Knox, 1999), 165.

4. Ellen van Wolde, "Texts in Dialogue with Texts: Intertextuality in the Ruth and Tamar Narratives," *BibInt* 5 (1997): 2.

5. Julia Kristeva, *Revolution in Poetic Language*, trans. Margaret Waller (New York: Columbia University Press, 1984), 59–60.

6. Literary gaps, permanent or temporary, are a common feature in any written work, but at times they can undermine comprehension: "A gap is a lack of information about the world— an event, motive, causal link, character trait, plot structure, law of probability ... and gap-filling consists exactly in restoring the continuity that the narrator broke. For all our attempts at restoration, however, the breaches remain ambiguous—the hypotheses multiple—as long as the narrator has not authoritatively closed them. The storyteller's withholding of information opens gaps, gaps produce discontinuity, and discontinuity breeds ambiguity." Meir Sternberg, *The Poetics of Biblical Narrative: Ideological Literature and the Drama of Reading*, ISBL (Bloomington: Indiana University Press, 1985), 235–36.

narrative inconsistencies[8] are significant features in the way the Judg 19 narrative is constructed. The high prevalence of these elements functions to disorient the reader in the world of the text and undermines attempts to identify a singular, unifying theme.[9] Amidst this textual ambiguity, the narrative strategy of Judg 19 evidences numerous textual echoes and allusions. These intertextual interactions lend a further literary dimension to interpretation: A text may "allude to an earlier text in a way that evokes resonance of the earlier text beyond those explicitly cited. The result is that the interpretation of [a text] requires the reader to recover unstated or suppressed correspondences between the two texts."[10] Stefan Alkier astutely observed: "Not everything is intertextuality, and the concept of intertextuality is not the answer to all questions of textual research."[11] Without question, intertextuality has limitations. Yet, its conceptualization of the text as existing within an encyclopedic environment allows for textual interactions to inform meaning, which in turn has the potential to explicate literary gapping, elucidate lexical multivalence, and resolve narrative inconsistencies.

## Methodological Considerations and Findings

The current project delimits intertextual interactions along the lines of shared lexical, thematic, and syntactic markers between Judg 19 and other texts within the literary environment of the Old Testament. Within these parameters, particular attention is paid to unique lexical occurrences, distinctive word combinations, and rare expressions. Unique literary events are quantified as occurrences in Judg 19 and no more than three other

---

7. Multivalence obscures meaning as words come to signify multiple designations, and without the necessary textual context to affirm either, this feature further increases textual ambiguity.

8. Information either appears to contradict or be disconnected from prior textual data, or it inverts tropes and themes of texts echoed or alluded to. In either instance, reader expectations are subverted.

9. With regard to Judg 19, there seemingly exist as many proposals as there are scholars.

10. Richard B. Hays, *Conversion of the Imagination: Paul as Interpreter of Israel's Scripture* (Grand Rapids: Eerdmans, 2005), 2–3.

11. Stefan Alkier, "Intertextuality and the Semiotics of Biblical Texts," in *Reading the Bible Intertextually*, ed. Richard B. Hays, Stefan Alkier, and Leroy A. Huizenga (Waco, TX: Baylor University Press, 2009), 11.

texts. This particular emphasis on unique and rare lexical occurrences extends the list of literary contacts between Judg 19 and texts beyond the previously acknowledged intertextual interactions exhibited by the chapter. With this previous work, the current approach confirms significant intertextual contact between Judg 19 and the following texts: Gen 19 (Lot), Gen 22 (Akedah), 1 Sam 11:7 (Saul and oxen), 2 Sam 13 (Tamar), Deut 13:14 and 1 Sam 1:16 (בני־בליעל), and Deut 22:13–21 (sexual trespassing).[12]

Besides those texts previously identified by scholarship, the current project identifies additional intertextual contacts. Lexically and thematically unique literary occurrences shared between Judg 19 and just one other additional text or story were identified in the following texts: Hagar's abandonment in Gen 16:8 (מזה באת ואנה תלכי) and Gen 21:12 (אמתך used by third party); Rebekah's betrothal in Gen 24:25 (מספוא תבן) and Gen 24:4 (אכל, שתה, and לין); Abimelech's usurpation in Judg 9:19 (ironic use, שמח) and Judg 9:27 (אכל שתה, only other occurrence in the book of Judges); and Absalom's usurpation in 2 Sam 15:16, 20:3 (אשה פילגש), and 2 Sam 16:1 (וצמד חמרים). In each of these instances, intertextual interaction was determined via a shared unique lexical feature, either in wording or context, between Judg 19 and the second text. In all of these instances, interaction was further distinguished by repeated contact across the respective stories. In each interaction, unique lexical and syntactic events established exactly two contacts between Judg 19 and the respective story. The key themes that emerged by means of these interactions were abandonment of a foreign maid or wife, hospitality and feasting in the context

---

12. Most recently, Cynthia Edenburg affirmed the following texts as significant: Gen 18–19; 1 Sam 1:16, 11:7; Deut 13:14, 22:13–21; and 2 Sam 13:11–17 (*Dismembering the Whole: Composition and Purpose of Judges 19–21*, AIL 24 [Atlanta: SBL Press, 2016], 174–320). On Gen 19, see Daniel I. Block, *Judges, Ruth*, NAC 6 (Nashville: Broadman & Holman, 1999), 532–34; Susan Niditch, "The 'Sodomite' Theme in Judges 19–20: Family, Community, and Social Disintegration," *CBQ* 44 (1982): 365; Block, "Echo Narrative Technique in Hebrew Literature: A Study in Judges 19," *WTJ* 52 (1990): 326. On Gen 22, see Trible, *Texts of Terror*, 80. On 1 Sam 11:7, see Gale A. Yee, "Ideological Criticism: Judges 17–21 and the Dismembered Body," in *Judges and Method: New Approaches in Biblical Studies*, ed. Gale A. Yee, 2nd ed. (Minneapolis: Fortress, 2007), 155; Edenburg, *Dismembering the Whole*, 221. On 2 Sam 13, see Edenburg, *Dismembering the Whole*, 249–54. On Deut 13:14 and 1 Sam 1:16, see Edenburg, *Dismembering the Whole*, 231. On Deut 22:13–21, see Yee, "Ideological Criticism," 152; Edenburg, *Dismembering the Whole*, 244.

of betrothal, and usurpation of the throne. These three themes deserve more detailed attention.

Exactly four intertextual contacts exist between Judg 19 and accounts about usurpation. In a narrative world characterized by the absence of a king or YHWH's rule, this preponderance constitutes a significant textual phenomenon, thematically linking the events of Judg 19 to a subtheme of usurpation.[13] The stories of Abimelech and Absalom describe the inglorious careers of sons usurping their father's thrones, or implied claim thereto (Judg 9), amidst a wake of destruction and suffering. Both stories have their inceptions in fratricide (seventy brothers on one stone, Judg 9:5; Amnon, 2 Sam 13:28–32), bring suffering to others (people of Shechem, Judg 9:45, 49; David's wives, 2 Sam 15:16), and ultimately lead to the disgraceful death of the usurper (Abimelech is mortally wounded by a woman, Judg 9:53; Absalom is left dangling from a tree branch in 2 Sam 18:9, until he is run through by spears and clubbed to death in 2 Sam 18:14, 15). These stories paint a grim picture of the consequences resulting from usurpation. The intertextual contact between these accounts and Judg 19 introduces themes of rightful rule, justice, and the consequences of usurpation as a potential subtext. Within the narrative threats of chapter 19 as well as Judges as a whole, these topics offer a plausible and satisfactory reading.[14]

Themes of hospitality and feasting alluded to in the contact with the Rebekah stories highlight the seemingly nonsensical interaction between the Levite and father-in-law (Judg 19:5–9) as well as the absurd enumeration of provisions by the guests in their encounter with their future host (19:19). The intertextual interaction between these accounts seems to suggest that "things are not as they ought to be." And, in fact, the duration of five days for a drinking feast (19:5–9) is unique within the context of the Old Testament and puzzling, unless it is considered in light of practices related to the *marzēaḥ* feast. This practice is known from Ugarit, Israel, Samaria, Judah, Elephantine, Palmyra, rabbinic references,

---

13. Gregory T. K. Wong presents a convincing argument that Judg 19 employs the word מלך to denote YHWH. Gregory T. K. Wong, *Compositional Strategy of the Book of Judges: An Inductive, Rhetorical Study*, VTSup 111 (Leiden: Brill, 2006), 191–223.

14. Alluding to Hays's seventh criteria concerning the validity of textual echoes: "Does the proposed reading make sense?" (Richard B. Hays, *Echoes of Scripture in the Letters of Paul* [New Haven: Yale University Press, 1989], 29–31).

and the Madaba map mosaic.[15] Yet, despite this extensive attestation, questions remain concerning the precise character of the feast. Stefan Schorsch, working with extrabiblical evidence, identifies "Wein und Essen" and "Zeitangabe" as characteristic components in the extant evidence.[16] Importantly, the feast transpired over numerous days: "Es währte zwischen 5 und 30 Tage lang, wurde wegen seines z.T. orgiastischen Charakters mehrfach verboten."[17] The specific time frame associated with this feast is also corroborated by John L. McLaughlin: "The four and five day *marzēaḥ* feasts mentioned in the Piraeus inscription and the Be'eltak tessera would have required great financial resources."[18] A minimum of four to five days filled with food and alcohol was a characteristic duration for a *marzēaḥ*. This information may provide the clue to the vexing problem presented by verses 5–9. In light of the fact that Hebrew narrative eschews verbosity, the temporal characteristic associated with a *marzēaḥ* and its literary representation in form of redundant repetition in chapter 19 combine to ensure that no one reading the story misses the fact that eating and drinking extended for five days, like any other *marzēaḥ*, and the feast bodes ill within the context of Judg 19.

Lastly, the theme of abandonment of a foreign wife or maid, introduced via repeated intertextual interaction with the Hagar stories, rings paramount within the narrative content of Judg 19 where the dual designation of the female character as both אשה and פילגש (19:1) has introduced multivalence and obscured interpretation. Judges 19 is unique as it squarely places the identity of a פילגש within terms taken from family law: "*lāqaḥ lô ʾiššāh* (take to wife), *ḥōtēn* (father-in-law), *ḥātān* (son-in-law)— used in conjunction with *pilegeš*, suggest[s] a marriagelike relationship that does not correspond to the picture painted by other texts."[19] This textual oddity might be reasonably explained by the fact that the woman is foreign-born, as is indicated by the additional "from Bethlehem in Judah" in verse 1, so as to underscore this literary clue. Namely, despite the fact

---

15. Susan Ackerman, "A *Marzēaḥ* in Ezekiel 8:7–13?," *HTR* 82 (1989): 275. Also, H. J. Fabry, "מִרְזֵחַ," *TDOT* 9:10–15.

16. Stefan Schorsch, "Die Propheten und der Karneval: Marzeach—Maioumas—Maimuna," *VT* 53 (2003): 402.

17. Schorsch, "Die Propheten und der Karneval," 404.

18. John L. McLaughlin, *The Marzēaḥ in the Prophetic Literature: References and Allusions in Light of the Extra-Biblical Evidence*, VTSup 86 (Leiden: Brill, 2001), 68.

19. Karen Engelken, "פִּלֶגֶשׁ," *TDOT* 11:550.

that some of the women who are both designated as אשה and פילגש were originally introduced into the family structures as maids or female servants, "the theory that concubines were always former maids or slaves is not persuasive."[20] Often these women were simply of non-Israelite origin (Judg 19:1; 8:31; 1 Chr 1:32; 7:14).[21] In the case of the woman in Judg 19, she is from Judah—thus a foreign-born wife aptly designated as a פילגש. This fact is further hinted at in the intertextual correspondence between Judg 19 and Gen 16 and 21. Hagar is also a foreign-born woman who will find herself abandoned.

Characterized by less symmetrical intertextual contacts, equally noteworthy textual events were identified in the next three verses:

(1) Verse 3 and the following texts: Gen 50:21 (וידבר על־לבם), which describes Joseph's reception of his brothers, during which his speech reinstates familial relations and assures the brothers of his kindness toward them; Isa 40:2 (דברו על־לב ירושלם), where the prophet pronounces comfort at the implied conclusion of the people's hard service for their sins; and Hos 2:16 (ודברתי על־לבה), where YHWH seeks the return of a wayward nation.[22] These texts combine thematically as a subtext that presents literary portraits of a variety of outcomes when mending relationships.

(2) Verse 17 and Gen 18:2 (וישא עינו וירא), which describes Abraham looking up and seeing three messengers. The phrase וישא עינו וירא occurs frequently, with the implication of "looking up and noticing." Of its thirty-four additional occurrences, nineteen usages take place to describe a vision context.[23] On four occasions, the phrase is used for noticing either land or a place.[24] Three texts list items, and in eight cases the texts list people as the object of notice.[25] Of the texts in which the

---

20. Engelken, "פִּלֶגֶשׁ," 11:550.

21. Barry L. Bandstra, "Concubinage," in *Dictionary of Scripture and Ethics*, ed. Joel B. Green (Grand Rapids: Baker Academic, 2011), 160.

22. I thank Hyun Chul Paul Kim for noting the textual interactions between verse 3 and Gen 50:21 and Isa 40:2.

23. Gen 31:10, 12; Num 24:2; Deut 4:19; Josh 5:13; Isa 40:26; 49:18; 60:4; Jer 3:2; 13:20; Ezek 8:5 (x2); Dan 8:3; 10:5; 1 Chr 21:16; Zech 2:1; 5:1, 9; 6:1.

24. Gen 13:10, 14; 22:4; Deut 3:27.

25. Items: Gen 22:13 (ram); Gen 24:63 (camels); 1 Sam 6:13 (ark). People: Gen 18:2 (Abraham sees travelers); 24:64 (Rebecca sees Isaac); 33:1 (Esau and four hundred men), 5 (women and children); 37:25 (caravan of Ishmaelites); 43:29 (Jacob sees Benjamin); 2 Sam 13:34 (many people); 18:24 (messenger).

phrase is applied to noticing people, only Gen 18 appears in the context of receiving strangers.

(3) Verse 27 and Prov 31:20 (ידים + possessive feminine ending): In Prov 31:20, the woman opens her palm to the poor and sends her hands to the oppressed; in Judg 19, the female character is the oppressed, and her hands are stretched out in need. The dual form ידים is ubiquitous, but it occurs only a few times with the possessive feminine ending: women's hands are described as exercising power (Gen 16:9); as objects to be adorned (Gen 24:2, 47); as a means of production (Prov 31:19, 31); as a chain that encumbers men (Eccl 7:26); and as a means to distribute blessings to the poor and needy (Prov 31:20). The language in Prov 31:20 is reminiscent of verse 27: כפה פרשה לעני וידיה שלחה לאביון.

In each of these examples, the textual events are characterized by unique lexical, syntactical, and thematic features shared between chapter 19 and the respective secondary texts. Moreover, in each instance a case can be made that the texts alluded to in the interaction significantly contribute in content to the themes of the primary text: the attempted restoration of relationship, the noticing and hosting of visitors, and a literary portrait of a woman "who extends her hands." However, the relationship between the content of Judg 19 and these echoed texts is nonlinear. As the events of the chapter unfold, these themes are represented in a twisted manner: relationships are shattered amidst violence, guests are not provided for, and the "extended hands" signify need. While subtle, this apparent subtext is critical to the work of interpreting the events in Judg 19.

The intertextual findings across all thirty verses are tabulated in the following table in order to present a visual representation of the textual data discussed above.

| Verse | Expression | Textual Contact | Theme |
|---|---|---|---|
| 1 | אשה פילגש | 2 Sam 15:16; 20:3 | David's wives; Absalom's usurpation of throne via rape in a public forum: "in the sight of all Israel" (2 Sam 16:22). |
| 2 | ארבעה חדשים | Judg 20:47 | Six hundred Benjamites hiding for ארבעה חדשים. |
| 3 | הלך אחרי | 2 Sam 3:16 | Paltiel following after Michal |
|   | לדבר על־לבה | Gen 50:21 | Joseph reassures his brothers of his kindness |

# Hidden in Plain Sight

| | | | |
|---|---|---|---|
| 3 cont. | | Isa 40:2 | Comfort to the nation following hard service |
| | | Hosea 2:16 | YHWH seeking return of wayward nation |
| | וצמד חמרים | 2 Sam 16:1 | Ziba brings food to David; Absalom usurpation of throne |
| | הנערה | Deut 22:13–21 | Word used of married woman; sexual trespasses |
| | שמח | Judg 9:19 | Used ironically; Abimelech's usurpation |
| 4 | שלשת ימים | Judg 14:14 | Samson's riddle during wedding |
| | שתה, אכל, and לין | Gen 24:54 | Rebekah's marriage negotiations and **feast** |
| | שתה and אכל | Judg 9:27 | Shechemites before Abimelech's revenge |
| 15 | רחוב | Gen 19:1 | Beginning literary contact between Judg 19:15–24 and Gen 19:1–8; Lot; **Levite sitting in square** |
| 17 | וישא עינו וירא | Gen 18:2 | Abraham sees the three messengers |
| | אנה תלך ומאין תבוא | Gen 16:8 | Hagar's encounter with the messenger; **word order** |
| 19 | מספוא and תבן | Gen 24:25, 32 | Rebekah's betrothal scene; **offering fodder** |
| | אמתך | Gen 21:12 | Used by third party; YHWH speaks to Abraham about Hagar |
| 22 | בני־בליעל | Deut 13:14; 1 Sam 1:16 | Those who would lead others to follow after foreign gods |
| | | Gen 19:4 | The men of the city surrounded the house of the host |
| 23 | | Gen 19:6 | Lot; the man went out to them |

| 23 cont. | | Gen 19:7 | Plead with townsfolk "not to act wickedly" |
| --- | --- | --- | --- |
| 24 | ענה in the *piel* and נבלה | 2 Sam 13:12 | Tamar's rape by Amnon |
| | | Gen 19:8 | Lot offering his two daughters, or host offering two women |
| 25 | ולא־אבו האנשים לשמע לו | 2 Sam 13:14a | Unwillingness to listen |
| | ויחזק האיש בפילגשו | 2 Sam 13:14b | Seizing of the female victim; **no divine intervention (Gen 19)** |
| | שלח *piel* | 2 Sam 13:15 | Tamar pleads not be sent away |
| 27 | ידים + feminine possessive | Prov 31:20 | Contact in word and motif; **outstretched palms** |
| 29 | המאכלת | Gen 22:6, 10 | Knife used by Abraham; **no divine intervention** |
| | נתח | 1 Sam 11:7 | Saul divides a bull into twelve pieces; **no divine command** |

Of the overall thirty intertextual interactions identified in the table, some more significant than others, eight cases were unique in that the narrative content of Judg 19 deployed the themes and tropes of the secondary text in an inverted or distorted manner.[26] Verse 4 portrays a protracted feast at the conclusion of what amounts to be nuptial negotiations, possibly a *marzēaḥ*, distorting the alluded one-night feast following Rebekah's betrothal (Gen 24:54). Verse 15 portrays the Levite and travel party sitting in a square, which inverts the scene of Lot sitting in the square (Gen 19:1). Verse 17 utilizes the wording of Gen 16:8 but inverts the word order when the old man speaks. Verse 19 inverts roles of host and guest in terms of provisions: in Gen 24, Rebekah is enumerating, while here the Levite lists his own provisions. Verse 25, in the absence of any divine intervention, reports the abandonment of the female character to the mob, distorting and rupturing contact with the events in Gen 19:10. Verse 27, while being inconclusive as to the state of the woman, utilizes language from Prov 31:20 to describe the battered

---

26. Identified in bold in fig. 1.

condition of the woman. Verse 29 utilizes language from Gen 22:11, but in the absence of divine intervention, the knife-wielder does cut the human body. Verse 29 also utilizes the imagery of Saul's dividing the oxen into twelve pieces to send all over Israel. Yet here, the Levite divides the body without a divine command, and his actions incite fratricide in subsequent chapters.

Of these eight cases, verses 25 and 29 are notable. In both instances, the chapter creates a textual event with secondary texts in which the respective victims are spared by divine intervention (Gen 19 and 22). In a dramatic departure from a theme of divine intervention, chapter 19 employs literary representations of violence to rupture the intertextual contact established with these texts. In the case of verse 25, the additional lexical and thematic interaction with the Tamar story (2 Sam 13) provides a literary clue that divine intervention may not be the expected course of action (Gen 19). Verses 25 and 29 are the most notable examples of a literary technique that seems to intentionally invert and distort echoed texts. However, in each of the overall eight instances listed above, contact with secondary texts—established via lexical, thematic, and syntactical means—was nonlinear, as themes and tropes of the secondary texts were presented in a distorted or inverted manner. The prevalence of this technique throughout the chapter suggests intentionality and must be considered as significantly contributing to meaning.

## Literary Gaps, Narrative Inconsistencies, and Lexical Multivalence

Literary crises rely on reader engagement for resolution. The reader is forced to add information, gap-fill, or otherwise make meaning of the literary event. However, within the literary landscape of Judg 19, such a task becomes an insurmountable challenge. The chapter evidences scores of literary gaps, textual inconsistencies, and multivalence, adding to the complexity of the task.

Judges 19 evidences permanent literary gaps in the following areas. The pervasive anonymity of the chapter prevents relational activity on a textual level (19:1–3, 16).[27] The chapter introduces a secondary wife with no literary evidence of a primary one (19:1).[28] There is inconclusive

---

27. See Don Michael Hudson, "Living in a Land of Epithets: Anonymity in Judges 19–21," *JSOT* 64 (1994): 54.
28. A fact that lends weight to reading "foreign-born wife" here.

evidence to ascertain the nature of the familial constellation of the protagonists (19:1–2). It is the only text that appears to place a פילגש squarely within familial terminology. Judges 19 provides inconclusive evidence to establish the nature of the inciting incident (19:2).[29] Additionally, it includes a passage of an inexplicable time period (19:2).[30] There is literary preoccupation with geographical locations, yet textual failure to enumerate the Levite's place of origin (19:16), and inconclusive textual evidence concerning the state of the woman following the violent assault (19:27–29).[31]

These permanent gaps are exacerbated by conflicting intratextual data in the following verses: a Levite in a setting without YHWH (19:1);[32] a father's rejoicing at the sight of his daughter's would-be accuser (19:3); a delayed departure that catches the travelers unexpectedly searching for shelter (19:14); and a curiously delayed offer of shelter (19:20).

Finally, these features combine with lexically multivalent vocabulary, further increasing textual ambiguity. Of the thirty verses that make up the chapter, twenty verses contain at least one lexically multivalent word in a literary context that provides insufficient data to definitively ascertain signification.[33] Of the overall twenty-one words identified as lexically

---

29. Irene E. Riegner, *The Vanishing Hebrew Harlot: The Adventures of the Hebrew Stem ZNH*, StBibLit 73 (New York: Lang, 2009), 5.

30. A fact further emphasized by J. Alberto Soggin, who suggests following Palestinian vocalization, "*yāmīm weʾarbāʿāh ḥedāšīm*," which translates to report that the woman stayed for "one year and four months." J. Alberto Soggin, *Judges*, OTL (Philadelphia: Westminster, 1981), 284 n. 1.

31. The Masoretic text allows for the fact that she may yet be alive, while the Greek manuscript adds that "she was dead" (LXX).

32. Wong, *Compositional Strategy*, 212–23.

33. Verses 1 (king/YHWH—מלך; פילגש—secondary/foreign wife), 2 (זנה—adultery/participate in non-Yahwistic praxis), 3 (שוב—return/repent, become apostate; הלך אחרי—to follow after / [depending on context] to follow YHWH in religious faithfulness or to run after foreign gods; שמח—to rejoice [in common life]/rejoice [religiously], used ironically in Judg 9:19 with negative implication), 10 (Jebus—place name/בוס, to be high, with the implication of "religious worship, true or false," including the high places of Baal worship), 11 (Jebus), 12 (Gibeah—place name/גבעה, which means "hill," carries the connotation of "especially as place of illicit worship"), 13 (Ramah—place name/רמה, also bears the meaning of "height, high-place" with the particular implication of "shrine [for illicit worship]," also: Gibeah), 14 (Gibeah), 15 (Gibeah), 16 (Gibeah), 18 (multivalence as a result of text-critical issues: ביתי versus בית יהוה—the Levite is returning to "his house" or from "the sanctuary"), 19

multivalent, eleven words contain a secondary meaning that allows for a signification that included cult practices, illicit worship, or non-Yahwistic worship practices as follows:[34]

1. זנה: adultery/participate in non-Yahwistic praxis
2. שוב: return/repent (become apostate)
3. הלך אחרי: to follow after/when followed by a double infinitive, as is the case here, it takes on a religious signification and, depending on context, means to follow YHWH in religious faithfulness or to run after foreign gods
4. Jebus, Ramah, and Gibeah: place names/to be high, with the implication of "religious worship, true or false," including the high places of Baal worship; "height, high-place" with the particular implication of "shrine (for illicit worship)"; especially "as place of illicit worship"
5. ויבל (instead of תבן and מספוא in 19:19): mixed fodder/"mixing of cakes or flour" in the technical term for sacrifices
6. בני־בליעל: evil men/those who lead others to worship idols
7. נבלה: abomination or evil thing/thing done by "nations cast out from land" (Lev 18:22–24)
8. ענה: oppress, violate/transgression of norms
9. נתח: cutting up/of the seven occurrences outside Judges, four describe the cutting up of animals as part of a burnt offering (Exod 29:17; Lev 1:6, 12; 8:20)

---

(מחסר—secular want/related theologically to obedience or sin), 21 (ויבל [instead of תבן and מספוא in verse 19]—mixed fodder/"mixing of cakes or flour" in the technical term for sacrifices), 22 (בני־בליעל—evil men/those who lead others to worship idols; ידע—secular/religious use of ידע), 23 (נבלה—abomination or evil thing/thing done by "nations cast out from land" Lev 18:22–24), 24 (ענה—oppress, violate/transgression of norms), 25 (שלח—sent away/set free from captivity), 26 (האשה—woman/wife), 29 (המאכלת—knife/sacrificial knife; נתח—cutting up/of the seven occurrences outside Judges, four describe the cutting up of animals as part of a burnt offering; see Exod 29:17; Lev 1:6, 12; 8:20), and 30 (ראה—to see/regard; versus "everyone does what is right in his own eyes").

34. Verses 2, 3 (2x), 10, 11, 12, 13 (2x), 14, 15, 16, 21, 22, 23, 24, and 29. Note the multiple occurrences of the place names for Jebus (19:11, 12) and Gibeah (19:12, 13, 14, 15).

The prevalence of multivalence weakens the literary reliability of Judg 19 as words turn out to be increasingly unstable vehicles of data.

Charting the frequency of these features by verse illustrates the general instability of the text:

| Verse | Literary Gaps | Lexical Multivalence | Narrative Incoherence | Intertextual Echoes | Other |
|---|---|---|---|---|---|
| 1 | + | + | + | + | |
| 2 | + | + | | + | |
| 3 | | + | + | + | |
| 4 | | | + | + | |
| 5 | | | | | marzēaḥ |
| 6 | | | | | marzēaḥ |
| 7 | | | | | marzēaḥ |
| 8 | | | | | marzēaḥ |
| 9 | | | | | marzēaḥ |
| 10 | | + | | | |
| 11 | | + | | | |
| 12 | | + | | | |
| 13 | | + | | | |
| 14 | | + | + | | |
| 15 | | + | + | + | |
| 16 | + | + | | | |
| 17 | | | + | + | |
| 18 | | + | | | |
| 19 | | + | + | + | |
| 20 | | | + | | |
| 21 | | + | | | |
| 22 | | + | | + | |
| 23 | | + | | + | |
| 24 | | + | | + | |
| 25 | | + | | + | narrative pacing |
| 26 | | + | | | |
| 27 | + | | | + | |
| 28 | + | | | | false ending |
| 29 | + | + | + | + | |
| 30 | | + | | | breaking fourth wall |

Of the thirty verses that make up Judg 19, all but five (19:5–9) exhibit at least one literary feature whose inherent characteristic it is to undermine text stability. The chart illustrates the prevalence of these narrative techniques throughout the overall chapter, presenting a visual representation of a phenomenon long hinted at by others.[35] The text is riddled with elements that subvert reader comprehension. The quantification of results highlights not only the ubiquitous but also the systematic distribution of these features, suggesting intentionality.

Verses 5–9 do not overtly exhibit destabilizing literary elements. An analysis of these verses above suggests that they present a literary portrait of a *marzēaḥ* feast, spanning a five-day duration. This being its singular feature, and in the absence of textual data concerning the type of drink and meat consumed, the literary portrait of the feast does not permit a definitive identification. Yet, the excessive proportions of the narrated meal within the context of the pervasive themes that dominate the scene—namely, marriage and impending death—appear to mimic characteristics typically associated with a *marzēaḥ* feast. And, as is incumbent to "mimicking" features, they provide only a faint hint of something beyond the obviously narrated. Thus, the text goes to great lengths to paint a portrait which ultimately leaves the reader guessing as to the true nature of that which it intends to portray. In the absence of positively determinative data, the reader is unable to resolve the literary crisis. This, in effect, works similarly to the other twenty-five verses of the chapter, calling upon the reader to resolve conflicting information in the absence of pertinent details.

Analyzing Judg 19 along the lines of narrative features that destabilize the text has affirmed the prevalence of literary gaps, lexical multivalence, and narrative inconsistencies as integral parts of this composition. Within the overall narrative, these features combine to permit multiple meanings. As a text bounded within the encyclopedic environment of the Old Testament, not all interpretations are equally convincing, but in a textual world rife with multivalence, they are permissible.

---

35. Robert Polzin, *Moses and the Deuteronomist: A Literary Study of the Deuteronomic History*, part 1, ISBL (Bloomington: Indiana University Press, 1980), 18–20; J. Cheryl Exum, "The Centre Cannot Hold: Thematic and Textual Instabilities in Judges," *CBQ* 52 (1990): 412.

## Of Themes and Patterns

Previous work in Judg 19 has sought to identify internal structures and unifying themes which could provide an explanatory model for this enigmatic chapter. The resultant offerings have been diverse and varied. This project did not set out to discover a unifying literary thread which would neatly tie up the themes of this chapter. Thus, it was surprising when, during the ongoing discovery phase, lexically multivalent words bearing secondary significations of illicit worship/non-Yahwistic practices began to surface. Lexical multivalence is one of the significant tools used by the text to subvert meaning. Yet, within the number of multivalent words, a theme emerged. In all, sixteen occurrences of eleven lexically multivalent words in a total of fourteen separate verses permitted an inference of illicit worship practices. These occurrences combined with a literary portrait permitting an association with non-Yahwistic practices in Judg 19:5–9. When charting the frequency of these occurrences against the textual evidence of themes previously recognized, and unquestionably present in the story, a pervasive undercurrent of lexical and literary clues presented as follows:

---

Notes to the chart on page 69:

36. Implications may be established via lexically multivalence permitting a secondary meaning, or literary portrait of non-Yahwistic practices.

37. See, for example, Hermann-Josef Stipp, "Richter 19: Ein Frühes Beispiel Schriftgestützter Politischer Propaganda in Israel," in *Ein Herz so weit wie der Sand am Ufer des Meeres*, ed. Susanne Gillmayer-Bucher and Annett Giercke, ETS 90 (Würzburg: Echter, 2006), 141; and Edenburg, *Dismembering the Whole*, 327.

38. See, for example, Trible, *Texts of Terror*, 65; and Jan P. Fokkelman, "Structural Remarks on Judges 9 and 19," in *"Sha'arei Talmon": Studies in the Bible, Qumran, and the Ancient Near East Presented to Shemaryahu Talmon*, ed. Michael A. Fishbane, Emanuel Tov, and Weston W. Fields (Winona Lake, IN: Eisenbrauns, 1992), 43.

39. See, for example, J. Cheryl Exum, *Was sagt das Richterbuch den Frauen?*, SBS 169 (Suttgart: Katholisches Bibelwerk, 1997), 10–12, 58–59; Ilse Müllner, "Tödliche Differenzen: Sexuelle Gewalt als Gewalt gegen Andere in Ri 19," in *Von der Wurzel Getragen: Christliche-feministische Exegese in Auseinandersetzung mit Antijudaismus*, ed. Luise Schottroff and Marie-Theres Wacker, BibInt 17 (Leiden: Brill, 1996), 96–98; Frank M. Yamada, *Configurations of Rape in the Hebrew Bible*, StBibLit 109 (New York: Lang, 2008), 2.

| Verse | Possible Implication of Illicit Worship[36] | Anti-Saulide/ Benjaminite[37] | Hospitality[38] | Travel/ Transit | Threat/ Violence[39] |
|---|---|---|---|---|---|
| 1 | | | | | |
| 2 | + | | | + | |
| 3 | + | | | + | |
| 4 | | | + | | |
| 5 | + | | + | | |
| 6 | + | | + | | |
| 7 | + | | + | | |
| 8 | + | | + | | |
| 9 | + | | | | |
| 10 | + | | | + | |
| 11 | | | | + | |
| 12 | + | + | | + | |
| 13 | + | + | | + | |
| 14 | + | + | | + | |
| 15 | + | + | | + | |
| 16 | + | + | | | |
| 17 | | | | | |
| 18 | + | | | | |
| 19 | + | | | | |
| 20 | | | + | | |
| 21 | + | | + | | |
| 22 | + | + | + | | + |
| 23 | + | | | | + |
| 24 | + | | | | + |
| 25 | + | | | | + |
| 26 | | | | | |
| 27 | | | | | |
| 28 | | | | + | |
| 29 | + | + | | | + |
| 30 | | | | | |

Frequency may be an inconclusive measure of validity. However, an undercurrent of secondary significations which systematically point to topics of illicit worship significantly amplifies the narrated reality of a literary world described at the outset as without or in the absence of YHWH and YHWH's rule. As such, this finding is significant. Independent vignettes about travel, feasting, and violence, appearing oddly disjointed from each other within the narrative progression of the story, all evidence lexical, syntactical, or thematic content with secondary significations implying illicit worship practices. Intertextual interactions with secondary texts, pervasive throughout the chapter, systematically invert or distort echoed or alluded texts and their themes, thereby representing in its literary construction the narrated reality of a world in which "things are not how they ought to be." However, importantly within a text that is largely unstable, intertextual contact with other texts also introduces themes of usurpation, feasting, and abandonment. In a narrative world in which a pervasive secondary signification of multivalent words indicts the nation's illicit worship practices as having usurped the rule of YHWH, intertextuality might provide a subtext which provides the leitmotif. Rightful rule has been usurped by illicit practices, and in the resultant narrative world, nothing is "as it ought to be."

## Literary Representations of Sexual Violence

This project set out to discern the literary function and meaning of the narrated violence so characteristic of this chapter. Tools borrowed from narrative criticism confirmed the text of Judg 19 to be riddled with permanent literary gaps, lexically multivalent words, and textual incoherence. While any text evidences a certain amount of these literary phenomena, in Judg 19 the sheer number of these features combine to render the text largely unstable. In such a literary landscape, words and narrative facts become unreliable vehicles of data, calling upon the reader to supply information in order to resolve literary crises. However, amidst the textual ambiguity, the reader's work of meaning-making is perpetually subverted. This phenomenon, in light of the sheer number of literary crises evidenced in the chapter, may explain the varied treatments and interpretations this particular text has received from scholarship. Literary gapping and lexical multivalence invite the reader to interject, or read into, the text a vast number of assumptions and personal viewpoints, resulting in a nearly kaleidoscopic array of interpretive maneuvers.

Yet, the interpretive possibilities, opened by gapping and multivalence, are not as boundless as they may appear. Tools borrowed from intertextuality permit a reading that places the chapter within the encyclopedic environment of the Old Testament canon while exploring intertextual events as a means with which the text introduces a subtext of meaning. The chapter evidences numerous intertextual contacts with other texts. These textual events introduce the topics of usurpation, abandonment, and the absence of divine intervention as key themes. These themes—all of which are significant within the context of tenets evidenced in the book of Judges as a whole—combine with a narrative style that systematically distorts or inverts the themes and tropes of texts interacted with in order to represent in its very composition a narrative reality in which "things are not as they ought to be." Fascinatingly, this pattern is underscored with a pervasive secondary signification of multivalent words pointing to "illicit worship practices" as a literal subtext to the narration. Thus, intertextuality is able to provide a sort of leitmotif to a literary construction in which illicit worship practices usurp YHWH's rule, culminating in the breakdown of humanity.

Against this backdrop, the sexual nature of the literary representation of violence against the female character gains in importance. Judges 19 presents a husband who delivers his wife to be gang raped and subsequently dismembers her with the use of a knife. These are disturbing images, undoubtedly designed to shock. But they are also significant theologically within the context of the ideal set forth in Gen 1:27 and Gen 2:24. Not only does the creation narrative in Gen 1:26–31 recount the creation of male and female in the likeness of God, but it also implies a very particular understanding concerning the mutuality in which this creation took place and in which "men and women together image God in their differences and sameness."[40] Created in duality, men and women in mutuality image God. This ideal finds practical fulfillment in Gen 2:24, where unity is expressed in intimacy and given expression when male and female are described as becoming one flesh in matrimony. Though fractured amid shame (Gen 3:7) and obscured by hierarchy (Gen 3:16), this creation ideal may provide a lens through which to understand the literary significance of narrated acts of sexual violence.[41] Acts of sexual violence and intimate

---

40. Erin Dufault-Hunter, "Sex and Sexuality," in Green, *Dictionary of Scripture and Ethics*, 719.

41. Dufault-Hunter, "Sex and Sexuality," 719.

femicide are entirely destructive of the mutuality envisioned for a husband and a wife, specifically, and for women and men living in community in general. Thus, the very fact that the violent acts against the woman are of a sexual nature, rupturing the intimacy of the marriage ideal, come to impact how these literary characters "image God." In a literary world rife with illicit worship, the narrated relationship between YHWH and his people finally fractures in the literary representation of shattered human mutuality. Rape and dismemberment constitute the ultimate distortion of human mutuality and consequently of how male and female image God. This concluding episode of narrated sexual violence represents the final literary distortion in a chapter presenting a literary portrait of a world in which "things are not how they ought to be."

Judges 19 is an enigmatic text. The current analysis does not attempt to resolve its issues definitively, nor does it attempt to offer an all-encompassing interpretation. This writing is merely one more contribution to the growing literature addressing the issues raised by the chapter in light of an intertextual approach. As such, it confirmed what others have noted previously: The text of Judg 19 "cannot hold."[42] However, the literary abyss so noted is not quite as dramatic as one may suspect. Intertextual literary events introduce themes of usurpation, abandonment, and divine absence. These are significant themes within the context of a book narrating the persistent apostasy, repentance, deliverance, and repeated backsliding of a nation, culminating in what appears to be the cessation of YHWH's raising up of deliverers. Judges 19, then, as the center chapter of what constitutes the final five chapters of the book of Judges, presents in content and structure the narrative reality of a society disintegrating in apostasy. As such, the chapter does not shy away from portraying the grim reality of humanity—its duality in mutuality—as destroying its very self and, consequently, its ability to image God to the world. Against this literary portrait, the ensuing fratricide of chapters 20 and 21 are merely the literary representation of a narrative reality already presented in chapter 19.

---

42. Exum, "Centre Cannot Hold," 410–29.

# Ancestral Voices and Disavowal: Poetic Innovation and Intertextuality in the Eighth-Century Prophets

*Francis Landy*

## Texts and Intertexts

Three issues will concern me in this paper: (1) The prophets were living in a sea of texts. Every word is evidence of a highly literate society, which we may associate, in the case of the eighth century prophets, with the development of states in Judah and Israel, but which draws on much more ancient resources.[1] (2) Prophetic books are demarcated, bounded texts, with strong evidence of intentional composition and individual authorship, however one may understand that. (3) *Intertextuality* is a term with different meanings, applicable to a wide variety of fields, such as music and translation studies, and one whose heyday has perhaps passed. One must be careful as to what one means by it and how to use it, while being open to its polysemy.

I will elaborate on these below: (1) One does not know how much writing there was in ancient Israel. What there is evidence for is a literary habit of mind, shown through inscriptions, school texts, and a scribal tradition, as demonstrated, for instance, by Christopher A. Rollston;[2] there is also a vast panoply of texts, written and oral, on which poets and prophets could draw and which conditioned expectations. For example, if Isaiah

---

1. By this, I do not imply a high rate of literacy, which is extremely improbable, merely a society in which texts were valued and pervasive.
2. Christopher A. Rollston, *Writing and Literacy in the World of Ancient Israel: Epigraphic Evidence from the Iron Age*, ABS 11 (Atlanta: Society of Biblical Literature, 2010). Rollston argues on the basis of epigraphic evidence for formal scribal training, at least among the elite.

is commanded: "Go and say to this people" (Isa 6:9), one knows what to anticipate; Amos and Hosea, at least, see themselves as the heirs of a prophetic tradition. Whether this tradition was in writing or not, we cannot know.[3] Finally, there is a world saturated with texts and images that had a greater or lesser impact on Israel. The most pertinent example is Assyrian imperial texts.[4]

(2) It is a truism that prophetic books are something new in the ancient Near East and differentiate Israelite prophecy from its Assyrian coevals.[5] Once you start to have a book, you begin also to have literary complexity. Amos and Hosea, at least, have strongly marked structural boundaries.[6] In Amos, the formulaic sequence of oracles against the

---

3. David M. Carr, *The Formation of the Hebrew Bible: A New Reconstruction* (Oxford: Oxford University Press, 2011), traces the beginnings of Israelite literature to early state formation, in the tenth to ninth century, including some early pentateuchal traditions, psalms, and wisdom literature. Mark Leuchter, *The Levites and the Boundaries of Israelite Identity* (Oxford: Oxford University Press, 2017), 20–23, argues for the continuity of scribal culture from the Late Bronze Age into prestate Israel and that some literary texts are very early.

4. It is widely accepted that Israelite literature of the eighth century was influenced by, and a response to, Assyrian imperial propaganda. See William M. Schniedewind, *How the Bible Became a Book* (Cambridge: Cambridge University Press, 2004), 45, 64–84; and Schniedewind, *A Social History of Hebrew: Its Origins through the Rabbinic Period*, AYBRL (New Haven: Yale University Press, 2013), 73–97. The classic contribution on the influence of Assyria on Isaiah is Peter Machinist, "Assyria and Its Image in First Isaiah," *JAOS* 103 (1983): 719–37. Hanna Liss, *Die Unerhöhrte Prophetie: Kommunikative Strukturen prophetische Rede im Buch Yesha'yahu* (Berlin: Evangelische Verlagsanstalt, 2003) examines at length how Isaiah defamiliarizes and reverses Assyrian imperial imagery. See also Friedhelm Hartenstein, *Das Archiv des verborgenen Gottes: Studien zur Unheilsprophetie Jesajas und zur Zionstheologie der Psalmen in assyrische Zeit* (Neukirchen-Vluyn: Neukirchener Verlag, 2011); and Seth L. Sanders, *The Invention of Hebrew* (Urbana: University of Illinois Press, 2009), 148–55.

5. See, for instance, Reinhard G. Kratz, *The Prophets of Israel*, trans. Anselm C. Hagedorn and Nathan MacDonald, CSHB 2 (Winona Lake, IN: Eisenbrauns, 2015), 28. A further distinction is that oracles from Assyria have only been recovered from the royal archives and clearly are preserved as part of the royal agenda. See the detailed study of Matthijs J. de Jong, *Isaiah among the Ancient Near East Prophets: A Comparative Study of the Earliest Stages of the Isaiah Tradition and Neo-Assyrian Prophets*, VTSup 117 (Leiden: Brill, 2007).

6. This is a powerful argument against the thesis that the Minor Prophets constituted an independent Book of the Twelve. See Ehud Ben Zvi, "Is the Twelve Hypothesis Likely from an Ancient Reader's Perspective?," in *Two Sides of a Coin: Juxtaposing*

nations at the beginning is matched by the series of visions at the end; in Hosea, the tripartite structure (Hos 1–3, 4–11, and 12–14) is framed by the concentricity of chapters 2 and 14 and the alternation of matching chapters in the central section.[7] Isaiah 1–12 has long been recognized as having a double concentric structure, and similar patterns can be observed for the rest of the book, for instance in the series of *hoy* oracles that unify chapters 28–33.[8] It may be the case that these structures have been retrospectively imposed by editors of the books in the way that the final editors or composers of the book of Isaiah self-consciously matched beginning and end, but equally they may be the work of original composers.[9] The very tight organization of Hosea, Amos, and Isa 1–12 suggests intentional design at some stage of the compositional process. Poets may compose prospectively and retrospectively—with an eye to the past as well as the future—as part of a career, a trajectory. One has to read an image in the light of its occurrences elsewhere. This renders any poem intertextual. There are methodological issues I have not yet discussed, notably the questions of orality, supplementation, and style. Nonetheless, the point is that in a strong sense, the early prophetic writings are *texts*, not intertexts, even though they may be intertextually connected to others, retrospectively and prospectively, and even though they are unified by connections which may be intertextual as well as intratextual, if we are dealing with originally separate compositions.

---

*Views on the Book of the Twelve/The Twelve Prophetic Books*, ed. Ehud Ben Zvi and James Nogalski (Piscataway, NJ: Gorgias, 2009), 41–96, especially 72–80; and my comments in Francis Landy, "Three Sides of a Coin: In Conversation with Ben Zvi and Nogalski, *Two Sides of a Coin*," *JHS* 10 (2010): 1–21.

7. Francis Landy, *Hosea*, 2nd ed., Readings (Sheffield: Sheffield Phoenix, 2011), 4–5, provides a detailed structural breakdown.

8. Erhard Blum, "Jesajas prophetisches Testament: Beobachtungen zu Jes 1–11," *ZAW* 108 (1996): 547–68; 109 (1997): 12–29; Jörg Barthel, *Prophetenwort und Geschichte: Die Jesajaüberlieferung in Jes 6–8 und 28–31*, FAT 19 (Tübingen: Mohr Siebeck, 1997), 43–56; Andrew H. Bartelt, *The Book around Immanuel: Style and Structure in Isaiah 2–12*, BJSUCSD 4 (Winona Lake, IN: Eisenbrauns, 1996); Gary Stansell, "Isaiah 28–33: Blessed Be the Tie that Binds (Isaiah Together)," in *New Visions of Isaiah*, ed. Marvin A. Sweeney and Roy F. Melugin, JSOTSup 214 (Sheffield: Sheffield Academic, 1996), 68–103.

9. Contra Eva Mroczek's thesis that the concept of the book is anachronistic in ancient times. See Eva Mroczek, *The Literary Imagination in Jewish Antiquity* (Oxford: Oxford University Press, 2016), 10–11.

(3) Julia Kristeva defines intertextuality as "the *passage from one sign system to another*."[10] It need not be textual or even linguistic at all. Her parade example is the transposition of the semiotics of the carnival into the dialogic novel.[11] Moreover, in *Revolution in Poetic Language*, she drops the term in favor of *transposition*, because "intertextuality" can be used banally to refer to allusion or influence. Accordingly, she holds that every work of art is the confluence of several sign systems and thus plural:

> If one grants that every signifying practice is a field of transpositions of various signifying systems (an inter-textuality), one then understands that its "place" of enunciation and its denoted "object" are never single, complete, and identical to themselves, but always plural, shattered, capable of being tabulated. In this way polysemy can also be seen as the result of semiotic polyvalence—an adherence to different sign systems.[12]

Transposition means the "abandonment" of the old sign system, its transference to a new one, and, most importantly, the articulation of the new system with its new "representability," which she defines as "the specific articulation of the semiotic and the thetic for a sign system."[13] The semiotic, a key term for Kristeva, is the traces or marks of drive energy in the body, manifest for instance in vocalic play; its complement, in the signifying process, is the symbolic—the order of language, law, and society.[14] The thetic is the bridge between them, the condition for the establishment of propositional truth. In poetry, the semiotic is transferred to the symbolic and vice versa; there are constant interactions of sound and sense. The heterogeneity of the semiotic and the symbolic, of drive energy and the order of language, renders a poem fundamentally disunified. As "a field of transpositions" it is "shattered," polyvalent, but at the same time, it is a process, an interaction,

---

10. Julia Kristeva, *Revolution in Poetic Language*, trans. Margaret Waller (New York: Columbia University Press, 1984), 59, emphasis original.
11. This is explored most thoroughly in her essay, "The Bounded Text," in Julia Kristeva, *Desire in Language: A Semiotic Approach to Literature and Art*, ed. Leon S. Roudiez, trans. Thomas Gora, Alice Jardine, and Leon S. Roudiez (New York: Columbia University Press, 1980), 36–63. It clearly shows the influence of Mikhail M. Bakhtin.
12. Kristeva, *Revolution in Poetic Language*, 60.
13. Kristeva, *Revolution in Poetic Language*, 60.
14. Kelly Oliver, *Reading Kristeva: Unraveling the Double-Bind* (Bloomington: Indiana University Press, 1993), 18–48, provides a succinct account of Kristeva's concepts of the semiotic and the symbolic and her differences with Lacan.

whereby vocalic clusters may acquire symbolic meaning and language as signification is felt sensually. Kristeva is, in fact, close to Roman Jakobson, in his insistence that the "poetic function" of language is the "set (*Einstellung*) towards the MESSAGE as such," the actual verbal medium.[15]

Michael Riffaterre writes that "the very idea of textuality is inseparable from and founded upon intertextuality" and continues with the following definition: "Intertextuality is a mode of perception, the deciphering of the text by the reader in such a way that he identifies the structures to which the text owes its quality of a work of art."[16] Unlike Kristeva, he sees it as primarily a literary and aesthetic phenomenon and as the work of the reader rather than the writer, though in the examples he gives, it is hard to see why it should be so. It is a perception of underlying structures beneath the variants that constitute individual works of art.[17] For Riffaterre, every word is double-sided, or in his terminology, *sylleptic*, referring to something both literally and figuratively.[18] It points both to an object in the "real" world and to an intertextual field. For example, Wordsworth's sonnet, "Composed Upon Westminster Bridge, 3 September, 1803," is both a description of London at dawn and a comment on the pastoral tradition; a competent reader must be aware of that tradition to understand it.[19] There is thus a double mimesis, of the outside world and of other texts, either complementarily—when the text accords with its intertexts—or negatively, when it rejects them. Riffaterre also discusses the role of the intertextual unconscious, when a text's overt meaning may conflict with its hidden and subversive meanings derived from other texts.[20]

---

15. See especially her essay, "The Ethics of Linguistics," in Kristeva, *Desire in Language*, 23–35, emphasis original. She admires Roman Jakobson for his interest in verbal play, as part of her critique of Structuralism as lacking an awareness of the emotional and sensual intensity of language; Roman Jakobson, "Closing Statement: Linguistics and Poetics," in *Style in Language*, ed. Thomas A. Sebeok (Cambridge: MIT Press, 1960), 357.

16. Michael Riffaterre, "Syllepsis," *CI* 6 (1980): 625.

17. It could thus be seen as similar to form or genre criticism, though it is clear that Riffaterre means it more broadly.

18. Riffaterre, "Syllepsis," 629. The term is borrowed from Derrida, though the usage goes back to 1750. In a syllepsis, one meaning is literal and primary and the other metaphorical.

19. Michael Riffaterre, "Intertextual Representation: On Mimesis as Interpretive Discourse," *CI* 11 (1984): 149–59.

20. Michael Riffaterre, "The Intertextual Unconscious," *CI* 13 (1987): 371–85.

In this essay, following Kristeva and Riffaterre, I am not going to be primarily concerned with allusion and influence, fascinating as they might be, with the texts as part of a literary history.[21] I will focus on the different "sign systems" present in the prophetic books, on the cultural competence they assume; the tension between the heterogeneity and unity of the prophetic books; and, finally, on the close readings the interpretation of intertextuality demands. On one level, it is a global phenomenon, but it is only manifest through local effects.

## Types of Intertextuality

I will confine myself to the so-called eighth-century prophets, more for convenience than anything else and without any confidence that we can isolate eighth-century texts from others in the prophetic tradition. All texts are products of a complex process. I will outline the different sign systems present in the texts before turning to specific examples. Inevitably, the list is somewhat ad hoc, and can never be exhaustive:

(1) The ritual system. The prophetic books assume a background of the ritual system, as a mode of communication both with God (or other deities) and the rest of society. Their relationship to the ritual system may be positive or, more conspicuously, polemical.

(2) History. The prophetic books are comments on and interpretations of historical events and processes. From a retrospective point of view, the prophetic books and the Deuteronomistic History are entirely interdependent.[22] The historical books validate prophecy; the prophetic books require a consciousness of history. Projecting back onto an earlier period, it is evident that the prophets interpreted current events in the light of the past, or particular versions of the past. This may also include myth; the repetition of primordial events, such as creation; theomachy; and the exodus.

---

21. For the difference between allusion and intertextuality, see Benjamin D. Sommer, *A Prophet Reads Scripture: Allusion in Isaiah 40–66*, Contra (Stanford, CA: Stanford University Press, 1998), 6–10. Riffaterre, "Syllepsis," 627, helpfully comments that influence refers to a vertical relationship between text and its past, while intertextuality refers to the lateral relationships between texts and other texts in its present. Confusion between allusion and intertextuality is rampant, however, including in biblical studies. I prefer to see allusion as a subset of intertextuality.

22. Ian D. Wilson, *Kingship and Memory in Ancient Judah* (Oxford: Oxford University Press, 2017) focuses on the mutual emplotments of history and prophecy.

(3) All we have are texts, infused through and through with the spirit of writing. Yet, as F. W. Dobbs-Allsopp points out, these texts grew up in a profoundly oral culture, the vast bulk of whose poetic production has disappeared along with the singers and hearers.[23] In an oral world, as in the contemporary folk scene, every performance offers the possibility of revision and improvisation, an ever-changing interaction between artist and audience. The standard model sees oral performance as primary and writing as a secondary development in response to the perceived failure of the prophet's teaching. Texts such as Isa 8:16 and Jer 36 and 45 would support this. But if literature were "interfacial," in Dobbs-Allsopp's felicitous phrase, orality was as penetrated by literacy as vice versa.[24] Especially in an elite culture, such as eighth-century Jerusalem or Samaria, one can imagine prophets writing for posterity, as a means of composition, or to assert the significance of the divine word, its transcendence of any human situation. The difference between oral and literary composition, as well as the interactions between them, makes the text polyphonic; it evokes a culture and all previous or subsequent performances. Every text is only one of the many texts that might have been; moreover, every text, especially in antiquity, reverts to orality as soon as it is written, being transmitted, for example, through memory.

(4) Similar considerations affect processes of redaction and editing; prophetic books may be supplemented or abbreviated, with radical shifts of meaning. The new text may coexist uneasily with the old one. This is evidently an issue with major collections such as Isaiah. The more one writes, the more difficult it will be to achieve poetic unity. The text is fundamentally heterogenous.

(5) Prophetic poetry is part of a practice in which every action has potential significance and in which we must imagine numerous engagements with disciples, with institutions, with family, and so on. If a prophet is characterized by "an alternate state of consciousness," which has a therapeutic function, this consciousness would pervade all spheres of life.[25]

---

23. F. W. Dobbs-Allsopp, *On Biblical Poetry* (Oxford: Oxford University Press, 2015), 234.

24. Dobbs-Allsopp, *On Biblical Poetry*, 318. The term actually goes back to Jack Goody, *The Interface between the Written and the Oral* (Cambridge: Cambridge University Press, 1987).

25. Prophets participate in what Pieter F. Craffert calls "the shamanic complex," common to all Mediterranean societies (and probably worldwide). The shamanic com-

We have traces of this in prophetic "signs." In any case, we must suppose minute interactions between the prophet's biography, as a set of sign systems, and the text, as another set of sign systems. This may apply also to successors, scribes, and editors.

(6) The personality of the prophet and of the speaking voice in the poem is split between the voice of God, whose message the prophet supposedly transmits, and the human voice and allegiances of the prophet—between the shamanic and the ordinary self. This sometimes expresses itself in prophetic resistance, when the prophet speaks on behalf of condemned humanity. The text is then a translation, or a set of translations, of vision into voice, of divine speech into human understanding. At times we have reference to a book of YHWH, which may or may not be coterminous with our book.[26]

(7) For Kristeva, as we have seen, the two fundamental sign systems that intersect in the poetic text are the *semiotic* and the *symbolic*. In the prophets, this interaction may take various forms. Drive energy (i.e., the semiotic) may be manifested in phonemic play, pleasure in language for its own sake. The prophetic message may be burdensome, horrific, but also beautiful. At the same time, alliterative patterns may, and often do, acquire symbolic significance. Moreover, since the prophet speaks on behalf of a deity who destroys the world—and with it the entire symbolic, cultural order—as well as being its creator and redeemer, he expresses a profound ambivalence, whereby death is as powerful as life. The prophet imaginatively and prospectively annuls the world he loves and of which he is part.

---

plex is characterized by an alternate state of consciousness, a transformative or therapeutic function, and communication with an alternative mode of reality. See Pieter F. Craffert, "Shamanism and the Shamanic Complex," *BTB* 41 (2011): 66; and Craffert, "Alternate States of Consciousness and Biblical Research: The Contribution of John Pilch," *BTB* 47 (2017): 100–10. The definition is adapted from Geoffrey Samuel, *Civilized Shamans: Buddhism in Tibetan Societies* (Washington, DC: Smithsonian Institution Press, 1993), 8. James L. Kugel, *The Great Shift: Encountering God in Biblical Times* (New York: Houghton Mifflin Harcourt, 2017), 18, 107–8, similarly contrasts the "revelatory state of mind" of the prophets with the modern Cartesian self. See also my unpublished paper, Francis Landy, "Shamanic Poetics: With Stammering Lips and Another Tongue Will He Speak to This People" (paper presented at the International Meeting of the Society of Biblical Literature/European Association of Biblical Studies, Berlin, Germany, 11 August 2017).

26. Examples are Isa 34:16 and Mal 3:16.

(8) The prophet may be unaware of the meaning of his words. In other words, there may be unconscious meanings and an irreducible polyvalence. If the poet speaks on behalf of an Other, of an exigent alterity, as Maurice Blanchot and Emmanuel Levinas each claim,[27] then it threatens the foundations of the ego. As Kristeva says, we are strangers to ourselves, inhabiting, at least imaginatively, a strange new world.[28]

## Examples

I will now turn to specific examples. Ideally, one should cite whole books, instead of which I will take a verse—chosen almost at random—and a chapter, and then draw together texts chosen from two books. My concern will be with textual and intertextual boundaries and one particular issue I have not referred to above, though it is implicit in all of the systems I have noted: the tension between tradition and innovation, between the prophet as the temporary incarnation of prophecy and as an individual voice.

Amos 1:2

ה׳ מציון ישאג ומירושלם יתן קולו ואבלו נאות הרעים ויבש ראש הכרמל
YHWH roars from Zion, and from Jerusalem he gives forth his voice, and the meadows of the shepherds mourn, and the summit of the Carmel is dry.[29] (Amos 1:2)

This is the introductory verse of Amos, following the very interesting superscription in verse 1, and like every introduction, it is supposed to

---

27. See Maurice Blanchot, "Prophetic Speech," in *The Book to Come*, trans. Charlotte Mandell (Stanford, CA: Stanford University Press, 2003), 82, 84; Emmanuel Levinas, *Otherwise than Being or Beyond Essence*, trans. Alphono Lingis (Pittsburgh: Duquesne University Press, 1981), 149. See also Francis Landy, "Maurice Blanchot on Prophetic Speech," in *Welcome to the Cavalcade: A Festschrift in Honour of Rabbi Professor Jonathan Magonet*, ed. Ellie Tikvah Sarah, Colin Eimer, and Howard Cooper (London: Kulmus, 2013), 356–67; and Landy, "Levinas on Prophecy," in *Making a Difference: Essays on the Bible and Judaism in Honor of Tamara Cohn Eskenazi*, ed. David J. A. Clines, Kent H. Richards, and Jacob L. Wright, HBM 49 (Sheffield: Sheffield Academic, 2012), 179–203.

28. Julia Kristeva, *Strangers to Ourselves*, trans. Leon S. Roudiez (New York: Columbia University Press, 1991). See also Oliver, *Reading Kristeva*, 12–13.

29. Unless indicated otherwise, all biblical translations are mine.

introduce the book and to mark the boundary between inside and outside. What interests me is the way it shifts the discourse.[30] Zion only appears once elsewhere in the book (6:1) and is decidedly second fiddle to Samaria. It may, of course, be what Sara J. Milstein calls "revision through introduction" and be analogous to the Judah-centric conclusion.[31] But it also makes YHWH an outsider, comparable to Amos as outsider, to the busy world of northern Israel. Zion is opposed to Carmel; Carmel comes back in 9:3 as a place from which one cannot hide from God. We might suppose Zion to be the representative of the south and Carmel of the north.[32] The shepherds may be a conventional metaphor for rulers; it thus leads us to expect a polemic against the north as schismatic.[33] Zion is YHWH's true place, Jerusalem the city from which he sends forth his voice; his wrath is directed against the dissident north—in other words, it evokes the mainstream Deuteronomistic narrative, of which there is not a trace in the rest of the book.[34] But there are other implications. The metaphor of the lion recurs in 3:3–8 as part of a series of rhetorical questions: "Will the lion roar from the forest, when it has no prey? Will the young lion give forth its voice from its den when it has caught nothing?" (3:4); and "The lion roars, who will not fear? My Lord YHWH has spoken, who will not prophesy?" (3:8).

Prophecy here is both a response to the lion's roar—elsewhere in the sequence, the prophet is analogous to a shofar, warning the people of

---

30. It is odd that no one notices this. Most scholars see 1:2 unproblematically as the "motto" of the book. Examples are James R. Linville, *Amos and the Cosmic Imagination*, SOTSMS (Farnham, Surrey, UK: Ashgate, 2008), 43; Karl Möller, *A Prophet in Debate: The Rhetoric of Persuasion in the Book of Amos*, JSOTSup 372 (Sheffield: Sheffield Academic, 2003), 170; and Göran Eidevall, *Amos: A New Translation with Introduction and Commentary*, AYBRL (New Haven: Yale University Press, 2017), 90.

31. Sara J. Milstein, *Tracking the Master Scribe: Revision through Introduction in Biblical and Mesopotamian Literature* (Oxford: Oxford University Press, 2016).

32. Carmel has rich intertextual associations, for instance with Elijah's triumph over the priests of Baal. It is unclear how this might contribute to an understanding of the verse, for instance as a place of prophetic judgment.

33. Pietro Bovati and Roland Meynet, *Le Livre du Prophète Amos* (Paris: Cerf, 1994), 30.

34. Representative of the view that it emanates from a Judean, Deuteronomistically inspired redaction, perhaps from the reign of Josiah, is Hans Walter Wolff, *Joel and Amos*, trans. Waldemar Janzen, Sean D. McBride, and Charles A. Muenchow, Hermeneia (Philadelphia: Fortress, 1977), 121. See also John Barton, *The Theology of the Book of Amos* (Cambridge: Cambridge University Press, 2012), 142–44.

danger—and an articulation of it, since he is YHWH's servant and messenger. But the lion is in the forest, not in the city; YHWH is both an external threat and an inner violence. According to 3:6, there is no evil in the city that YHWH has not done. Then at the heart of Zion, in the holy of holies, at the center of the sacred city, is something wild, a denizen of the forest, as it were, a minotaur.

Of course, there are other texts, with different images of YHWH, especially the so-called doxologies: "For behold, the one who forms mountains and creates wind, and tells human being what is its thought" (Amos 4:13). From the formed mountains we go to the formless wind and then to speech, in what seems to be a regress, possibly to the thought of creation. The subject of "its thought" (שחו) is ambiguous: it could be humanity, or it could be God.[35] If the latter, then it refers to prophecy, but as a universal propensity; if humanity (אדם) is the subject, God reveals to human beings what their own thoughts are—his is the hidden speech of which theirs is a reflection. In either case, language is the discourse of an Other; to return to Kristeva for a moment, we are strangers to ourselves.

Hosea 12

Hosea 12 is as complicated as any chapter in the book, characterized by extreme transitions between past and present, Judah and Ephraim, condemnation and hope. I will concentrate on the twinning of Jacob and Moses and the prophets, and the status of the chapter as metaprophetic.

> There is a contention of YHWH with Judah, to visit upon Jacob his ways and to requite his deeds. In the womb he gripped his brother, and in his virility he strove with God. He strove against the angel, and he prevailed; he wept and begged mercy from him; at Bethel he would find him; and there he will speak with us. And YHWH, God of Hosts, YHWH is his remembrance. (Hos 12:3–6)[36]

Most discussion of this enigmatic passage has focused on Hosea's sources and on whether the characterization of Jacob is positive or negative. From

---

35. Many commentators note the ambiguity, and rather casually dismiss the former possibility, probably because it seems too strange.

36. Translation follows my commentary (Landy, *Hosea*, 168–69), which also provides the basis for the subsequent discussion.

an intertextual point of view, however, what matters is the transposition of the Genesis text, in all its complexity, onto the prophetic one. Hosea 12:3–6 is entirely ambiguous.[37] We do not know who wept, who begged mercy, whether God would find Jacob at Bethel or vice versa, whether עִמָּנוּ means "with us," as the MT punctuation suggests עִמּוֹ, "with him."[38] Most seriously, we do not know whether the *rib* against Judah, which is immediately transferred to Jacob, refers to his uterine struggles. Are the deeds which are to be requited his ancestral wiles or his present malfeasance? Was Jacob/Israel originally pernicious? Is God, as the parallelism might indicate, equivalent to Esau? However, in Gen 25:22–23, the strife of the twins is ordained by God, and Jacob's success is the subject of a divine oracle. Both events provide etiologies of his name and thus his character: Jacob is the one who "heeled" (עָקַב) his brother and strove (שׂרה) with God—he is the fighter and the trickster. The trajectory from Jacob to Israel suggests a transformation, as with other changes of name.[39] Bethel is the site of Jacob's theophanies (Gen 28:10–22; 35:1–15), his formative encounters, and thus of his (or YHWH's) remembrance, which may mean the ritual recitation of his name or the recollection of the deep past. The name Bethel contrasts with Hosea's usual derisive Beth-Awen, the house of folly; it may suggest that it is still the house of God, despite its corruption. Past and present intermesh.

Why Judah?[40] It may be inclusive, as some commentators propose, but it is also a distraction. It may evoke, for instance, Judah's own murky history or indicate that God's wrath will not be exhausted by his condem-

---

37. Ehud Ben Zvi, *Hosea*, FOTL 21A (Grand Rapids: Eerdmans, 2005), 249–51, provides an exhaustive exposition of the different possibilities and their putative effect on the readership (which for him is postmonarchic). See also Landy, *Hosea*, 173. Others opt for a one-sidedly negative interpretation, for instance Mayer Gruber, *Hosea: A Textual Commentary*, LHBOTS 653 (London: Bloomsbury, 2017), 499–501.

38. Many correct to עִמּוֹ, but this is hardly necessary.

39. Else K. Holt, *Prophesying the Past: The Use of Israel's History in the Book of Hosea*, JSOTSup 194 (Sheffield: Sheffield Academic, 1995), 39, suggests that it is a conversion narrative.

40. This is often corrected to "Israel." Gruber is a typical example, with an interesting reconstruction of the history of the change (*Hosea*, 498). Ben Zvi thinks that, in a postmonarchic setting, it stresses the inclusivity of Jacob/Israel as incorporating both Judah and Ephraim (*Hosea*, 247–48). The status of Judah throughout Hosea is ambiguous; it is both an "other" to the northern kingdom and shares in its destiny.

nation of Ephraim. As elsewhere in Hosea, and as with Jacob and Esau, the fraternal rivals become indistinguishable.

Toward the end of the chapter, Jacob returns, coupled with Moses:

> And Jacob fled to the country of Aram, and Jacob toiled for a wife, and kept watch for a wife. And through a prophet YHWH brought Israel out of Egypt, and through a prophet it was watched over. (12:13–14)

Again, this is often thought to be to Jacob's discredit: Jacob kept watch for a *mere* woman.[41] But the parallels are startling: Moses, like Jacob, fled, found his wife by a well, and was a shepherd. Moreover, the passage cannot be read except against the background of Jacob's self-vindication in Gen 31:38–41. He is a precursor of Moses whose commitment to his wife anticipates that of Moses, or the prophet more generally, to his descendants.

Hosea sees himself as being at the end of a long line of destructive prophets, for instance in 6:5. Here there is another image: that of the prophet as the true and faithful shepherd. Jacob's virility (און) manifests itself in erotic desire, which recollects that of YHWH for Israel at the beginning of the book.

In 12:11, there is another image of prophecy:

> And I spoke through the prophets, and I multiplied vision, and through the prophets I would be compared.

The context is YHWH's continued care for Israel since the exodus ("I am YHWH your God from the land of Egypt" [Hos 12:10]), parallel to that of the prophet in verse 14, the condemnation of the proliferation of cult sites (12:12), and the desire to return to a primordial communion, as in 2:16, of which festivals, especially the festival of Sukkot, may be a reenactment: "once more I will make you dwell in tents, as in the days of the appointed festival" (12:10). In this connection, YHWH's speech, which renews the initial relationship, is accompanied by the multiplication of vision. The speech is presumably all the same, though in different words, and equivalent to the vision. The silent vision is always translated and comprises

---

41. An example is Hans Walter Wolff, *Hosea*, trans. Gary Stansell, Hermeneia (Philadelphia: Fortress, 1974), 216. For a positive reading of the parallel, see A. A. Macintosh, *Hosea: A Critical and Exegetical Commentary*, ICC (London: Bloomsbury, 2014), 508–13.

an aspect of the passage's intertextuality. The connection between speech and vision is confirmed by wordplay: דברתי ("I spoke") is permutated in הרביתי ("I multiplied"). The many words and the many visions merge, attesting to an underlying musicality, the crossover between the semiotic and the symbolic. The prophet's task is to find images for the imageless ("through the prophets I would be compared"), to trace the vision back to the invisible.

The word for "compare" (דמה) is the same as that for "destroy," and the two meanings coalesce, for instance in 10:7 and 10:15.[42] The care of the prophets, and of YHWH who brought Israel out of Egypt, is the obverse of their destructiveness. Repeatedly, words have double and contradictory meanings: און, "virility," for instance, is homonymous with און ("folly" or "iniquity") and און ("wealth").[43] The words and visions emanate from YHWH and return to him; the book is full of images of transitoriness. It exemplifies the fundamental conflict between life and death, doom and hope. All words and images are subject to erasure; since all are inadequate, all may acquire opposite connotations. The poetic process is one of creation and destruction.

Micah and Isaiah

Isaiah 2:2–4 is almost identical to Mic 4:1–3, and Isa 2:7–8 has some similarities with Mic 5:9–14. I am not concerned here with the priority of one over the other, with the question of why Isaiah grew to become the book it is, or with why there is a book of Micah at all.[44] The common material

---

42. For the ambiguity, see Ben Zvi, *Hosea*, 254. I do not agree with Ben Zvi, however, that על could also mean "against" (the prophets) in this context. A further meaning of דמה is "silence"; speech reverts to speechlessness.

43. Michael Fishbane, *Biblical Interpretation in Ancient Israel* (Oxford: Clarendon, 1985), 379, comments on this chain as an example of Hosea's midrashic interpretation of the Genesis narrative.

44. Peter R. Ackroyd, "Isaiah I–XII: Presentation of a Prophet," in *Congress Volume: Göttingen 1977*, ed. John A. Emerton, VTSup 29 (Leiden: Brill, 1978), 16–48. Ackroyd argued that more and more material was attributed to Isaiah because of the authoritative status, communicated especially through his presentation in chapters 1–12, and that at one time Micah might have been the more prestigious prophet. See also Ehud Ben Zvi, "Isaiah, a Memorable Prophet: Why Was Isaiah So Memorable in the Late Persian/Early Hellenistic Periods? Some Observations," in *Remembering Biblical Figures in the Late Persian and Early Hellenistic Periods: Social Memory and*

clearly blurs the boundaries between the two texts so that neither is completely autonomous. Yet the passages are integral to the respective books, contributing to their overall unity and coherence, such as it is. Isaiah 2:2–4 is a second introduction to the book of Isaiah, corresponding to the climax in chapter 66, and is marked as such by the new superscription in 2:1.[45] Micah 4:1–3 begins a new section of the book of Micah, which is closed by 5:9–14. In both cases, moreover, it is connected to the preceding section. In Isaiah, 2:2–4 follows the restoration of Zion to its original state and the perdition of sinners in 1:26–31, so much so that some commentators see it as a conclusion to chapter 1.[46] Micah 4:1–3 reverses the prediction of Zion's destruction in 3:12 in a sudden peripeteia.

But the contexts are very different. Isaiah 2:2–4 and 2:6–22 (including 2:7–8) are juxtaposed as programmatic alternative futures: the pilgrimage of the nations to Zion to learn the ways of the Torah and establish universal peace is contrasted with the terrifying vision of the day of YHWH. Micah 4:1–3 and 5:9–14 frame a section which is essentially positive, contrasting with both the previous and succeeding parts of the book.[47] The difference can be seen in the respective continuations of Isa 2:2–4 and Mic 4:1–3:

---

*Imagination*, ed. Diana V. Edelman and Ehud Ben Zvi (Oxford: Oxford University Press, 2013), 383 n. 54, who suggests that from the point of view of social theory, Micah might have been squeezed out by Isaiah. Burkard M. Zapff, "Why Is Micah Similar to Isaiah?," *ZAW* 129 (2017): 536–54, proposes that Micah was constructed as representative of Isaiah in the Book of the Twelve.

45. H. G. M. Williamson, *The Book Called Isaiah: Deutero-Isaiah's Role in Composition and Redaction* (Oxford: Clarendon, 1994), 153–154; Williamson, *Isaiah 1–5*, ICC (London: T&T Clark, 2006), 165, 172. See also Marvin A. Sweeney, *Isaiah 1–39 with an Introduction to Prophetic Literature*, FOTL 16 (Grand Rapids: Eerdmans, 1996), 45, who thinks it introduces chapters 2–33. Isaiah 1 is frequently held to have been composed subsequently as an introduction to the entire book, a suggestion first made by Georg Fohrer, "Jesaja 1 als Zusammenfassung der Verkündigung Jesajas," *ZAW* 74 (1962): 251–68. On chapter 66 as a fulfillment of the oracle of 2:2–4, see Ulrich F. Berges, *The Book of Isaiah: Its Composition and Final Form*, trans. Millard C. Lind, HBM 46 (Sheffield: Sheffield Phoenix, 2012), 502.

46. See, for example, John Goldingay, "Isaiah I 1 and II 1," *VT* 48 (1998): 330–32; and Joëlle Ferry, *Isaïe: "Comme les mots d'un livre scellé" (Is 29, 11)*, LD 212 (Paris: Cerf, 2008), 43–45.

47. Mignon R. Jacobs, *The Conceptual Coherence of the Book of Micah*, JSOTSup 322 (Sheffield: Sheffield Academic, 2001), 70–79 provides a good overall summary of the structure.

O house of Jacob, come, let us go in the light of YHWH. For you have abandoned your people, house of Jacob. (Isa 2:5–6a)

For each will sit under his vine and under his fig tree, and there will be none to make afraid, for the mouth of YHWH of Hosts has spoken. For all the peoples go, each in the name of their god(s), and we go in the name of YHWH our god for ever and ever. (Mic 4:4–5)

In the first case, we do not know if the "house of Jacob" is the same or different from the "house of the God of Jacob" in Isa 2:3, in whose ways the peoples wish to walk.[48] That the prophet (if that is who the speaker is) urges the house of Jacob to go in the light of YHWH suggests that perhaps they need to do so, that they are separated from the other nations who say "come let us go to the mountain of YHWH" (2:3), that they are alienated from themselves if "the house of the God of Jacob" expresses their proper values. The impression is reinforced by the next line, in which the subject is either YHWH, who abandoned his people, or the hypostatized house of Jacob, which is thus distinguished from and rejects its members or inhabitants. In either case, Jacob is a potential exception from the desire of all peoples to learn from his ways; Jacob alone is not at home in his house. The impression is reinforced by the succeeding verses, in which the people—either YHWH's or Jacob's—consult mediums (עננים) "like the Philistines," are "filled from the east," "clap hands with the children of foreigners" and thereby are culturally or spiritually miscegenated.

In Mic 4:4–5, the prediction that all peoples will recycle their weapons and cease to learn the arts of war is followed by a reassuringly familiar image of untroubled contentment: "each will sit under his vine and under his fig tree," which may either refer to all peoples or to Israel. The statement that all people walk in the name of their god(s) and we walk in that of YHWH, "our god," either implies that we are one with those peoples or superior to them.[49] In any case, the injunction to walk in the light of YHWH in Isa 2:5 is here no longer required.

---

48. I have examined the ambiguities of this passage in Francis Landy, "Isaiah 2: Torah and Terror," in *Far from Minimal: Celebrating the Influence of Philip R. Davies*, ed. Duncan Burns and John W. Rogerson, LHBOTS 484 (New York: T&T Clark, 2012), 269.

49. Ehud Ben Zvi, *Micah*, FOTL 21B (Grand Rapids: Eerdmans, 2000), 101–2, examines the ambiguity, concluding that there is no reason "to prefer one option over the other" (102).

Isaiah 2:7–8 introduces the day of YHWH section:

And its land is filled with gold and silver, and there is no end to its treasures; And its land is filled with horses, and there is no end to its chariots; And its land is filled with non-gods; they worship the work of their hands, that which their fingers have made.

Riches, military hardware, and idols are symptomatic of human pride and thus the objects of God's wrath. In Mic 5:9–14, in contrast, the cutting off of horses, chariots, and more is preliminary to God's triumph over his enemies and by implication the restoration of Zion.[50] This is shown, for example, by enjambment:

And all your enemies shall be cut off [יכרתו]. And on that day, says YHWH, I will cut off [הכרתי] your horses. (Mic 5:8–9)

The passage shows many lexical correspondences with Isa 2:6–22, but it looks backward rather than forward. Moreover, it recollects the universalist vision of Mic 4:1–3 as well as the triumphalist one suggested by the ambiguity of Mic 4:5, "we walk in the name of YHWH our god." It is preceded by two parallel extended similes, in which the remnant of Jacob among the nations is compared first to dew and then to a ravaging lion—the one fructifying, the other destroying. The tension is possibly exemplified by the last verse of the section: "And I will enact vengeance in wrath and fury against the nations who have not listened" (Mic 5:15), which might suggest that the nations who do obey will be spared. At all events, the eradication of horses, chariotry, cities, fortresses, and cult places corresponds to the vision of devastation in Mic 1–3 and thus to destruction of the kingdom(s) and exile as a precondition for reconstitution.

Intertextuality here, in its narrow sense of the interrelation and comparison of these two texts, shows the different ways in which the same oracle(s) can be developed: the similarity is there for the sake of the difference. Perhaps the same might be true for the books of Micah and Isaiah.

---

50. Jacobs, *Conceptual Coherence*, 155–56. Others think the addressees are the nations, for instance Julia M. O'Brien, *Micah*, WisC 37 (Collegeville, MN: Liturgical Press, 2015), 69. Ben Zvi argues for the polyvalence of the passage (*Micah*, 139). It seems to me that the primary reference, given the second person singular address, must be Israel. This does not exclude encompassing the nations "who do not listen" in the oracle.

Every argument is contingent; every text is a selection from among myriad ways not taken. Both texts, moreover, are temporary and chance incarnations of the prophetic voice. As Amos seems to suggest, everyone could and should be a prophet (Amos 3:8). The underlying continuity is indicated by the affirmation, "for the mouth of YHWH has spoken," which links Mic 4:4 to Isa 1:2 and 1:20.

There are other texts: the text of Torah, written or spoken, the text of the culture that is to be erased. The book may be a transcription of that Torah, and the voice or word of YHWH, and a memorial to the culture. One may note other elements: the pleasure in destruction,[51] for instance, the sheer *jouissance* indicated by the parallelisms in Isa 2:6–22 and Mic 5:9–14, or the thrill of aesthetic achievement in the twin similes of Mic 5:6–7. But that is material for another day.

---

51. I have, for instance, discussed the importance of rhythm and alliteration in Isa 2 in Landy, "Isaiah 2," 263–64.

# Bloodshed and Hate: The Judgment Oracle in Ezek 22:6–12 and the Legal Discourse in Lev 19:11–18

*Klaus-Peter Adam*

Intertextuality

Intertextuality studies ponder the particular overlapping relations between texts and seek to describe the connection of the outsides of texts with other texts.[1] Ezekiel and the Holiness Code (H), Lev 17–26, are among the textual areas that for a long time have been in the focus of intertextuality studies. The relationship between these two textual areas connects with wider areas of biblical studies—for instance, with the problem of the relationship between prophets and the law in general. Ezekiel stands in priestly and in prophetic tradition associated with the Babylonian era;[2] H is among the latest stages of the long-lived stream of pentateuchal law,[3] a legal tradition that likely intends to supersede and to replace earlier law.

---

1. See, for instance, B. J. Oropeza, "Intertextuality," *OEBI*, 453–63.
2. Assessing the priestly role of Ezekiel is beyond the scope of this contribution. The focus on "instruction," תורה, as a priestly task in Ezek 7:26 (dependent on Jer 18:18b; Zeph 3:3–4) presupposes the inclusion of legal material in priestly teaching; more specifically, a form of making informed distinctions (Lev 10:10–11) is understood as the essence of Ezekiel's priestly role; see Jacob Milgrom, *Leviticus 1–16*, AB 3 (New York: Doubleday 1991), 615, in regard to Lev 10 and Ezek 22:25–29. On the reconstruction of the priestly identity of Ezekiel, see Andrew Mein, "Ezekiel as a Priest in Exile," in *The Elusive Prophet: The Prophet as a Historical Person, Literary Character and Anonymous Artist*, ed. Johannes C. de Moor, OtSt 45 (Leiden: Brill 2001), 203.
3. See the attempt to embed biblical law in ancient Near Eastern law as demonstrated in David P. Wright, *Inventing God's Law: How the Covenant Code of the Bible Used and Revised the Laws of Hammurabi* (Oxford: Oxford University Press, 2009); Eckart Otto, *Der Wandel der Rechtsbegründungen in der Gesellschaftsgeschichte des antiken Israel: Eine Rechtsgeschichte des "Bundesbuches," Exodus XX 22–XXIII 13*,

The lexicographic and thematic overlap between the laws of the Holiness Code and of Ezekiel suggests five ideal-typical explanatory models:[4] (1) Ezekiel's authorship of both H and Ezekiel,[5] (2) H draws upon Ezekiel,[6] (3) both used a common source,[7] (4) both underwent a history of mutual influence,[8] and (5) Ezekiel used H.[9] All models develop a macroperspective

---

StudBib 3 (Leiden: Brill, 1988). Insights in the development of biblical law are of particular help to interpret later stages of the law, such as the Holiness Code. On H seeking to replace earlier law, see the overview in Jeffrey Stackert, "Holiness Code and Writings," *OEBL*, 389–96, esp. 392.

4. On a different level than the models that consider the textual overlap are interpretations of the identity of Ezekiel. To consider the attempt to determine the priestly identity of Ezekiel as an individual, see the overview in Karl-Friedrich Pohlmann, *Ezechiel: Der Stand der theologischen Diskussion* (Darmstadt: Wissenschaftliche Buchgesellschaft, 2008), 203–5. On scholarship on Ezekiel in general, see the collection of Stephen L. Cook and Corrine L. Patton, eds., *Ezekiel's Hierarchical World: Wrestling with a Tiered Reality*, SymS 31 (Atlanta: Society of Biblical Literature, 2004). On models, see Michael A. Lyons, *From Law to Prophecy: Ezekiel's Use of the Holiness Code*, LHBOTS 507 (New York: T&T Clark, 2009), 35–46; see also brief overviews in Pohlmann, *Ezechiel*, 197–201; Nancy R. Bowen, "Ezekiel," *OEBB* 1:282–300.

5. This theory was put forward by Karl Heinrich Graf, *Die geschichtlichen Bücher des Alten Testaments: Zwei historisch-kritische Untersuchungen* (Leipzig: Weigel, 1866), 81–82, and was criticized and rejected by August Klostermann, "Ezechiel und das Heiligtumsgesetz," in *Der Pentateuch: Beiträge zu seinem Verständnis und seiner Entstehungsgeschichte*, ed. August Klostermann (Leipzig: Böhme, 1893), 386. Klostermann suggested instead that Ezekiel found a pattern of language in H which influenced him in his use of language without giving up his own.

6. Julius Wellhausen, *Prolegomena to the History of Ancient Israel*, trans. J. Sutherland Black and Allan Menzies (New York: Meridian Books, 1957), 378. Wellhausen suggested that much of the material in Lev 17–26 was preexilic from the time immediately after D's composition and the reform of Josiah, while he dated his compositional stage to the exile or postexile (382). Finally, Wellhausen saw H quoting Ezekiel and suggested, based among other things on assumptions of prophetic authenticity, Ezekiel precedes the Holiness Code which then precedes the Priestly Code (378). The mainstream assumption of a postexilic date of H is mainly based on its relationship to older law collections; see Klaus Grünwaldt, *Das Heiligkeitsgesetz Leviticus 17–26: Ursprüngliche Gestalt, Tradition und Theologie* (Berlin: de Gruyter 1999), 13–22; see also Eckart Otto and Christophe Nihan below.

7. Georg Fohrer, *Introduction to the Old Testament*, trans. David E. Green (Nashville: Abingdon, 1968), 142, suggests a common source of Ezekiel and H. Both, independently from each other, took as their point of departure "extant or developing individual collections and complexes, if not a first combined edition."

8. A proponent of this model is Walther Zimmerli's commentary on Ezekiel, sug-

on the relationship between the two books in their entirety. The controversial result warns from oversimplification and from generalization, assuming complex source-critical relations between H and Ezekiel. Rather, this complexity presents an opportunity to consider one segment of a semantic overlap along with the ideological parallels and along with the analogies of the content of Ezekiel and P in general, and with H in particular.

In light of the fundamentally relational nature of texts and their complex overlap, this essay concentrates on Lev 19:11–18 in its relation to Ezek 22:6–12.[10] It probes the explanatory models for a relationship between both that is based on the parallels and the differences between the individual passages. Juxtaposing Lev 19 and Ezek 22 illustrates the differences between the genre of both texts, one of them being a judgment oracle of a prophetic composition with a literary context in the book of Ezekiel targeting the city of Jerusalem. In comparison, Lev 19:11–18 is a sequence of injunctions in the form of prohibitives with predecessors and close parallels in the legal tradition, as the over-imposed typical framework of H it now presents. This juxtaposition of a prophetic passage with a roughly contemporary tradition of H seeks to map out the shared lexicographic field between both texts and its typical overlap of idiomatic language. The juxtaposition of Ezek 22 and Lev 19 thus offers a window into the diverse discourses on Jewish ethics that span from the Babylonian through the Persian time. Their shared reflection of priestly legal tradition and their ethos of mutual benevolence yields astonishing parallels in the lexicography of both.[11]

---

gesting a shared, complex process of composition over an extended time line. Zimmerli rejects any unilateral literary dependence and suggests a reciprocal relationship, in which to a large extent Ezekiel used H, with the exception of Lev 26, a later layer in H influenced by Ezekiel. Walther Zimmerli, *Ezekiel 1*, trans. Ronald E. Clements, Hermeneia (Minneapolis: Fortress, 1979), 52.

9. Ezekiel borrowed from the Holiness Code; see among others, L. E. Elliott-Binns, "Some Problems of the Holiness Code," *ZAW* 67 (1955): 26–40; Daniel I. Block, *The Book of Ezekiel: Chapters 1–24*, NICOT (Grand Rapids: Eerdmans, 1997), 40; L. B. Paton, "The Holiness-Code and Ezekiel," *PRR* 26 (1896): 98–115; and Lyons, *From Law*, 44n108, which lists more representatives of this position.

10. Intertextual analysis between biblical texts needs scope and limitation. An example of a comprehensive approach is Georg Steins, *Die "Bindung Isaaks" im Kanon (Gen 22): Grundlagen und Programm einer kanonisch-intertextuellen Lektüre*, HBS 20 (Freiburg im Breisgau: Herder, 1999); but see the critical review by James L. Crenshaw, *JBL* 121 (2002): 152–54, esp. 153, the question about the criteria for the selection of the relevant hypotexts.

11. The comparison and the overlap between both raise questions about the

Thematically, Lev 19:11–18 reflects on actual or potential conflicts and on the ways of avoiding and of settling conflicts. The behavioral roles and themes have parallels in Ezekiel's judgment oracle. At the same time, stylistically, both reflect their literary context. Leviticus 19:11–18 lists predominantly prohibitives, while Ezek 22:6–12 is kept in the accusatory tone of judgment prophecy. I probe the relational models between the texts in the comparison between the two quintessential passages on private conflict settlement and on enmity in their respective contexts and in their diverse types of communal ethos as frame of reference. An initial comparison between Ezek 22:6–12 and the laws of Lev 19 demonstrates conceptual and lexicographic similarities. First, this opens up an informed look at Ezek 22, in particular at the ways it draws on the laws of Lev 18–20. This is worthwhile, as it reveals how prophetic priestly cycles reflected on law and how they adjusted it to their specific situation.[12] The comparison also ponders the differences between the alleged audiences. The lexicographic and the thematic overlap between particularly Lev 19:11–18 and the judgment oracle against the city of bloodshed in Ezek 22:6–12 offers an interesting perspective on the overlap between Ezekiel's prophetic tradition and law. Second, naming the textual overlap between the sources while bracketing out questions of priority leads to the identification of legal themes and their relevance in diverse bodies of literature. Ezekiel 22:6–12 and Lev 19:11–18 present themselves as a litmus test for the relevance of intertextual considerations about the two sources.[13] The result of this debate contributes to clarifying the development of biblical law and elucidates its reception and discussion in the prophetic-priestly tradition of Ezekiel.

The lexicographic and thematic overlap of Lev 19:3–4, 11–18 and of Ezek 22:6–12 with the Decalogues are extensive.[14] The Decalogues first

---

coherence of a theory of the strict literary dependence of Ezekiel from H. While this is beyond the scope of this contribution, the extended time span of the alleged redaction of the book of Ezekiel and, to a slightly lesser extent for H, covers a period of time that allows for parallel and for mutually overlapping processes of reflection in both literary corpora. Consequently, a parallel history of the composition of H and of Ezekiel seems plausible, with phases of mutual interdependence between them, as suggested by Gustav Hölscher, *Hesekiel: Der Dichter und das Buch; Eine literarkritische Untersuchung*, BZAW 39 (Berlin: de Gruyter, 1924), 31.

12. See an overview in Lyons, *From Law*, 115–16.

13. The relationship between both texts has often been noted; see, among others, Block, *Book of Ezekiel*, 707–8.

14. They would require a separate study; I merely mention a selection.

share with Lev 19:3–4, 11–18 and Ezek 22:6–12 their concern about the use and the religious value of foreign material, cultural objects. More generally, they share the concern about the use of idols or images seen as not genuinely Yahwistic in their nature (Exod 20:4–5; Deut 5:7–9; Lev 19:4).[15] Second, they specifically share the profanation of the Sabbath as festival day (Exod 20:8–11; Deut 5:12–15; Lev 19:3, 30 plural suffix, first-person singular). Third, they are both concerned about the disrespect of the traditional structures of parental authority as one important way that ensures the stability of kinship-based society (Exod 20:6; Deut 5:16; Lev 19:3). Fourth, they share the theme of homicide within the community with the specific verb רצח (Exod 20:13; Deut 5:17), while Lev 19:16 also refers to homicide in the community, framing it differently as prohibition of standing against the blood of a community member—which also represents a core theme of Ezek 22:6, 9, 12, and 13. Fifth, they share various forms of false accusation of a community member (Exod 20:16; Deut 5:20); swearing falsely; lifting YHWH's name to false accusation (Exod 20:7; Deut 5:11; Lev 19:15); and, specifically, acting as a slanderer רכיל (Ezek 22:9; Lev 19:16). Sixth, various forms of men gaining illegitimate control over women are shared: either breaking a neighbor's marriage (Exod 20:14; Deut 5:18), attempting to steal a neighbor's wife (Exod 20:17; Deut 5:21), or illegitimately giving a daughter up for prostitution (Lev 19:29).

These themes are distinctively framed and reflected on from various vantage points. Ezekiel 22:6 considers the theme of homicide ("bloodshed") in an accusation directed against the ruling elite. In Lev 19:16, the prohibition of standing against the blood is followed in Lev 19:17–18 by prohibitions against more comprehensive forms of retaliation in favor of mutual benevolence. The passage addresses the concerns about far-reaching patterns of interaction with a neighbor. It names specific patterns of retaliatory interaction such as hate (שנא), revenge (נקם), and bearing a grudge (נטר), and commands to instead exercise mutual benevolence (אהב). The case for H as the historically latest law collection is stimulating within the discourse on intertextuality, namely because it specifies how Ezekiel relates to the laws of H partaking in a Persian era discourse—a highly interesting theme given H's alleged intention to revise earlier legal tradition in the Covenant Code and in Deuteronomy. This character of H

---

15. See also the rejection of turning toward the spirits (Lev 19:31) and the emphasis on YHWH's holiness (19:2b).

as revision would namely invite a comparison of Lev 19:11–18 with the content and with the function of the Sinaitic Decalogues that themselves serve as summaries of legal traditions and as prologues to the law collections of the Covenant Code (Exod 21:2–23:19) and the law collection of Deuteronomy (Deut 12–26).[16]

## The Outline of Lev 19 and Its Relevance for the Question at Stake

For the array of legal collections in the Pentateuch, the attempt to retrieve the literary contexts and the compositions of the collections is at the heart of understanding their legal thought. It is therefore appropriate to briefly consider the composition of Lev 19 in H. Bookended by rules about the social structure in Lev 18 and 20, the chapter itself presents a variety of laws, some of which are arranged around the criterion of "purity" and of "mixture." Leviticus 19:11–18, which is at the core of this comparison with Ezek 22:6–12, consists of four pairs of two verses framed by the short introductory formula "I am YHWH," which closes each set of two verses (19:11–12, 13–14, 15–16, 17–18). As is the case in Lev 19:11–18, the entire chapter of Lev 19 also reveals a clear outline. Leviticus 19 can be understood as a diptych consisting of two panels, both of which exhibit a symmetric arrangement of introductory general exhortation to holiness (19:2abβb, 19aα) and a sequel of three commands that can be summarized as:

1. fundamental prescriptions: Sabbath, idolatry (19:3–4); the prohibition of mixtures (19:19aβ, γ, b);
2. casuistic laws: sacrifice (19:5–8); gleaning of fields (19:9–10); sacrifice (19:20–22); harvesting of trees (19:23–25);

---

16. Leviticus 19:11–18 and the Decalogues show significant textual overlap and both summarize earlier law. Also, the form of a row of prohibitives in Lev 19:11–18 has invited thoughts about its relationship to other Decalogues in general and the reconstruction of an old core of a Dodecalogue or a Decalogue; see, for instance, J. Morgenstern, "The Decalogue of the Holiness Code," *HUCA* 26 (1955): 1–27; Karl Elliger, *Leviticus*, HAT 1.4 (Tübingen: Mohr Siebeck, 1966), 254; and the overview in Jacob Milgrom, *Leviticus 17–22*, AB 3A (New York: Doubleday, 2000), 1600. Specifically, the thematic and the lexicographic overlaps between the rows of prohibitives (Lev 19:11–18) and the two versions of the Decalogues (Exod 20 and Deut 5) witness a vivid discourse between both texts.

3. other mixed prescriptions: the benevolence toward fellow community members (19:11–18); and corresponding prescriptions of cultural separation (19:26–32).

A summary exhortation to keep and practice all statutes and ordinances in verse 37 concludes Lev 19.[17]

| panel 1 | panel 2 |
|---|---|
| general exhortation to holiness: (2aβ.b) | transition to new exhortation: *Keep my statutes!* (19aα) |
| (a) fundamental prescriptions: parents Sabbath prohibition of apostasy, idolatry (3–4) | (a′) fundamental prescription: prohibition of mixtures (19aβ, γ, b) |
| (b) casuistic laws: sacrifice (5–8) gleaning fields; leaving harvest (9–10) | (b′) casuistic laws: sacrifice (20–22) harvesting trees; leaving harvest (23–25) |
| (c) other prescriptions: benevolence toward fellow community member (11–18) | (c′) other prescriptions: cultural separation (26–32) benevolence toward resident alien (33–34) benevolence/fairness in trade (35–36a) |

Concluding exhortation: "keep and practice all my statutes and all my ordinances!" (37)

Recent studies have considered the outline of this legal collection as relevant for its interpretation. Seen through a compositional lens, Lev 19 juxtaposes verses 11–18 with the countercultural practices verses 26–32 describe. Therefore, when viewed in their relation to verses 26–32, the set of behavioral expectations in verses 11–18 functions on a compositional

---

17. See this outline first in Eckart Otto, "Das Heiligkeitsgesetz Leviticus 17–26 in der Pentateuchredaktion," in *Altes Testament: Forschung und Wirkung; Festschrift H. Reventlow*, ed. Peter Mommer and Winfried Thiel (Frankfurt: Lang, 1994), 73.

level as the corresponding counterpart to the expectations of a non-Yahwistic behavior seen in Lev 19:26–32.

In more detail, part (c) of the first panel (19:11–18) presents the aspects of mutual malevolence and benevolence in the community of the Holiness Code. All of the prohibitives are apodictic and largely without rationale: verses 11–12 concern the deception of a fellow countryman, which would amount to desecrate YHWH; verses 13–14 aim at a general protection of the socially weak, such as the day laborer or people with disabilities; verses 15–16 request fair and just conflict settlement in the community; and verses 17–18 explicitly reject inimical, hateful behavioral patterns, such as seeking revenge or bearing a grudge, and request an active attitude of mutual benevolence in the interaction. The context and the addressees of this passage are relevant for its precise understanding. Four categories of terms designate the community members. The first verse pair (19:11–12) mentions the compatriot (עמית in 19:11), and the second (19:13–14) refers to the companion/neighbor (רע in 19:13). The third verse pair (19:15–16) uses again compatriot (עמית in 19:15) and refers to "your people" (19:16aα) and then to "companion/neighbor" (19:16aβ). The final double verses (19:17–18) combine four terms: "brother" (אח in 19:17aα); "compatriot" (19:17aβ); the "sons of your people" (בני עם) and "companion/neighbor" (רע), both in 19:18a; and, finally, "companion/neighbor" (19:18b).[18] The meticulous nuances of the addressees in Lev 19:11–18 reveal the sophisticated perception of the social structure. The variants mirror a nuanced understanding of how precisely interpersonal responsibility would be defined and how it would play out among various community members.[19]

---

18. Unless otherwise stated, all translations are my own.

19. For interpersonal responsibility, see also Christophe Nihan, *From Priestly Torah to Pentateuch*, FAT 2/25 (Tübingen: Mohr Siebeck, 2007), 475. It is disputed whether the command in 19:18 is originally a command to love one's enemies. This is the suggestion of Hans-Peter Mathys, *Liebe deinen Nächsten wie dich selbst: Untersuchungen zum alttestamentlichen Gebot der Nächstenliebe (Lev 19,18)*, OBO 71 (Göttingen: Vandenhoeck & Ruprecht, 1986), 82. The matter requires more attention; in short, I assume that verse 18 systematically excludes the category of enmity as a form of continuous mutual malevolence in the closely knit community that Lev 19:11–18 addresses.

## The Themes of Foreign Images, Sabbath, and Conflict Settlement in General in Lev 19

Widening the scope from 19:11–18, the opening passage (a) at the beginning of the first panel refers to two fundamental commands: keeping the Sabbaths as festival day (19:3) and the prohibition of apostasy and idolatry (19:4). The subsequent casuistic commands on offerings (19:5–8) and the laws that demand maintaining options for gleanings for the socially disadvantaged after the harvest of fields and vineyards in verses 9–10 form part (b). Both parts (a) and (b) intend to govern fundamental aspects of communal life: the weekly rhythm through the festival day and fundamental responsibilities for the disadvantaged in the community. Seen in the larger context of the focus of the implied addressees of the laws of H, Lev 19 seeks to essentially provide laws for the community it addresses.[20] The prohibitives in Lev 19:11–18 that in detail relate to interpersonal behavior in the community closely connect these ethical ideals more specifically to religious ideals, such as the observance of YHWH-Sabbaths and the exclusion of apostasy and idolatry—all of which are hallmarks of the identity of "holiness" for the community. In fact, Lev 19:11–18 considers lying to a community member as a form of "desecration" of the name of YHWH (19:12) and considers cursing a deaf person or being a stumbling block for the blind as expressions of a lack of YHWH-fear (ירא in 19:14). With the use of the adjective "holy," H labels these ethical rules as part of the distinct, exclusive concept of Yahwism.

## The Outline of Ezek 22:6–12 and Its Relevance for This Question

Ezekiel 22 is an arrangement of three units: 22:1–16, 17–22, and 23–29. An idiomatic formula, "the word of YHWH came" (22:1, 17, 23), introduces each of these larger units and serves as the delineation between them.[21] Three diverse thematic foci are apparent. The first of these core units con-

---

20. The reference to vineyards and fields in Lev 19:9–10, together with the laws for fruit trees in 19:23–25, has led to the understanding that the Holiness Code presupposes a rural or an agricultural community as its audience. The priestly ideals would not exclude these addressees from labor on the fields.

21. Friedrich Pohlmann, *Der Prophet Hesekiel/Ezechiel Kapitel 20–48*, ATD 22 (Göttingen: Vandenhoeck & Ruprecht, 2001), 329, assumes verses 23–31 have inspired verses 1–16 and verses 17–22 are an addition.

sists of two oracles (22:6–12 and 1–5); the latter functions as introduction to the former. The final part (22:23–29) adds another oracle. The three core units as such can be broken down further. Verses 1–5 arrange variations on the themes of accusation of homicide and idolatry in Jerusalem.[22] In detail, the passage breaks down to a comprehensive accusation of Jerusalem, the "city of blood" (עיר הדמים), in an introduction in verses 1–5. The structure of this introduction can be retrieved in detail; following an introductory formula (22:1–2), there is a command to the prophet to act as judge, that is, a summons (22:3aβ–5). Therefore, when seen through the lens of a compositional analysis, Ezek 22:1–5 seemingly condenses older passages that now follow later in the current composition.[23]

The first judgment oracle (22:6–12) is of interest here. It mentions a specific addressee. First, 22:6 singles out the "princes" or "rulers of Israel." The subsequent verses list the more detailed accusations. The content and the arrangement of this core unit and its accusations are essential for the larger unit (Ezek 22:1–12*). Verses 6–7 are key to the concept of 22:1–12*. Verse 6 addresses Israel's rulers with the title נשיא.[24] In the context of this verse, the oracle addresses the rulers of the city ("in you"), holding accountable the city rulers for the ethical conduct characterized by bloodshed. Beyond these authorities, Ezek 22:6–12 adduces more than one accusation. Its attention shifts toward an exposure of the officials' disrespect for (assumingly traditional) kinship organization.

Verses 6–12 present in itself a complex unit. Verses 13–16 adduce the consequences of the behavior addressed in verses 6–12 in an announcement of judgment. From a compositional viewpoint, verses 13–14 add a new passage. The interjection "but see" (והנה) in 22:13 marks its beginning, and its tone demonstrates the character of verses 13–14 with a new intention. The *qatal* form in 22:13a holds an announcement for the imme-

---

22. Without the classic subforms of prophetic "accusation" and "threat." Frank-Lothar Hossfeld, *Untersuchungen zu Komposition und Theologie des Ezechielbuches*, 2nd ed., FB 20 (Würzburg: Echter, 1983), 111–16, esp. 112, 148, conveys of the passage as close to preexilic prophetic accusations of homicide in, for example, Mic 3:10 and Hab 2:12, and therefore assumes it is part of the basic layer. He suggests the closest parallel is in the command to proclaim in Ezek 20:4–5 and in a redactional version in Ezek 23:36.

23. I follow largely Hossfeld, *Untersuchungen*, 99–152.

24. Hossfeld, *Untersuchungen*, 149, ascribes the basic layer (22:1–5, 6, 9a, 12) to the time shortly before the Babylonian era in 587 BCE, yet he admits that dating the prophecy of Ezekiel based on this layer remains difficult.

diately impending future: "But see, I will smite."[25] These two verses draw the consequences of the aforesaid accusations in the form of an indictment and doom that are missing from the previous verses, 22:6–12.[26] Two objects follow, and both reference the dishonest gain and bloodshed. The following question in 22:14 is symmetric: "Can your heart endure, or can your hands be strong?" The idiomatic "I, YHWH, have spoken, and I will act" functions as a closure of this passage.

After this closure, Ezek 22:15–16 carries forward as an opening of a new unit. This passage addresses the problems from a wider angle, and it speaks in two regards about a context that exceeds the level of the city of Jerusalem and the level of Israel as an ethnic entity. This overarching level exceeds the limits of the city of Jerusalem and takes them to the international forum of the nations (גוים) and the countries (ארצות), into which Israel will be scattered. As is the case in 22:13–14, the passage relates to the future. Syntactically, verses 15–16 consist of a chain of four qatal-x sentences that announce the future; verse 16b adds a final formula of knowledge. This second bookending of the judgment oracle looks ahead to the forum of the nations.[27] Verses 13–14 and 15–16 add different foci, with both containing words that widen the scope beyond the more confined society of Jerusalem.[28] Compositionally, we can distinguish distinct elements in the first unit (22:1–16).[29] Verses 13–16 take up the keyword בצע

---

25. As is the case in the LXX and Ezek 21:19, 22, the form is to be read "I smite my hand at."

26. Hossfeld, *Untersuchungen*, 149.

27. Verses 17–22 are a metaphoric discourse on metallurgy that constitutes a separate unit. Verses 23–29 arrange accusations of five groups of addressees with a specific rebuke. First, it addresses "the land" (22:24), then the prophets (22:25), the priests (22:26), the princes (22:27), the prophets (22:28), and, finally, the people of the land (22:29).

28. From a source-critical perspective, these units can be understood as a first and a second addition (Hossfeld, *Untersuchungen*, 149–50).

29. A nuanced source-critical reading of Ezek 22:1–12 suggests a basic exilic layer and passages that are part of a successive, later reworking of the prophetic book. See, for instance, Hossfeld, *Untersuchungen*, 109, 148–52, 524–29. For 22:1–12, he suggests a core of sentences with the refrain "in order to shed blood" in verses 6, 9a, 12a, and 12b, including verses 1–5. He sees this basic layer from exilic time in close analogy to preexilic judgment prophecy, and, at the same time, it is in its semantic profile closely related to Ezekiel's core units: a first addition of disciples of the prophet Ezekiel in 22:13–14; and a third layer in 22:15–16 added after the fall of Jerusalem, but not filling in the plethora of cultic concerns as the subsequent layer. A fourth layer, representing

("unfair gain") from verse 12 in verse 13. Another term that functions as a bridge between both passages is "blood" in 22:12a and 13b. Verses 13–16 leave the context of the city as such and extend the judgment prophecy to a wider context. Seen through a source-critical lens, the more specific accusations in 22:6–12 appear to be a concise oracle. The explicit threat of impending judgment in 22:13–16 is assumingly later, and the unit was further enlarged through an introduction.[30]

1–2 Announcement of Judgment
    1 Then the word of YHWH came to me saying,

Summary, rhetorical question:
    2 And you, son of man, will you judge, will you judge the *bloody* city? Then cause her to know all her abominations.

3–5 Summons
    3 And you shall say,
    "Thus says my Lord YHWH,
    A city *shedding blood* in her midst, so that her time will come,
    and that makes 'scarabs,' against her, for her defilement!

Framework: Bloodshed, Defilement, the Nations:
    4 You have become guilty by the *blood* which you have *shed*, and defiled by your 'scarabs' which you have made. Thus you have brought your day near and have come to your years.
    Therefore, I have made you a reproach to the nations, and a mocking to all the lands.
    5 Those who are near and those who are far from you will mock you, you of ill repute, full of turmoil.

6–12 Against Israel's Leaders
    6 Behold, the rulers of Israel, each according to his power, have been in you, for the purpose of *shedding blood*.

---

Ezekiel's roots in the Jeremiah/D tradition, is found in the genre of "statements" ("*Feststellungen*") and commandments in analogy to Lev 20 in Ezek 22:7, 9aβ, 10; it presents an equilibrium of both social and cultic misdemeanors. A fifth layer in Ezek 22:9bβ, 11 exhibits an increasing influence of priestly law (P$^G$ and H) and priestly language and is interested in listing the complete perception of misdemeanors. Potentially, this layer echoes Jer 5:7–9; 9:1; 23:10, 14. Finally, sixth, the concern for the Sabbath was added in 22:8.

    30. Zimmerli, *Ezekiel 1*, 455.

7 They have treated father and mother lightly within you.
The alien they have oppressed in your midst; the fatherless and the widow they have wronged in you.
8 You have despised my holy things and profaned my Sabbaths.
9 Slanderous men have been in you for the purpose of *shedding blood*, and in you they have eaten on the mountains. In your midst they have committed lewdness.
10 In you they have uncovered *their* fathers' nakedness; in you they have humbled her who was unclean in her menstrual impurity.
11 And one has committed abomination with his neighbor's wife,
and another has lewdly defiled his daughter-in-law.
And another in you has humbled his sister, his father's daughter.
12 In you they have taken *bribes* to *shed blood*;
you have taken interest and profits,
and you have injured your neighbors for *dishonest gain* by oppression,
and you have forgotten Me,"
declares my Lord YHWH.

13–16 Word of Threat/Doom
13 "Behold, then, I smite my hand at your *dishonest gain* which you have acquired, and at your *blood* which is among you.
14 Can your heart endure, or can your hands be strong, in the days that I shall deal with you? I, YHWH, have spoken and shall act.
15 And I shall scatter you among the nations, and I shall disperse you through the lands, and I shall consume your uncleanness from you.
16 And you will profane yourself in the sight of the nations, and you will know that I am YHWH."

17–22 Purification Metaphor

23–29 Paraenesis for Various (Privileged) Classes:
    25 Prophets: conspiracy
    26 Priests: use of violence
    27 Officials/princes: homicide
    28 Prophets: false, misleading visions
    29 People of the land: oppression, robbery, oppression of poor, sojourner
    30–31 YHWH speech: "I sought for a builder of the wall"

Final announcement of doom: "Therefore"

## Thematic Analysis

The judgment oracle references accusations against incidents in the city of Jerusalem. The passage's focus is on the city's community and its reality as social space. The two spatial markers locate the described behavior in the entity of the city in a defined area, referencing the population in it with the terms "in your midst" (בתוכך) and "in you" (בך). The passage Ezek 22:6–12 repeats these spatial markers ten times.[31] This emphasis on the communal life and on its proceedings highlights that these problems pertain to the city as the center of the community. The heading of Ezekiel's oracle addresses the ruling elites in Israel, the rulers (נשיאי ישראל) and their respective executive power (זרע). In the context of Ezek 22, these rulers refer to the guilt of the urban elites whom the prophetic oracles hold responsible for incidents in the city precincts. Pointing to the city rulers, the passage refers to the theme of hierarchy and highlights the unacceptable mechanisms of behavior of the inhabitants of the city itself. The attack on the city rulers as urban elite finds an interesting complementary aspect in the rejection of the traditional authorities in a kinship-based society, notably the clan elders, both female and male. Ezekiel 22:6–7 connect the rulers' bloodshed in 22:6 with the disrespect of the traditional order of the kinship-based society. The rulers seek to increase bloodshed in the community by ruling for their own good. As a consequence, the members of the society whose primary community of solidarity is shattered—such as widows and orphans, who experienced a loss of a next of kin—are wronged. Ideally, in a kinship-based society, members of the same kin would help such individuals.

Besides the destruction of the primary community of solidarity, the internal structure of the weekly order is also broken, including the disruption of the Sabbath celebration. A closer look at the emphasis of the accusations of 22:6–12 indicates that they pair the theme of bloodshed in the city as the most far-reaching consequence with other transgressions of the order in 22:6–8, 9–11, and 12. The internal structure of each of these three sections is regular. All three passages begin with the accusation of homicide they label as "bloodshed" in 22:6, 9, and 12 as a primary intention of Israel's rulers. The themes of Ezek 22:6–12 relate to the violation of

---

31. Ezek 22:7 (3x), 9 (3x), 10 (2x), 11b, and 12a. Additionally 22:13 mentions בתוכך.

the communal order as opposed to traditional kinship order (22:6–7), as well as the violations of Yahwistic customs and of fair conflict settlement (22:9a), in a variation in 22:12. The theme of unfair conflict settlement brackets a relatively elaborate central passage (22:9b–11) that refers to the violation of the kinship order and results in the intentional deviation of patterns of appropriate intimate relationship between the members of a kinship group, to which the text refers with the term זמה, "lewdness."

Ezekiel 22 puts the violation of rules through individual acts in the larger context of constituting a violation of genuine Yahwistic customs. Verse 8 refers to the "holy things, Sabbaths," and the subscript in verse 12b sees the behavior in contradiction to Yahwism in essence.

| | symptom | category/cause |
|---|---|---|
| 22:6 | rulers aim at *bloodshed* | violation of communal order |
| 22:7 | disrespect against parents *oppression* of the sojourner wronging orphan and widow | violation of traditional kinship order |
| 22:8 | despise YHWH's holy things and Sabbaths | violation of Yahwistic customs |
| 22:9a | slanderous men with purpose of *bloodshed* | violation of fair conflict settlement |
| 22:9bα | eating on the mountains committing "*lewdness*" | violation of religious rules violations of kinship order |
| 22:10 | uncovering father's nakedness humbling unclean women in their menstruation period | |
| 22:11 | committing "abomination" with neighbor's wife "*lewdly*" defiling daughter-in-law humbling one's sister, father's daughter | |
| 22:12a | taking bribes with the purpose of *bloodshed* | violation of fair conflict settlement |

| | | |
|---|---|---|
| 22:12bα | taking interest and profits | violation of fair economy |
| 22:12bβ | injuring neighbors for gain by *oppression* | violation of fairness in community |
| | forgetting YHWH | rejection of Yahwism |

A number of accusations in Ezek 22:6–12 also play a role in Lev 19:3–4, 11–18; others have parallels in Lev 18 and 20. Both texts significantly overlap with regard to two themes and one semantic field. First, they both urge to respect the hierarchical frame of reference of the traditional kinship in Judah. Ezekiel 22:6 first accuses the rulers of their intentional homicide that they reference as "bloodshed," a term that reflects on the general priestly principle of talionic retribution for bloodshed in Gen 9:6. Ezekiel 22:6–7 puts this next to the reproach against the rulers who seek their personal gain with the climate of disrespect for the traditional kinship authorities. It associates this posture with certain members who find themselves systemically at a disadvantage, but about whom a functional kinship society would have to care—namely, the sojourner, the orphan, and the widow. Leviticus 19:3a also mentions the urge to value the traditional patterns of authority in the kinship in the first position of chapter 19. Notably, both Ezek 22 and Lev 19 mention both authorities separately: mother and father (Lev 19:3a); father and mother (Ezek 22:7a). Second, both Ezek 22:8 and Lev 19:4 frame the themes of general conduct within a broader critique of an aberration from Yahwistic practices, notably a critique on neglecting Sabbath observance. Third, Ezek 22:9bα–11 covers aberrations from an established order. They first reference the problematic offering practices and subsequently the prohibited practices of intimate relationships within a kinship society.

The passage relates this theme to the slanderous subversion caused by a group of ideal-typical nonconformists (אנשי רכיל), whose intentional killings undermine any sense of security in the society. Their deliberate malice (זמה) is a threat to the city's order and is paired with their religious opposition to Yahwism as the accusation of having meals on the mountains in the city in 22:9bα. Verse 10b refers to the violations of family law when a man would force a woman in her menstruation to have intercourse. With the term זמה twice repeated in 22:9bβ, 11b, the passage points to a type of inappropriate, intentional malevolence that here plays out specifically in the intimate relationship between kin members. Intimate relationships of one individual with members of another generation are prohibited. Verse 11b enforces the notion of a religious undertone or criticism with the term "abomination" (תועבה), a term that is also used in Lev 18:26 as an element of the bookending or framing of the prohibitions in Lev 18:6–23 through the passages Lev 18:24–30 and Lev 18:1–5.[32] The term for "wicked intention" (זמה) has further parallels in three passages in the Holiness Code. Leviticus 18:17 uses זמה for inappropriate intimate relationships to both mother and daughter; in Lev 19:29, it specifically designates the pollution of a daughter through giving her up for prostitution. In conjunction with "abomination" (תועבה), the term is also used in Ezek 22:8 and in Lev 20:13 for the rejection of male-male sexual interaction. It is followed by a prohibition of marriage to both a mother and her daughter (Lev 20:14). A technical term for problematic intentional practices of intimacy that are in the authority of the kin, זמה, is predominantly found in Ezekiel, typically as a priestly designation for the misuse of (male) authority within the kin, failing to protect its weakest (female) members in the patriarchal hierarchy.[33]

## Function of the Terminology of Bloodshed שפך דם in Ezek 22:3, 4, 6, 9, 12, 13, 26

While not a direct parallel between Ezek 22:6–12 and Lev 19:11–18, the tradition of the accusation of bloodshed in Ezek 22 builds on earlier prophetic oracles that present the same accusation of homicide as Ezek 22:6–12. These preceding lists are less elaborate yet thematically related. Jeremiah 7:6, for instance, presents a short accusation of bloodshed, bundling a triad of the oppression of the stranger, the fatherless, and the widow together with shedding innocent blood and with "walking after

---

32. S. Steingrimsson, "זמם," *TDOT* 4:89–90, distinguishes a meaning "plan" in six instances, mostly in wisdom literature, with the negative connotation of scheming: Isa 32:7; Ps 119:150; Prov 10:23; 21:27; 24:9; Job 17:11. The only positive connotation of "plan" is found in Job 17:11. From this, Steingrimsson discerns the meaning "wickedness, lewdness" found three times in H; in Judg 19:6 and Ps 26:10; possibly also in Hos 6:9; and in Ezekiel and Jer 13:27, where the wicked plan of "whoring" refers to prostitution in a comparison with neighing horses.

33. Thirteen out of twenty-two references are from Ezekiel, mostly alluding to what is seen as non-Yahwistic intimate behavior. The term is used in Ezek 22, as Steingrimsson ("זמם," 90) suggests, to associate cases as outlined in Lev 18–20. The term is also used, for instance, in the retrospective historiographic oracle against the personified Jerusalem in Ezek 16:27, 43, 58 (with the parallelism זימה—תועבה).

other gods." In variation, the accusation of bloodshed in Jer 22:3 combines three misdeeds: delivering someone who has been robbed from the power of his oppressor; acting violently against the stranger, the orphan, or the widow; and shedding innocent blood in the city ("this place"). Jeremiah 22:17 arranges a group of four transgressions: gain (בצע), shedding innocent blood, oppression, and violence.

Another short version of an accusation against the collective is a judgment oracle about conflict settlement procedure in Isa 59:1–7. The core in Isa 59:3–7 refers to multiple facets of problematic behavior. In 59:3 and 7, "bloodshed" is bookending the judgment oracle, while 59:4 focuses on unfair lawsuits and conflict settlement and 59:6b singles out the particular problem of violence:

3   blood guilt defiles (גאל, niphal)
    false speech, a tongue that mutters wickedness
4   unfair lawsuits with lies; trust in worthlessness; iniquity as a result
5–6 metaphors: eggs, spider web
    violence in their hands
7   "evil"; hastening to shed innocent blood, iniquity
    devastation and destruction as consequences

Accusations of shedding innocent blood are also used for foreign collectives, such as Edom (Joel 4:19) or the "nations" (Ps 79:3). Israel and Judah as collectives are accused in Ezek 23:45 of having blood on their hands. Jerusalem is accused in Ezek 16:38. Notably, the criticism of the house of Israel in both Ezek 33:25 and 36:18 is the object of the criticism of the defilement of the land through non-Yahwistic idols (גלולים*), and it becomes a part of the religious self-identity of the addressees, that is, of the population.[34] The oracles see the practices of bloodshed against the backdrop of adopting foreign religious habits. In a wider sense, they perceive them as foreign cultural habits. Prophetic tradition in Joel 4:19 accuses the close neighbors of Egypt and Edom of bloodshed, holding them accountable for killings amongst Judeans. The judgment prophecy

---

34. The personal suffix, second-person plural, highlights the connection of the accusation to the people as an ethnic entity.

in Zeph 1:17 announces the pouring out of the blood of the guilty on the day of YHWH.

Ezekiel 22 offers a more complex and specific context of bloodshed as related to city authorities and forms of greed. Ezekiel 24:6-8 echoes the accusation of bloodshed of Jerusalem and, in the reading order of the book, already Ezek 9:9 anticipates this same accusation.[35] Furthermore, in the larger context of Ezek 18:5-18, verse 10 is a reference to blood guilt, yet specifically to the subcase of blood guilt that was incurred in a conflict with an individual of one's own kin.

Shedding blood is an idiom for violence that incurs guilt. It is used outside of prophetic literature in Lam 4:13 for the priests as well as for the prophets who are blamed for shedding blood in connection with the fall of Jerusalem. Two areas spell out the combination of "shedding blood" with other transgressions: the wisdom tradition in Prov 1:8-17 and 6:17, which points to it; and a cultural custom that Ps 106:38 associates with foreigners. These passages originated in the Persian or the Hellenistic era. The terminology of "bloodshed" has, in some instances, secondarily entered Deuteronomy's law. Both Deut 21:7 and Deut 19:10 use the terminology of "bloodshed." The latter is an addition to Deut 19:1-12 as a reference to homicide in priestly language. Priestly law equally uses the idiomatic bloodshed in association with the pollution of the land. Late priestly homicide law in Num 35:33 points to the "pollution" of the land through bloodshed: "So you shall not pollute [חנף, *hiphil*] the land in which you are; for blood pollutes [חנף, *hiphil*] the land and no expiation [כפר, *pual*] can be made for the land, for the blood that is shed on it, except by the blood of him who shed it." Seen through an intertextual lens in comparison with Lev 19:11-18, bloodshed is an extreme expression of personal hate that the city prophecy of Ezek 22 rejects; this extreme category of priestly thought is absent in the rules of H in Lev 19:11-18.

## Comparison and Conclusion

Ezekiel 22:6-12 mingles priestly and prophetic traditions, while Lev 19:11-18 springs from genuine legal traditions and discourses. In their respective forms, Ezek 22:6-12 represents a distinctive composition of a

---

35. This relates to 2 Kgs 21:16, echoing Deut 19:10, in an accusation of Manasseh of having shed blood until he had filled Jerusalem with blood.

judgment oracle, while Lev 19:11–18 aligns four double verses predominantly about the forms and the constellations of fair and unfair conflict settlement. From an intertextual perspective, the terminological and ideological overlap between both texts is apparent. Ezekiel 22:6–12 and Lev 19 both urge parental honor, admonishing to keep in place traditional rules of kinship that ideally the authority of the elders would guarantee. Written from a city perspective,[36] Ezek 22 blames the city "nobles" as the authorities responsible for the deviation from traditional values of kinship. Ezekiel 22 highlights the value of kinship in the tradition of urban prophecy that addresses the ruling elites.[37]

Different from this, Lev 19:2 addresses the congregation (עדה) of the Israelites as an insider group, and, consequently, Lev 19 may well be compared to a rule book of a lay community in a rural setting. The core of the intertextual overlap may further be seen in the function of Ezek 22:6–12 as an application of the principles to a city context in a literary context of a prophetic corpus. It is plausible that aspects of Ezek 22, namely Sabbath and parental authority, would be derived from H. Yet beyond this dependence between both texts, when reading the prohibition of mutual hate and the command of mutual love in Lev 19:17–18 in juxtaposition with Ezek 22:6–12, clearly the latter addresses the consequences of physical bloodshed in the city from a priestly point of view. Leviticus 19:11–18 urges a fundamental change in attitude among the members of the community.

---

36. The city perspective is evident, for instance, in the comparison between the Isaianic accusation of the city in Ezekiel and in Deutero-Isaiah; see among others, Dieter Baltzer, *Ezechiel und Deuterojesaja: Berührungen in der Heilserwartung der beiden großen Exilspropheten* (Berlin: de Gruyter, 1971), 41–47, 50–71; and Brian Neil Peterson, *Ezekiel's Message Understood in Its Historical Setting*, PTSMS 182 (Princeton: Princeton University Press, 2012), 94, with reference to Baltzer.

37. In contrast, a number of aspects in H point toward a rural milieu: (1) the use of the expression "people of the land"; (2) the rare references of cities in H as compared with Deuteronomic law; (3) the preceding regulations on harvesting leaving the gleaning (Lev 19:9–10) and the regulations about fruit trees (Lev 19:23–25); (4) in the larger context of H, the redemption laws (Lev 25:25–55); (5) the emphasis on agriculture and country life; (6) the Sabbath and jubilee year rules that presuppose land use as a necessity for freedom from slavery; (7) the focus of the blessings on fertility and harvest in Lev 26 that point to a rural context; and (8) the use of מושבה for dwelling places (Lev 23:3, 14, 17, 21, 31) rather than cities. All of these suggest an (envisioned) provincial setting of H as pointed out by Jan Joosten, *People and Land in the Holiness Code: An Exegetical Study of the Ideational Framework of the Law in Leviticus 17–26*, VTSup 67 (Leiden: Brill, 1996), 137–65.

The passage addresses the need for a generally constructive interaction in the closely knit community that H addresses, not pointing to the extreme outcome of hate but to the widespread, destructive attitude of unfair mutual interaction among community members.

# Anthology as Intertext:
# Ambiguity and Generative Interpretation in Qoheleth

*Hans Decker*

## On Collecting

In the epilogue of Ecclesiastes, the writer comments that Qoheleth has sought out דברי־חפץ, "charming sayings" (12:10).[1] But the following verse undermines this optimistic assessment of the preceding work by describing the effect of the collection (12:11):

דברי חכמים כדרבנות וכמשמרות נטועים בעלי אספות נתנו מרעה אחד
The words of the wise are like goads, and like planted nails are the collections of sayings given by one shepherd.

Qoheleth has gathered sayings together and arranged them, but the collections taken together prove to be provocative. Ecclesiastes' self-presentation as a troubling work has certainly proven true in its reception, where the interpretations of his words have been diverse and often contradictory. Even if the collections have been fixed, their meaning remains elusive. In this paper, we will examine the anthological form and how it shapes our process of reading in a way that embodies these uncertainties of Qoheleth's worldview. In order to understand the effect of Qoheleth's anthologies, we may begin our argument with a brief examination of collecting as a cultural practice. This will provide us with a helpful prism through which we can recognize the purpose and effect of an anthology.

---

1. In this paper I have adopted the convention of referring to the biblical book as Ecclesiastes and the persona of the narrator as Qoheleth. Additionally, I have used the masculine pronoun for Qoheleth, following the character's identification in 1:1 as the "son of David." All translations of texts are my own.

In her discussion of collecting, Susan Stewart argues that the constituent elements have meaning through their relationship to the other objects in the collection: "There are two movements to the collection's gesture of standing for the world: first, the metonymic displacement of part for whole, item for context; and second, the invention of a classification scheme which will define space and time in such a way that the world is accounted for by the elements of the collection."[2] Objects are selected as representative of a larger body, and the differences between them are given significance through their arrangement in relation to the rest of the collection. The collection becomes an accessible model of the world; the chronology of origin and the diversity of production or use collapse into the simultaneity of the collection. As Stewart says: "Those great civic collections, the library and the museum, seek to represent experience within a mode of control and confinement. One cannot know everything about the world, but one can at least approach closed knowledge through the collection."[3]

As literary collections, anthologies also manifest these features. James L. Kugel notes that the wisdom tradition in the ancient Near East tends to gather samples of wisdom into a literary collection.[4] The body of knowledge represented in the collection, Kugel notes, is inaccessibly large. No student of wisdom can fully master it, but the collection still gives a meaningful impression of the whole. As literary works, anthologies represent the worldview of wisdom—they articulate the principles that give events meaning and enable the wise to live well. The diverse wisdom tradition offers different views on the consistency and accessibility of these principles, but as collections, the anthologies of these sayings model the worldview they represent.

## Overview of the Argument

This raises an important question: How does the anthological character of wisdom literature shape the interpretive process? In this paper, we will examine the way that Qoheleth assembles collections of sayings as a representative embodiment of his worldview. We will look closely at two brief

---

2. Susan Stewart, *On Longing: Narratives of the Miniature, the Gigantic, the Souvenir, the Collection* (Durham, NC: Duke University Press, 1993), 162.

3. Stewart, *On Longing*, 161.

4. James L. Kugel, "Wisdom and the Anthological Temper," *Proof* 17 (1997): 9–32.

collections of משלים in order to explore the way that Qoheleth utilizes the ambiguity of the sayings he has chosen in order to create a miniature world of uncertainty.

As proverbs, the sayings from these anthologies could stand as independent literary texts. The generic archetypes, unadorned metaphors, and poetic structures that allow these miniaturized texts to be understood without context also leave room for a wide range of interpretations and applications. When such open texts are gathered together into a collection, however, each proverb exercises some influence over the way that we read the surrounding proverbs. The anthology becomes a self-contained series of intertexts that together provide a multifaceted worldview. The boundaries between texts are blurred in the collection, and readings of sayings often become entangled.

Qoheleth composes or quotes these proverbs as a set, and so they stand together, unified by the single voice of his narrative persona. Contrasting or contradictory points of view are not presented as the product of multiple authors, or even as changes in Qoheleth's own view over time. Instead, the complexity of the model world is presented in the paradoxical relationship of the sayings themselves. In order to read a collection as a coherent body of literature, we look for interpretations that draw connections between these different sayings which hold them together into a coherent account of the world. The difficulty inherent in generating coherent interpretations of Qoheleth's collection is not necessarily characteristic of wisdom anthologies; rather, it mirrors Qoheleth's unique account of his struggle to find wisdom.

## Ecclesiastes 10:5–11 as an Anthology

### A Calamity Observed

In Eccl 10:5–7, Qoheleth describes some problematic observations that he has made during his quest for wisdom:

יש רעה ראיתי תחת השמש כשגגה שיצא מלפני השליט נתן הסכל במרומים רבים ועשירים בשפל ישבו ראיתי עבדים על־סוסים ושרים הלכים כעבדים על־הארץ

There is an evil I have seen under the sun, like a mistake that comes from a ruler: the fool is set in many high places, and the wealthy sit in humiliation. I have seen servants upon horses, and princes walking like servants on the ground.

If these verses were separated, we could interpret Eccl 10:6 and 10:7 as traditional aphorisms. The book of Proverbs includes warnings against seeking out honors above one's station (e.g., Prov 26:6–7), while the book of Esther tells of a prince on the ground leading a servant on a horse as an expression of poetic justice (Esth 6:7–11). But when these verses are read as a running text, Eccl 10:6–7 is subordinate to the opening clause of 10:5. Qoheleth observes an evil, which he explores through two examples of inverted social order. The generic figures and representative situations in these verses illustrate the principle that worth does not guarantee position.

Pits of Our Own Making

Whatever the origins of the previous two verses, Eccl 10:8 clearly functions as a traditional distich proverb:

חפר גומץ בו יפול ופרץ גדר ישכנו נחש
The one digging a pit will fall into it; and the one breaching a wall will be bitten by a snake.

While the previous verses were marked by their shared imagery of inverted social order, this proverb focuses on actions and consequences. The imagery of falling into one's own pit is a familiar expression for being undone by one's own plots (e.g., Prov 28:26). The parallel structure of the saying encourages a similar reading of breaking through a wall as a criminal enterprise. A robber digs a pit as a trap in order to get someone else to fall into it, while a vandal knocks down a boundary wall in order to destroy a vineyard. In this way, the proverb offers a tidy assurance that the wicked will be hoist with his own petard. This interpretation is consistent with numerous other biblical passages describing those who fall into their own pits (Prov 26:27; 28:26; Pss 7:15; 9:15; 35:7–8; 57:6). The משל on its own is a traditional moral aphorism warning that, in the words of another sage, evil people will reap what they sow.

Contextual Reshaping

With this interpretation of Eccl 10:8 in our minds, we may return to the context, searching for ways in which to integrate this saying into the collection Qoheleth has already started. Perhaps 10:8 should be understood as a qualifying interpretation of the preceding situations. In this reading, the situations described in 10:6–7 are merely temporary wrinkles in the moral fabric of society that will soon be smoothed out under the irresistible weight of natural consequence. This reading of 10:8 does not contradict the legitimacy of Qoheleth's observations. They remain true, but the proverb in 10:8 reframes them under a larger principle. The slave may ride on horseback above his nobler counterparts, just as the bandit may lay traps for the innocent, but he is bound to fall from grace, just like the unstable edge of the pit will give way under the feet of the criminal. The sequence of the collection replaces narrative chronology. The observation and the principle are understood to be true simultaneously, but the assurance in 10:8 provided by what Klaus Koch called the *Tun-Ergehen-Zusammenhang* limits the implications of the רעה that Qoheleth has witnessed.[5]

Taken as a set, we can easily reimagine the paradigmatic situations in Qoheleth's observations as proverbial warnings. We may see situations where the wicked prosper, Qoheleth warns, but do not mistake such scenarios for evidence of moral anarchy. The destruction of the wicked will come upon them. In this way, by providing a new setting for the proverbs, the anthology could qualify problematic situations as temporary and reformulate the initial cynical observations about unworthy rulers as warnings about their impending demise. The collection generates additional significance in the proverbs through their juxtaposition.

Accidental Consequences

Qoheleth continues with a similar theme in Eccl 10:9:

מסיע אבנים יעצב בהם בוקע עצים יסכן בם
The one quarrying stones will be injured by them; the one splitting timber will be harmed by it.

Here we have the same kind of consequential reflex represented in both halves of the משל, where the subject is harmed by his actions. Strong parallels with the preceding verse indicate this saying belongs to the collection, but the implications are less clear. Both quarrying stone and splitting timber are dangerous activities, but neither is criminal. Some version of

---

5. See Klaus Koch, "Is There a Doctrine of Retribution in the Old Testament?," in *Theodicy in the Old Testament*, ed. James L. Crenshaw, IRT 4 (Philadelphia: Fortress, 1983), 57–87.

Koch's *Tun-Ergehen-Zusammenhang* may be at work, but without ethical grounding: accidents just happen.[6]

The juxtaposition of these two proverbs compromises the ethical interpretation of Eccl 10:8. As we noted in the introduction, difference may generate significance in a collection, but here the simultaneity of these contradictory principles creates a paradox. We reevaluate 10:8 in light of 10:9. Qoheleth has noted that everyone faces occupational hazards: the vandal may be bitten by a snake, but the stonemason may just as easily be crushed by the rock he is cutting. Or perhaps we have misread 10:8; maybe it describes the benign activities of a farmer digging a cistern or repairing a boundary wall.[7] Either way, the ethical dimensions of our first reading of verse 8 have been reshaped by the harsh reality of pointless accidents in verse 9.[8] What we interpret to be justice when it happens to the wicked is actually indistinguishable from the fate of the ordinary hard worker.

Verse 9 has shifted the center of gravity in this miniature world embodied by the collection, which means that our reevaluation of verse 8 must mean as well a reevaluation of verses 5–7. Here is a great moral evil

---

6. In Koch's interpretation, the consequences of an action are present in seed form in the deed, and God does not personally administer justice. Others argue against Koch that the Hebrew Bible manifests a tradition of divine intervention in the administration of justice, even if this operated in harmony with a more automatic view. See, for example, John Barton, *Ethics in Ancient Israel* (Oxford: Oxford University Press, 2014), 212–17. In Ecclesiastes, these different possibilities represent alternative objections that Qoheleth might be raising: either the natural order has broken down, or God himself has failed to administer justice properly.

7. See, for example, Tremper Longman III, *The Book of Ecclesiastes*, NICOT (Grand Rapids: Eerdmans, 1998), 244; or Michael V. Fox, *Qohelet and His Contradictions*, JSOTSup 71, BLS 18 (Sheffield: Sheffield Academic, 1989), 268. Even if we concluded that this verse does not speak of criminal activity, the entire argument for that reading would rest on rereading it in light of the surrounding passage, since the trope of falling into one's own pit is otherwise so well attested in the wisdom tradition.

8. The Aramaic targum of Ecclesiastes approaches this problem from the opposite angle, overlaying the proverb in Eccl 10:9 with ethical dimensions by imagining cutting stone and splitting wood as references to the crafting of idols. See Alexander Sperber, ed., *The Hagiographa: Transition from Translation to Midrash*, vol. 4A of *The Bible in Aramaic: Based on Old Manuscripts and Printed Texts*, ed. Alexander Sperber (Leiden: Brill, 1968), 165. Like Longman and Fox, the rabbis have read the sayings alongside one another as a means of generating a sense of coherence between the sayings, though they have done so by moralizing 10:9 rather than reimagining 10:8 as a description of benign activities.

Qoheleth has witnessed: prosperity and destruction come to the righteous and the wicked alike, without any discernible reason for their disparate fortunes. In this reading, verses 8–9 are not an interpretation or justification of the רעה that Qoheleth observes in 10:5; they are an extension of it. The entire collection embodies the evil he has seen. But how does the משל in 10:8 describe an evil? Has Qoheleth grouped 10:8–9 together, identifying as evil the lack of distinction between the death of the wicked and the innocent? Are we meant to reimagine 10:8 as a description of the death of undeserving workers—one digging a cistern, and the other reworking a boundary wall? Or has the decay of moral order meant that even the misfortunes that hamper the wicked have been robbed of any meaningful sense of goodness?

Polishing the Blunted Blade: A Possible Solution?

Qoheleth continues to expand his collection with another proverb (Eccl 10:10):

אם־קהה הברזל והוא לא־פנים קלקל וחילים יגבר ויתרון הכשיר חכמה

Each clause in verse 10 is beset with philological and interpretive difficulties, which are reflected in the apparent confusion of the ancient translators.[9] The ambiguity of this verse presents a problem for the purposes of this present analysis, since each possibility opens different interpretive pathways. We do not have the space here to explore them all.[10] We may begin with an interpretation suggested in the following translation: "If the iron is dull, and someone does not polish the edge, he must increase strength, but the profit of wisdom is success." Taken as an independent saying, this reading of the proverb encourages timely effort at the outset in order to

---

9. The LXX, for example, translates the verse: ἐὰν ἐκπέσῃ τὸ σιδήριον καὶ αὐτὸς πρόσωπον ἐτάραξεν καὶ δυνάμεις δυναμώσει καὶ περισσεία τοῦ ἀνδρείου σοφία ("If the axe head should fall off, and a man has injured a person, and he shall strengthen strength and the advantage of diligence is wisdom"). The first clause may be influenced by the language of Deut 19:5, which describes accidental homicide, while the second clause lacks the negative particle found in the Hebrew, which changes the logic of the verse.

10. For a summary of the various problems in this verse, see Timothy J. Sandoval and Dorothy B. E. A. Akoto, "A Note on Qohelet 10,10b," *ZAW* 122 (2010): 90–95.

save greater effort along the way—something like the traditional English aphorism: "A stitch in time saves nine."

As we read the collection, we look for ways of integrating this principle or pattern of thought into Qoheleth's larger collection of sayings about deed and consequence. If Qoheleth is indeed encouraging us to sharpen our tools to lighten our workload, the saying may offer a flash of optimism. When we read this verse in light of the previous proverbs about the dangers of manual labor, we may find additional significance in the imagery. Cutting wood, for example, is far safer when done with a sharp instrument than a dull one, since the keen axe is less likely to be deflected in unexpected directions. Perhaps Qoheleth has offered us a kind of solution to the problem he has raised: wisdom helps us avoid danger. Taken by itself, this reading offers corresponding conventional wisdom similar to our original reading of verse 8.

Our reading of this passage, however, has been defined by the context of the collection: Qoheleth is exploring the breakdown of the moral order through this collection of proverbs. How does this proverb fit into his anthology? Wisdom understood as foresight might help good people avoid dangerous errors, but it could as easily help the wicked succeed in their schemes. Does the statement about the value of preparation serve as a cynical explanation of the rise of the unworthy—even a little effort at the right time enabled their success? Or is it, rather, an indictment of those otherwise worthy of rule—the failure to act wisely in a timely manner makes maintaining the moral order impossibly difficult? Or is it perhaps spoken as advice for the potential solution to the problem—only timely wisdom can reverse the effects of moral corruption?

What if we have misread the Hebrew? Perhaps we should read this verse more in the tradition of Rashi, rendering the Hebrew differently: "Even if the iron is dull, and someone does not brighten its face, it will still strengthen the warriors—so the profit of success is skill." In other words, even a rusty hammer still pounds nails. Does that mean, as Rashi suggests, that wisdom might take the form of an ugly sage, but it still leads to success (see Rashi, Eccl 10:10)? Or should we read it in a more sinister fashion, suggesting that power, even when it is untempered by discipline or wisdom—an unpolished axe, as it were—still gives strength to the powerful? Power begets power, ensuring the oppressed remain oppressed.

The ambiguity of the construct relationships in Qoheleth's final line in Eccl 10:10 likewise lends itself to a range of interpretations. If the construct chain in ויתרון הכשיר חכמה is broken, as Anthony Frendo argues, the phrase praises the efficacy of wisdom.[11] This fits well as a summary of the reading of the verse where foresight improves effectiveness. Perhaps the saying presents an optimistic assessment of Qoheleth's crisis: even if the vindication of the righteous has been temporarily hampered, wisdom will ultimately lead to success.

However, if the construct chain is unbroken, the saying is more troubling: "The profit of success is wisdom." In other words, success reinforces right behavior. How does this address the apparent failure of the moral order? If the success of the wicked only improves their skill, then how can the moral inversion be reversed? After all, perhaps even the dull axe will "strengthen the strong," which means that those who should be princes are doomed to remain subservient to their unfit superiors.

The Serpent's Bite

Qoheleth's confused vision continues in Eccl 10:11:

אם־ישך הנחש בלוא־לחש ואין יתרון לבעל הלשון
If the serpent bites when it has not been charmed, there is no advantage for a charmer.[12]

---

11. Anthony Frendo has argued that the three words may be interpreted as a broken construct chain, a grammatical phenomenon noted in a short article by David Noel Freedman. See David Noel Freedman, "The Broken Construct Chain," *Bib* 53 (1972): 534–36. See Frendo, "The 'Broken Construct Chain' in Qoh 10,10b," *Bib* 62 (1981): 544–45.

12. The Hebrew verb לחש and the Greek translation ψιθυρισμῷ are ambiguous. They could refer to the muttered magical incantations of a snake charmer or to the "whispering" of the snake itself—that is, its hissing. Either way, the first half of the verse seems to refer to unexpected catastrophe—whether the snake bites before the chant of the charmer or the hiss of the snake, there is no way of escaping the danger. The phrase לבעל הלשון is also unclear and otherwise unattested. In the Greek, the phrase is translated and interpreted with the word ἐπᾴδοντι, which refers to singing charms. However, in the Hebrew, we could also interpret it in reference to the snake itself—if the snake bites before it hisses, there is no advantage to its skill with the tongue. In this reading, the proverb could function as a critique of the fool so prone to violence that his words are useless to him. This reading ties in well with the verses that follow in 10:12–14, and we might draw connections between the tendency toward senseless violence expressed in the traditional reading of 10:8 and the moral disarray in 10:6–7.

Taken on its own, the proverb could be understood as a warning that those who expose themselves to danger will eventually be harmed. In this reading, snake charming is pure foolishness because it willingly seeks danger. Thus, for example, Ben Sira notes: "Who will pity the charmer [חובר] when he is bitten?" (12:13). This may offer an interpretation of the inverted social order: those in high places have further to fall. Even if Qoheleth is not condemning climbing the ladder of power as immoral, perhaps the verse praises the wisdom of avoiding that ladder altogether.

However, as with the rest of the verses in this passage, we read this saying in conversation with the other sayings in the collection. We are not merely asking questions about avoiding risk; we are trying to understand the inversion of the moral order. Perhaps this verse too expresses the רעה that Qoheleth laments. We could reinterpret snake charming as a metaphor for being wise: wisdom helps to avert disaster, but once it strikes, such skills are useless.[13] This reading reinterprets the didactic force of the detached proverb as a bleak assessment of wisdom's inability to save us from the vicissitudes of fate.

Reading the First Collection

In our process of interpreting this anthology, we have explored different possible readings of the proverbs. The point of this exercise is not merely to highlight ambiguity in the wisdom tradition for its own sake. Rather, we have examined the way that the new context of the משלים in the collection creates an intertextual web that reorients the sayings toward one another. The miniature world of Qoheleth's collection highlights the ambiguity of the sayings by undermining their traditional readings and inspiring new imaginative interpretations. Qoheleth's framing narrative

---

13. As Fox notes, "Skills, including magical knowledge, are included in *hokmah*." The snake charmer, then, can be understood to be someone who has developed a particular magic or skill as a manifestation of their wisdom. See Fox, *Qohelet and His Contradictions*, 268–69. Indeed, if this interpretation is correct, the use of the Hebrew phrase לבעל הלשון in this context reduces wisdom to mere talent with words, which does not prevent disaster. Once destruction comes, many words only make the speaker look foolish. This cynical assessment of wisdom is consistent with the overall disillusionment and confusion that we have uncovered in our interpretation of the collection to this point. If we had additional space in this paper, we could explore the way that this reading might reorient the subsequent traditional proverbs of Qoheleth's collections about foolish talk to become sayings about the inadequacies of wisdom.

creates the impression of continuity and coherence, but the meaning of the משלים continues to shift as new possibilities emerge. The coherence of the worldview embodied in the collection is not one of interpretive stability but of consistent uncertainty. The unresolved tension between the traditional and novel interpretations is itself part of the meaning of the passage as a whole; the world manifested in the collection mirrors the complexity of Qoheleth's articulation of the human experience.

## Ecclesiastes 7:1–3 as a Collection

### Is Death Better than Birth?

In the opening verses of chapter 7, we can see another example of the way that disparate sayings in an anthology interact with one another to form a paradigmatic representation of a worldview. Here, Qoheleth once again observes the world through aphorism, this time focused on issues of life, death, happiness, and grief, which Qoheleth summarizes at the end of chapter 6 with a series of such questions (6:12):

כי מי־יודע מה־טוב לאדם בחיים מספר ימי־חיי הבלו ויעשם כצל אשר מי־יגיד לאדם מה־יהיה אחריו תחת השמש
For who knows what good thing there is for humanity in their lives, among the few days of the life of their vapor? They are like a shadow. Who will tell a person what will be after him under the sun?

Immediately following these questions, Qoheleth shifts in chapter 7 into a series of traditional משלים, gathered together into an anthology. He begins with an unusual proverb (7:1):

טוב שם משמן טוב ויום המות מיום הולדו
A good name is better than good oil, and the day of death than the day of birth.

The first half of this proverb is extremely conventional, echoing similar sentiments in the book of Proverbs (22:1):

נבחר שם מעשר רב מכסף ומזהב חן טוב
A name is to be chosen rather than great wealth, and good favor more than silver or gold.

The traditional motif in the first half of the verse is paired with an unusual second line, forcing a difficult marriage between old and new.[14] How is the day of death better than the day of birth? We must reexamine our interpretation of the first half of the verse and use it as a rubric to help make sense of the second line. In his exploration of the phenomenon of biblical parallelism, Kugel offers his own ingenious interpretation of the verse. Oil, he notes, spoils easily, while a name is incorporeal and thus free from decay. In the same way, "the newborn child is like the precious oil in that he is entirely physical—no qualities, no character, in fact, *no name*, at least not for a while."[15] Only when a person has died will this process of constructing the intangible and incorruptible name be complete. In line with Kugel's interpretation, we might read this saying as a warning: as long as we remain alive, we have the power irrevocably to destroy our own reputations.

In light of the questions at the end of chapter 6, perhaps we can understand this as a partial answer: What good thing is there for a person in the course of his life?[16] The capacity to establish a pristine reputation. In this

---

14. This fits well with the theory of the folk origins of proverbs put forward by Otto Eissfeldt. See Otto Eissfeldt, *Der Maschal im Alten Testament: Eine wortgeschichtliche Untersuchung nebst einer literargeschichtlichen Untersuchung der lvm genannten Gattungen "Volkssprichwort" und "Spottlied"* (Giessen: Töpelmann, 1913), 47. Subsequent scholars have critiqued Eissfeldt's methodology for relying on arbitrary criteria. See Carole R. Fontaine, *Traditional Sayings in the Old Testament: A Contextual Study*, BLS 5 (Sheffield: Almond Press, 1982), 3–7. In this particular case, however, Eissfeldt's paradigm may well account for the awkward shift between the smooth (and highly traditional) first line and comparatively awkward (and surprising) second line.

15. James L. Kugel, *The Idea of Biblical Poetry: Parallelism and Its History* (New Haven: Yale University Press, 1981), 10. Kugel's reading has its roots in Jewish interpretive tradition. See, for example, Mekhon ha-Midrash ha-Mevo'ar, *Qohelet Rabbah*, vol. 15 of *Midrash Rabbah HaMevo'ar* (Jerusalem: Ḥavre ha-Makhon ha-Midrash ha-Mevo'ar, 1995), 351–52. James L. Crenshaw makes a similar observation, noting a parallel with Ben Sira 11:28, which claims no one should be called blessed before they die, since misfortune may always strike. See James L. Crenshaw, *Ecclesiastes: A Commentary*, OTL (Philadelphia: Westminster, 1987), 133–34.

16. This reading of the opening of Eccl 7:1 as Qoheleth's tentative answer to the questions raised in 6:12 is reflected in rabbinic interpretation: אשר מי יגיד לאדם וגו אמר שלמה אני אגיד לך מה טוב מכלן טוב שם משמן טוב. See Mekhon ha-Midrash ha-Mevo'ar, *Qohelet Rabbah*, 341. Of course, taken as it is written, the midrash relies on the very traditional moralistic interpretation of the first half of the verse without reference to the complicating development it receives in 7:1b and the subsequent verses.

interpretation, the day of one's death is considered good, not in itself, but because it cements the reputation of the righteous in perpetuity. What will still remain after someone dies? In the words of Qoheleth Rabbah: ושם טוב לעולם.[17]

Rethinking Death

As we move on to the second verse, however, doubts about this interpretive direction emerge (Eccl 7:2):

טוב ללכת אל־בית־אבל מלכת אל־בית משתה באשר הוא סוף כל־האדם
והחי יתן אל־לבו

Better to go to the house of sorrow than to go to the house of feasting, for in it is the end of all humanity, and the one who is alive should keep this in mind.

There are clear syntactical and conceptual parallels between the two verses that invite us to read them together. Kugel's interpretation made sense of 7:1 on its own, but there is nothing in 7:2 about establishing a reputation to form a point of continuity between the verses. Here, Qoheleth seems to be praising mourning a death rather than rejoicing (over birth?). Both verses make counterintuitive claims, but 7:2 lacks the mechanism for Kugel's clever turn. Instead, Qoheleth drives his point home: "For in it is the end of all humanity, and the one who is alive should keep this in mind." Maybe Qoheleth is merely praising stoic realism over mindless frivolity. We return to the first verse. We could try to interpret it in line with our reading of the second verse: the person who would establish a good name would do well to consider where she is going rather than where she is from.

But Eccl 7:1 says nothing of how we ought to feel about death; it only tells us that the day of death is better than the day of birth. Perhaps we have misinterpreted 7:2. Does Qoheleth simply mean that we ought to see death as obviously superior to birth, as we know our reputation to be better than a jar of ointment? After all, Qoheleth argued in the previous chapter that the stillborn child is better off than the person who fails to enjoy life: "It has not seen the sun or known anything, yet it finds rest rather than he" (Eccl 6:3). Here, though, he eschews enjoyment itself in favor of sorrow. Perhaps death is superior to life because in death we escape the endless

---

17. Mekhon ha-Midrash ha-Mevo'ar, *Qohelet Rabbah*, 342.

toil of wisdom and finally have rest, which otherwise eludes us (e.g., Eccl 8:16–17; 1:18).[18] Maybe the second half of verse 1 seems jarring to us only because we have failed to acknowledge life's pervasive misery and wrongly feared the deep sleep of death.

This new interpretation of 7:1 in light of 7:2 reorients the worldview modeled in Qoheleth's collection. We had suggested that cultivating a good reputation was of great value, in part because this reputation would continue on after death. But if Qoheleth is saying that death is better than life because life is not worth living, then he has answered his questions in a very different manner: what good thing is there for a person during the days of his life? Nothing but the certainty of the grave. What remains after him? Who knows? Maybe nothing at all.

More Frustration

The third verse continues in this same theme (Eccl 7:3):

טוב כעס משחק כי־ברע פנים ייטב לב
Better frustration than laughter, for sadness of face makes better the heart.[19]

The first half of this verse fits with the theme established in the previous two verses: Qoheleth lifts up what we would otherwise view as undesirable and claims that it is superior to what we would otherwise crave. Here, though, he offers a slightly different twist in the second line, distinguishing between the sadness of one's face and the happiness (יטב) of the heart. This introduces a new uncertainty into our attempt to understand these verses: how can we be in mourning and happy at the same time? We could

---

18. Longman favors this reading, arguing specifically against interpretations like that of Kugel that "the best reading of the second [half of the verse] is that it expresses Qohelet's relief that life is finally over. In the context of his speech as a whole, this relief arises not because of work completed and well done but because death means escape from life's oppression and meaninglessness" (Longman, *Book of Ecclesiastes*, 182). Longman draws a direct connection between 7:1 and 7:2.

19. The meaning of some of the vocabulary is ambiguous. כעס means "frustration," "vexation," or "anger," while רע פנים is a common expression for sadness. The degree to which these two phrases are meant to overlap is uncertain; is Qoheleth suggesting, as some translations have favored, merely that mourning is superior to laughter, or does he intend to favor indulging in anger as a means of relieving anxiety? See Crenshaw, *Ecclesiastes*, 134.

invent ways of reconciling this problem. For example, we could understand this grief to be superficial, occurring only on the face, as opposed to the deep-seated joy in the heart. But this strains credibility, given that the previous two examples have involved coming face-to-face with death, which is hardly a matter for superficial sadness.

Perhaps we should follow Graham Ogden, who reads in the tradition of the targum: "Better frustration than laughter, for sadness of face improves the mind."[20] Misery builds character. In this reading, of course, there is no contradiction or paradox at all; instead, in a Nietzschean twist, bad experiences are good for you because they make you a person of stronger character. However, while Ogden's reading of improved moral fiber softens the paradoxical nature of the expression, the phrase יטב לב is elsewhere attested clearly as merriment or gladness.

Maybe Qoheleth does mean to say that a sad face can make the heart glad (cf. Prov 14:13); an awareness of our encroaching death imbues the experience of joy with greater significance. This helps us to make sense of the distinction between the sorrowful face and the happy heart: the difficulty of facing our impending death brings renewed vibrancy to the pleasures of the moment. This also makes sense of the second verse: Qoheleth has pointed out that the grave is the inevitable end of all and that the living should lay this to heart. Perhaps he is explaining that only when we do so are we enlivened to the happiness of the present. In that sense, then, we can reinterpret the house of feasting as mere superficial happiness devoid of any significance beyond fleeting pleasure. The house of mourning causes us to hold our loved ones closer.[21]

---

20. Graham Ogden, *Qoheleth*, Readings (Sheffield: Sheffield Academic, 1987), 103. This tradition is also reflected in the targum. See Sperber, *Hagiographa*, 159.

21. It may be helpful to read this passage in conversation with 4Q417 2 I, 10–12: ואל תשׂמח באבלכה פן תעמֹל בחיכֿ[ה. הבט ברז] נהיה זקח מולדי יִשׁע ודע מי נוֹחל כבוד וֹעָמֹל. הֹלואׁ] שׂים ששון לנכאי רוח] ולאבליהמה שמחת עולם. ("But do not rejoice in your time of mourning lest you should toil in your life. Trust the mystery of the way things are, and take hold of the source of salvation, and know who will inherit glory and toil. Has rejoicing not been established for the contrite of spirit, and for those who sorrow, eternal joy?") Reconstructed text from John Strugnell, Daniel Harrington, and Torleif Elgvin, *Qumran Cave 4: XXIV Sapiential Texts, Part 2; 4QInstruction (Mûsār Lĕ Mēvîn): 4Q415 ff.*, consult. Joseph A. Fitzmyer, ed. Emanuel Tov, DJD 34 (Oxford: Clarendon, 1999), 173. Both 4QInstruction (4Q418) and Qoheleth urge their readers in these passages to eschew rejoicing and embrace mourning in light of the future, but their reasoning is diametrically opposed. In 4Q418, the speaker is urging his readers

While this reading makes sense of Eccl 7:2–3 together, verse 1 does not fit well in the same paradigm. How can we understand the day of death to be better than the day of birth if no happiness is to be found in the grave? We could force readings that would bring it into conformity: it is better to contemplate the day of our death than the day of our birth because it will remind us to live a more fulfilling life (thereby establishing a good name). But there is little to recommend such readings aside from our desire to bring our own sense of coherence onto the flow of Qoheleth's thoughts.

## Reading the Second Collection

We uncovered multiple possible readings for these proverbs. The shared theme of valuing sorrow more than happiness (not to mention the טוב מן construction they hold in common) invites us to read them together, searching for ways in which we can understand Qoheleth's insights to address the questions that he has raised, but the differences between the proverbs hinder a unified reading. Of course, we should not misunderstand Qoheleth's collection of proverbs in this chapter as a tightly constructed argument, and in that sense, we do not need to uncover a single logical thread connecting his different observations.[22] Rather, we read these proverbs together because they all address the same questions: who knows what good thing there is for humanity in their lives? Who will tell a person what will be after him under the sun? Each משל becomes a unique prism through which we can study the same questions. The individual proverb, when read alone, invites us to exercise our creativity in order to make sense of the metaphors, comparisons, and contrasts. But just as internal ambiguity allows us to generate multiple interpretations, so also when we read these proverbs alongside one another as a set of intertexts, Qoheleth's observations inform one another, reshaping our understanding as a

---

to live in light of eschatological hope; Qoheleth, on the other hand, seems to anticipate only death. Curiously, though they disagree about the future, both teachers urge a kind of internal happiness: 4Q418 finds it in unwavering flame of eschatological hope, while Qoheleth seems to argue that the heart shines brighter in the present by an awareness of the impending darkness.

22. As Longman points out, "Such harmonization is only needed if one understands Qohelet to be a perfectly orthodox and consistent wisdom teacher," which Longman rejects (*Book of Ecclesiastes*, 183). Even though such difficulties do not need to be forcibly excised from the literature, when we read, we naturally look for ways to understand tensions, even if they remain unresolved.

way of moving us closer to wisdom. The collection as a whole embodies a worldview of death; the tensions between the different משלים express the complexity and uncertainties of Qoheleth's vision.

## Conclusion

In Ecclesiastes, משלים are often so ambiguous that a single saying can be interpreted in contradictory ways. Interpretation is the distillation of coherence from the possibility of meaning, but in the anthology, these possibilities multiply. Intertexts shape the direction of our reading but also problematize our interpretations. Within the collection, how ought we to define the boundaries between texts? Where does one text properly end and another begin? On the one hand, the overlap in potential meaning between any two proverbs narrows the semantic range of those sayings to their points of intersection. On the other hand, the more sayings are collected together, the more overlapping readings there are to be discovered that destabilize our process of reading. The intertextual relationship of each new proverb in the collection suggests new possible avenues of interpretation.

The intertextual readings we have explored are not part of a project of harmonization. Qoheleth is rightly famous for his contradictions. But we cannot see the tensions in his writings unless we read the sayings together and ask how they relate to one another. This generates imaginative readings that may contrast or harmonize different insights represented in the collection, but these produce opaque suggestions rather than definitive clarity. Our difficulties in interpreting the collection have mirrored the challenges Qoheleth himself relates in his search for wisdom. The collection of proverbs establishes a mimetic world, miniaturizing Qoheleth's problematic experiences and insights. If literature is an imitation of reality, as Erich Auerbach argued, then reading is an echo of living.[23] Even when the collection contains contradictions, gives voice to competing insights,

---

23. Erich Auerbach, *Mimesis: Dargestellte Wirklichkeit in der Abendländischen Literatur*, SD 90 (Bern: Francke, 1971), 26. Though Qoheleth's anthologies are not narrative, Auerbach's insights provide a useful framework for understanding Qoheleth's mimesis of reality that he constructs in his collection. What Auerbach called the "*Vieldeutigkeit und Deutungsbedürftigkeit*" produces greater uncertainty but also a greater sense of realism. By way of contrast, the transparent idealism sometimes expressed in the book of Proverbs strikes a decidedly different note: those collections model a

or expresses confusion, we read these verses together as a collection in order to understand the problems Qoheleth is articulating—not necessarily to resolve them, but to grasp the nature of the contradiction that he has observed. Wisdom is not found in the individual saying any more than one correct insight makes someone wise. Only when the sayings have been brought together into a collection of intertexts do they trace the outline of wisdom. Only when the illusion of certainty has been lost can we cease to be wise in our own eyes and begin to pursue wisdom. As Stewart notes, "the point of the collection is forgetting—starting again in such a way that a finite number of elements create, by virtue of their combination, an infinite reverie."[24] In the world of Qoheleth, wisdom is elusive, and so the shifting shapes represented in his collections never resolve into greater clarity. As we interpret, we lose ourselves in a miniaturized version of the same maze Qoheleth himself has been wandering.

---

comparatively perfect world that exists as the projection of moral imagination rather than lived experience.

24. Stewart, *On Longing*, 152.

# Prophetic and Proverbial Justice: Amos, Proverbs, and Intertextuality

*Timothy J. Sandoval*

In an erudite 2014 article, John L. McLaughlin revisited a question that many Hebrew Bible scholars have long puzzled over: whether the prophet Amos belonged to the circle of the wise.[1] As McLaughlin helpfully explains, the thesis that Amos did in fact belong to the wise was first robustly argued by Hans Walter Wolff in his short book, *Amos' Geistige Heimat*, though he was anticipated in this endeavor by Samuel Terrien.[2] These scholars identified what they believed to be features of Amos that suggested a rela-

---

1. John L. McLaughlin, "Is Amos (Still) among the Wise?," *JBL* 133 (2014): 281–303.
2. Hans Walter Wolff, *Amos' Geistige Heimat*, WMANT 18 (Neukirchen-Vluyn: Neukirchener Verlag, 1964). Translated as Wolff, *Amos the Prophet: The Man and His Background*, ed. John Reumann, trans. Foster R. McCurley (Philadelphia: Fortress, 1977). Samuel Terrien, "Amos and Wisdom," in *Israel's Prophetic Heritage: Essays in Honor of James Muilenburg*, ed. Bernhard W. Anderson and Walter J. Harrelson (New York: Harper & Brothers, 1962), 108–15. Many of Wolff's claims about Amos and wisdom are also evident (and somewhat developed) in Wolff, *Joel and Amos*, trans. Waldemar Janzen, Sean D. McBride, and Charles A. Muenchow, Hermeneia (Philadelphia: Fortress, 1977). Subsequent studies on "Amos and Wisdom" include: James L. Crenshaw, "The Influence of the Wise upon Amos: The 'Doxologies of Amos' and Job 5:9–16, 9:5–10," *ZAW* 79 (1967): 42–52; and J. Alberto Soggin, "Amos and Wisdom," in *Wisdom in Ancient Israel: Essays in Honour of J. A. Emerton*, ed. John Day, Robert P. Gordon, and H. G. M. Williamson (Cambridge: Cambridge University Press, 1995), 119–23. Scholarly investigations of wisdom's impact on prophetic works in the twentieth century are usually traced back to J. Fichtner, "Jesaja unter den Weisen," *TLZ* 74 (1949): 75–80, translated as Fichtner, "Isaiah among the Wise," in *Studies in Ancient Israelite Wisdom*, ed. James L. Crenshaw (New York: Ktav, 1976), 429–38. Wisdom influence has often been detected in other biblical works as well. See Crenshaw, "Method in Determining Wisdom Influence on 'Historical' Literature," *JBL* 88 (1969): 129–42. Gerald T. Sheppard argues wisdom scribes redacted much of the

tionship between that text and the wisdom tradition.³ For both Terrien and Wolff, Amos's words and thoughts were in some sense thought to belong to, or borrow from, the social-historical context of those early clan leaders whose originally oral, wise notions and rhetoric would come to be enshrined in books like Proverbs, Job, and Ecclesiastes.

McLaughlin's article systematically reviews the main arguments put forward by Terrien and Wolff regarding the geographical links between Amos and wisdom traditions, the presence of wisdom forms in Amos, the wisdom terminology that the prophet employs, and the wisdom ideas in Amos that might suggest sapiential influence on the prophet. If other scholars after Terrien and Wolff sought to reign in and/or modify the thesis of wisdom's influence on Amos, McLaughlin seeks to put the claim fully to rest. He strives to demonstrate that all of the principal arguments put forward by Terrien and Wolff are unconvincing.

I will not here explicitly defend either Terrien and Wolff, on the one hand, or McLaughlin, on the other, regarding the possible influence of wisdom circles on Amos. Rather, I offer an effort to reframe the question of the relations between wisdom books and the text of Amos more fully in terms of theories of intertextuality, while also limiting my consideration to the relations between Amos and that paradigmatic wisdom text, Proverbs.

More specifically, the analysis that follows builds on a set of ideas and critical terms developed by Mikhail M. Bakhtin and his interpreters having to do with, among other matters, authors, discourse, and intertextuality. As is well known, the modernist, critical terminology of *influence* has become problematic in light of contemporary discussions of textuality and intertextuality. However, I hope to show—via a Bakhtinian critical orientation—that the distinct utterances or discourses of Amos and Proverbs are related to each other, especially in regard to their articulation of closely aligned moral-theological visions in which justice rhetoric plays a key role. The moral visions of each book, I suggest, drew on a broad, shared

---

Hebrew Bible. See Sheppard, *Wisdom as a Hermeneutical Construct: A Study in the Sapientializing of the Old Testament*, BZAW 151 (Berlin: de Gruyter, 1980).

3. A number of scholars have recently fundamentally questioned the coherency of the concept of a "wisdom tradition," focusing instead on questions of literacy, text production, and education in the ancient world. See Mark R. Sneed, ed., *Was There a Wisdom Tradition? New Prospects in Israelite Wisdom Studies*, AIL 23 (Atlanta: SBL Press, 2015).

moral discourse, and each text accentuated and inflected aspects of that discourse in its own ways, toward its own particular rhetorical ends, and in its own distinct social and historical context. It is conceivable that Amos was, after all, influenced by a wisdom work like Proverbs; or, perhaps, the opposite—that Proverbs was influenced by Amos. In either case, however, the way that one understands influence will have shifted significantly from the way Terrien, Wolff, and McLaughlin have deployed the term.

## The Influence of Terrien, Wolff, and McLaughlin

The arguments presented by Terrien and Wolff regarding Amos's relatedness to wisdom or the wise are often complex and are largely offered as responses to the critical orthodoxy of the mid-twentieth century regarding the provenance of Amos. Amos's thought and language—or as Wolff put it, his "Geistige Heimat"—was believed to be found in early covenant and cultic-legal traditions and social circles.[4] Terrien thus could note that some scholars had long suggested that the preexilic prophet Amos had influenced wisdom texts like Proverbs, a work that had been firmly assigned a postexilic date.[5] He believed, however, that "proper emphasis on the early date of an oral tradition among the wise may reopen the question of the influences which the prophets received."[6] Instead of Amos influencing Proverbs, early wisdom may have influenced the prophet.

Wolff's arguments regarding the influence of wisdom circles on Amos were significantly more thoroughgoing and polemical than Terrien's efforts. Wolff, for instance, was more concerned to upend the thesis that Amos belonged to covenant-oriented, cultic-legal circles than was Terrien. Like Terrien, Wolff assumed a late date for the book of Proverbs and suggested that Amos belonged to, or was influenced by, the early oral wisdom traditions of the clan, which was apparently discernable in and through later wisdom texts like Proverbs. Neither Terrien nor Wolff, however, says much about how, methodologically, one might discern older clan wisdom in the literary expression of texts like Proverbs, which, in the form that we

---

4. Terrien, "Amos and Wisdom," 113; Wolff, *Amos the Prophet*, 1–5.
5. Terrien, "Amos and Wisdom," 108; Terrien is citing, apparently, a 1910 edition of the work of William R. Harper, *A Critical and Exegetical Commentary on Amos and Hosea*, ICC (New York: Scribner's Sons, 1905), 137.
6. Terrien, "Amos and Wisdom," 109.

have them, surely were produced and transmitted by learned urban scribes likely associated with central institutions of court and temple.[7]

Few commentators have wholly accepted Terrien's and Wolff's claims, though aspects of their arguments have occasionally been affirmed.[8] Others, like McLaughlin, have viewed the connections between Amos and wisdom works identified by Terrien and Wolff as tenuous, superficial, and often too general—belonging too broadly to Amos's social-historical context—to warrant the claim that the prophet belonged to circles of the wise or that early clan wisdom directly influenced his words.

The precise nature, or terms, upon which scholars like Terrien, Wolff, and their critics carried out their debates regarding relations between Amos and the wise is important to recognize. Although their approaches are never explicitly articulated in theoretical terms, Terrien and Wolff were essentially looking to identify, if possible, something like the literary sources of Amos's ideas and language in wisdom texts. However, as this search for the clear literary dependence of Amos on wisdom works could not be sustained, the quest took the form of identifying more generally different sites and sorts of influence on Amos—genres, terms, ideas, and so forth—that could be said to have been derived or taken over from wisdom works and thought. On the first two pages of McLaughlin's article critiquing Terrien's and Wolff's position, for example, the term influence appears twelve times (including the abstract)—a textual tick that gestures toward the modernist theoretical terms upon which all these scholars have explored the question of the literary and ideological relations between Amos and wisdom.[9] On this understanding of textual relations, authors intentionally cite, or otherwise clearly allude to, the works of other authors and so can be said to be substantively impacted—or influenced—by them.

## Influence and Intertextuality

The term *intertextuality* is now widely deployed in a range of academic disciplines, including biblical studies. It is, however, regularly used in

---

7. A version of the methodological problem continues in Proverbs studies in the debate over whether the origin of the sentence sayings of Prov 10–29 "was the scribal school or village life." Michael V. Fox, *Proverbs 1–9: A New Translation with Introduction and Commentary*, AB 18A (New York: Doubleday, 2000), 7.

8. See Crenshaw, "Influence of the Wise," 51.

9. McLaughlin, "Is Amos (Still) among the Wise?," 281–82.

multiple ways. It can, for instance, serve as a gloss to describe the essentially modernist quest to discover the influence of one text or author upon another—the sort of work that Terrien, Wolff, McLaughlin, and others have long pursued in biblical studies. As was intimated, intertextuality in this sense means that a precise literary source for one author's text can be identified in the work of another author; or, in less explicit fashion, it describes the way one text alludes to or echoes another.[10] Such a view is quintessentially modern in that it presupposes self-contained subjects as authors of texts that easily refer to things and embed intended meanings. Such texts and authors can thus sometimes be thought purposely and substantively to impact each other.

The chief debates in this way of understanding relations between authors or texts are thus methodological. As Jay Clayton and Eric Rothstein explain, scholars investigating the influence of one text on another regularly worry "how to discriminate genuine influences from commonplace images, techniques, or ideas that could be found in almost any writer of a given period."[11] Unless there is explicit acknowledgment in one text (by one author) of influence by another text (author), or a critic finds something close to a verbatim citation of one text in a second text, disputes over influence are inevitable and inevitably interminable. Where one critic of a work claims influence and hears allusion to, or echo of, a second text, another critic will insist that any similarity between works is due not to the influence of one author or text on another but, for example, to a common context or shared world of ideas, or something else.

This is precisely how the debate regarding wisdom's influence on Amos takes shape. As J. Alberto Soggin says in his own contribution to the "Amos and wisdom debate," "the problem ... seems to me to be one of method: if a wisdom text and a non-wisdom text use the same idiom, does it automatically follow that the latter has been influenced by wisdom?"[12] Indeed, Wolff did not see in the author/text called Amos sufficient evidence to warrant concluding that the prophet was directly or substantively impacted by cultic-legal thinking and rhetoric. Instead, Wolff discerned

---

10. See Jay Clayton and Eric Rothstein, "Figures in the Corpus: Theories of Influence and Intertextuality," in *Influence and Intertextuality in Literary History*, ed. Jay Clayton and Eric Rothstein (Madison: University of Wisconsin Press, 1991), 3–36; and Gregory Machacek, "Allusion," *PMLA* 122 (2007): 522–36.

11. Clayton and Rothstein, "Figures in the Corpus," 5.

12. Soggin, "Amos and Wisdom," 122.

the substantive and clear impact of wisdom ideas and rhetoric on Amos. This argument, however, was subsequently rejected by others, including most recently, McLaughlin, who set out to contest, robustly, the claim that Amos was influenced by wisdom circles, notions, and texts. The relations between Amos and wisdom that Wolff attributed to the impact of early clan wisdom on the prophet can be, for McLaughlin, (better) explained otherwise. At most, McLaughlin admits—as one would expect in disagreements of this sort—that Amos and wisdom works might have shared a common cultural background. Although Wolff and Terrien often do not seem to be claiming a whole lot more than this, McLaughlin's evaluation of their arguments for wisdom influence on Amos nonetheless reveals the modernist theoretical presuppositions—implicit as they might be—of the entire debate regarding how relations between texts can be understood.

On the typical modernist understandings of influence upon which Terrien and Wolff implicitly carried out their projects and upon which McLaughlin somewhat more explicitly engages their work, there turns out to be—as will become clear below—remarkably little to quibble with in McLaughlin's essay. McLaughlin is right; or, at least, it is hard to say that Wolff and Terrien unambiguously demonstrated the correctness of the thesis that Amos belonged among the wise. Yet one might nonetheless wonder why Terrien and Wolff discerned a relationship between Amos and wisdom works in the first place, especially since the terms upon which they sought to demonstrate this relationship seem to have failed, and rather spectacularly so according to McLaughlin. I suspect it was simply Terrien's and Wolff's deep familiarity with the language, forms, and ideologies of a wide range of biblical books that triggered their exegetical instincts regarding an intertextual relation of influence between Amos and the wise. Yet, if the theoretical mode of understanding the relations between wisdom works and Amos that was available to them was inadequate to demonstrate convincingly the relationship they sensed, it may be that other theoretical tools can be deployed, in part, to rehabilitate their theses. Other notions of intertextuality, which move beyond questions of influence, can help reframe questions and arguments regarding the relations between books like Amos and Proverbs.

### Textuality and Intertextuality

Rather than focusing on quests for sources and influence, contemporary discussions of intertextuality often involve thoroughgoing claims about textuality in general and thereby shift considerably the terms of the discussion of intertextuality itself. Robust postmodern articulations of (inter)textuality that insist upon inevitable relations between texts are usually associated with such theoretical heavyweights as Julia Kristeva, Jacques Derrida, Roland Barthes, and others.[13] Deriving from Kristeva's encounter with the work of Bakhtin and poststructuralist critiques of Saussurean linguistics, the conception of (inter)textuality that emerges from these thinkers recognizes that, as signifier slides under signified, authors vanish into sites of discourse, multiplicity of meaning bursts the bonds of simple claims about reference and truth, and all texts are revealed to be intertextually related to all other texts. As Simon Dentith has put it:

> This version of intertextuality seeks to do away with our common sense ideas of authors and texts and replace them with a sense of the underlying productiveness of writing itself; from the perspective of "textuality" any actual text is merely a particular density among a myriad [of] codes or discourses, whose origins cannot be traced and which stretch to the horizon in all directions.[14]

Despite these claims about intertextuality from the world of critical theory, modernist, diachronically oriented biblical (or other) critics may, of course, continue to see the influence of one author or text on another—Amos intentionally alluding to or echoing wisdom teaching, for instance. As Dentith explains, "There is nothing wrong with this kind of criticism except that it does not go nearly far enough" in explaining relations between texts.[15] By contrast, synchronically minded, postmodern intertextual critics might simply insist theoretically on the inevitable

---

13. Key texts include, but are hardly limited to: Julia Kristeva, "Word, Dialogue, and Novel," in *Desire in Language: A Semiotic Approach to Literature and Art*, ed. Leon S. Roudiez, trans. Thomas Gora, Alice Jardine, and Leon S. Roudiez (New York: Columbia University Press, 1980), 64–91; Jacques Derrida, *Of Grammatology*, trans. Gayatri Chakravorty Spivak (Baltimore: Johns Hopkins University Press, 1976); Roland Barthes, *Writing Degree Zero*, trans. Annette Lavers and Colin Smith (New York: Hill & Wang, 1977); Barthes, "The Death of the Author," in *Image, Music, Text*, trans. Stephen Heath (New York: Hill & Wang, 1977), 142–48; and Barthes, *S/Z*, trans. Richard Miller (New York: Hill and Wang, 1974).

14. Simon Dentith, *Bakhtinian Thought: An Introductory Reader*, CRTP (London: Routledge, 1995), 95.

15. Dentith, *Bakhtinian Thought*, 95.

intertextual relationship between Amos's language and the rhetoric of wisdom works and point to some of the available intertexts. Regardless of any demonstrable direct, historical relationship between wise clan elders (or the book of Proverbs) and Amos, on this model, all that is really necessary to identify and warrant claims of intertextual relations between Amos and wisdom traditions is a reader who gestures to them.

However, for many critics, the so-called high theory notions of intertextuality articulated by Kristeva, Barthes, and others turn out to be not all that helpful for practical analysis of literary works. As Clayton and Rothstein have put it in relation to Barthes's views in particular, such theories "do not provide the critic with a particularly effective tool for analyzing literary texts."[16] With the wielding of this sort of critical instrument alone, one does not learn much about specific texts and the relation between works except for the fact that they are (inevitably) intertextually related and can be said *not* to mean what one might have, in an earlier epoch, thought their authors to have intended them to mean. Historically minded biblical scholars might reach the conclusion (warranted or not) that this sort of intertextual work evidences a lack of rigor in a critic's textual analysis, or they might suspect a renunciation of any concerns with history and the history of texts—whether or not good arguments for skepticism about different historical projects and diachronic relations between literary products are articulated.[17] Put otherwise, for some, this version of intertextuality grants too little theoretical space for recognizing real, material, and social actors, whose subjectivity and texts may not be as unified and coherent as once thought but whose utterances are nonetheless articulated in specific social and historical contexts that matter.

It will not do, however, simply to refuse the postmodern and return cheerfully to modernist views and practices of interpretation and its intertextual search for sources and influences. One cannot unring the bell of poststructuralism or the announcement of inevitable textual relations. How, then, to proceed with a notion of intertextuality that is both useful for understanding specific works and relations between texts and which has learned, or at least has been critically informed by, the lessons of Derrida, Kristeva, and Barthes regarding textuality?

---

16. Clayton and Rothstein, "Figures in the Corpus," 22–23.

17. See Benjamin D. Sommer, "Exegesis, Allusion and Intertextuality in the Hebrew Bible: A Response to Lyle Eslinger," *VT* 46 (1996): 479–89.

One way forward is to (re)turn to Bakhtin.[18] In articulating a foundational notion of intertextuality, Kristeva drew on, and famously altered, aspects of Bakhtin's musings by wedding these to French poststructuralism.[19] As Dentith, among others, has noted, Kristeva's work is focused differently than Bakhtin's. The criticism of the modernist or "the 'classic realist' text" associated with Kristeva and French poststructuralism is largely epistemological; it is concerned "to show the impossibility of the 'truth-speaking' authorial voice escaping the same deconstructive considerations which afflict all language."[20] By contrast, for Bakhtin, the "deconstruction of the apparent unities of authorship, or the apparent obviousness of reference is always towards the heterogeneity of the historical process, and never towards the paradoxes that can be generated by considering epistemology in the abstract."[21]

For a Bakhtinian perspective on intertextual relationships, heteroglossia—the different varieties of any single language (e.g., regional dialects, class inflections, and so forth)—and polyphony—the multiple points of view and perspectives of others that are already present in any(one's) utterance—are key concepts. As Bakhtin explains:

> At any given moment, languages of various epochs and periods of socio-ideological life cohabit with one another … at any given moment of its historical existence, language is heteroglot from top to bottom: it represents the co-existence of socio-ideological contradictions between the present and the past, between differing epochs of the past, between different socio-ideological groups in the present, between tendencies, schools, circles and so forth, all given a bodily form…. Therefore, languages do not exclude each other, but rather intersect with each other in many different ways.[22]

---

18. Jonathan D. Culler has suggested another way forward: limiting intertextual relations to those emerging from logical and pragmatic presuppositions in a text. Jonathan D. Culler, "Presupposition and Intertextuality," in *The Pursuit of Signs* (Ithaca, NY: Cornell University Press, 1981), 100–18. See also Clayton and Rothstein, "Figures in the Corpus," 24–25.

19. See Dentith, *Bakhtinian Thought*, 95–98; Clayton and Rothstein, "Figures in the Corpus," 17–21.

20. Dentith, *Bakhtinian Thought*, 94.

21. Dentith, *Bakhtinian Thought*, 95.

22. Mikhail M. Bakhtin, *The Dialogic Imagination*, ed. Michael Holquist, trans. Caryl Emerson and Michael Holquist (Austin: University of Texas Press, 1992), 291.

In a Bakhtinian mode of reflection, real authors are not superfluous, not mere useful fiction or intersection of various discourses. However, an "author's intentions" are in fact "always refracted through one or more historically specific languages" that a writer, in a sense, activates by engaging other discourses that are likewise historically and socially situated.[23] Superficially, a Bakhtinian approach to understanding relations between texts might thus sound as if it has not moved too far from notions of shared cultural background or context, or even influence, that critics both of an earlier generation like Wolff and Terrien, and others still today, deploy in their efforts to describe relations between texts. Yet the differences between Bakhtinian notions and traditional understanding of textual influence are significant.

On the one hand, a Bakhtinian perspective regarding relations between texts "radically transforms the question of sources, making them a matter not of individual influences or borrowing but of the socially located languages that each and every text manages in its own particular way."[24] Different authors or texts (sometimes struggling against other voices) seek to accent, or inflect, already at hand, socially marked languages in ways appropriate to each one's particular rhetorical ends. *Dialogue* (or dialogism or the dialogic), not influence, thus best describes the nature of relations between texts. Bakhtin writes:

> Each word tastes of the context and contexts in which it has lived its socially charged life.... The word in language is half someone else's. It becomes one's "own" only when the speaker populates it with his own intentions, his own accent, when he appropriates the word, adapting it to his own semantic and expressive intention. Prior to this moment of appropriation, the word does not exist in a neutral and impersonal language ... but rather it exists in other people's mouths, in other people's contexts, serving other people's intentions; it is from there that one must take the word, and make it one's own.[25]

On the other hand, Bakhtin's insistence upon the particularity of such social-historical language also "undoes the unstoppable indeterminacy of 'textuality'" (at least provisionally) and warrants efforts to speak

---

23. Dentith, *Bakhtinian Thought*, 91–92.
24. Dentith, *Bakhtinian Thought*, 95.
25. Bakhtin, *Dialogic Imagination*, 293–94.

of the historical and social conditions, contexts, and institutions associated with particular discourses.²⁶ Bakhtin points not to "the unstoppable indeterminacy of 'textuality,'" but to an irrepressible dialogism, moments in the history of which criticism can gesture toward:

> There is neither a first nor a last word and there are no limits to the dialogic context (it extends into the boundless past and boundless future). Even *past* meanings, that is those born in the dialogue of past centuries, can never be stable (finalized, ended once and for all)—they will always change (be renewed) in the process of subsequent, future development of the dialogue. At any moment in the development of the dialogue there are immense, boundless masses of forgotten contextual meanings, but at certain moments of the dialogue's subsequent development along the way they are recalled and invigorated in renewed form (in a new context) [emphasis original].²⁷

## The Discourse of Justice in Proverbs and Amos

As noted above, Wolff was concerned to demonstrate the influence of early clan wisdom on Amos in a variety of ways. His argument regarding geographical connections is the most speculative and thus the least compelling. In light of Bakhtinian notions of texts and their relations, however, the connection between Amos and wisdom in regard to literary forms, terminology, and especially motifs merits further consideration.

Wolff dedicated nearly eight pages of his little book on Amos and wisdom to exploring the specific motif and language of justice and righteousness (including fair marketplace practices); he adds nearly another five pages of analysis of other themes that can also be said to belong to the biblical rhetoric of justice—concern for the "poor and needy" and the censuring of "an extravagant life."²⁸ All this suggests that the best chance of a productive reconsideration of the relations between Amos and Proverbs may be precisely through a review of each text's moral rhetoric of justice.

---

26. Dentith, *Bakhtinian Thought*, 95.
27. Mikhail M. Bakhtin, *Speech Genres and Other Late Essays*, ed. Caryl Emerson and Michael Holquist, trans. Vern W. McGee, UTPSS 9 (Austin: University of Texas Press, 1986), 170.
28. Wolff, *Amos the Prophet*, 70–75.

To demonstrate that Amos was influenced by the wise, Wolff pointed especially to the pairing of the important words "justice" and "righteousness" in Amos (three times) and the appearance of "justice" by itself on one further occasion:

Ah, you that turn justice [משפט] to wormwood,
  and bring righteousness [צדקה] to the ground! (Amos 5:7)[29]
But let justice [משפט] roll down like waters,
  and righteousness [צדקה] like an ever-flowing stream. (Amos 5:24)
But you have turned justice [משפט] into poison
  and the fruit of righteousness [צדקה] into wormwood. (Amos 6:12bc)
Hate evil and love good,
  and establish justice [משפט] in the gate. (Amos 5:15a)

Wolff believed that the "justice and righteousness" rhetoric of Amos 5:15 appears in a "wisdom type of exhortation speech," while in 6:12 it is expressed within a "wisdom didactic question."[30] However, he is most concerned to point out that Amos's terminology of justice and righteousness not only appears in wisdom forms; it appears frequently throughout wisdom books.[31]

Wolff likewise thought Amos's concern for honest weights, measures, and balances was influenced by repeated, similar concerns in Proverbs. If Amos 8:5b has oppressors claim, "We will make the ephah small and the shekel great, and practice deceit with false balances," verses such as Prov 11:1 (cf. Prov 16:11; 20:23) insist, "A false balance is an abomination to the LORD, but an accurate weight is his delight."[32] So too, for Wolff, wisdom's prioritizing of justice over cultic activity likely shaped the prophet's words.[33] Just prior to calling down justice and righteousness in Amos 5:24, for example, in verses 21–22 the prophet has the Lord proclaim,

---

29. Unless otherwise noted, biblical translations are from the NRSV.
30. Wolff, *Amos the Prophet*, 60.
31. Wolff cites only Prov 16:8 (Wolff, *Amos the Prophet*, 62). However, the term צדקה appears eighteen times (צדק nine times) in Proverbs while משפט occurs twenty times. In Prov 1:3; 2:9; 8:20; 16:8; and 21:3, the terms appear together (משפט with either צדק or צדקה). See Prov 18:5; 21:15; and 31:9, where forms of the two roots also appear together.
32. Wolff, *Amos the Prophet*, 62–63.
33. Wolff, *Amos the Prophet*, 63.

> I hate, I despise your festivals,
>   and I take no delight in your solemn assemblies.
> Even though you offer me your burnt offerings and grain offerings,
>   I will not accept them;
> and the offerings of well-being of your fatted animals
>   I will not look upon.

Similarly, Prov 21:3 (cf. Prov 15:8 and 21:27) states:

> To do righteousness [צדקה] and justice [משפט]
>   is more acceptable to the Lord than sacrifice.

Wolff also highlighted the concern with the poor and needy in both Amos and wisdom contexts. In Amos, the דל (Amos 2:7; 4:1; 5:11; 8:6), the אביון (Amos 2:6; 4:1; 5:12; 8:4, 6), and the עני/ענוים (Amos 2:7; 8:4) are all mentioned, and sometimes in word pairs (Amos 2:7; 4:1; 8:4, 6). Wolff was keen to point out that this same terminology is also regularly found in Proverbs, sometimes also in pairs (e.g., Prov 14:31; 22:22; 30:14; 31:8).[34]

Finally, Wolff was concerned to point to the warning in both Proverbs and Amos against extravagant living.[35] In Amos, for example, he highlights 2:8, 4:1, 5:11, and 6:6, the last of which rebukes those "who drink wine from bowls, and anoint themselves with the finest oils." Amos's sentiments, Wolff believed, are shared by verses such as Prov 21:17, 23:29–35, and 31:4, which warn one against becoming an excessive lover of wine and other fine things.

McLaughlin, as was intimated, interrogates Wolff's arguments and is persuaded that none of them necessarily indicate wisdom influence on the prophet. The features of Amos's justice rhetoric described by Wolff may be traced instead to other sources: to biblical legal works, to other prophetic texts, or perhaps to a broad literary and ethical ancient Near Eastern tradition. There is no unambiguous intertextual relation of influence between wisdom and Amos. When it comes to Amos's view of justice, then, McLaughlin has, on the modernist terms of the debate sketched above, successfully rebutted Wolff's arguments that Amos fell under the influence of the wise.

---

34. Wolff, *Amos the Prophet*, 70–73.
35. Wolff, *Amos the Prophet*, 74–75.

However, on the terms of that distinct, postmodern discourse of intertextuality discussed above, another ironic conclusion is possible. One can also say that McLaughlin's rebuttal of Wolff's claims, which regularly suggests that features of Amos can be found in a range of works besides wisdom books, has in fact pointed to a robust set of intertextual relationships that Amos has with any number of other texts. McLaughlin's work can be said to reveal that Amos's discourse of justice represents, as was said above, "a particular density among a myriad [of] codes or discourses, whose origins cannot be traced and which stretch to the horizons in all directions"—whether to wisdom works, the Pentateuch, other prophets, or cognate texts in the ancient Near Eastern world.[36]

## Amos and Proverbs in Bakhtinian Dialogue

Yet besides arguing about influence, and beyond ironically gesturing toward signs of inevitable (inter)textuality, there is a third way to explore the (intertextual) relations between Amos and Proverbs. It is, recall, the Bakhtinian route that understands dialogic relations between texts to include not only points of agreement or similarity but also the ways social-historical voices or discourses disagree or struggle with one another, how texts accent in unique ways a broader historically and socially grounded discourse that authors or speakers find at hand. On modernist terms, dialogic differences or disagreements between texts like Amos and Proverbs might be regarded as support for the claim that Amos did not substantively fall under the influence of wisdom. For a Bakhtinian mode of intertextual analysis, however, they clarify the complex nature of the dialogic relations between the works.

Despite similarities between Amos's and Proverbs' justice rhetoric that Wolff highlighted (and which McLaughlin rejected as evidence for wisdom's influence on the prophet), significant differences between the moral discourses of Amos and Proverbs are evident. Most obvious is the near complete absence in Amos of a central feature of Proverbs' moral rhetoric—its discourse of "two ways," each populated by particular moral types. One path in Proverbs is trod by the wise and righteous (and others aligned with such types); on the second path, one finds the foolish and wicked (and others aligned with those types). In Amos, none of the three

---

36. Dentith, *Bakhtinian Thought*, 95.

common wisdom terms for the way or path—ארח, נתיבה, or דרך—occur. Wolff identified only a single term in Amos, deployed only once, that might be said to belong to this aspect of Proverbs' moral discourse. But he made much of it. Although Wolff was correct that "A man can betray what his cultural home is with a single characteristic word," it is not as clear that the single word he identifies in Amos 3:10a—נכחה ("right," "straight")—is so revelatory.[37] Wolff claimed that it "occurs frequently in wisdom," but it is attested only twice in Proverbs (8:9; 24:26) and once in Sirach (11:21; MS A 11:19), though Wolff appears to believe the word's appearances in Isaiah are also in wisdom contexts (at least Isa 30:10; cf. Isa 26:10; 57:2; 59:14).[38] Although the term certainly belongs broadly to a wisdom rhetoric of the morally right way—and in Amos 3:10, one can identify other terminology important to wisdom discourse—its isolated appearance in Amos underscores less wisdom's impact on the prophet and highlights more a relation of difference between the two discourses.

Terminology derived from roots such as צדק, כסל, אול, בין, חכם, and רשע clearly mark Proverbs' moral discourse.[39] Indeed, Proverbs' understanding of justice is linked closely to the way of life of certain virtuous and vicious characters described by this rhetoric—the wicked and the just, the foolish and wise. Human subjects are reckoned as just (and wise) or wicked (and foolish) precisely insofar as they embody (or not) wisdom's virtues, including the social virtues of justice and righteousness. Together, different verses in Proverbs sketch profiles of virtue and vice corresponding to the characters of just and wicked persons. For example, the just are teachable (Prov 9:9) and possess a practical knowledge (10:32; 11:9) that includes the ability to speak rightly and honestly to particular moments (10:11, 20, 21, 31; 13:5), and they care for even nonhuman members of the community (12:10). Their desires and thoughts are rightly ordered (11:23; 12:5; 15:28), and hence they correctly understand the value of wealth (11:28), are just toward the poor (29:7), and are rightly oriented to the divine (15:29), as well as toward justice (in which they rejoice, 21:15) and iniquity (which they abhor, 29:27). In short, they are people of integrity (20:7) in that they possess and exercise a full range of (social) virtues. Indeed, when one who

---

37. Wolff, *Amos the Prophet*, 56.
38. Wolff, *Amos the Prophet*, 58–59.
39. Terms derived from צדק appear ninety-four times; רשע eighty-seven times; חכם one hundred-three times; בין forty-eight times; אול forty-two times; and כסל fifty-one times.

is thought to be just fails to act well and boldly (28:1) and "give[s] way before the wicked," the quality of that person's character can be called into question, reckoned as "a muddied spring or a polluted fountain" (25:26). By contrast, the wicked, who often stand in parallel to the just in Proverbs, are typically characterized in opposite moral terms. They are iniquitous evildoers (5:22; 14:32; 19:28) who do not listen to rebuke (9:7). Their desires are wrongly structured (11:23; 12:12; 21:10) and their (practical) knowledge is lacking (10:20; 12:5), something evident in their morally problematic utterances (10:6, 11, 32; 11:11; 12:6, 26; 15:24). They are religiously suspect (15:8–9, 29; 21:27) and full of vice, being characterized as cruel (12:10), unreliable (13:7), haughty and proud (21:4), violent (21:7), and merciless (21:10). They do not understand the rights of the poor (29:7) and, indeed, take bribes to pervert justice (17:23).

Despite Proverbs' wide-ranging moral rhetoric, most of the book's key moral terminology is conspicuously sparse in Amos. The righteous (or just) person (צדיק) appears only twice, in Amos 2:6 and 5:12 (צדקה is attested three times), while the figure of the wicked (רשע) is completely absent. Words derived from the other key roots in Proverbs noted above are likewise not attested in Amos. What is more, the emphasis in the prophetic book is not on the just person's moral subjectivity or character but on other subjects who act in particular negative ways upon the just (and others). The צדיק in Amos is inflected differently than in Proverbs. Such a person is less the morally rotund individual of the wisdom book and more simply an "innocent" person, associated with the "needy" (אביון), whom others unjustly afflict in the social-economic realm.[40] As Amos 2:6b (cf. 5:12b) says, "they [Israel] sell the righteous [צדיק] for silver, and the needy for a pair of sandals."

Proverbs' moral-theological discourse is distinct from Amos in other ways, too. The wisdom book's teaching, though variously aligned with the divine (e.g., the fear of the Lord; Prov 1:8 and fifteen further times) and grounded in the creation (Prov 3:19–20; 8:22–31), is cast primarily as human teaching—as instructional poems uttered by teachers or parents to children or students, or as short sayings that evoke communal, folk wisdom, even if such sayings equally, or ultimately, are the product of urban scribes.[41] By contrast, the book of Amos is cast as the prophet's

---

40. Of course, Proverbs can deploy צדיק in the sense of "innocent" as well (cf. Prov 17:26; 18:5).

41. See note 7 above.

report of divine visions and messages. The book's superscription speaks of Amos's prophetic "seeing" (חזה), and in Amos 7:12 he is called a "seer" (חזה), perhaps alluding to the visions recounted elsewhere in the book, which however are described with forms derived from ראה (Amos 7:1–9; 8:1–3; 9:1–4). The prophet's own utterances, moreover, are cast as divine words against the nations (כה אמר יהוה/נאם יהוה), including Israel (e.g., Amos 2:6–16). Such revelatory terms are not absent in Proverbs, but they are rare. Only in Prov 29:18 do we find חזון in the sense of a prophetic vision (though the root with the usual meaning, "to see," is more common), while נאם appears a single time, introducing Agur's words (Prov 30:1).

In addition, if there is a central or controlling moral term in Amos's discourse, it is not one that is central to Proverbs. Rather it is arguably פשע, "transgression." The root appears twelve times in Amos and is largely used to connote broad and severe political and social-economic outrages. Most of the crimes against humanity in the initial oracles against the nations are described as transgressions, as is Israel's social-economic failing (Amos 1:3, 6, 9, 11, 13; 2:1, 4, 6; 3:14; 5:12; cf. the two verb forms in 4:4). According to Wolff, all of the nominal forms of פשע appear "in authentic oracles" of the prophet, except for 1:9, 11; and 2:4.[42] The root is hardly unknown in Proverbs. The noun occurs twelve times and a verbal form appears twice. However, only in Prov 18:19; 28:2; and 29:16 are political connotations easily discernable, and only in 29:16 does the term gesture toward the sort of political or social-economic moral failing that Amos associates with the word. All its other usages in Proverbs suggest a more individualized conception of ethical failure.

Although other differences between Proverbs and Amos might be discerned, enough has been said to illustrate that the broader moral-theological rhetoric of the two books is distinct in significant ways. These differences, however, do not necessarily imply no intertextual relation between the moral-theological vision of the two works. It rather invites further description of the dialogic relations—similarities, agreements, as well as other points of difference—between the two books.

One obvious way to conceptualize how Amos and Proverbs inflect in distinct ways an already at hand, socially and historically specific moral discourse is to say that Proverbs, as an ancient instruction, and Amos, as prophetic utterance, are directed toward distinct rhetorical situations.

---

42. Wolff, *Hosea and Amos*, 152.

Though the precise moral language of the way of the just and the wicked, so prevalent in Proverbs, is absent in Amos, the underlying vision of justice in the two books is not unrelated conceptually or in terms of each text's broader moral rhetoric. Through its descriptions of the wicked and righteous and their respective destinies and benefits, Proverbs is concerned to form and motivate individuals who embody a range of virtues—including social virtues like kindness and generosity toward the poor, fairness in economic practices, and so forth—all of which can be gathered under the signs of righteousness and justice. Amos, by contrast, announces divine judgment on humans whose (wrongly formed) characters and whose lack of social virtue have resulted in their oppressing the poor and their treacherous dealings in the marketplace. The wise of Proverbs exhort readers and hearers to cultivate (social) virtue, highlighting the value of this wisdom.[43] The prophet rails against the absence of justice and righteousness among those in his social world who ought to embody it, but do not.

What is more, although Amos does not use the word רשע, his upbraiding of his audience paints them with hues very close to what one finds in the portrait of the wicked (and other travelers of the wrong path) that Proverbs presents. Unlike the just in Proverbs, those whom Amos addresses have, in their domination of the poor and through cheating in the market, failed to walk a path characterized by social virtue. As Wolff also somewhat discerned, like Proverbs' wicked, those to whom Amos preaches do not heed the exhortations and rebukes they are offered (Amos 5:4–6, 10, 14–15), are religiously suspect (Amos 2:12; 4:4–5; 5:21–25; 8:5), and can easily be characterized as haughty, violent, and merciless (e.g., Amos 1:3–2:3; 2:7; 3:9–10; 4:1; 5:11; 6:3; 8:4, 6).[44]

## Further Points of Dialogic Relations

A few further characteristics of Amos and Proverbs can be added to the data set one considers when discerning how the moral rhetoric of Proverbs and Amos might be understood as standing in dialogic relation with one other. A couple of these points of connection were already mentioned by

---

43. The value and desirability of wisdom is expressed primarily via the rhetoric of desirable wealth, social status, and sexual attraction. See Timothy J. Sandoval, *The Discourse of Wealth and Poverty in the Book of Proverbs*, BibInt 77 (Leiden; Boston: Brill, 2006), 71–100.

44. Wolff, *Amos the Prophet*, 44–53.

Wolff, however only briefly. They were not contested much by McLaughlin, though they surely could be dismissed on the same modernist terms upon which the debate about Amos's dependence on wisdom has usually been carried out.

Wolff, for example, noted that Amos condemned certain of his hearers for their extravagant lifestyle. One aspect of this concern that Wolff does not emphasize, but which might also suggest that the prophetic text stands in a positive dialogic relation with Proverbs, is Amos 6:1's characterization of those who pursued such a lifestyle as feeling "at ease" (שאנן) and "secure" (בטח). Words formed from the second root, "to trust," are fairly common in Proverbs, appearing fourteen times, mostly in contexts that alert hearers or readers to trustworthy and deceptive loci of trust. The Lord (Prov 3:5; 28:25; 29:25) and wisdom's virtues (Prov 3:23; 10:9; 11:5; cf. 28:26) provide genuine security, while one's own intellect (לב; Prov 28:26) and riches (Prov 11:28) are unreliable. Indeed, elsewhere in Proverbs the "rich" are described like those against whom Amos preaches. They are not only said to be merciless, extravagant in their lifestyle, arrogant, and greedy (Prov 18:23; 21:17; 22:7; 28:11, 20, 22); they are also characterized as those whose trust is misplaced.[45] On the one hand, in Proverbs the advantages that wealth secures the "rich" are acknowledged. The protection riches provide is compared to city fortifications like those that would have adorned places such as Samaria, one of the places where Amos surely prophesied:

The wealth of the rich is their fortress. (Prov 10:15b)

The wealth of the rich is their strong city. (Prov 18:11a)

On the other hand, however, the rich person's refuge of wealth is also described as illusory and contrasted with the genuine security YHWH provides:

In their imagination it [wealth] is like a high wall. (Prov 18:11b)[46]

---

45. As R. Norman Whybray has said, "the rich man (*ʿāšîr*) is always regarded with hostility" in Proverbs. R. Norman Whybray, *Wealth and Poverty in the Book of Proverbs*, JSOTSup 99 (Sheffield: JSOT Press, 1990), 63.

46. The expression וכחומה נשגבה במשכיתו is difficult. For a discussion and a defense of the above sense of the line, see Michael V. Fox, *Proverbs 10–31: A New*

The name of the LORD is a strong tower;
  the righteous run into it and are safe. (Prov 18:10)

However, it is Prov 1:33 that hints more fully at a dialogic relation between Amos and Proverbs, as it also deploys both of the key terms the prophet uses in Amos 6:1. Yet, for the Proverbs verse, it is not an apparent secure existence in Zion or on Samaria attained via "a reign of violence" (Amos 6:3) that can ultimately put one at ease. Instead, it is an attainment of wisdom. As Woman Wisdom herself proclaims:

Those who listen to me will be secure [בטח]
  and will live at ease [שאנן], without dread of disaster. (Prov 1:33)

A further intertextual connection between Amos and Proverbs that Wolff did not much emphasize can also be noted. In Amos 3:8, the prophet connects the inevitability of his prophesying the divine word with the fear one necessarily feels upon hearing a lion's roar. Although Wolff recognized that "the fear of God" was an "ultimate characteristic of wisdom," he did not believe the prophet was "aware of the theme" among the early wise.[47] Wolff's modernist understanding of the nature and extent of the evidence necessary to establish one text as the source of, or source of influence upon, another text surely cut short his analysis of this possible point of connection between the prophet and wisdom. The fact that the root ירא appears only once in Amos (3:8), and only to characterize divine speech, was simply not sufficient evidence for Wolff to claim (or explore) wisdom's influence on the prophet when it came to the motif of fear of the divine.

Yet on a Bakhtinian approach to intertextuality, it may be worth considering a possible dialogic relationship around the rhetoric of fear and "fear of the divine." Proverbs, for example, twice says a king's anger is similar to the "growling of a lion" (19:12a; 20:2a), while Prov 24:21–22 likewise exhorts one to "fear the Lord and the king ... for disaster comes from both suddenly and who knows the ruin both can bring?" Such an assertion calls to mind both Amos's fearsome announcements of the Lord's "day" (Amos 5:18–20) and God's severe punishment of Israel (e.g., Amos 1:5, 7–8, 10, 12, 14–15; 2:2–3, 5, 9, 13–16; 3:11, 14–15; 4:2, 6–12; 5:16–17; 6:7, 9–11, 14;

---

*Translation with Introduction and Commentary*, AB 18B (New Haven: Yale University Press, 2000), 1018–19.

47. Wolff, *Amos the Prophet*, 76.

7:17; 8:3, 8; 9:1–4) as well as Proverbs' confidence that the wicked will face disastrous consequences for their immorality.

Although "fear of YHWH" in Proverbs is often thought to entail essentially a kind of pious respect or religiosity, it surely also includes a genuine physical-emotional trepidation of the divine as the powerful guarantor of the moral order the book proffers. As Yoder notes, the concept includes "dread of God's disapproval or punishment."[48] A fearful stance toward a potentially terrifying deity motivates adherences to the book's instruction and offers protection from death and security from harm (Prov 19:23; cf. 1:33). By contrast, the unhappy fate of wrongdoers—their elimination (or something close to this)—is implied in verses like Prov 1:18–19, where the robbing sinners lose their lives. What is more, over and over one reads of the inevitable demise of the wicked and sinners in Proverbs. They will be "cut off from the land" or "rooted out of it" (Prov 2:22; cf. 10:30); they will "not go unpunished" (11:21) and will be "repaid for their iniquities" (11:31), "condemned" by God (12:2), "overthrown" (12:7), "filled with trouble" (12:21), and so on (cf. 14:32; 15:6; 15:10; 16:4; 18:12; 21:7; 29:1).

When Proverbs' social-economic concerns for fairness in the marketplace and right treatment of the poor are combined with other aspects of the book's moral-religious vision, such as its emphasis on "fear of the Lord" and the inevitable punishments that await the wicked, it is not a big step from wisdom's moral vision to Amos's proclamation of the coming divine judgment and destruction of Israel for its social-economic misdeeds. In Bakhtinian terms, all the above similarities and differences between Proverbs' and Amos's rhetoric illustrate each book's particular inflection of an already at hand historically and socially anchored moral discourse; it reveals, too, that the keenest point of intersection between each book's moral discourse is to be discerned in its rhetoric of social justice. Again, none of this is to suggest one can prove Proverbs' direct influence on Amos, or vice versa, along the lines Wolff and McLaughlin have carried on the debate. Rather, it is to say the two works stand in a Bakhtinian dialogic relation and thus can well be said to be intertextually related.

---

48. Christine R. Yoder, *Proverbs*, AOTC (Nashville: Abingdon, 2009), 6. See Fox, who makes similar observations about the "real fear" involved in Proverbs' conception of fear of the Lord (*Proverbs 1–9*, 69–71).

# Genres, Intertextuality, Bible Software, and Speech Acts

*Tim Finlay*

The concept of genre, whether in biblical literature or elsewhere, is certainly a tricky one.[1] In my desperation to find ways to make my Bachelor of Science in mathematics relevant to my biblical interpretation class, I sometimes write upon the board an integral equation and ask the puzzled students what genre it is. Some say it is mathematics, which is more of a discipline than a genre. Others might point out that it is an example of calculus, and by the Socratic method, we arrive at the genre of mathematical

---

1. Some of the major works dealing with genre outside the discipline of biblical studies include the following: Thomas O. Beebee, *The Ideology of Genre: A Comparative Study of Generic Instability* (Toronto: University of Toronto Press, 2004); Seymour Benjamin Chatman, "On Defining 'Form,'" *NLH* 2 (1971): 217–28; Heather Dubrow, *Genre* (London: Methuen, 1982); Alastair Fowler, "The Life and Death of Literary Forms," *NLH* 2 (1971): 199–216; Fowler, *Kinds of Literature: An Introduction to the Theory of Genres and Modes* (Cambridge: Harvard University Press, 1982); Fowler, *A History of English Literature: Forms and Kinds from the Middle Ages to the Present* (Oxford: Blackwell, 1987); Mary Gerhart, "The Dilemma of the Text: How to 'Belong' to a Genre," *Poet* 18 (1989): 355–73; and Jean-Marie Schaeffer, "Literary Genre and Textual Genericity," in *The Future of Literary Theory*, ed. Ralph Cohen (New York: Routledge, 1989), 167–87. Fowler's contention that the concept of genre is fussy is similar to Rolf P. Knierim's argument discussed later in this paper. Gerhart aims to avoid prescriptivism in genre categorization. Schaeffer's structural model is so opposed to essentialism and to maintaining that everything which exists is material that he is willing to bite the bullet and say that meaning does not exist. A full discussion of genre has metaphysical implications. Early form critics discussed concepts of genre and form in a manner that often presupposed Platonic realism. At the other extreme are approaches that assume conceptualism or nominalism. My own approach assumes the moderate realism of the Aristotelian-Thomistic tradition, which also recognizes the crucial difference between artifacts (and genres are definitely artifacts) and natural essences.

equation (integral equation in a very good year). At this point, I tell them that it could be read as a limerick and then chant out the following:

> The integral of zee squared dee zee
> From one to the cube root of three
> Times the cosine
> Of three pi over nine
> Equals the log of the cube root of e.[2]

This is an example of the same conceptual content being conveyed via two very different surface structures: that of integral equation and of limerick. We typically think of works being in the same genre only if they have the same surface structure, yet works with similar conceptual content but different structures obviously can be discussed intertextually. Moreover, some standard genre terms, such as genealogy, are content categories. Most genealogies in the Hebrew Bible are conveyed in lists, but Gen 29:31–30:24 is a genealogy conveyed through a narrative. Today, most genealogies are conveyed through charts.

Rolf P. Knierim argues for expanding the concept of genre "to include a diversity of possible typicalities by which texts can be constituted."[3] In writing my forthcoming book on genres, I have observed that different texts relate to each other in a bewildering variety of useful ways. Legal genres can be categorized according not only to surface structure considerations (the traditional form-critical categories of apodictic law, case law, prescription, prohibition, and so forth) but by theological considerations (natural law, divine law, human law), whose behavior is being regulated (laws for women, priests, the king, and so forth) whether the law is part of civil law or criminal law, the severity of punishment allotted (death penalty laws, temporary banishment laws, financial restoration laws, and so forth), and the actual content of the law (calendrical laws, poverty laws, sex laws, and so forth).

---

2. The mathematics works out because the particular integral is equal to two thirds, the cosine of three pi over nine (i.e., one third of pi radions, which is equivalent to sixty degrees) is equal to one half, and the natural log of the cube root of e (an important irrational number approximately equaling 2.718, which occurs in population growth and radioactive decay) is equal to one third. I thank Robert E. Long for bringing my attention to this equation/limerick.

3. Rolf P. Knierim, "Old Testament Form Criticism Reconsidered," *Int* 27 (1973): 456.

I have glossary entries in all of these categories of law. Each mode of categorization of a passage leads to a different assortment of texts, both within the Bible and outside it, that have intertextual connections to the passage in question. Hence, there is a strong connection between genre and intertextuality. It has long been standard practice to look for parallels in the literature of the ancient Near East when examining texts in the Hebrew Bible, and these parallels are not limited to what we frequently think of as genre but also include similarity of topic or content.

In dealing with the genres in the book of Job, I have glossary entries on Bildad speech, Elihu speech, Eliphaz speech, Job speech, and YHWH speech. So, this is a genre with a further characterizing principle: that of the speaker. In Aristotelian terms, it is characterized by its efficient cause.[4] In theory, one could have glossary entries for the speeches of every character in the Bible, but this would seldom be of use to pastors or biblical scholars. However, in the majestic drama that is Job, it does make sense to discuss each character's speeches as a whole, as the scholarly literature verifies.

Similarly, in my chapter on Psalms genres, I have glossary entries on psalms of Asaph and psalms of the sons of Korah, and the bibliographies accompanying these glossary entries demonstrate the validity of that choice. Related to this is the genre of prayer, which is categorized by addressee, namely God. Many other categories that we associate with the Psalms, such as hymn and adoration, typically involve God as the addressee. Many of Job's speeches are initially addressed to whichever of Eliphaz, Bildad, or Zophar gave the previous speech, but at some point in the speech, Job switches addressee and directs his remarks to God. "Job's addresses to God" is an entirely suitable topic for intertextuality. Further, as mentioned previously, laws can be categorized as to whose behavior is being regulated—in other words, by indirect addressee.[5]

---

4. Aristotle discussed four causes with reference to material objects: the material, formal, efficient, and teleological causes. The material cause of a bronze statue of a wrestler back in ancient Greece would be the bronze from which it was made; the formal cause, the form of a wrestler in action; the efficient cause, the sculptor sculpting the statue; and the teleological cause perhaps to inspire young Greek boys to acquire the manliness of wrestlers. With modification, these causes can be applied to various pieces of human communication or "speech acts." The efficient cause would typically be the speaker or writer. I shall discuss the other causes later.

5. Logos Bible Software has an interactive resource named "Commandments of the Law" that has various sorting possibilities of the 613 commandments, including

## Bible Software

This is a useful point at which to switch to the third item in the article title: Bible software. Azusa Pacific Seminary students are required to use Logos Bible Software—so the remarks I make concern that software—but many of them also apply to other Bible software. The search capacities in Bible software are increasing all the time. One can now right-click within a verse of the NRSV, say, and a menu appears that contains numerous search options (including basic concordance searches on the English word, the Hebrew lemma or root, or the morphological form such as feminine plural noun).

Several recent additions to the right-click menu aid either genre work or intertextual work. If I right-click on a word within a speech by Rebekah to Jacob, from the ensuing menu I can opt to search for all the speeches where Rebekah is the speaker (or opt to search for all the speeches where Jacob is the addressee, for that matter). This ties in to the previous discussion of genre and intertextuality as they can relate to speaker and addressee.

There are also at least three right-click options that help for genre comparison. One is the literary type option, which relies on how that verse has been tagged in the *Lexham Glossary of Literary Types*. This has the potential to be extremely helpful but is presently limited by assigning only one literary type to each verse. Hence, if one searches for "account, vocation,"[6] it picks up the accounts in Isa 6, Jer 1, and Ezek 1–3, but not the accounts in Exod 3–4 or Judg 6, which are categorized as legend and history, respectively.

A second option that is frequently helpful for investigating clause level genres (and for subclausal searching also) is searching by the terms contained in *The Lexham Propositional Outlines Glossary*. This includes very general terms such as "action," "condition," and "experience," but also some more specific terms as "arrival" and "beatitude." A third option is that of Longacre genre, but I have not found it to be as useful.

---

which group of people is being regulated. The Proverbs explorer resource likewise includes a sort feature on implied addressee along with type of parallelism and major themes. There are some other interactive resources related to genre and/or intertextuality also, but many more could and hopefully will be developed not just in Logos but by other software companies as well.

6. There are other ways one can perform any of the searches in the right-click menu. One does not have to know a particular example of a genre or a speech by Michal, for instance, in order to search for all the examples of that category.

## Speech Act Theory

A fourth option, but presently only available for New Testament texts, is that of searching by speech act—also the fourth and final item in the title of this article. The dataset behind this search option employs the categories of assertives, information questions (usually regarded by speech act theorists as a subcategory of directive), directives, commissives, expressives, and declaratives. These are the main categories of what John L. Austin, in his posthumously published *How to Do Things with Words*, calls "illocutionary speech act," to be distinguished from locutionary act and perlocutionary act. Austin gives the following example of locutionary act: "He said to me 'Shoot her!' meaning by 'shoot' shoot and referring by 'her' to *her*."[7] The corresponding *illocutionary act* would be: "He urged me to shoot her."[8] The corresponding *perlocutionary act* would be: "He persuaded me to shoot her."[9] The perlocutionary act depends upon cooperation from the hearer. By contrast, the illocutionary act could be said to have been achieved if the hearer recognized the illocutionary force intended by the speaker, whether or not the hearer then acted on it.

Even when the hearer does not cooperate with the speaker, one can talk of the perlocutionary intent of the speech act. The perlocutionary intent is, in Aristotelian terms, the teleological cause of the speech act. Much of this is common sense. In our legal structures, we acknowledge the importance of intention—the same action may be sexual harassment or a necessary medical examination according to the intention of the actor, and that can only be determined by context. Good exegesis of the biblical text necessarily involves an attempt to construct the author's intentions, however difficult this may be. Meir Sternberg writes, "From the premise that we are not people of the past, it does not follow that we cannot approximate this state by imagination and training," and "once the choice turns out to lie between reconstructing the author's intention and licensing the reader's invention, there is no doubt where most of us stand."[10]

---

7. John L. Austin, *How to Do Things with Words* (Cambridge: Harvard University Press, 1962), 101, emphasis original.
8. Austin, *How to Do Things*, 102.
9. Austin, *How to Do Things*, 102.
10. Meir Sternberg, *The Poetics of Biblical Narrative: Ideological Literature and the Drama of Reading*, ISBL (Bloomington: Indiana University Press, 1985), 10. Of course,

Although this approach may disallow some of the more radical strands of the text-centered new criticism, or versions of reader-response theory that ignore the author's intention, the words of the text are still important:

> In the performance of an illocutionary act in the literal utterance of a sentence, the speaker intends to produce a certain effect by means of getting the hearer to recognize his intention to produce that effect; and furthermore, if he is using words literally, he intends this recognition to be achieved in virtue of the fact that the rules for using the expressions he utters associate the expression with the production of that effect.[11]

So meaning is not entirely intention-driven; the efficient cause of a speech-act is partially constrained by the conventional use of language. Moreover, context is important in determining what a speaker meant by a sentential act in a particular situation. If a proposal to go to a movie is met with the response, "I have to study for an exam," the context will likely determine that this response is a rejection of the proposal.[12] John R. Searle calls this an indirect speech act. A similar role to context in speech act theory is played by "setting" in form-critical studies.[13]

William P. Alston builds on Austin's work and uses a slightly different categorization using sentential act, illocutionary act, and perlocutionary act.[14] For Alston, a sentential act is simply the act of uttering a sentence

---

one can always choose to counterread the Bible, to read the text in a manner opposite to the Bible's norms, whether those norms are stated or presupposed.

11. John R. Searle, *Speech Acts: An Essay in the Philosophy of Language* (Cambridge: University Press, 1969), 45.

12. John R. Searle, *Expression and Meaning: Studies in the Theory of Speech Acts* (Cambridge: Cambridge University Press, 1979), 30–32.

13. There has been a movement in form criticism away from Hermann Gunkel's primary consideration of setting as the *Sitz im Leben* of the original genre toward a consideration of the literary setting of the pericope to be exegeted and also the historical situation of the event described in the pericope, when applicable. See, for example, the setting sections in Marvin A. Sweeney, *Isaiah 1–39 with an Introduction to Prophetic Literature*, FOTL 16 (Grand Rapids: Eerdmans, 1996).

14. Austin argued that to perform a locutionary act was certainly to perform a "phonetic act," the action of uttering certain noises, and a "phatic act," the act of uttering certain vocables (words) as belonging to a particular vocabulary and arranged conforming to a particular grammar (Austin, *How to Do Things*, 92). But Austin also thought that there was a "rhetic act," which consisted of using the pheme (Austin's term for the output of phatic act) with a more or less definite sense and reference

(or part of a sentence uttered elliptically for a sentence, or a gesture that counts as a sentence surrogate).[15] One of the main purposes of my forthcoming book on formulae and genres is to identify the various formulae used in the Old Testament. A formula is a short, fixed word association used frequently in a particular context. "And the land had rest for X years" is a phrase typically used in the book of Judges to conclude an account of a judge's leadership and is thus a formula.[16] It is the (largely) invariant sentential act that defines a formula. And sentential acts are, in Aristotelian terms, the material cause of a speech act.[17]

Although formulae are sentential acts, most genres are subcategories of illocutionary acts—they are significantly determined by whether the speakers are asserting something about the way the world is, urging others to do something, committing to some future action themselves, expressing their emotions, or bringing about through their speeches a new social fact (e.g., "I pronounce you man and wife"). Alston respectively calls these five main categories of illocutionary acts assertives, directives, commissives, expressives, and exercitives (otherwise known as declaratives).[18] Alston

---

but which still stopped short of an illocutionary act. The difficulties in distinguishing between the rhetic act, as Austin conceived it, and the illocutionary act have been pointed out by Searle, *Speech Acts*; and P. F. Strawson, "Austin and 'Locutionary Meaning,'" in *Essays on J. L. Austin*, ed. Isaiah Berlin (Oxford: Clarendon, 1973), 47–49.

15. William P. Alston, *Illocutionary Acts and Sentence Meaning* (Ithaca, NY: Cornell University Press, 2000), 28.

16. I was able to construct a syntax search in Logos for this formula by searching for all clauses consisting of a past tense of the Hebrew verb שקט followed by any subject that was a geographical noun, followed by any immediate constituent clause that was a time point or time interval. This yielded five results: Judg 3:11, 30; 5:31; 8:28; and 2 Chr 13:23. Most formulae can be searched for in Logos by using the syntax search, but it does require some practice. I have created several Camtasia videos on how to use this tool for my Hebrew classes at Azusa Pacific Seminary.

17. This is actually a simplification of the topic.

18. Alston devotes several pages of analysis concerning each of these categories, and it is impossible to give precise definitions here without doing injustice to the topic. For his partly sympathetic critique of Searle's category of commissives, see Alston, *Illocutionary Acts*, 51–80; for Alston's own preliminary analysis of commissives and exercitives, see Alston, *Illocutionary Acts*, 85–89; for his further analysis of exercitives, see Alston, *Illocutionary Acts*, 89–95; for his further analysis of commissives, see Alston, *Illocutionary Acts*, 95–97; for his analysis of directives, see Alston, *Illocutionary Acts*, 97–103; for his analysis of expressives, see Alston, *Illocutionary Acts*, 103–13; and for his analysis of assertives, see Alston, *Illocutionary Acts*, 114–43. These categories are

gives a list of verbs associated with these categories, from which could be derived the following partial list: assertives include allegations, reports, claims, denials, admissions, predictions, and reminders; directives include requests, suggestions, proposals, commands, and prohibitions; commissives include promises, bets, guarantees, and offers; expressives include apologies, compliments, commiserations, thanksgivings, and expressions of contempt, relief, agreement, opposition, or delight; and exercitives include adjournments, namings, appointments, nominations, sentencings, acquittals, and firings.[19] Martin J. Buss notes that there is considerable overlap between the classifications within different categories of speech acts and the various genres listed in the FOTL series.[20] In Aristotelian terms, illocutionary acts correspond to the formal cause of a particular speech act.

## Aristotle's Four Causes Applied to Speech Acts

The four Aristotelian causes of a speech act, then, are as follows: the teleological cause of the speech act is the intended purpose of the writer or speaker in giving the speech act, thus the cause of all the other causes; the efficient cause is the speaker or writer; the material cause is the sentential act;[21] and the formal cause is the illocutionary act. Just as Aristotle's analysis of sensible objects had the material and formal causes in an inseparable composite—the doctrine of hylomorphism—so every speech act is a composite of sentential act and illocutionary act.[22] Austin pointed out that "to

---

almost identical to the five categories (assertives, directives, commissives, expressives, and declaratives) previously developed by Searle, *Expression and Meaning*, 1-29. Searle's contribution to speech act theory is immense, and Alston largely adopts Searle's insights not only into the various categories of speech acts, but also in his notions of drama and fiction being "parasitic" speech acts, his understanding of indirect speech acts, and his explanation of how metaphor and irony work in terms of speech acts. Where I think that Alston's work has the advantage over Searle's is in its exposition of the relationship between sentential act, illocutionary act, and perlocutionary act.

19. Alston, *Illocutionary Acts*, 34.

20. Martin J. Buss, "Potential and Actual Interactions between Speech Act Theory and Biblical Studies," *Semeia* 41 (1987): 127. Buss specifically refers to the categories of Searle, but the same is true of Alston's categories.

21. The sentential act is itself a hylomorphic composite, consisting of the phonetic act (material cause) and phatic act (formal cause).

22. Perhaps the most rigorous contemporary exposition of the Aristotelian-

perform a locutionary act is in general, we may say, also and *eo ipso* to perform an illocutionary act" and that an illocutionary act cannot be performed without performing a locutionary act.[23]

I may or may not be the first biblical scholar to discuss speech act theory in terms of Aristotelian causes, but speech act theory itself has long been used in the discipline of biblical studies. One volume of *Semeia* was devoted to applications of speech act theory and biblical studies.[24] Several biblical scholars have also written full monographs making good use of speech act theory, including Jim W. Adams, Richard S. Briggs, Donald D. Evans, Timothy Polk, and Steven T. Mann.[25]

Going back to the Bible software, what I have found helpful is combining searches of speech act categories with searches of basic sentence types (declarative, interrogative, and imperative), which are also only available for New Testament in Logos at the moment. When they become available for the Hebrew Scriptures, one should be able to search the Psalms for expressives that are questions—most of which will be hymnic or adoration genres.[26] However, what is really needed is not just tagging each clause

---

Thomistic doctrine of hylomorphism is David S. Oderberg, *Real Essentialism*, SCP 11 (London: Routledge, 2008).

23. Austin, *How to Do Things*, 98; it might be objected that an illocutionary act can be performed without saying or writing anything but instead through a gesture. However, Alston counts such gestures as sentential acts (Alston, *Illocutionary Acts*, 27–28).

24. See Charles E. Jarrett, "Philosophy of Language in the Service of Religious Studies," *Semeia* 41 (1988): 143–59, for a summary and critique of the other essays in that volume.

25. Jim W. Adams, *The Performative Nature and Function of Isaiah 40–55*, LHBOTS 448 (New York: T&T Clark, 2006); Richard S. Briggs, *Words in Action: Speech Act Theory and Biblical Interpretation* (Edinburgh: T&T Clark, 2001); Donald D. Evans, *The Logic of Self-Involvement: A Philosophical Study of Everyday Language with Special Reference to the Christian Use of Language about God as Creator*, LPT (London: SCM Press, 1963); Timothy Polk, *The Prophetic Persona: Jeremiah and the Language of Self*, JSOTSup 32 (Sheffield: JSOT Press, 1984); Steven T. Mann, *Run David Run! An Investigation of the Theological Speech Acts of David's Departure and Return (2 Samuel 14–20)*, Siphrut 10 (Winona Lake, IN: Eisenbrauns, 2013). I am particularly indebted to the works of Adams and Mann, two colleagues, for my understanding of how speech act theory can be utilized in prophecy and narrative, respectively.

26. My glossary of genres distinguishes hymnic language (third person praise for God) from adoration language (second person praise). It also distinguishes imprecations proper from predictions of the demise of the wicked.

and sentence with one of the five general illocutionary act categories but tagging with more specific genre terms, which are subcategories of them.

## Intertextuality beyond the Bible

So far, I have only discussed intertextuality within the Bible.[27] However, some features aid intertextual work with nonbiblical works. The ancient literature section in the passage guide of the Logos software is particularly helpful in this respect. This section looks for ways that other ancient literature parallels the biblical passage in question. The currently available corpora used for comparison are ancient Near Eastern material (e.g., Ugaritic material, context of scripture, ancient Near Eastern texts, Amarna letters), apostolic fathers, church fathers, Dead Sea Scrolls (sectarian material), Judaica (Babylonian Talmud, Jerusalem Talmud, Mishnah, Mekhilta, and so forth), Old Testament pseudepigrapha, Nag Hammadi codices, New Testament apocrypha, works of Josephus, and works of Philo. Regarding modes of intertextuality, it has categories of quotation, allusion, echo, historical, topical, phrase, and lexical.

In my "Biblical Interpretation: Exploring Genesis" class, I include a specific assignment where students compare Gen 37–50 with Josephus's account of the Joseph story, another assignment where they compare Gen 25–36 with the parallel in Jubilees in James Charlesworth's *The Old Testament Pseudepigrapha*, and another assignment where they compare Gen 12–24 with the Genesis Apocryphon in their edition of the Dead Sea Scrolls.[28] Then we explore James B. Pritchard's *Ancient Near Eastern Texts*, and I have them look at works such as Enuma Elish, Tale of Adapa, and Epic of Gilgamesh and compare and contrast them with Gen 1–11.[29] It is usually only after they have become familiar with some of the primary resources that I explain how the ancient literature section of the passage guide works.

The second most important tool for intertextual work outside the Bible is the Cited By tool, which searches for all the places in which a particular

---

27. We often overlook the fact that basic resources such as a harmony of the gospels, a synopsis of the Old Testament, or a collection of Old Testament quotations and allusions in the New Testament are doing intertextual work of a kind.

28. James H. Charlesworth, ed., *Old Testament Pseudepigrapha*, 2 vols. (New York: Doubleday, 1983–1985).

29. James B. Pritchard, ed., *Ancient Near Eastern Texts Relating to the Old Testament*, 3rd ed. (Princeton: Princeton University Press, 1969).

verse, chapter, or book is cited in the various resources in one's library. I have made collections such as a Wesley collection and a C. S. Lewis collection, and the Cited By tool enables me to see where my favorite authors have cited a particular chapter or verse of the Bible.[30]

Building collections such as this also enables topical intertextuality, as one can search for words or phrases anywhere in the collection or limit the search to the section headings or large print within the book. I can search my biblical theology collection for sections that include "covenant" or "blessing" in the subheading.

Logos also has a concordance tool that was designed for Bible versions but can also be used for any resource in one's library. When used in a Bible version, it has various settings. The lemma setting enables one to make lists such as *hiphil* verbs containing energic *nun*, broken down via lemma. Other settings are sense (such as all the instances where "flesh" in the sense of "tissue" occurs), root (broken down by the lexemes associated with that root), or biblical entity (such as a shepherd's staff or the remnant of Israel).[31] Within other resources, it understandably only has the word setting, broken down by language. However, if sometime in the future the concordance tool can be applied to collections of resources, this would be another tool for intertextuality.

## Tagging

What makes many of these tools possible is tagging. At the basic level, each word segment of each Hebrew[32] word in the Lexham Hebrew Bible (whose surface text is simply that of *BHS*) is tagged so that it can be searched according to manuscript form, lemma, root, or morphology (e.g., *qal* perfect third feminine singular). Searches on any of these can be done simply

---

30. Observe that these are collections categorized according to author. Other collections are by publisher. Both of these types of collections are instances of categorizing by efficient cause. Other standard collections, such as systematic theology or Bible encyclopedia, would be clearly according to genre.

31. This does mean relying on the tagging decisions made by the software company. The tagging on "sense" is important because it shows up not only in the concordance tool but in the Bible word study guide and in the Bible sense lexicon. And decisions on the sense of a word in a particular context are more subjective than tagging its morphology or grammatical role.

32. Similar tagging of Greek words is done for the LXX, NA[28], and UBS[5], among others.

by right-clicking on a word and choosing the appropriate search option from a menu. This tagging also enables more sophisticated morphological searches, such as searching for all the *hiphil lamed-aleph* verbs in the Deuteronomistic History, to be accomplished fairly easily through the morph search feature. But Logos has also tagged in the Lexham Hebrew Bible each noun and pronoun according to its referent, grammatical role, and semantic role.[33] This enables the clause search feature to search for all clauses where Rachel is the agent or Jerusalem is the place.

Some of the most sophisticated tagging is on the Andersen-Forbes Analyzed Text (AFAT) and accompanying Andersen-Forbes Phrase Marker Analysis (AFPMA) created by Francis I. Andersen and A. Dean Forbes.[34] In AFAT, each noun is tagged according to one of twenty-eight categories of noun semantics (abstract concept, furniture, body part, building, color, human, and others), and each portion of text is categorized according to one of forty-nine basic genres. Andersen and Forbes have also tagged the Pentateuch according to Otto Eissfeldt's source designations and Jeremiah according to Sigmund Mowinckel's source designations. In AFPMA, phrases are categorized into eight main types (verbal, substantival, conjunctive, prepositional, adjectival, adverbial, or other) and seventy subtypes (e.g., concessive, reason, or adverb of manner). At the larger level, each clause consists of several clause-individual constituents which are categorized into some seventy-three subtypes (e.g., discourse level sequential-*waw*, finite verb, subject, direct object, accompanier, beneficiary, movement origin, time interval, cost, instrument, vocative). There are also supraclausal categories that handle protasis-apodosis and other constructions.

This tagging makes possible very sophisticated syntax searches. For example, one can construct a syntax search to find all the examples of the call to attention formula: "Hear, Personal Name, Message," or "Hear Message, Personal Name." Syntax searches search for similar sentential acts. But the identical sentential act can be used on different occasions to perform different illocutionary acts. My colleague Mann discusses how "strike" can be used as an assertive, a commissive, a directive, an exerci-

---

33. Other software companies, such as Concordance and Bibleworks, have similar tagging schemes.

34. Their approach is expounded in great detail in Francis I. Andersen and A. Dean Forbes, *Biblical Hebrew Grammar Visualized*, LSAWS 6 (Winona Lake, IN: Eisenbrauns, 2012).

tive, and an expressive by different people at a baseball game.[35] This is an example of different sentence tokens of the same sentence type having different meanings. Alston argues—I think correctly—that the meaning of a sentence type is its illocutionary act potential.[36] There is no mechanistic way of determining which illocution (formal cause) is actually performed in a particular sentential act token (material cause). It involves looking at the context or setting to determine the likely perlocutionary intent (teleological cause) of the speaker (efficient cause).

## Intertextual Readings of Ruth

I conclude this essay by exploring the book of Ruth: first analyzing just a portion of Ruth from the perspective of speech act theory and then discussing various intertextual approaches that have been taken with Ruth. Throughout this exploration, I shall comment on presently available Bible software capabilities and what I hope to see in the future.

In Ruth 1, Naomi's directive for her daughters-in-law to return to Moab is followed by an expressive in which she wishes them well (Ruth 1:8–9). Ruth and Orpah respond negatively with a commissive (Ruth 1:9); Naomi repeats her directive and follows up with rhetorical questions that function as assertives giving a reason for the directive (Ruth 1:11–13); and Orpah is convinced. Naomi starts her third speech with an assertive that Orpah has returned, which gives rhetorical backing to her final directive for Ruth to return to Moab (Ruth 1:15). Ruth begins her famous speech with a counter-directive, requesting Naomi not to entreat her anymore. Only then does she launch into her powerful compound commissive, affirming her identification with Naomi's people, God, and burial place (Ruth 1:16–17). This speech is powerful in isolation but is more so as a response to three successive directives. I have not yet found a way to search easily for all commissives that are in response to a series of three or more directives and look forward to when Bible software has advanced enough to support that sort of searching.

We are now ready to look at several different intertextual approaches to the book of Ruth. When looking at the marriage scene in Ruth 4, the invocation of the people at the gate, "through the children that the Lord

---

35. Steven T. Mann, "Performative Prayers of a Prophet: Investigating the Prayers of Jonah as Speech Acts," *CBQ* 79 (2017): 20–40.
36. Alston, *Illocutionary Acts*, 147–309.

will give you by this young woman, may your house be like the house of Perez, whom Tamar bore to Judah" (Ruth 4:12 NRSV), virtually begs the reader to do intertextual work between Ruth and the Tamar-Judah story in Gen 38. The stress on Ruth's Moabite origins in Ruth 4:5, 10 further suggests that a comparison of Ruth with the story of Moab's origins (Gen 19) may be in order.[37] Harold Fisch takes up this challenge and argues for intertextuality between the stories of Lot and his daughters, Judah and Tamar, and Boaz and Ruth based on the following paradigm: (1) descent—Lot to Sodom, Judah from his brothers, Elimelech for Moab; (2) disaster—destruction of Sodom, deaths of Judah's wife and two sons, deaths of Elimelech and two sons; (3) abandonment—Lot's daughters unable to acquire men, Tamar remaining widowed in father's house, Orpah and Ruth left widowed; (4) redemption—Lot, Judah, and Boaz as *go'el*; (5) bed-trick—Lot deceived into cohabiting with daughters, Tamar disguised as prostitute, Ruth coming secretly to threshing floor; (6) celebration—Lot made drunk, Judah attending sheep-shearing festivity, Boaz eating and drinking at barley-festival; (7) Levirate union—Lot's daughters conceiving from their father, Judah recognizing justice of Tamar's claim, Boaz acquiring property of dead kinsman (including Ruth); and (8) offspring—Moab (ancestor of Ruth) and Ben-ammi, Perez (ancestor of Boaz) and Zarah, and finally Obed (ancestor of David).[38]

There are some excellent observations here, but the paradigm needs modifying. The celebration comes before the bed-trick in all three cases. Only Boaz is called a *go'el*, only in the Judah story is the term "descend" used, and the levirate union is not really present in the Lot story.

Even taking these factors into account, the fact that both Ruth 4:17b and Ruth 4:18–22 interpret the significance of the story of Ruth as leading toward David suggests that Fisch's decision to analyze the stories of Gen 19, Gen 38, and Ruth in parallel as stories that are part of the same geneal-

---

37. Both Gen 19 and 38 appear in the cross-references section of the passage guide to Ruth in Logos. My experience with the cross-references section is that it includes more than I want, but that may be difficult to avoid. It does reveal how numerous intertextual connections are for so many biblical passages.

38. Harold Fisch, "Ruth and the Structure of Covenant History," *VT* 32 (1982): 425–37. Fisch bases his methodology on that of Claude Lévi-Strauss's analysis of different generations in the Oedipus corpus. Claude Lévi-Strauss, *Structural Anthropology* (New York: Basic Books, 1963), 213–19. I would like to see Bible software eventually pick up better on parallels between the Hebrew Scriptures and texts of antiquity in both the classical world and the Far East.

ogy is well motivated.³⁹ But we must not stop there but instead ask what insights into Ruth itself do the parallels yield: How does Ruth contrast with the other stories? With regard to the bed-trick, Fisch does note the crudity and directness of Lot's daughters, Tamar's veiling herself and Judah's concern for public opinion, and Ruth's cleansing and anointing herself as well as referring to the rite of redemption. Yet this aspect is still understated in Fisch's study. Boaz's concern for the welfare of Ruth in Ruth 2 could not be more different from Lot's utter lack of regard for his daughters in Gen 19:1–30. And although Boaz may have been merry in the night encounter with Ruth, he is not dead drunk and acts with appropriate decorum and concern for proprieties throughout. Finally, YHWH is entirely absent from the birth narratives of Gen 19 and 38, but in Ruth it is YHWH that gives Ruth conception (Ruth 4:13).⁴⁰ This provides a partial fulfillment of the expressive/directive of the townspeople, "And may your house be like the house of Perez, whom Tamar bore to Judah, from the seed that YHWH will give to you from this woman" (Ruth 4:12, my translation). The Bethlehem community expresses well-founded faith in YHWH, whom they presumably see as having directed the Judah-Tamar story, and YHWH explicitly grants their request by giving Ruth conception, as narrated in the very next verse. The book of Ruth becomes not just about the redemption of Naomi, Ruth, and the land but of unsavory events in the past.

This first approach to intertextuality involves one text citing or alluding to another. A second approach concerns passages that are the same genre. Ruth is an example of a marriage story, as are Gen 24:10–67 and Gen 29:1–30.⁴¹ The Genesis marriage stories share the following structure:

---

39. The various patterns that Lévi-Strauss had observed in different generations of Oedipus's line are as follows: overrating of blood relations (Cadmos seeks his sister, Europa; Oedipus marries his mother, Jocasta), killing of blood relations (Oedipus kills his father, Laios; Eteocles kills his brother, Polynices), slaying of monster (Cadmos kills the dragon; Oedipus kills the sphinx), and etiologies associated with difficulties in walking (Labdacos means "lame"; Laios means "left-sided"; Oedipus means "swollen-foot").

40. I have created a passage list in Logos of all the birth narratives, and this is the only example of YHWH being active in the conception element of a birth report.

41. Robert Alter has an insightful discussion of what he calls "the betrothal typescene," in which he primarily discusses Gen 24:10–61; 29:1–20; and Exod 2:15–21. See *The Art of Biblical Narrative* (New York: Basic Books, 1981), 47–62. In the latter part of the chapter, he mentions Ruth as a possible inversion of the scene, with the woman going to the foreign country and with the permission to drink from where the young

(1) The man goes to the foreign country, having previously been told to take a wife from there (Gen 24:10; 29:1); (2) the man arrives at a well (Gen 24:11; 29:2); (3) a difficulty or test with regard to the watering of livestock occurs (Gen 24:12–14; 29:8); (4) a woman comes to the well, and her name and heritage are mentioned (Gen 24:15; 29:10); (5) the test is passed or obstacle overcome, and the livestock are watered (Gen 24:16–20; 29:10); (6) the man and woman interact, and family identity is revealed (Gen 24:22–25; 29:11–12a); (7) the woman runs to tell her family the news (Gen 24:28; 29:12b); (8) the woman's guardian quickly welcomes the man (Gen 24:29–31; 29:13–14); (9) the man dialogues with the woman's guardian, who agrees to give her as a bride (Gen 24:34–51; 29:15–19); (10) some sort of bride-price or gift-giving takes place (Gen 24:53; 29:20); (11) there is a meal or feast (Gen 24:54; 29:22); (12) a complication arises which threatens the marriage (Gen 24:55; 29:23–24); (13) after further dialogue, the complication is resolved (Gen 24:56–59; 29:25–27); and (14) the bridegroom takes his wife (Gen 24:62–67; 29:28–30).

With respect to Ruth as an inverted marriage story with the woman as the protagonist, we see: the journey to the foreign country in Ruth 1; the narrator emphasizes the man's name and identity in Ruth 2:1; the agricultural obstacle is the danger that Ruth would be reproached or hindered from gleaning (Ruth 2:15–16), which is overcome by Boaz's directives to his men (Ruth 2:9, 15–16); the well element is alluded to in Ruth 2:9; the interaction and discussion of identity takes place in Ruth 2:10–11; and Ruth tells Naomi the news in Ruth 2:19. There is no initial agreement of marriage, but there is a feast/meal (Ruth 3:7) followed by Boaz explaining a complication which would threaten a possible marriage (Ruth 3:10–12), a crucial dialogue which resolves the complication (Ruth 4:1–12), and the bridegroom taking his wife (Ruth 4:13).

What is gained by the intertextual comparison here? In Gen 24, the main characters are Abraham's servant, Rebekah, and Laban. In Gen 30, the main characters are Jacob, Rachel, and Laban. In Ruth, the main characters are Ruth, Boaz, and Naomi. The prominence and characterization of Ruth and Naomi counter the supposed trend of declining female agency in marriage narratives.[42] Nor is this agency limited to its main characters. The

---

men had drawn (Ruth 2:9) substituting for the well element. By extending the analysis to the full pericopes (Gen 24:10–67 instead of just 24:10–61 and Gen 29:1–30 instead of just 29:1–20), we shall see further evidence that supports Alter's claim.

42. Esther Fuchs argues that the decreasing role of the woman in the betrothal

unnamed townswomen greet Naomi at the beginning of the story (Ruth 1:19), pronounce a blessing upon her toward the end (Ruth 4:14–15), and are the subjects of the last action in the book of Ruth proper—naming Ruth's child (Ruth 4:17). Read as a marriage narrative, Ruth provides a model of positive female initiative which many women have found inspiring for centuries.

A third approach is to read Ruth in its various canonical settings. Most Christian Bibles situate Ruth between Judges and Samuel, and this leads to interesting canonical readings also.[43] Ruth begins "in the time when judges judged" (Ruth 1:1) thus situating it historically in the Judges period, and it concludes with a genealogy leading toward David, the major character in Samuel. Timothy J. Stone notes two other verbal connections between Ruth and the epilogue of Judges: the geographical marker "from Bethlehem of Judah" (Judg 17:8, 9; 19:1, 2, 18; Ruth 1:1, 2) and that Judg 21:23 and Ruth 1:4 use the contextually rare verb נשא rather than the standard לקח in the phrase "took a wife."[44] Marvin A. Sweeney has argued that Judges functions in part as an argument that if kingship comes, all tribes other than Judah fail to show the necessary qualities to be the ruling tribe.[45] The book of Ruth complements this by portraying David's ancestors and even the entirety of his hometown of Bethlehem as highly Torah-observant in contrast to the behavior in Judg 17–21, which is a virtual catalogue of the sins that YHWH had warned against. The perlocutionary intent of Ruth becomes a proleptic apology for Davidic kingship.

If the standard Christian Bible order provides a very good intertextual reading of Ruth, so too does the Jewish Bible, which understands it as the second of five festival scrolls read at Passover, Weeks (Shavuot), Tisha

---

type-scene reflects patriarchal values. Esther Fuchs, "Structure, Ideology and Politics in the Biblical Betrothal Type-Scene," in *A Feminist Companion to Genesis*, ed. Athalya Brenner, FCB 2 (Sheffield: Sheffield Academic, 1993), 273–81. Fuchs's analysis is valid if one only looks at Gen 24, Gen 29, and Exod 2.

43. Logos has a neat canon comparison tool, which displays the canonical orders of the Jewish Bible, Anglican Bible, Lutheran Bible, Protestant Bible, Roman Catholic Bible, Eastern Orthodox Bible, Leningradensis, Ethiopian Orthodox Bible, and others.

44. Timothy J. Stone, *The Compilational History of the Megilloth*, FAT 2/59 (Tübingen: Mohr Siebeck, 2013), 120–24. I have performed some syntax searches for clauses throughout the Hebrew Bible containing the relevant verbs נשא and לקח, plus "wife" or "wives," as the direct object and can affirm Stone's conclusions.

45. Marvin A. Sweeney, "Davidic Polemics in the Book of Judges," *VT* 47 (1997): 517–29.

B'Av, Tabernacles, and Purim, respectively. Ruth takes place in the weeks between the beginning of the barley harvest (Ruth 1:22) and the end of the wheat harvest (Ruth 2:23), and Boaz is probably celebrating Shavuot in Ruth 3:7. Shavuot is also called the feast of harvest (Exod 23:16), and Ruth has more harvest activity than any other biblical narrative. Further, Shavuot celebrates the giving of the law on Mount Sinai, and Ruth becomes a model of how a gentile becomes a part of the Jewish community by identifying with YHWH and YHWH's people. The book of Ruth is thus in dialogic tension with Ezra-Nehemiah, where Jews have to divorce their non-Jewish wives, and with Num 25:1–9, where Moabite women lead Israelite men to commit apostasy. Along with Isa 56:1–8, Ruth argues that the prohibition against Moabites becoming part of Israel in Deut 23:4–7 is not absolute but a norm that can be overcome by factors such as Sabbath observance (Isa 56:1–8) and absolute identification with YHWH and YHWH's people (Ruth 1:16–17).[46] Actions, not ethnicity, count. The perlocutionary intent of Ruth in the Jewish Bible is to interpret torah correctly, to exemplify torah observance, and, by example, to encourage it.

The canonical setting of Ruth for most biblical scholars is determined by its order in *BHS* (i.e., Leningradensis), where it appears immediately after Proverbs. Proverbs warns the young man against the lures of the נכריה (foreign woman) but ends in the acrostic poem devoted to the אשת חיל (woman of honor).[47] Ruth demonstrates that this contrast is not absolute. Ruth wonders why Boaz, whom the narrator describes as איש גבור חיל (a mighty man of honor) and portrays as respected in the city gates (Ruth 4:1–2; cf. Prov 31:23), shows favor to her, a foreign woman (Ruth 2:10). Boaz later states that Ruth is "a woman of honor" (actually the only woman specifically designated a woman of honor in the Bible) who has not gone after young men (Ruth 3:10–11)—she has not acted in the fashion that Proverbs attributes to the foreign woman. In this reading, Ruth also shows

---

46. Given that some important Christian Old Testament theologies, such as those by Brevard Childs and Rolf Rendtorff, also use the Jewish canonical order, an exploration of what Ruth contributes to an understanding of what happens at Shavuot/Pentecost in Acts 2 might be fruitful, and I hope to write on this topic at another time.

47. Stone discusses some other connections between Proverbs and Ruth (Stone, *Compilational History*, 130–36). Stone also discusses a reading of Ruth in the order prescribed by the Talmudic tractate Bava Batra. I find this less useful, since no actual community reads the Bible in this order.

that action, not ethnicity, is what matters, but it is more a hermeneutic regarding wisdom and universal virtues than Torah observance as such.

In my opinion, all the above intertextual readings of Ruth legitimately highlight certain features of the text, as do numerous others not explored here. What is crucial is that we not absolutize any one reading at the expense of all others. Many biblical narratives (and laws, proverbs, and so forth) concern the realities of everyday life, and we should expect to see parallels to these passages in all sorts of places. Great preaching is largely about connecting the biblical narratives to present-day situations that have certain similarities with them; hence, the same passage becomes a legitimate basis for very different sermons. But there are constraints; once we have generated possible parallels, we have to check how close those parallels are, we have to pay attention to the differences, and we must not limit our analysis to showing connections but discover what insights it yields into the passage (or the present situation, in the case of preaching). Bible software is already of great help in finding parallels and in analyzing the locutionary level of different texts, but much still needs to be done, especially in the area of speech act theory and in tagging other works of antiquity. These are exciting times for scholars doing intertextual work.

# Part 2
# Postbiblical Intertextuality

# Mikhail M. Bakhtin and Dialogical Approaches to Biblical Interpretation

*Patricia K. Tull*

In biblical studies as elsewhere, the term *intertextuality* appears quite slippery. People who use the word in homage to its creator, Julia Kristeva, tend toward viewing it as an overarching observation that no act of communication is independent, no text is an island. As Kristeva famously said, "Any text is constructed as a mosaic of quotations; any text is the absorption and transformation of another."[1] For her, even an author is "no more than a text rereading itself as it rewrites itself."[2]

Beginning from ambiguities inherent in her formulations, various literary critics and philosophers immediately took the concept and term intertextuality into quite distinct directions.[3] These discussions quickly underscored the truth of Kristeva's own theory about the endless interrelatedness of texts and, consequently, the loss of authorial control over the meaning of their own words, even for Kristeva herself, when others read them. Kristeva's disciple Leon S. Roudiez, for instance, claimed that intertextuality had "nothing to do with matters of influence by one writer

---

1. Julia Kristeva, *Desire in Language: A Semiotic Approach to Literature and Art*, ed. Leon S. Roudiez, trans. Thomas Gora, Alice Jardine, and Leon S. Roudiez (New York: Columbia University Press, 1980), 66.

2. Kristeva, *Desire in Language*, 86–87. For a fuller treatment of the origins of intertextuality and discussion of some earlier works in inner-biblical exegesis, see Patricia K. Tull, "Intertextuality and the Hebrew Scriptures," *CurBS* 8 (2000): 88–119.

3. For early developments, see discussions concerning Roland Barthes, Michael Riffaterre, Jonathan D. Culler, Gérard Genette, and Foucauldian critics in Jay Clayton and Eric Rothstein, "Figures in the Corpus: Theories of Influence and Intertextuality," in *Influence and Intertextuality in Literary History*, ed. Jay Clayton and Eric Rothstein (Madison, WI: University of Wisconsin Press, 1991), 21–29.

on another, or with the sources of a literary work."[4] But many readers, including many biblical scholars, ignored this demurral even while adopting the term. Although more purely Kristevan applications are available, intertextuality has frequently been used in biblical studies to refer to interpretations of scripture occurring within scripture, or inner-biblical exegesis. Diversity in defining intertextuality seems to underscore the truth of its basic insight that no utterance survives unaffected by other utterances. But the fact that so many people mean so many different things by the word does create confusion.

As most students of intertextuality are aware, Kristeva first coined the term in response to Mikhail M. Bakhtin's writings about dialogism and the polyphonic nature of novels, especially those of Fyodor Dostoevsky. But as Kristeva described Bakhtin's work, she modified his ideas by utilizing French theorists, especially Jacques Derrida and Jacques Lacan, as "unacknowledged intertexts."[5] Like Bakhtin, Kristeva viewed dialogical relationships as inevitable and inseparable from the very warp and woof of every discourse. But in using the word intertextuality as a stand-in for Bakhtin's *dialogism* and *polyphony*, she introduced more than a synonym. Both of Bakhtin's terms reflect hearing and sound. The dialogues that most often occupied Bakhtin's thinking were certainly to be found in written texts, but he never lost sight of these texts' social dimensions. He retained interest in people as people and not merely as texts.[6] Kristeva's substitute term intertextuality, in contrast, self-evidently derives not from *dialogue* but from *text*, a word she slipped into her restatement of Bakhtin's ideas in

---

4. Leon S. Roudiez, introduction to *Desire in Language: A Semiotic Approach to Literature and Art*, by Julia Kristeva, ed. Leon S. Roudiez, trans. Thomas Gora, Alice Jardine, and Leon S. Roudiez (New York: Columbia University Press, 1980), 15.

5. Clayton and Rothstein, "Figures in the Corpus," 19.

6. According to Barbara Green, "there is little in his thought that seems patient with texts talking to texts; Bakhtin liked to think of particular readers, historically situated, as juxtaposing texts" (Barbara Green, *Mikhail Bakhtin and Biblical Scholarship: An Introduction*, SemeiaSt 38 [Atlanta: Society of Biblical Literature, 2000], 23–24). This gravitation toward the personal is especially evident in his religious formulations, as Paul J. Contino and Susan M. Felch pointed out: "The movement in Bakhtin is always away from the abstract toward the personal, interactive, committed, responsible life—from faith, as an object that one possesses, to a feeling for faith, the engagement with a personal subject" (Paul J. Contino and Susan M. Felch, "Introduction: A Feeling for Faith," in *Bakhtin and Religion: A Feeling for Faith*, ed. Susan M. Felch and Paul J. Contino [Evanston, IL: Northwestern University Press, 2001], 20).

repeated parentheses, saying: "Each word (text) is an intersection of words (texts) where at least one other word (text) can be read."[7] This contrast in emphasis, and the fact that Kristeva insisted on retaining authorial control of a theory that inevitably describes loss of authorial control, guided me long ago to ground my own work in the writings of her predecessor and muse Bakhtin, especially his essays "Discourse in the Novel" and "Author and Hero in Aesthetic Activity."[8] Bakhtin's insistence on the social dimensions of language make his ideas amenable to studies of the Bible, which has never existed as a text for its own sake but for the sake of the lives of real readers interacting with the poets, prophets, artists, and sages who inhabit its pages.

It is important to note that Bakhtin himself wrote little about scripture—an irony, given biblical scholarship's regard for him.[9] Yet according

---

7. Kristeva, *Desire in Language*, 66. As Clayton and Rothstein noted, "Though the parentheses imply that Kristeva is only supplying a synonym, or at most, a neutral expansion of Bakhtin's concept, this textualization of Bakhtin changes his ideas—changes them just enough to allow the new concept of intertextuality to emerge" (Clayton and Rothstein, "Figures in the Corpus," 19).

8. Mikhail M. Bakhtin, "Discourse in the Novel," in *The Dialogic Imagination*, ed. Michael Holquist, trans. Caryl Emerson and Michael Holquist (Austin: University of Texas Press, 1981), 259–422; Bakhtin, "Author and Hero in Aesthetic Activity," in *Art and Answerability: Early Philosophical Essays by M. M. Bakhtin*, ed. Michael Holquist and Vadim Liapunov, trans. Vadim Liapunov (Austin: The University of Texas Press, 1990), 4–256. David I. Yoon recently decried the fact that biblical scholars use Kristeva's word while ignoring her ideological agenda (David I. Yoon, "The Ideological Inception of Intertextuality and Its Dissonance in Current Biblical Studies," *CurBR* 12 [2012]: 58–76). Many biblical scholars reveling in intertextuality do indeed focus curiously and often woodenly on developing an intertextual method. But it is ironic to criticize departures from the "original intent" of a theorist whose work undermined the idea of original intent. The insight about the permeability of language that Kristeva passed on from Bakhtin fueled different interests than Bakhtin's in her work and, in turn, funds interests in biblical studies that are in many ways closer to Bakhtin's. While I agree that intertextuality is not a methodology (Yoon calls it an ideology; I would call it more simply an insight about language), I find it odd to claim that readers should not alter the usage of a term that "was created with a distinct purpose of deconstructing the authority of meaning from the author to the reader" (Yoon, "Ideological Inception," 72).

9. Green pointed out that Bakhtin's scattered remarks on the Bible "suggest that his assumptions about Holy Writ, as he called it, were far from those held today by those who work with the text professionally.... He considered it *the* authoritative (as distinct from innerly persuasive) text and did not approach it as he did 'novelistic'

to those who knew him, he was a deeply devout Orthodox Christian, and his early works, such as "Author and Hero," which appeared in English some time after his later books, especially reveal a theological bent permeating his understanding of language, communication, and human communion.[10] His theology was thoroughly incarnational and relational, and his interest in dialogue has often been compared with that of Martin Buber, whom he admired.[11]

Although scholarship continues to pour forth based on individual aspects of his ideas and on the idea of intertextuality in general, it has been almost twenty years since Barbara Green summarized Bakhtin's contributions to biblical studies in *Bakhtin and Biblical Scholarship*. My contribution, which was first requested as a paper for the 2015 consultation on Intertextuality and the Hebrew Bible, is not intended to cover the entirety of Bakhtin's contributions to biblical studies but simply to reintroduce a few dimensions of his understanding of dialogism, particularly in reference to interrelationships among biblical texts. After a brief discussion of his personal history, I will draw attention to the use of his theories in exploring individual inner-biblical relationships, on the one hand, and in constructing scriptural hermeneutics and biblical theology, on the other.

Bakhtin developed his thinking in the midst of experiences consonant with those of biblical writers—suffering, deferred hope, exile and return, and even, in a sense, death and resurrection. This may partially explain why the ideas he developed have resonated with Christian thinkers.[12] Born

---

discourse" (Green, *Mikhail Bakhtin and Biblical Scholarship*, 24, emphasis original). Given this assumption born of his piety, she says, it is perhaps fortunate that he did not say too much about it. Timothy K. Beal pointed out a similar assumption about the Bible as a nondialogical text in Kristeva's work ("The System and the Speaking Subject in the Hebrew Bible: Reading for Divine Abjection," *BibInt* 2 [1994]: 171–89).

10. For the theological dimensions of Bakhtin's writings, see especially Alexander Mihailovic, *Corporeal Words: Mikhail Bakhtin's Theology of Discourse*, SRLT (Evanston, IL: Northwestern University Press, 1997); Ruth Coates, *Christianity in Bakhtin: God and the Exiled Author*, CSRL (Cambridge: Cambridge University Press, 1998); Green, *Mikhail Bakhtin and Biblical Scholarship*; and Felch and Contino, *Bakhtin and Religion*.

11. For an in-depth discussion of Bakhtin's relationship with Martin Buber, see Caryl Emerson, *The First Hundred Years of Mikhail Bakhtin* (Princeton: Princeton University Press, 1997), 225–32.

12. For his full biography, see especially Katerina Clark and Michael Holquist,

in 1895 and reared in a Russian family valuing education and the arts, he suffered poor health and chronic physical disabilities. As a young Russian Orthodox intellectual and teacher in pre-Stalinist Russia, he flourished in circles engaged in theological and philosophical exploration. But several years of increasingly severe government repression forced religious societies to disband or go underground. In the midst of intense Stalinist attacks on both intellectuals and practicing Christians, he was arrested in 1929 for membership in a Christian intellectual society. Held for several months, he was finally exiled with his wife Elena in the town of Kustanai in Kazakhstan. Barred from teaching, he made his living for many years as a bookkeeper and wrote during extended periods of unemployment.

It is a wonder that the frail scholar survived these days at all, and even more remarkable that his writings did. His casual approach to his works was famously encapsulated in the story of his using one of his own manuscripts for cigarette paper. His doctoral dissertation, submitted in 1940, found in the writings of Rabelais "a hilarious, irreverent celebration of all that was pompous, authoritarian, official, repressed, and silenced."[13] Such interests were so out of step with the Soviet state that he was fifty-six before he finally received his Doctor of Philosophy degree and seventy by the time the work was published.

But he outlived the purges, partly because he avoided the spotlight and partly because he sought to coexist even with ideological foes.[14] He taught quietly in the faraway town of Saransk for years until, in the late 1950s, university students discovered his early work on Dostoevsky and then found to their surprise that he was still alive. He enjoyed brief renown before his death in 1975. The vast majority of English translations of his works have appeared posthumously. Poignant lines among the very last he wrote certainly describe the near loss and revival of his own writings: "Nothing is absolutely dead: every meaning will have its homecoming festival."[15]

---

*Mikhail Bakhtin* (Cambridge: Harvard University Press, 1984). For briefer presentations, see Green, *Mikhail Bakhtin and Biblical Scholarship*, 11–23; and Emerson, "Bakhtin at 100: Art, Ethics, and the Architectonic Self," *CR* 39 (1995): 397–418.

13. Green, *Mikhail Bakhtin and Biblical Scholarship*, 21.
14. Clark and Holquist, *Mikhail Bakhtin*, 254.
15. Mikhail M. Bakhtin, "Toward a Methodology for the Human Sciences," in *Speech Genres and Other Late Essays*, ed. Caryl Emerson and Michael Holquist, trans. Vern W. McGee, UTPSS 9 (Austin: University of Texas Press, 1986), 170.

Bakhtin's writings reflect his kindly and even forgiving disposition. But they also reflect his mistrust of authoritarian speech and suspicion toward overly neat systems. Covert critiques of totalitarian ideology suffuse his analyses of language and speech. Rightly so, for as Katerina Clark and Michael Holquist have observed: "The way discourse is ordered in a given society is the most sensitive and comprehensive register of how all its other ideological practices are ordered, including its religion, education, state organization, and police. Cultures can be classified as open or closed according to the way in which they handle reported speech."[16]

In all his writings, Bakhtin kept front and center the reality that language is not simply self-contained and given but is contextually shaped and intensely relational. What we say is said in answer to the words of others, is filled with speech heard from others, and anticipates responses from others. Language reflects the quest for communion, and it is largely through language that relationships with others shape how we see both ourselves and the world around us.

Bakhtin's literary studies enrich biblical interpretation in several diverse ways. He has been helpful in the study of polyphonic texts, comprising more than one point of view, or even more than one authorial voice.[17] Although strong differences in viewpoint are inherent to encounters between biblical figures from the garden of Eden on, one contribution Bakhtin makes via his appreciation of Dostoevsky's novels is the recognition that an author can choose—or choose not—to invite readers to observe the situated truth inherent in the viewpoints of more than one person. The episodes surrounding Abram, Sarai, and Hagar, for instance, read with Bakhtin in mind, offer enough support to the viewpoints of all three figures to encourage readers to see the story from all sides—even

---

16. Clark and Holquist, *Mikhail Bakhtin*, 237.

17. On polyphonic texts, see in particular Carol A. Newsom, "The Book of Job as Polyphonic Text," *JSOT* 97 (2002): 87–108; and Newsom, *The Book of Job: A Contest of Moral Imaginations* (Oxford: Oxford University Press, 2003). See also Raj Nadella's study of Luke as a polyphonic book: Raj Nadella, *Dialogue Not Dogma: Many Voices in the Book of Luke*, LNTS 431 (London: T&T Clark, 2011); and Charles William Miller's study of the two voices in Lam 1: Charles William Miller, "Reading Voices: Personification, Dialogism, and the Reader of Lamentations 1," *BibInt* 9 (2001): 393–408. Since the corpus of biblical studies responding to Bakhtin has become vast, I will mention illustrative publications but will not attempt to list all or even most of the important works that merit attention. An earlier bibliography may be found in Green, "Bakhtin and the Bible: A Select Bibliography," *PRSt* 32 (2005): 339–45.

if our own social location prompts us to identify with only one.[18] Similarly, biblical writers sometimes played with such monologic speech on the part of characters within stories to undermine their messages with what Bakhtin called "double-voicing": one intent becomes evident from the speaker's viewpoint while the author is busy promoting a very different message through the character's own speech. The Assyrian Rabshakeh in 2 Kgs 18–19 and Isa 36–37, sent to taunt and demoralize Hezekiah and his supporters, for instance, sounds not terrifying but arrogantly hollow when his claims of Assyria's power over Judah's God are read by an audience who is rooting for Hezekiah and knows the story's outcome.[19] Additionally, Bakhtin's discussions of the distinctions between dialogic and monologic texts help us recognize that while some biblical texts invite multiple and ambivalent sympathies, others do all they can to discourage our interest in rival truth claims.[20]

Further, Bakhtin's sensitive considerations of the complex, compassionate relationship between author and inscribed character, or hero, help us sort out ways in which the psalms, for instance, while speaking in the voice of an individual, invite an audience to read them not only as the words of someone else but also, simultaneously, as our own potential words, as believers instinctively do.[21] His distinctions between authoritative discourse and internally persuasive speech help interpreters make our way through some of the Bible's more imperious sections and offer insight

---

18. In a somewhat different but related vein, see L. Juliana M. Claassens, "Laughter and Tears: Carnivalistic Overtones in the Stories of Sarah and Hagar," *PRSt* 32 (2005): 295–308.

19. Paul S. Evans offered an insightful analysis of double-voicing and polyphony in this story in "The Hezekiah-Sennacherib Narrative as Polyphonic Text," *JSOT* 33 (2009): 335–58. Similarly, Susanne Gillmayr-Bucher attends to the double-voicing that occurs in the stories of the book of Judges in "Framework and Discourse in the Book of Judges," *JBL* 128 (2009): 687–702; see also Benjamin J. M. Johnson, "David Then and Now: Double-Voiced Discourse in 1 Samuel 16.14–23," *JSOT* 38 (2013): 201–15.

20. Christopher B. Hays, for example, explored the monologism of Ezra 7–10 in "The Silence of the Wives: Bakhtin's Monologism and Ezra 7–10," *JSOT* 33 (2008): 59–80.

21. I explore this aspect of Bakhtin's work in relation to the Psalms in Patricia K. Tull, "Bakhtin's Confessional Self-Accounting and Psalms of Lament," *BibInt* 13 (2005): 41–55. See also in this regard Elizabeth Boase, "Grounded in the Body: A Bakhtinian Reading of Lamentations 2 from Another Perspective," *BibInt* 22 (2014): 292–306.

into internal struggles within texts.[22] His ideas about chronotope and the carnivalesque have likewise lent sensitivity to the ways we consider certain biblical texts.[23]

But since this particular volume concerns intertextuality rather than other possibilities from Bakhtin's rich treasures, I want to touch on just two of the ways that thinking about the Bible's dialogical nature has enriched our interpretation of what goes on between biblical texts. The first is fairly diachronic in orientation while the second is more synchronic. First, Bakhtin brings a sharper focus to considerations of inner-biblical exegesis. And second, his views help us in shaping theological and ethical claims.

The first has served as a much-needed corrective to an overvaluation of original speech. Most of us were told in high school and college to read other people's writing and then express it in our own words, documenting everything that we derived from elsewhere, since failure to do so was plagiarism, subject to serious repercussions. Especially for young thinkers for whom every thought is derivative, the challenge to digest and regurgitate the words of others in our own original speech often seems perplexing, making it difficult to distinguish what required a footnote from what did not. Though documentation is a crucial practice to learn and teach, I find myself sympathetic to students who have trouble deciding whether they can write a sentence without offering multiple, often meaningless, citations.

The privileging and protection of originality, however, is relatively recent, dating to the mid-eighteenth century in literary studies, when originality began to be viewed as "the only true sign of an author's genius."[24] This prejudice about originality found its way from literary criticism into biblical source criticism in the mid-1800s and continued to trouble readings of composite biblical books for a century. Scholars reading the

---

22. See, for instance, Miriam J. Bier, "'We Have Sinned and Rebelled; You Have Not Forgiven': The Dialogic Interaction between Authoritative and Internally Persuasive Discourse in Lamentations 3," *BibInt* 22 (2014): 146–67.

23. Nehama Aschkenasy, for instance, points out these particular features of the book of Ruth while simultaneously reading its dialogical engagement with other biblical stories. See "Reading Ruth through a Bakhtinian Lens: The Carnivalesque in a Biblical Tale," *JBL* 126 (2007): 437–53.

24. Clayton and Rothstein, "Figures in the Corpus," 5, citing Edward Young (*Conjectures on Original Composition*, 1759, reproduced in Hazard Adams and Leroy Searle, eds., *Critical Theory Since Plato*, 3rd ed. [Belmont, CA: Wadsworth, 2004]) and William Duff, a Scottish Presbyterian minister (*An Essay on Original Genius*, 1767).

prophets, for instance, worked hard to isolate supposed original oral speeches of true prophets from so-called accretions of later scribes, considered detectable by the mere fact that they contained repetitions or echoed other texts.[25] Privileging originality deterred study of narrative texts in a somewhat different way, as scholars found it difficult to say much more about Chronicles, for instance, than that it was a tendentious rewriting of Samuel-Kings which, despite its own complex history of composition and frequent references to earlier documents, was viewed as original.

But the ground shifted in biblical studies when scholars read Bakhtin pointing out that originality has not actually belonged to anyone since Adam first spoke. "In the everyday speech of any person living in society," Bakhtin opined with amusingly fabricated precision, "no less than half … of all the words uttered by him will be someone else's words … transmitted with varying degrees of precision and impartiality (or more precisely, partiality)."[26] In fact, every word proceeds from, and responds to, words that came before. On this I would like to quote a well-known passage from "Discourse in the Novel" at some length to highlight the evocative nature of his language and especially its potential nuance for biblical studies:[27]

> Between the word and its object, between the word and the speaking subject, there exists an elastic environment of other, alien words about the same object, the same theme…. Indeed, any concrete discourse (utterance) finds the object at which it was directed already as it were overlain with qualifications, open to dispute, charged with value, already enveloped in an obscuring mist—or, on the contrary, by the "light" of alien words that have already been spoken about it…. The word, directed toward its object, enters a dialogically agitated and tension-filled environment of alien words, value judgments and accents, weaves in and out of complex interrelationships, merges with some, recoils from others, intersects with yet a third group…. The living utterance, having taken meaning and shape at a particular historical moment in a socially spe-

---

25. On this peculiar wrinkle in early modern interpretation of Isaiah, see Patricia Tull Willey, *Remember the Former Things: The Recollection of Previous Texts in Second Isaiah*, SBLDS 161 (Atlanta: Scholars Press, 1997), 11–22.

26. Bakhtin, "Discourse in the Novel," 339.

27. Quoting passages from Bakhtin such as this seems to be fairly typical for his followers, including myself, since his speech is difficult to summarize without reducing its impact and resonance. As Green has pointed out, "his complexity and 'non-systemness' resists such efforts" ("Mikhail Bakhtin and Biblical Studies," *PRSt* 32 [2005]: 242).

cific environment, cannot fail to brush up against thousands of living dialogic threads, woven by socio-ideological consciousness around the given object of an utterance; it cannot fail to become an active participant in social dialogue.[28]

Creators of new words cannot help but invoke antecedents. However, as Bakhtin pointed out and as Kristeva both demonstrated in relation to Bakhtin and was dismayed to discover among her followers, this does not mean that authors or speakers are constrained by their antecedents. Even as they redeploy precursors' words in various ways, new speakers and writers make their bid to rearrange what will be understood in the future. Such dialogical engagement is active, vigorous participation in a society's meaning-making, in its very construction.

We know that the biblical corpus that was passed down through history to us, complex as it is, is only a sliver of ancient Israel's writing corpus. And even the countless writings that were lost are only a slice of the communication that shaped ancient Israel's language and thought. We possess so little from which to understand so much. Bakhtin's descriptions of the thick contexts surrounding all utterances help us to remain humbly aware that the biblical writers were engaging in disputes that are largely lost and silent for us today, disputes that can only be reconstructed, if at all, from the fragments left to us. Yet though we know that any intertextual fibers we find are only threads and not the whole cloth, the notion that one utterance is a rejoinder to another beckons us to try to reconstruct elements of these conversations. Thus, the field of inner-biblical exegesis, often explicitly indebted to Bakhtin, has flourished for the past generation.[29]

This reality about the dialogues erupting among ancient texts is valuable not only for students writing dissertations. It also reorients the religious imagination in relation to sacred scripture. Many Christians were raised on a Bible that seemingly fell leather-bound from heaven sometime in the distant past, a unified divine message, "the word of God," mediated through human messengers speaking in unison, infallible wisdom

---

28. Bakhtin, "Discourse in the Novel," 276–77.

29. My own doctoral dissertation involved Second Isaiah's use of previous authoritative texts to help construct an argument for reconciliation with Israel's God and return to Jerusalem (*Remember the Former Things*). Many other studies of specific inner-biblical relations, more or less based in Bakhtin's writings, have followed, varying greatly in their sophistication and literary sensitivity.

for all generations and each individual reader. Glimpsing the writers of what was to become scripture not simply as mouthpieces of messages from God but rather as readers and recipients of other religious texts that were becoming authoritative—readers often compelled to update or improve on what preceded them—makes the Bible spring wide open, to resemble less a finished unity to which to submit and more a theological symposium that readers throughout the centuries have found themselves invited to overhear and even join. Many individual findings have delighted scholars pursuing inner-biblical exegesis. But perhaps more significant for the ongoing history of biblical reception is the renewing of the imagination, funded by such specifics, to see prophets and poets as having themselves been immersed in a compelling tradition against which they nevertheless struggled. This larger vision renders the world of ancient Israel more recognizable in terms of our own world, with its vigorous and even violent rhetorical rough and tumble.

As a student of Second Isaiah, I find hope for social impasses today by recognizing specific, rhetorically charged ways in which the poet invoked the past to advocate for bold and unprecedented, perhaps even Quixotic, acts of faith, such as the rebuilding of the ruined city of Jerusalem. Whenever history seems at a dead end, a very new vision is needed—not the old story repeated again. But at such a crisis point, visions that ignore the old story are not likely to gain traction. So, grounding Second Isaiah's vision in words from the past, molding those words into new forms, and using old cadences to sing new songs became one prophet's way of claiming that what might sound entirely novel was actually implicit all along. The gospel writers performed similar acts of alchemy when they grounded Jesus's new story in traditional genealogies, ancient miracle accounts, unlikely birth narratives, encounters at public wells, and so on.

As with the search for gold or oil, as with many methodological inquiries, diminishing returns tend to set in over time with inner-biblical exegesis. If the "so what" questions can be satisfyingly addressed, study of intertextual allusion can be fruitful. But otherwise such studies can devolve into what Kristeva and her supporters disdainfully called "banal source hunting," demonstrating nothing more, over and over again, than that no text is an island indeed. Finding that one biblical writer engaged dialogically with another is nice; better is to ask what that writer was seeking to say, and more importantly, to do or make happen in that engagement, and what the effect of that engagement has been in the history of interpretation.

Another value to Bakhtin's ideas in the area of inner-biblical study has to do with biblical theology, including its implications for religious ethics. Carol A. Newsom pointed this out in her 1996 article "Bakhtin, the Bible, and Dialogic Truth," suggesting that Bakhtin's understanding of dialogic truth can honor the particularity of divergent biblical texts while also giving theologians "something to work with."[30] Acknowledgement that biblical writers do not speak in unison, but rather sponsor competing claims, and recognition that scripture does not hand constructive theologians prooftexts to plug into their systems, but rather elucidates tensions in human self-understanding, may give readers pause before electing certain biblical perspectives as central while ignoring others that merit a hearing alongside them.

A widespread example of such prooftexting—though rarely recognized as such—which has made its way over the centuries beyond theologians and deep into congregational and even secular culture, with alarming consequences, involves Gen 1:26–28: "Let us make humankind in our image, according to our likeness; and let them have dominion" (NRSV). Even among environmentalists troubled by the notion, this passage is widely considered the Bible's first, last, and primary word about divine intent for humans in relation to nature. In the past generation or so, as environmental degradation has become increasingly worrisome, the idea of dominion has been softened from "domination" to "stewardship." But what remains the same is the misperception that we humans not only understand creation but somehow uniquely rule it. From a biological standpoint, the notion is nonsense, of course. Though our knowledge about the biosphere continues to grow, human activity is also rapidly destroying species we have not even discovered, much less understood or protected. From an exegetical standpoint, unless we use some extrabiblical measuring rod to determine that Gen 1 was intended by those who assembled the canon to be central to biblical thought and theology in a way that other biblical passages describing creation such as Gen 2, Ps 104, Isa 40:12–31, and Job 38–42 are not, we are compelled to acknowledge that scripture presents multiple distinct and defensible interpretations of the place and role of humans in creation, some of these more easily confirmed by our experience than others.[31]

---

30. Carol A. Newsom, "Bakhtin, the Bible, and Dialogic Truth," *JR* 76 (1996): 290–306.

31. On Bakhtin's contribution to theological ethics, see Michael G. Cartwright, "The Uses of Scripture in Christian Ethics—After Bakhtin," *ASCE* (1992): 263–76. For

Although theology has traditionally valued monologic truth claims, the field of theology and the thinking of theologians can benefit from the rich dialogical fund the Bible offers when examined through a Bakhtinian lens. Unlike monologic truth, a dialogic sense of truth, as Bakhtin said, "requires a plurality of consciousness ... [that] in principle cannot be fitted within the bounds of a single consciousness."[32] Peter Slater, meditating on Bakhtin's significance for a theology of the divine word, wrote: "Far from expecting to be addressed directly by a single voice from on high, Bakhtin reminds us, we most hear God's voice when we mull over with others what is both true to our tradition and true in our present situation."[33] According to Newsom, dialogic truth "exists at the point of intersection of several unmerged voices."[34] It is an embodied truth—it does not belong to everyone and therefore to no one in particular. It is more event than system, dynamic rather than unified, coming to life in its tensions and qualifications in relation to other ideas. Thus, it is always open, unfinished, and unfinalizable—just as the work of theology over the centuries has proven to be.

I recently took part in a conversation among people from various faith traditions reflecting on a tour led by an environmental justice group through an area of Newark, New Jersey, where homes are interspersed with heavily polluting industries. Reflecting together on what had ostensibly been a shared experience, participants uncovered its multifaceted nature as they described what they saw and its impact on them. For some, the industrial wasteland inspired anger; for others, the vast, polluted shipping port provoked consumer guilt; for still others, the stories of neighborhoods organizing to protect themselves inspired hope. Some observations were choked by emotion, others were profound and arresting. The shared experience was recognizable, but the rich personalities refracting it defied its containment in a single consciousness. This was an example of truth as event. Fortunately for its richness, no one tried to monologize the conversation with a summary or consensus. Such freedom to explore the

---

specific discussion of the dominion debate, see Patricia K. Tull, "Jobs and Benefits in Genesis 1 and 2," in *After Exegesis: Feminist Biblical Theology*, ed. Patricia K. Tull and Jacqueline E. Lapsley (Waco, TX: Baylor University Press, 2015), 15–29.

32. Mikhail M. Bakhtin, *Problems of Dostoevsky's Poetics*, ed. and trans. Caryl Emerson (Minneapolis: University of Minnesota Press, 1984), 81.

33. Peter Slater, "Bakhtin on Hearing God's Voice," *MTh* 23 (2007): 14.

34. Newsom, "Bakhtin, the Bible, and Dialogic Truth," 294.

vast dialogical realities surrounding human experience could well save theology from some of its more unrealistic truth claims, and indeed, the introduction of a broader range of conversation partners in both theology and biblical studies has begun to do so.

Newsom's observations about dialogism's value for biblical theology have been followed by those of others, most notably Dennis T. Olson, Ben Quash, and L. Juliana M. Claassens. Since Bakhtin insisted on the unfinalizability of all truth quests, Olson suggested that all our theology too can only be "provisional monologization" as a first step in ongoing dialogue.[35] Quash offered the "tent of meeting" as a scriptural image of the virtual space created by the scriptures and their readers for doing theology, saying: "This tent is not a permanent home.... It is a mobile and temporary space, always determined by the specifics of texts and readers at a given moment of encounter."[36] This space for "recognizing competing voices without making any single voice normative," Claassens pointed out, is particularly valued by feminist thinkers.[37]

When Jacqueline E. Lapsley and I began planning the volume published in 2015 by Baylor University Press called *After Exegesis: Feminist Biblical Theology*, we wanted our book, organized in Newsom's honor, to try inner-biblical dialogue and the symposium idea in the service of feminist theological soundings. We gathered a group of female scholars, most of whom had been Newsom students, to write provisional theologies on a variety of themes, some traditional and some not, by selecting diverse biblical texts that concern the theme they were exploring and observing what they might learn from these texts' quarrels with one another. The participants met at successive Society of Biblical Literature meetings to discuss the project and to hear how one another's discordant texts were being arbitrated.

---

35. Dennis T. Olson, "Biblical Theology as Provisional Monologization: A Dialogue with Childs, Brueggemann, and Bakhtin," *BibInt* 6 (1998): 162–80.

36. Ben Quash, "Heavenly Semantics: Some Literary-Critical Approaches to Scriptural Reasoning," *MTh* 22 (2006): 404.

37. L. Juliana M. Claassens, "Biblical Theology as Dialogue: Continuing the Conversation on Mikhail Bakhtin and Biblical Theology," *JBL* 122 (2003): 127, citing Dale M. Bauer and S. Jaret McKinstry, "Introduction," in *Feminism, Bakhtin, and the Dialogic*, ed. Dale M. Bauer and S. Jaret McKinstry (Albany: State University of New York Press, 1991), 2, 6.

Some of our authors were Christians, some Jews, some secular. Some welcomed the invitation to do theology, while others resisted calling themselves theologians of any kind. We used a variety of exegetical methods, from source criticism to literary studies, and appealed to several authorities, from the Bible itself to current sociological studies to recent events. To give some examples, Carleen Mandolfo pondered God's judgment through examining Psalms over against parts of Job. Katie Heffelfinger set Ps 62 and Isa 51–52 side by side to explore biblical salvation themes. Cameron Howard compared two foreign queens—Jezebel and Esther—who exercised authority through authorship. Julie Galambush juxtaposed pentateuchal texts displaying contrasting ethics toward outsiders. Amy Merrill Willis engaged parts of both Isaiah and Daniel to find a description of hope. The result was "a dialogical approach that does justice to the compositional and ideological complexity of biblical texts and that attends to intersections between them that generate new insights."[38]

When guided by Bakhtin's dialogism, intertextuality is more an angle of vision on textual production and reception than an exegetical methodology, more a set of insights than an ideology. There are certainly important roles to be played both by the more diachronic intertextual studies represented by inner-biblical exegesis and by a variety of synchronic studies, such as the theological explorations I described. In addition, open recognition of—and theoretical tools for unlocking—the dialogues inherent among the many ancient writers who contributed to scripture encourages those introduced to these insights to value the Bible's nature as a living, human document, brimming with religious debate, that invites its audience not simply to submit to monologic authority, but instead actively to join the collective task of interpreting the scriptures that Jewish and Christian faith communities have inherited.

---

38. Frances Taylor Gench, review of *After Exegesis: Feminist Biblical Theology*, ed. by Patricia K. Tull and Jacqueline E. Lapsley, *Int* 70 (2016): 347–48.

# Between Abandoned House and Museum: Intertextual Reading of the Hebrew Bible as Embracing "Abjection"

Soo J. Kim

Reading is an activity, always in process. Diversified experiences mingle together. Readers struggle but enjoy the process by accepting and denying authoritative manuals; they feel repressed but relieved, resisting some experiences but preferring others and even creating their own. Although readers are unaware, this process itself is intertextual recognition. Further, modern readers of the Hebrew Bible are born too late to avoid any intertextual engagement. Hence, despite the general, contentious mood of scholars over this matter,[1] this paper maintains that the Hebrew Bible's innately ambivalent nature automatically drives readers toward the ongoing process of

---

An earlier version of this study, "Confinement and Ironic Exclusion: Intertextual Reading of Jeremiah, Cassandra, and Margot as the Act of Reader's Release," was presented to the "Intertextuality and the Hebrew Bible" section at the Annual Meeting of the Society of Biblical Literature (Boston, MA, November 2017).

1. Gary A. Phillips, "Sign/Text/Difference: The Contribution of Intertextual Theory to Biblical Criticism," in *Intertextuality*, ed. Heinrich F. Plett, RTT 15 (Berlin: de Gruyter, 1991), 78–97; Benjamin D. Sommer, *A Prophet Reads Scripture: Allusion in Isaiah 40–66*, Contra (Stanford, CA: Stanford University Press, 1998); Patricia K. Tull, "Rhetorical Criticism and Intertextuality," in *To Each Its Own Meaning: An Introduction to Biblical Criticisms and Their Application*, ed. Steven L. McKenzie and Stephen R. Haynes, rev. ed. (Louisville: Westminster John Knox, 1999), 156–80; Carol A. Newsom, *The Book of Job: A Contest of Moral Imaginations* (Oxford: Oxford University Press, 2003); Richard Bautch, "Intertextuality in the Persian Period," in *Approaching Yehud: New Approaches to the Study of the Persian Period*, ed. Jon L. Berquist, SemeiaSt 50 (Atlanta: Society of Biblical Literature, 2007), 25–35; Geoffrey D. Miller, "Intertextuality in Old Testament Research," *CurBR* 9 (2011): 283–309; Ziony Zevit, ed., *Subtle Citation, Allusion, and Translation in the Hebrew Bible* (Sheffield: Equinox, 2017).

intertextual moments. To explicate the argument, I discuss in detail aspects of the Hebrew Bible and some essentials of the reading process. Especially in the case of the Hebrew Bible, the different levels of accessibility between scholars and laypeople have not been fully recognized; this study fills that lacuna and facilitates further discussions.[2]

The hierarchy established among the readers of the Hebrew Bible consists of two distinct groups: one of scholarly experts and the other of laypeople.[3] How do these two groups relate to one another? Imagine, if you will, the Hebrew Bible as an abandoned house of treasures. Scholarly experts in the relevant fields explore the house inside and out and then (re)organize its contents to display the house as a museum for laypeople to tour.

Intertextuality in the Hebrew Bible is concerned with two diachronic issues. First, the multiple implied authors in a single text preserves the intertextual signals of the ancient, original writers. The process of editing or collecting the Hebrew Bible into its current form has a complicated history that encompasses the text's compositional growth up to the present. Consequently, the present text is full of the tensions and contradictions between its many implied authors. Interestingly, this multiplicity of authorship is not an issue in modern literary works, which prompts us to take this unique aspect of the Hebrew Bible seriously. The second diachronic concern is with the relationship between intertextuality and source or redaction criticism: Should we or should we not include allusion, influence, or subtle citation as intertextual categories?

Meanwhile, the typical layperson's reading experience is similar to a tour-guided visit to the museum. I label this a directed reading because the implied reader and the layperson's religious community exert a bit more influence than the scholarly tour guide. Like other sacred books, the Hebrew Bible has been regularly read, memorized, interpreted, and used for dogmatic assertions in the community of faith. This more or less religious setting defines individual readings more forcefully than often recognized. The interpretive communities' directions dominate the reading process strongly, systematically, and persistently.[4] In my

---

2. *Laypeople* in the broadest sense refers to nonordained or nonprofessional people but those who identify themselves as religiously oriented readers.

3. As a Hebrew Bible scholar and a leader of a religious community, I identify myself as a transporter of the treasures from the house to the museum.

4. Consider R. W. L. Moberly, *Old Testament Theology: Reading the Hebrew Bible*

view, intertextual reading with a heuristic attitude can provide rereading opportunities that relativize and counterbalance this initial dominance. The significance of this reading strategy lies, first, in the fact that the ongoing, interactive, and dialogic reading process inculcates an ethical, communicative attitude in readers who practice it; second, it helps readers to narrow the scope of intertextual reading to a manageable extent, which might otherwise become unlimited.

### 1. Guests of the Abandoned House of Treasures

This section will discuss two unique aspects of the Hebrew Bible: multiple elusive implied authors and the issue of a diachronic approach. These topics are more appealing and accessible to experts than to laypeople. The experts of the field—biblical archeologists, linguists, exegetes, and commentators—are the primary guests of the abandoned house of treasures.

#### 1.1. Multiple Elusive Implied Authors and Intertextual Reading

As Thomas R. Hatina notes, our discussion on intertextuality may start from "the relationship between written texts, primarily as the imbedding of fragments of earlier texts within later texts."[5] This definition is descriptive enough and a convenient way to understand modern literature, whose chronological order of compositional dates is readily known. However, with ancient literature such as the Bible, the matter is more complicated, which makes Hatina's definition an impossible place to start our discussion of intertextuality.

First, the Hebrew Bible text often does not have a single or single-minded author(s) but rather multiple elusive and complicated implied authors. The final editors preserved the complicated reading environment to set up different target readers. From the reader's perspective, this means that different readers in different situations may evoke and recognize different implied authors.[6]

---

*as Christian Scripture* (Grand Rapids: Baker Academic, 2013); especially see the chapter "Educating Jonah," 181–210.

5. Thomas R. Hatina, *In Search of a Context: The Function of Scripture in Mark's Narrative*, JSNTSup 232, SSEJC 8 (London: Bloomsbury, 2002), 5.

6. Isabell Klaiber, "Multiple Implied Authors: How Many Can a Single Text Have?," *Sty* 45 (2011): 138–52.

Let me first clarify who or what the implied author means in our discussion. Paul R. House in his Zephaniah study defines the implied author as "the writer pictured by the reader," which still assumes human agencies in the composition and reception process.[7] Several scholars on narratology have already shown the impersonalizing tendency in defining the implied author. Wayne C. Booth, the inventor of this term, illustrates the implied author as "an ideal, literary, created version of the real man," while Seymour Benjamin Chatman describes it as "the source of the narrative text's whole structure of meaning."[8] These scholars characterize the implied author as the active initiator of meaning in the text, regardless of the personal or impersonal characteristic of the implied author.

Shlomith Rimmon-Kenan grants more passivity to the implied author; according to her, the implied author is a "depersonified" construct built by the reader's inference and imagination.[9] Mieke Bal goes even further, saying that "the implied author is the result of the investigations of the meaning of a text."[10] I disagree with the notion that the reader alone constructs the image of the implied author because the reader is constrained by the undeniable and unmovable domain of the implied author *in* the text. The implied author does not appear on the surface level of the text, as characters do, nor does the implied author exist outside the text, as the author does. Waiting for the reader's recognition, the implied author exists within the text and eventually nests in the mental space of the reader. In sum, in the broadest sense, we can use the term *implied author* as the one who sets the agenda behind the surface of the text.[11]

---

7. Paul R. House, *Zephaniah: A Prophetic Drama*, BLS 16 (Sheffield: Sheffield Academic, 1989), 82.

8. Wayne C. Booth, *The Rhetoric of Fiction* (Chicago: University of Chicago Press, 1961), 70–71; Seymour Benjamin Chatman, *Story and Discourse: Narrative Structure in Fiction and Film* (Ithaca, NY: Cornell University Press, 1978), 147.

9. Shlomith Rimmon-Kenan, *Narrative Fiction: Contemporary Poetics* (London: Methuen, 2002), 87–89.

10. Mieke Bal, "The Laughing Mice; or, On Focalization," *PT* 2 (1981): 209.

11. *The Oxford Dictionary of Media and Communication* defines implied author as "source of a work's design and meaning which is inferred by readers from the text" (*ODMC*, s.v. "Implied Author"); Tom Kindt and Hans-Harald Müller, *Implied Author: Concepts and Controversy*, trans. Alastair Matthews, Nar 9 (Berlin: de Gruyter, 2006), 151–60.

### 1.1.1. Abandoned House of Treasures

As mentioned above, the Hebrew Bible can be compared to an abandoned house of treasures. Despite the possibility of misleading by oversimplifying, the analogy makes it easier to understand the unique relationship of the author-text-reader. The owner who had abandoned the house is the author; the abandoned house of treasures is the Hebrew Bible, with many attractions and valuables; and the guests of the house are the readers, especially those trained for in-depth study.

When a guest opens the door of the house, complicated issues await. First of all, since the house has been abandoned for such a long time, the guest cannot be 100 percent sure who the owner is. Shall we limit the title *owner* to the original builder(s)? to the first residents? Given the fact that the house had many residents, to whom shall we attribute any repairs or remodeling? Are modifying adjectives such as *original* or *first* legitimate? Even if, like Roland Barthes, we define author as a scriptor or orchestrator, it is hard to delineate the concept of the author in a cumulative text.[12]

In addition to the owner issue, there is an issue with the guests themselves. No guest has stayed in the abandoned house throughout its history, so intertextual and intercultural reading is fundamentally a guessing job only possible with various imported methodologies, involving territorializing certain parts of the house by certain groups of guests.[13] As a result, many remarks by earlier guests often make latecomers feel muddled. Still, the inherent uncertainty defying *the* right answer bestows authority to either side. Some guests claim to have the same authority as the authorized tenants, arguing that they get the authorization from the original owner. Roman Catholic traditions under the papacy or some Christian traditions under a particular theory of inspiration have argued exaggerated authority of this kind in biblical interpretation. Unfortunately, institutional authority remains strong in directing the reading process of laypeople.

---

12. Roland Barthes, "The Death of the Author," in *Image, Music, Text*, trans. Stephen Heath (New York: Hill & Wang, 1977), 145; Barthes, "Theory of the Text," in *Untying the Text: A Post-Structuralist Reader*, ed. Robert Young, trans. Ian McLeod (London: Routledge, 1981), 31–47.

13. Julia Kristeva explains this interaction with a textual space of three-dimensions: the writing subject, the addressee, and other exterior texts. Julia Kristeva, "Word, Dialog and Novel," in *The Kristeva Reader*, ed. Toril Moi (New York: Columbia University Press, 1986), 37.

In conclusion, the boundaries separating all these groups—whether owners/renovators/guests of the abandoned house or authors/redactors/readers—is unavoidably blurry. I suggest that we use the term *users* to subsume all into one. This way we can avoid granting more power to one agent over another. The term users is expandable to include all the agents of the text, including flesh-and-blood authors, translators, editors, compilers, transmitters, scribes, implied authors, narrators, characters, literary audiences, implied audiences, and even the later groups of the audiences and readers throughout the ages. As Claudia D. Bergmann asserts, the possibility of recognizing a larger scope from the text depends on modern readers' awareness of all the previous users of the text.[14] This is the picture of the Hebrew Bible's intertextual reading environment.

### 1.1.2. Palimpsest

*The Oxford English Dictionary* defines *palimpsest* as "a manuscript in which later writing is written over an effaced earlier writing."[15] The inability to erase the former work in palimpsest is adopted by reading theorists as the ground to argue for intertextuality as quintessential in the reading process. Both Julia Kristeva's (text as "the absorption and transformation of another") and Barthes's (text as "a new tissue of past citations") definitions well reflect the notion of coexisting texts—in other words, intertextuality.[16]

I specify the general analogy by using two prepositions: *above* and *after*. With *above*, we pay attention to the later author's effort to erase earlier texts by putting newer texts above the earlier ones. With *after*, we see the later author's effort to invite readers to join what the author traditionalized via intertextual writings. These processes produce multiple implied authors, although they are very elusive. The vague though visible traces of forerunners on the surface level of the text are beyond recognition but informative enough to hint at their possible locations in history and society. Thus, biblical interpreters should not unthinkingly follow the general principle of modern literature in which readers presume one unified implied author at one point in time and place. In his book *Palimpsests*, Gérard Genette

---

14. Claudia D. Bergmann, *Childbirth as a Metaphor for Crisis: Evidence from the Ancient Near East, the Hebrew Bible, and 1QH XI, 1–18*, BZAW 382 (Berlin: de Gruyter, 2008), 6–8.

15. *Oxford English Dictionary*, s.v. "palimpsest."

16. Kristeva, "Word, Dialog and Novel," 37; Barthes, "Theory of the Text," 39.

rightly positions the reader as the significant agent of intertextual traffic in reading or writing and brings diachronic concerns to transtextuality.[17] As we shall discuss further in the next section, in diachronic reading(s), the full awareness of the reader's role and the appreciation of each voice of the multiple implied authors according to their historically, geographically, and theologically different agendas are truly significant.

The Cyrus edict quoted in Ezra 1 and the Cyrus Cylinder in the British Museum well exemplify the *above* intention in the palimpsest analogy. The author of Ezra 1 attempts to reduce the possibility of identifying the original Cyrus edict by replacing Marduk with YHWH. The author of Ezra 1 never erases all connections to the Cyrus edict but contextualizes it to the extent of fabrication according to his own theological agenda customized for his own intended audience.[18] In its final form, the later text of Ezra 1 declares that its own presentation is identical with the actual edict. However, it is possible to see in the traces left and preserved the lines of the author's intention. Another example of this type of writing is the Akitu festival in the book of Ezekiel. The return of YHWH, the God of Israel, implicitly alludes to the return of Marduk, the deity of Babylonia, to the throne that is erased.

The dynamic interrelationship of different implied authors in the book of Isaiah, which modern readers divide as the First, Second, and Third Isaiah, is a good example of *after* palimpsest-like textuality. No ancient manuscript explicitly includes paratextual information about these three different implied authors in the book of Isaiah. Isaiah is bound as one book under one implied author whose name is Isaiah. Still, when scholars read this one canonical book, they can easily surmise the high probability of at least three different implied authors. Furthermore, the substantial presence of the three can hardly be reduced to the three different voices of one implied author. Other *after* examples include: Ezek 43:18–19 and 44:8–16 provide different treatments of Levites and the Levitical priests of the family of Zadok; and two contrastive presentations of King Zedekiah/Sedekias in MT Jeremiah and LXX Jeremiah reflect the two or more implied authors who reconnect the texts according to their own different interests.[19] Incidentally, this last

---

17. Gérard Genette, *Palimpsests: Literature in the Second Degree*, trans. Channa Newman and Claude Doubinsky (Lincoln: University of Nebraska Press, 1982), 1–5.

18. I thank Jieun Yun for her insightful conversation with me regarding the detraditionalization and traditionalization of the authors of the later text.

19. For the study of comparative characterization and the history of research on the MT and LXX texts, see Shelley L. Birdsong, *The Last King(s) of Judah: Zedekiah*

example suggests that translation theories or reception criticism should be also considered in the discussion of intertextuality.

What do we learn from this? The existence of multiple implied authors proves that the Hebrew Bible itself is a collection of intertextual writings. Intertextuality is not a secondary matter but is the quintessential starting point for discussions of writing and reading, since it refers to an inherent quality working both in writers' and readers' mental spaces.

1.1.3. The Reader's Mental Space as the Space of (Inter)Textual Reading

By providing selectively constructed historical backgrounds to a text, some interpreters try to persuade their contemporaries to believe that they found the authors' original ideas. However, these assertions miss out on two salient facts: the interpreter as reader is not free from his or her reading agenda, and all of the synthetic process of reading occurs in the reader's mental space.

With this epistemological understanding, Wolfgang Iser further specifies the reader's mental space as a "virtual space," the space between reader and text that generates the meaning of the text. He points out the importance of the reader's role. When the text leaves many unexplained gaps as well as some clear signs, it is the reader, not the author, who engages in intertextuality.[20] Keeping the aesthetic balance between the gaps and signs is the secret key of the literary work. However, the balance is often interpreted differently from what the author originally intended. Since the comprehension stage is created when the implied author and the implied reader meet in the virtual space, regardless of the seemingly perfect presentation of the author, the recognition/appreciation of the work depends in large part on the reader's desires and abilities. Barthes's claim that the "birth of the reader must be at the cost of the death of the author" makes the same point.[21]

Still, this does not mean the complete denial of the existence of the author. I do not fully agree with the perspective of the European poststructuralism of the 1960s, which is the social background for the rise of

---

*and Sedekias in the Hebrew and Old Greek Versions of Jeremiah 37(44):1–40(47):6*, FAT 2/89 (Tübingen: Mohr Siebeck, 2017).

20. Wolfgang Iser's emphasis on the text's indeterminacy also supports this idea. Wolfgang Iser, *The Implied Reader: Patterns of Communication in Prose Fiction from Bunyan to Beckett* (Baltimore: Johns Hopkins University Press, 1974), 280–89.

21. Barthes, "Death of the Author," 148.

intertextuality.²² Authors existed and still exist through the text, although they left a long time before we modern readers gained access to that text. This requires, interestingly, a learning stage from Hebrew Bible readers where the text's syntactic and semantic dimensions are enlightened in the ancient settings. Authors are not dead, but their survival depends on readers. Readers have the responsibility to revive the authors.

## 1.2. Diachronic Approaches to a Bronze Mirror-Like Text

Geoffrey D. Miller, in his "Intertextuality in Old Testament Research," illustrates the animosity between two sides of scholars in the intertextual reading of the Hebrew Bible: "Those who practice an author-oriented approach accuse reader-oriented scholars with eisegesis, whereas those interested in reader-oriented studies claim that the other side runs the risk of speculation by focusing on something as elusive as authorial intent."²³ Marvin A. Sweeney argues that the intertextuality discussion of the Hebrew Bible in the twenty-first century has shifted from more diachronic approaches (author's intertextual intentions) to more synchronic ones (reader's perception of the text).²⁴ Gail R. O'Day's complaint about the exclusively diachronic tendency of the 1990s was dismissed for a long time, until the twenty-first century.²⁵ Meanwhile, different definitions for various terminologies cause significant confusion in this field. Demonstrating many definitions and usages by Lyle Eslinger and Benjamin D. Sommer, Magan Fullerton Strollo details how the inconsistency negatively affects the field.²⁶ Strollo's analysis over the confusion of terminologies also reflects questions

---

22. Susan S. Friedman, "Weavings: Intertextuality and the (Re)Birth of the Author," in *Influence and Intertextuality in Literary History*, ed. Jay Clayton and Eric Rothstein (Madison, WI: University of Wisconsin Press, 1991), 152.

23. Miller, "Intertextuality in Old Testament Research," 283–309.

24. Marvin A. Sweeney, "Isaiah 60–62 in Intertextual Perspective," in *Subtle Citation, Allusion, and Translation in the Hebrew Bible*, ed. Ziony Zevit (Sheffield: Equinox, 2017), 131–42.

25. Gail R. O'Day, "Intertextuality," *DBI* 1:547.

26. Lyle Eslinger, "Inner-Biblical Exegesis and Inner-Biblical Allusion: The Question of Category," *VT* 42 (1992): 52; Sommer contends that *allusion*, as used by literary critics, does "posit an earlier and a later text," so that the study of allusion is historically centered (Sommer, *Prophet Reads Scripture*, 25); Magan Fullerton Strollo, "The Value of the Relationship: An Intertextual Reading of Song of Songs and Lamentations," *RevExp* 114 (2017): 192.

about the fusion of many disciplines, in this case, whether or not historical criticism is included in the discussion of the intertextuality of the Bible. Some scholars define intertextuality in a much narrower sense and argue that source criticism, redaction criticism, and the tracing of a text's influence should not be part of the intertextuality discussion. I will deal with this topic in two separate subcategories: (1) the inclusion/exclusion of allusion and influence; and (2) the goal of intertextuality.

### 1.2.1. Allusion, Influence, and the Imagined Immaterial Text

David M. Carr criticizes any claim to offer a unified reading of a text as a subjective imposition or, at best, an illusion made by the readers and their interpretive communities.[27] I agree with his analysis, but with his logic Carr discourages any effort to discover authorial intertextuality. He argues that the fractures of the text do not have to be understood as the traces of the later text but that readers' perceptions suffice to explain the diverse readings.[28] As we shall see below, I do not necessarily reach the same conclusion. Gerrie Snyman also explicitly criticizes any attempt to include source criticism in intertextual reading by arguing that the earlier sources can be termed different "voices."[29] To Snyman, intertextuality seems to occur only between physically existing texts. In the discussion of allusions in Isa 40–66, Sommer opposes subsuming allusion and influence (how one text has influenced another) under the category of intertextual reading, and he identifies the two as "the study of inner-biblical allusion and exegesis."[30] For Sommer, intertextuality relates more to the synchronic approach—the reader-oriented interpretation—while allusion and influence refer to the author's activity through the text.[31] The world of the literary critic in earlier

---

27. David M. Carr, *Formation of the Hebrew Bible: A New Reconstruction* (New York: Oxford University Press, 2011).

28. David M. Carr, *Reading the Fractures of Genesis: Historical and Literary Approaches* (Louisville: Westminster John Knox Press, 1996), 23.

29. Gerrie Snyman, "Who Is Speaking? Intertextuality and Textual Influence," *Neot* 30 (1996): 428. He quotes Barthes's critique of interpreters' intentional confusion between the intertextual reading and source-hunting. But my point is that even if it is hunting for source, it is somebody's intertextual reading in his or her mental space with the imagined text.

30. Sommer, *Prophet Reads Scripture*, 10.

31. Sommer, *Prophet Reads Scripture*, 6–8. Also see pp. 28–30 for his definitions of allusion and influence.

generations is not much different. Kristeva, for example, refuses to include the concept of influence within intertextual reading due to the invisibility (subjectivity) or textlessness of the source to influence.[32]

However, points of comparison between texts are not always visible to intertextual readers. Most books in the Hebrew Bible, like other ancient texts, do not provide explicit paratext information to trace their proveniences. So when we think of source-critical issues of intertextuality, we need to ask whether source-critical study is reading or not. According to Ilana Elkad Lehman's definition that "reading is an active organization of readers' awareness of the various elements in the text," the source-critical activity is a reading activity.[33] As cognitive linguistic theorists recognize, blending of the information of the two texts occurs in the reader's mental space and produce varying outcomes according to the reader's ability and willingness.[34] Klaus Bruhn Jensen notes that the denotation of the text in recent days has expanded its definition up to all meaningful entities.[35] Thus, source-critical study is based on two texts: a visible text before the reader (hypertext); and an invisible imagined text (a supposed hypotext) made by the source-critical reader.[36] Genette includes even a theory of the text that expands in seeking its origins and uses in the intertextuality.[37]

---

32. Julia Kristeva, *Desire in Language: A Semiotic Approach to Literature and Art*, ed. Leon S. Roudiez, trans. Thomas Gora, Alice Jardine, and Leon S. Roudiez (New York: Columbia University Press, 1980), 29. George Aichele and Gary A. Phillips point out that the initial motive of intertextuality has its root in the social transformative characteristic or resistant tendency against the existing norm of the society at that time. George Aichele and Gary A. Phillips, "Introduction: Exegesis, Eisegesis, Intergesis," *Semeia* 69/70 (1995): 9.

33. Ilana Elkad Lehman, "Spinning a Tale: Intertextuality and Intertextual Aptitude," *ESLL* 5 (2005): 40.

34. George Lakoff and Mark Johnson, *Metaphors We Live By* (Chicago: Chicago University Press, 1980); Gilles Fauconnier and Mark Turner, *The Way We Think: Conceptual Blending and the Mind's Hidden Complexities* (New York: Basic Books, 2002).

35. Klaus Bruhn Jensen, "Text and Intertextuality," *IEC* 11 (2008): 5126–30.

36. Hans-Peter Mai, "Bypassing Intertextuality: Hermeneutics, Textual Practice, Hypertext" in *Intertextuality*, ed. Heinrich F. Plett, RTT 15 (Berlin: de Gruyter, 1991), 30–59. For the similar cultural environment of textless intertextuality, see Jonathan S. Burgess, "Intertextuality without Text in Early Greek Epic," in *Relative Chronology in Early Greek Epic Poetry*, ed. Øivind Andersen and Dag T. T. Haug (Cambridge: Cambridge University Press, 2011), 168–83.

37. Sayyed Ali Mirenayat and Elaheh Soofastaei, "Gérard Genette and the Categorization of Textual Transcendence," *MJSS* 6 (2015): 533.

Finally, we need to distinguish two different activities: the ancient author's intertextual reading, which we modern interpreters assume occurred during composition/redaction, and the modern interpreter's imagined intertextual reading in his or her own source-critical interpretation. Both are intertextual readings. The former is the more recent author's activity of intertextual entertainment that produced the present text in front of the modern interpreter. The latter, source-critical intertextual reading occurs when the interpreter *selects* the potential signals that she or he assumes the ancient author(s) intentionally/unintentionally left in the text and pursues the plausible source text(s). Still, the stark reality of our current situation remains: modern readers are never able to fully grasp the source texts. Who can dare say that J, E, D, P, H, and DtrH in the Hebrew Bible and Q in the New Testament are tangible texts?

1.2.2. The Goal of Intertextual Reading of the Hebrew Bible

Source- or redaction-critical study should not be the goal of intertextual reading. The final goal should be inclusive enough to embrace diachronic approaches, all of which are only one phase of the whole intertextual reading activity. Although many biblical interpreters mesh the two notions, the final destination and stopping points along the way must not be confused. Samuel D. Giere encourages making diachronic questions not a goal but "a window into the textual/language world of the ancient interpreter."[38] Jonathan D. Culler's statement expresses my position well: "The study of intertextuality is not the investigation of sources and influences, as traditionally conceived: it casts its net wider to include the anonymous discursive practices, codes whose origins are lost, which are the conditions of possibility of later texts."[39]

The potential problem in prioritizing the diachronic approach is, if I use the ancient bronze mirror analogy, that the interpreter cognizant of source criticism may easily scratch the surface of the bronze mirror (the text) and think that she or he sees clearly, deep inside, and masters the world(s) behind the present text. It often leads the reader to make self-deluding excuses to consider all theoretical assumptions as the real

---

38. Samuel D. Giere, *A New Glimpse of Day One: Intertextuality, History of Interpretation, and Genesis 1.1–5*, BZNW 172 (Berlin: de Gruyter, 2009), 9, 11.

39. Jonathan D. Culler, *The Pursuit of Signs: Semiotics, Literature, Deconstruction* (Ithaca, NY: Cornell University Press, 1981), 103.

intentions of the real authors. This is another reason why we should avoid setting diachronic study as the goal of reading. As we shall see in the next section, a heuristic approach provides a good alternative to prevent or minimize potential scratches from becoming permanent scars on the text.

## 2. Visitors to the Museum

While for expert guests the Bible is an abandoned house of treasures, for laypeople it is a well-organized museum.[40] Imagine a group of museum visitors who put group-identity stickers on the top of their shirts and follow a tour guide. They can hardly decide their length of stay in a specific room or the program of the tour. They are prohibited from touching the displayed material, lest an alarm go off. Experts and laypeople enjoy varying levels of access to the treasures and the ability to evaluate them. Though archeologists, linguists, exegetes, religious leaders, and laypeople are all in equal standing as contemporaries, the distribution of authority or power among them is not equal. Laypeople seldom play a role as the curators of the museum, even though they are generally more interested than the experts in putting into practice the knowledge contained in the museum.[41] Given this reality, laypeople should not be carelessly thought of as *casual* readers.

### 2.1. Intertextuality in the First Reading

The first task of any reading is to understand the text. For Hebrew Bible intertextual reading, learning the Hebrew language and its linguistic environment makes it possible to understand the text. Criticism occurs only after this primary comprehension process. Hence, the readers' first reading experience is to learn the syntactic and semantic dimensions of the Hebrew text. Samuel Taylor Coleridge's "suspension of disbelieving" dominates at this point, since the experts who know the language and culture

---

40. For the nature of museum in the shaping of knowledge nowadays, see Eilean Hooper-Greenhill, *Museums and the Shaping of Knowledge* (New York: Routledge, 1992).

41. Bal points that the Bible is both "totally religious" and "totally literary" in any occasion. Mieke Bal, "Introduction," in *Anti-Covenant: Counter-Reading Women's Lives in the Hebrew Bible*, ed. Mieke Bal, JSOTSup 81, BLS 22 (Sheffield: Almond Press, 1989), 11.

are the guides with the readers' trust.[42] Similarly, Kristeva's point about the readers' strong objection to any encounter with abject and strong tendency to abide by the rule of the text is applied here.[43] Kristeva argues that one abandons or at least sets aside so-called inappropriate elements to situate oneself as the appropriate entity.

How does one know which norm is appropriate? For Bible reading in general, the community of faith to which readers belong exercises the most influence in teaching, directing, encouraging, and enforcing what is appropriate or inappropriate. Especially when newcomers are socialized into a biblical community, the directed reading of religious leaders constitutes almost all parts of the discerning process.

Learning happens not only in the study session but also when participating in the culture of the community. For example, laypeople in a worship service of a local Protestant church stay not only for the sermon hour but also for the pre- and postprayers. The preprayer invokes the Holy Spirit to illuminate the true meaning of the Bible as well as to help the participants subdue any self-consciousness and reason to interrupt their concentration on God's voice through the sermon. During this prayer, participants learn two important lessons, eyes closed, hands folded, solemnly: (1) the Bible is the word of God, the house is not abandoned, and the original owner is still residing within it; and (2) the preacher, when filled with the Holy Spirit, is the agent delivering God's will in the sermon. Once more, the postprayer invokes the Holy Spirit to expel suspicious criticism and grant firm resolution to practice what was received, which works as the reinforcement of the notion of the house-Bible-preacher-sermon occupied rightly by God.

The following case study illustrates the passive dynamics of the Bible readers' first reading experience in reality. A class of ten undergraduate students reads Jer 38; it is the spring of 2017 in a Christian private university.[44] The course name is Introduction to Old Testament. All ten students identify as Christians who regularly attend church at least once a week.

---

42. Samuel Taylor Coleridge, *Biographia Literaria*, ed. Nigel Leask (London: Dent, 1997).

43. Julia Kristeva, *Powers of Horror: An Essay on Abjection*, trans. Leon S. Roudiez (New York: Columbia University Press, 1982).

44. A report from Sara Susswein shows a similar concern from the Jewish Bible education. Sara Susswein, "Teaching Biblical Scholarship in a Modern Orthodox High School," *TheTorah*, n.d., https://tinyurl.com/SBL03103a.

Eight students have read several books of the Bible, but two have never finished reading even one book. Accordingly, they fit the laypeople category with enough exposure to the directed readings from their church or other extended Christian communities. The classroom setting is another influence on the students' reading process.

Our first reading of Jer 38 identifies the central theme as Jeremiah's failure to persuade the people.[45] This reading comes after introductory lessons on the history of ancient Israel, prophetic literature, and the book of Jeremiah as a whole. When reading Jer 38 (JPS) together in the classroom, the first task is to understand the semantic level of the text. King Zedekiah's indecisive character, the temporary withdrawal of the Babylonian military, and the unknown destiny of Jeremiah all contribute to the liminal and indeterminate mode of the narrative until the narrator reveals the doom, the decisive sentence: the fall of Jerusalem. Immediately after, I have students listen to a dramatic reading of the text (NRSV) to help with their understanding of the characters' emotional interactions.

Although my teaching does not seem directional, it is. Students could read the assigned passage in many other ways. I choose one particular way, and other options are automatically excluded. Peter D. Miscall points out that the first produced mental image forms a network of various images between the reader and the text.[46] In these student readers' minds, various conceptual metaphors emerge in the first reading of Jer 38, possible for many intertextual readings.[47] However, I lead them to read twice Jer

---

45. Before introducing the text to my students, I, as a guest of the abandoned house of treasures, have explored the treasures and what the earlier guests have found so far in an attempt to figure out the best display for them. Those include its history of interpretation and issues from the scholarly discussions. For a short overview of this history of scholarship and some of the latest opinions on this topic, see Else K. Holt and Carolyn J. Sharp, *Jeremiah Invented: Constructions and Deconstructions of Jeremiah*, LHBOTS 595 (London: T&T Clark, 2015). See especially the introduction. For diachronic concerns of the book of Jeremiah regarding the doublets and recurring phrases, see Geoffrey H. Park-Taylor, *The Formation of the Book of Jeremiah: Doublets and Recurring Phrases*, SBLMS 51 (Atlanta: Society of Biblical Literature, 2000). For the intertextual nature of Jer 37–38, see Mary C. Callaway, "Black Fire on White Fire: Historical Context and Literary Subtext in Jeremiah 37–38," in *Troubling Jeremiah*, ed. A. R. Pete Diamond, Kathleen M. O'Connor, and Louis Stulman, JSOTSup 260 (Sheffield: Sheffield Academic, 1999), 171–78.

46. Peter D. Miscall, "Isaiah: The Labyrinth of Images," *Semeia* 54 (1991): 104.

47. For the relationship between the conceptual metaphor and intertextuality, see

38:28, the decisive moment for the destination of Jerusalem. My intention is to discuss the matter of the poetics of tragic synchronicity with which I explain the verse.

וישב ירמיהו בחצר המטרה עד־יום אשר־נלכדה ירושלם ס והיה כאשר נלכדה
ירושלם: פ

So Jeremiah abode in the court of the guard until the day that Jerusalem was taken. And it came to pass, when Jerusalem was taken. (JPS)

After reading the last verse in the JPS version, I show students several other English versions (ESV, LXX [45:28], NRSV, NLT, BSB, and ISV): they do not have the last clause. Our first guess is that the omission probably reflects a desire to avoid redundancy. Then we read other English versions (JPS, KJG, KJV, NIV, and ASV) that have the last clause in verse 28. Finally, I give students the handout that has the LXX and the NASB, both of which have different versifications. The LXX has JPS 38:28 as 45:28; the NASB moves the last clause of MT 38:28 to 39:1. At this point students recognize more obvious intention to the versions that include the last clause. The last clause deliberately directs the reader to believe the simultaneous relationship between prophet's confinement and the fall of Jerusalem.

I provide another example of tragic synchronicity from 1 Kgs 14, the story of Jeroboam's wife and her son Abijah. When the mother consults the prophet Ahijah regarding her ill son, she receives a curse instead: when she steps on the threshold, her son will die. I ask several questions: Who is responsible for the death of this innocent Prince Abijah, son of King Jeroboam? Who is responsible for having this mother experience the cruel tragedy? The students' blame list does not mention God or the prophet Ahijah. By accepting the position of the implied reader, the students' reaction is directed by the implied author of 1 Kgs 14. I limit my comments on this point at that time.

A week passes after our first reading of Jer 38. This week is significant for our reading project, since it is the passion week following Palm Sunday

---

Manfred Pfister, "How Postmodern Is Intertextuality?," in *Intertextuality*, ed. Heinrich F. Plett, RTT 15 (Berlin: de Gruyter, 1991), 207–24; and Elisabeth Piirainen, "Metaphors of an Endangered Low Saxon Basis Dialect: Exemplified by Idioms of Stupidity and Death," in *Engaged Metaphors*, ed. Elisabeth Piirainen and Anna Idström (Amsterdam: Benjamins, 2012), 343. For the logic of the common use of biblical metaphor in the later literary work, see Zoltán Kövecses, *Where Metaphors Come From: Reconsidering Context in Metaphor* (New York: Oxford University Press, 2015).

in the Christian calendar. This special occasion directs the students' reading in a certain way: five students identify themselves with the leaders of Judah and people who confine Jeremiah in prison; two compare themselves to King Zedekiah, who has power but does not use it properly and instead causes the people to suffer; one student identifies herself as the people who act as bystanders.

Surprisingly, no one situates himself or herself in the position of Jeremiah! Guilty feelings of being the offenders preoccupies, never the suffering victims. One student mentions the sermon on Isa 53, the song of the suffering servant, a popularly read message during passion week; another, the confession of the centurion, "truly the man was the son of God" (ἀληθῶς οὗτος ὁ ἄνθρωπος υἱὸς θεοῦ ἦν) in Mark 15:39. The bridges to link these two texts to Jeremiah are from the guilt to kill the innocent person and the contrition coming late, respectively. The students/readers' emotional identification with the guilty party gets stronger when the Messiah takes the role of other victimized characters.

Up to this point, the intertextual reading directed by the classroom teaching and the passion week work together in the same direction. The students' first reading in the class is reinforced by the religious community. The special occasion in a Christian tradition exerts great influences as a significant reading environment.

After spring break, during which the school observes Easter, another shift happens. Most students do not remain in the guilt. The resurrection of Christ changes their mood from the misery of the perpetrators to the joy of the forgiven. The fall of Jerusalem coinciding with the persecution of Jeremiah is not their fault but the Judeans' fault in the ancient days. Likewise, the readers' reality determines the identification process or the extent of the distance to the characters in the text. The change of the terms from "people of Judah" to "Judeans" reflects on the Gospel of John's description of the people involved with the crucifixion of Jesus, which relates to readers' import in reading. When the guilty mode during the passion week shifted to the victorious and appreciative mode at Easter, the students' identification tendency was quickly and radically shifted.

Another interesting phenomenon to observe is the way these ten students themselves become a new reading community that shares a common experience. Regardless of the possible limiting force of the power of community, the readers welcome the mutual influence on themselves by their choice. The flesh-and-blood readers cannot easily avoid others' distractions or influences before, during, and after the reading.

At this point I introduce Kristeva's abjection theory to encourage (direct) students to look back on what they abandoned, such as potential suspicions, hesitance, or any kind of second thoughts. I say:

> Every direction is possible, but not everything is recommendable, especially when your reading takes the position of hurting the innocent people. Ethical concerns like this should make any reading experience a more passive and careful one. In my case, as a teacher, my direction should be restricted only to help build the infrastructure of your mental space for your own intertextual reading. And, in your case, you should pause and reexamine all the data that led you to reach the conclusion. In a difficult terminology, this is called the heuristic attitude to embrace the past abjection with critical eyes. Critical examinations of your own reading process must continue on and on. Now, what do you think of your anti-Semitic reading of Jer 38?

2.2. Intertextuality in the Rereadings

Actual or real readers usually assume the role of the implied reader. When the actual reader is invited to become the implicated reader, she or he may be distressed. However, distraction is one of the essential abilities for the readers to build upon. Reading appears fruitful when readers identify and comply with the author's intention, following the lead of the authorial design and order of the text. While this first reading necessitates some extent of reader's voluntary self-confinement, intertextual rereading provides the readers with the chance to break the prohibition of the suspension of belief. The implicated readers start distracting themselves to look for other options.

For our reading of Jer 38, two other stories construct a model for the students' intertextual rereading experience. One is the Cassandra story as presented in Aeschylus's tragedy *Agamemnon*; the other is the Margot story in Ray Bradbury's *All Summer in a Day*. Jeremiah, Cassandra, and Margot all have exceptional perceptions but with tragic destinies provoked by their contemporaries' distrust. Accordingly, their blissful spiritual abilities trigger horrible physical confinements, leading to their ironic exclusion from the events of their prophecies. Just as in Kristeva's ostracism of abjection, all three characters are ostracized as the objects of abjection: Jeremiah as a laughingstock, Cassandra as a mad woman, and Margot as an outcast.[48]

---

48. Kristeva, *Powers of Horror*, 1982.

Key words for the bridging conceptual metaphors for all three characters include extraordinary knowledge for the future, rejection by one's own people, confinement, and ironic exclusion.

The goal of the students' intertextual rereading is to guide them to reflect on and challenge the abjections that happened in the first directed reading. Students switch their status from the targeted reader to the critical reader.[49] After reading the two stories together with Jer 38, one student asks: "If the people of Judah at that time had listened to the prophet Jeremiah's advice, the fall of Jerusalem would not have happened? I start doubting this logic." Once the initial question breaks out, we start asking more. How efficient is it to keep the tension of the plot until the end, to see its ending as the fatal tragedy, the fall of Jerusalem? How would this portion of Jer 38 contribute to the development of the plot? In other words, for what purpose does the text allot the narrative space for this confinement story? Could Jeremiah have prevented the fall of Jerusalem if he had not been confined? The answer is almost always no. The fall of Jerusalem/Judah was unavoidable already when Jeremiah spoke the oracle, or when the author wrote it.

The failure of Jeremiah's prophetic work is not the theme of the book. People's persecution is what the confinement story focuses on—the stubborn and sinful nature of the people calling out the wrath of YHWH until Jerusalem's destruction. If that is one of the primary targets of the authorial intention, the readers' guilty feeling must have been directed by one of the implied authors of the text.

Kristeva describes the feeling of abjection with the baby's experience of separating herself or himself from the mother. As the baby grows to accept detachment as the process to get to maturity, receivers must grow to separate themselves from senders. Although it seems impossible to think of the text without the author, we readers, with the help of intertextual reading, learn to say goodbye to the author and to stand independently. The producers cannot but wait and attempt to influence from the outside of the text, though they would manipulate the readers to agree to their own rigid illusion of their own uniqueness, kept only by shutting down all access to others.

One of the rhetorical and theological agendas in the confinement story of the prophet Jeremiah is, as my students' first reading experienced,

---

49. See Brian Richardson, "Singular Text, Multiple Implied Readers," *Sty* 41 (2007): 259–74.

to infuse an unfathomable guilty feeling in readers. For some readers, the release from the negative, intense tension comes from finding a more powerful character than Jeremiah to undo the damage, as shown in the Messiah example above. For others, not following the people's mistake creates an exit from the guilty feeling. In one way or another, this tragic story becomes a lesson for readers to make a better story of their own. The resolutions that they *will* practice are the only escape from the burdensome emotions of the tragic story.

When other intertextual rereadings are involved, what happens? By recognizing that Jeremiah is not the only one who is confined and that confinement and fruitless prophecy stories are popular throughout times and places, readers pause, receiving exactly what the implied reader intends for the actual reader. In other words, the force of the emotions effused from the rhetorical or theological agenda will be loosened, blurred, and lightened when the focal point of the text moves to another direction. Indeed, intertextual reading means entering into the big, real world, which promises new experiences in many levels of human cognition.

# Intertextuality in the Dead Sea Scrolls

*Lawrence H. Schiffman*

Any attempt to discuss the overall question of intertextuality in the Dead Sea Scrolls will immediately run into the problem of the various definitions that can be given to this term. Our study will actually take a maximalist approach, attempting to demonstrate that a wide variety of relationships between texts may be observed in the Qumran corpus. In order to bring order to this material, we propose to move from direct quotation through exegesis, allusion, harmonization, and shared text. Some of these examples will illustrate the relationship between the scrolls and the Hebrew Bible, some the relationship among Dead Sea Scrolls. We will omit discussion of the relationship of the scrolls to other Second Temple texts that simply share ideas and of some relationships of texts that we, as readers trained in ancient Judaism and Christianity, experience. (The latter are usually termed parallels.) Hence, we will not deal with examples in which the intertextual relationship is perceived only by modern readers but could not have possibly been intended by the author, as in the example of Qumran legal texts and the Talmudic corpus.

In our investigation, we will see over and over that material found in the corpus of the Dead Sea Scrolls is based on, continues, or in some other way reflects the body of literature of ancient Israel that came to be called the Bible. From our point of view, the reuse of this material in the Second Temple period is itself an indication of a type of canonicity, even if it is not exactly the same as that of the later Jewish and Christian traditions and even if the list of books in that protocanon is not exactly the same as the Tanakh (the Hebrew Bible) and the Protestant Old Testament.[1] Much

---

1. Lawrence H. Schiffman, *Reclaiming the Dead Sea Scrolls: The History of Judaism, the Background of Christianity, the Lost Library of Qumran* (Philadelphia: Jewish Publication Society of America, 1994), 162-69.

of the literature of the Dead Sea Scrolls needs to be seen as an attempt to modulate the biblical tradition so as to apply it to the circumstances of the Greco-Roman period. At the same time, we have to acknowledge that, to a great extent, the authors of some of the scrolls saw themselves as in some way continuing the biblical tradition or actually living in a sort of time-warped biblical Israel. Just a quick look at the contents of the collection that moderns have termed the Dead Sea Scrolls should indicate the enormous potential for observing intertextuality in these texts and among these texts.

The corpus of manuscripts found at Qumran consists of three approximately equal parts: (1) biblical texts, including parts or all books of the Hebrew Scriptures except Esther; (2) apocryphal compositions, namely, books like the Bible, rewriting the Bible, or continuing it; (3) sectarian works particular to the group that occupied Qumran and gathered the library, considered to be the Essenes by most scholars.[2] We will see that even within the biblical manuscripts from Qumran, intertextuality is operative, and that in the other two sub-corpora, apocryphal and sectarian, the role of intertextuality in the composition of these texts is great.[3] This phenomenon should clearly be expected in view of the formative role of the Bible in the development of the varieties of Second Temple Judaism and particularly among the Qumran sectarians, their self-understanding, and the subject of the literature they composed. Therefore, between this corpus and the Hebrew Bible—as well as inside the corpus—we should expect complex levels of intertextuality. Put simply, the Bible was formative for Second Temple literature and, hence, intertextuality was rampant.

---

2. Schiffman, *Reclaiming the Dead Sea Scrolls*, 31–35; Devorah Dimant, "The Qumran Manuscripts: Contents and Significance," in *Time to Prepare the Way in the Wilderness: Papers on the Qumran Scrolls by Fellows of the Institute for Advanced Studies of the Hebrew University, Jerusalem, 1989–90*, ed. Devorah Dimant and Lawrence H. Schiffman, STDJ 16 (Leiden: Brill, 1995), 23–58; Dimant, "Apocalyptic Texts at Qumran," in *The Community of the Renewed Covenant: The Notre Dame Symposium on the Dead Sea Scrolls*, ed. Eugene Ulrich and James C. VanderKam, CJAS 10 (Notre Dame: University of Notre Dame Press, 1994), 175–91. A classic statement of the Essene theory is found in Frank Moore Cross, *The Ancient Library of Qumran*, 3rd ed., BibSem 30 (Sheffield: Sheffield Academic, 1995), 54–87.

3. Eugene Ulrich, *The Dead Sea Scrolls and the Developmental Composition of the Bible*, VTSup 169 (Leiden: Brill, 2015), 29–45.

## The Bible as Intertext

We begin with two demonstrations of intertextuality in what are at least officially classified as biblical manuscripts. Our first example is a manuscript of Numbers, 4QNum[b].[4] This manuscript contains some interpolations from the book of Deuteronomy in order to provide further explanation of text in which Deuteronomy, in Moses's recapitulation speech, adds additional details not in Numbers. For example, after Num 20:13b, an interpolation from Deut 3:24–28 and 2:2–6 was inserted, before apparently continuing with verse 14.[5]

A further example, in which a supposedly biblical manuscript strays further from the text of Scripture, is in the case of 4QDeut[n].[6] In this text, actually a series of excerpts, Deut 8 precedes Deut 5. Our focus, however, in this example, is on the Sabbath commandment in Deut 5. Indeed, this text is often touted as the earliest example of the Ten Commandments. Here, when we arrive at the Sabbath commandment, we find that the text initially follows Deuteronomy in explaining the command of abstention from work on the Sabbath as resulting from the fact that the Israelites had been slaves in Egypt (Deut 5:15). This social and moral explanation of the Sabbath, specifically as regards giving rest to one's servants and animals, is then immediately continued with reference to the version of the Ten Commandments found in Exod 20 that requires abstention from work to remember that God rested after creating the universe in six days (Exod 20:11). What happened in this text is that two passages from the Hebrew Bible have been conflated to yield a new unity, in a perfect example of intertextuality.[7] In many ways, this example—even though it

---

4. Eugene Ulrich et al., eds., *Qumran Cave 4.VII: Genesis to Numbers*, DJD 12 (Oxford: Clarendon, 1994), 205–67.

5. Ulrich et al., *Qumran Cave 4.VII*, 225–26.

6. Eugene Ulrich et al., eds., *Qumran Cave 4.IX: Deuteronomy, Joshua, Judges, Kings*, DJD 14 (Oxford: Clarendon, 1995), 117–28. Cf. Sidnie A. White Crawford, "4QDt[n]: Biblical Manuscript or Excerpted Text?," in *Of Scribes and Scrolls: Studies on the Hebrew Bible, Intertestamental Judaism, and Christian Origins Presented to John Strugnell on the Occasion of His Sixtieth Birthday*, ed. Harold W. Attridge, John J. Collins, and Thomas H. Tobin (Lanham, MD: University Press of America, 1990), 13–20; Crawford, "The All Souls Deuteronomy and the Decalogue," *JBL* 109 (1990): 193–206; Esther Eshel, "4QDeut[n]: A Text That Has Undergone Harmonistic Editing," *HUCA* 62 (1991): 117–54.

7. The very same identification of the two versions of the Ten Commandments

is in a supposedly biblical text—shows the overall tendency of the scrolls to create what scholars call "rewritten Bible" by adapting the biblical text to other purposes.[8]

Another type of intertextuality takes place when a text quotes directly from the Hebrew Bible, essentially with no modification. In such cases, we always have to remember the existence among the Dead Sea Scrolls, apparently reflecting the situation in the land of Israel in general, of varying text forms of Scripture.[9] Sometimes, therefore, a text at some variance from the MT may be serving as the direct quotation.

---

is found in traditional Jewish ritual in the Friday night Kiddush prayer. In its earliest preserved version, it states that the Sabbath is "a remembrance of the act of creation, first of the holy convocations, a remembrance of the Exodus from Egypt." Amram Gaon, *Seder Rav 'Amram Ga'on*, ed. Daniel S. Goldschmidt (Jerusalem: Mosad Harav Kook, 1971), 66. This idea is framed in the Mekhilta de-Rabbi Ishmael, Yitro 7, which states, "Remember (*zakhor* [Exod 20:7]) and observe (*shamor* [Deut 5:11]) were said in one speech (utterance)" (H. S. Horovitz and I. A. Rabin, eds., *Mekhilta' de-Rabbi Yishma'el*, 2nd ed. [Jerusalem: Bamberger & Wahrman, 1960], 229 and parallels in n. 5). The concept here is that the two versions of the Sabbath command are to be seen as one entity that is constituted of the totality of both versions, all revealed simultaneously by God. The latter motif was later enshrined in the Friday night ritual of Welcoming the Sabbath in the hymn Lekhah Dodi, composed by Shlomo Halevi Alkabetz (ca. 1500–1576). On this hymn, that entered the liturgy in sixteenth century Safed, see Gershom G. Scholem, *On the Kabbalah and Its Symbolism*, trans. Ralph Manheim (New York: Schocken, 1965), 141–42.

8. Moshe J. Bernstein, "Rewritten Bible: A Generic Category Which Has Outlived Its Usefulness?," *Text* 22 (2005): 169–96. Also in Bernstein, *Reading and Re-reading Scripture at Qumran*, STDJ 107 (Leiden: Brill, 2013), 1:39–62; Bernstein, "4Q452: From Rewritten Bible to Bible Commentary," *JJS* 45 (1994): 1–27. Also in Bernstein, *Reading and Re-reading Scripture*, 1:92–125; George J. Brooke, "Genre Theory, Rewritten Bible and Pesher," *DSD* 17 (2010): 361–86; Brooke, "The Genre of 4Q252: From Poetry to Pesher," *DSD* 1 (1994): 160–79; Emanuel Tov, "Rewritten Bible Compositions and Biblical Manuscripts, with Special Attention to the Samaritan Pentateuch," *DSD* 5 (1998): 334–54. For a survey of this genre, see Sidnie A. White Crawford, *Rewriting Scripture in Second Temple Times*, SDSS 1 (Grand Rapids: Eerdmans, 2008).

9. Emanuel Tov, "Groups of Biblical Texts Found at Qumran," in *Time to Prepare the Way in the Wilderness: Papers on the Qumran Scrolls by Fellows of the Institute for Advanced Studies of the Hebrew University, Jerusalem, 1989–1990*, ed. Devorah Dimant and Lawrence H. Schiffman, STDJ 16 (Leiden: Brill, 1995), 85–102; Tov, "The Biblical Texts from the Judaean Desert: An Overview and Analysis," in *The Bible as Book: The Hebrew Bible and the Judaean Desert Discoveries*, ed. Edward D. Herbert and Emanuel Tov (London: Oak Knoll Press, 2002), 139–66.

The Sabbath code in the Zadokite Fragments (Damascus Document) has as its first prescription (CD 10:14–17) to begin the abstention from work on the Sabbath somewhat before the actual setting of the sun on Friday. In order to support this requirement, the text explicitly quotes Deut 5:12.[10] In this case, as in many examples throughout the scrolls, an actual quotation formula is used, כי הוא אשר אמר, "for this is what he said."[11] We will not give many examples since, in these cases, intertextuality is a sort of overstatement—we are dealing with explicit quotation. However, there are other uses of biblical verses that need to be noticed. The Temple Scroll constitutes in itself an exercise in biblical and postbiblical intertextuality.[12] This document represents a rewriting of much of the canonical Torah, starting with the command to build the tabernacle, replaced by a command to build a gargantuan temple, and continuing through the legal and sacrificial sections of the Pentateuch up through the middle of Deuteronomy. Throughout this document, the text combines commands in the various sections of the canonical Torah, thus providing a uniform text and harmonized halakic rulings. For this reason, many of the texts quoted here are in some way modified from their biblical original, even after we take into consideration the textual variants found in Hebrew Bible texts in the Qumran corpus.[13] One example of such a direct quotation with virtually no change is 11QT 65:2–5, the law requiring sending forth the mother bird before taking the young from the nest, simply a representation of Deut 22:6–7.[14] This passage should be contrasted with, for example, the

---

10. For an analysis of this passage, see Lawrence H. Schiffman, *The Halakhah at Qumran*, SJLA 16 (Leiden: Brill, 1975), 84–87.

11. See Moshe J. Bernstein, "Introductory Formulas for Citation and Re-citation of Biblical Verses in the Qumran Pesharim," *DSD* 1 (1994): 30–70.

12. Yigael Yadin, *The Temple Scroll*, 3 vols., rev. ed. (Jerusalem: Israel Exploration Society, 1983); Elisha Qimron, *The Temple Scroll: A Critical Edition with Extensive Reconstructions*, JDS (Jerusalem: Israel Exploration Society, 1996); Lawrence H. Schiffman, Andrew D. Gross, and Michael C. Rand, "Temple Scroll," in *Temple Scroll and Related Documents*, vol. 7 of *The Dead Sea Scrolls: Hebrew, Aramaic, and Greek Texts with English Translations*, ed. James H. Charlesworth, PTSDSSP 7 (Tübingen: Mohr Siebeck; Louisville: Westminster John Knox, 2011), 1–173, 266–405.

13. Yadin, *Temple Scroll*, 1:71–81; cf. Dwight D. Swanson, *The Temple Scroll and the Bible: The Methodology of 11QT*, STDJ 14 (Leiden: Brill, 1995), 9–14.

14. Yadin, *Temple Scroll*, 2:293; see also Lawrence H. Schiffman, *The Courtyards of the House of the Lord: Studies on the Temple Scroll*, ed. Florentino García Martínez, STDJ 75 (Leiden: Brill, 2008), 451–52.

use of Deut 13:2–6, the idolatrous prophet, reflected in 11QT 54:8–18, in which introduction of minor changes is intended to solve specific exegetical problems in the original text of the Hebrew Bible.[15]

Another important place in the scrolls in which direct quotation occurs is in the genre known as pesher, best defined as contemporizing biblical interpretation.[16] Here we have a literary form close to what we have come to expect from a commentary—lemma and explanation (פשר הדבר, "the interpretation of the matter is," or פשרו, "its interpretation is"). However, the interpretations are contemporizing explanations of the biblical passages (some of the Minor Prophets, parts of Isaiah, and a few psalms).[17] Sometimes the interpretations can take their cue from variant readings of the biblical text. This is the case in 1QpHab 1:16–2:5, where three interpretations of Hab 1:5 are all based on the textual reading בגדים, "treacherous ones," where the MT has בגוים, "among the nations."[18] It is possible to explain that one or another reading is a scribal error for the other. This illustrates the possibility that the biblical intertext may be at variance with MT. In any case, we have here a form of intertextuality in which there are explicit quotations and commentaries, but that is only possible in a community that accepted at the same time differing biblical readings.

So far, we have been talking about texts that explicitly quote Scripture. We now move to texts that echo biblical terms and phrases. Here we return to the Sabbath code of the Zadokite Fragments. A quick look at a series of regulations at the beginning of the code (CD 10:17–19)—regarding such issues as proper conversation on the Sabbath, not talking about business on the Sabbath, not conducting financial disputes, and not making preparations for things to be done after the Sabbath—will show that these are clearly based on Isa 58:13. At no point is this text actually quoted. What we have is the use of various words found in this biblical passage to construct the verbiage of the laws of the Dead Sea scroll document.[19] This situation

---

15. Yadin, *Temple Scroll*, 2:243–45; cf. Schiffman, *Courtyards of the House of the Lord*, 476–78.

16. The texts are all collected in Maurya P. Horgan, *Pesharim: Qumran Interpretations of Biblical Books*, CBQMS 8 (Washington, DC: Catholic Biblical Association of America, 1979).

17. Schiffman, *Reclaiming the Dead Sea Scrolls*, 223–31.

18. See B. Nitzan, *Megillat Pesher Ḥabakkuk mi-Megillot Midbar Yehudah (1Qp Hab)* (Jerusalem: Bialik Institute, 1986), 46–51.

19. Schiffman, *Halakhah at Qumran*, 87–90.

is common throughout the various legal codes in the Zadokite Fragments (Damascus Document) and in a variety of other halakic fragments found among the Cave 4 manuscripts. The key point here is not simply that words for these verses have been used to form legal formulations in the Qumran texts. Rather, the point is that close analysis of fragments of biblical verbiage indicates the actual exegetical derivation of the laws expressed in the Second Temple period document. In other words, intertextuality is the key to understanding the legal process. In this context, we should note also that although the early rabbis avoided derivation of such laws from the Prophets, the Dead Sea Scrolls sectarians had no such hesitation. Probably based on the later use of the Prophets in early Christianity, the rabbis adopted a polemical stance not anticipated in any way by the earlier Dead Sea Scrolls sectarians.

The nature of the legal exegesis that we have been discussing seems to have been clearly recognized by the ancient sectarians. The texts explicitly describe two types of law. The "revealed" is simply those laws that can be derived by reading the Bible. The "hidden" law is what can only be derived as a result of inspired biblical exegesis that takes place at the study sessions of the sectarians.[20] In the case of these laws, we can discern a much more sophisticated reading, often involving midrashic exegesis. We will look at a good example of such exegesis now, in which intertextuality occurs on a number of levels. First, biblical verses are linked one to another in an exegetical chain, part of which is a result of common language. Further intertextuality takes place because the verses are quoted, and the legal language of the Qumran text reflects the language of these biblical verses.

A fascinating and complex example of this phenomenon is CD 9:2–8.[21] The passage starts with quoting Lev 19:18, which prohibits taking vengeance or bearing a grudge. It then states that bringing a charge against someone without reproof for a previous offense of the same nature constitutes taking vengeance and bearing a grudge. Nahum 1:2 is then quoted (with intentional omission of the divine name) to prove that only God is permitted to bear a grudge. Finally, the text quotes Lev 19:17 to prove that one who fails to give reproof for a previous offense until he is for some reason angered at the offender violates the Torah's commandment of reproof and brings upon himself the guilt that would otherwise have been visited on the offender.

---

20. Schiffman, *Halakhah at Qumran*, 22–32.
21. Lawrence H. Schiffman, *Sectarian Law in the Dead Sea Scrolls: Courts, Testimony and the Penal Code*, BJS 33 (Chico, CA: Scholars Press, 1983), 89–92.

This legal midrash represents an exegesis of Lev 19:17–18 in light of Nah 1:2. However, the intertextuality is supported by the presence of similar verbiage in these two passages. This is often a feature of legal exegesis in the scrolls, as it was in later rabbinic interpretation. Further, this passage uses three different quotation formulae: "as to that which he said," "is it not written that," and "God who said to him." However, alongside these quotations, some biblical language appears in the author's own composition. Here we observe intertextuality between passages in the Hebrew Bible as well as between the words of the author and his biblical base texts.

A completely different kind of intertextuality takes place in the Genesis Apocryphon.[22] Here there is a form of rewritten Bible in which the biblical text lies at the base of a set of expanded narratives retelling and, in so doing, interpreting and expanding biblical stories.[23] This text, however, is in Aramaic translation. The intertextuality here lies in the relation of the Aramaic translated and expanded text to the Hebrew original. Any reader who knows the book of Genesis will see its Hebrew narratives as the intertextual background for this new and independent Aramaic text. However, someone who did not know the biblical text would feel that he or she was experiencing an independent, continuous narrative. An example of this phenomenon is Genesis Apocryphon 19:14–20. The text relates the content of Gen 12:10–13, in which Abram is commanded to go down to Egypt because of famine and which reports that Abram was concerned for his own safety because of the beauty of his wife Sarai. It then attempts to solve the problem of why Abram would lie about his wife by inserting an account of his having a dream, presumably sent by God, which instructed him to follow this eventually unsuccessful strategy.[24] We should note, however, that some parts of this document contain narratives that seem to have no basis in the biblical text.

Similar rewritten Bible is evident in the book of Jubilees. This Hebrew work from circa 180 BCE also represents expansions of the stories of

---

22. Joseph A. Fitzmyer, *The Genesis Apocryphon of Qumran Cave 1: A Commentary*, BibOr 18A (Rome: Biblical Institute Press, 1971); Daniel A. Machiela, *The Dead Sea Genesis Apocryphon: A New Text and Translation with Introduction and Special Treatment of Columns 13–17*, STDJ 79 (Leiden: Brill, 2009).

23. Moshe J. Bernstein, "Rearrangement, Anticipation and Harmonization as Exegetical Features in the Genesis Apocryphon," *DSD* 3 (1996): 37–57.

24. Machiela, *Dead Sea Genesis Apocryphon*, 70–72; Fitzmyer, *Genesis Apocryphon*, 99, 185–89.

Genesis and early chapters of Exodus.[25] Standing behind this text is certainly the text of Scripture. But here the intenseness of the intertextual experience is much stronger, since the entire text is in an imitation biblical Hebrew style.[26] Even though the work adds throughout the chronological framework of Jubilee years and the overall theme that the patriarchs observed the laws of the Torah, the overall form of the biblical narratives is maintained.[27] However, one sees behind this text two separate sets of biblical material. First, there is the underlying narrative of Genesis–Exodus. To this underlying narrative, there are added ritual descriptions for various holidays, sacrifices, and commandments that in actuality are found later in the Torah, from Exod 12 through Deuteronomy.[28] So here, intertextuality works on two simultaneous levels. There is the weaving together of other Torah material into the Genesis narrative on what might be termed the lower level, and then there is the placing of this material into the framework of the Jubilees narration. So, we can speak here of two-dimensional intertextuality.

Another work that demonstrates a similar two-dimensional intertextuality in many of its passages is the Temple Scroll. In the course of rewriting much of the Pentateuch, the author/redactor gathers up material on the same subject while at the same time making modifications to indicate his own interpretations and legal rulings.[29] So we have intertextuality here operating between related scriptural material, as in the case of

---

25. James C. VanderKam, ed., *The Book of Jubilees*, 2 vols., CSCO 511, SAeth 88 (Leuven: Peeters, 1989). For recent commentaries, see James L. Kugel, *A Walk through Jubilees: Studies in the Book of Jubilees and the World of Its Creation*, JSJSup 156 (Leiden: Brill, 2012), 1–205; C. Werman, *Sefer ha-Yovelim: Mavo', Targum u-Ferush, Between Bible and Mishnah* (Jerusalem: Yad Izhak Ben-Zvi Press, 2015).

26. See the Hebrew fragments in Harold Attridge et al., *Qumran Cave 4.VIII: Parabiblical Texts, Part I*, ed. Emmanuel Tov, DJD 13 (Oxford: Clarendon, 1994), 1–140.

27. See m. Qidd. 4:14 (end); cf. Chanoch Albeck, *Shishah Sidre Mishnah*, 6 vols. (Jerusalem: Bialik Institute; Tel Aviv: Dvir, 1952–59), Nashim, *Hashlamot ve-Tosafot*, 3:416; Albeck, *Das Buch der Jubiläen und die Halacha*, BHWJ 47 (Berlin: Hochschule für die Wissenschaft des Judentums, 1930).

28. It has recently been suggested that the Jewish legal material was added to an earlier layer consisting of rewritten Bible. See Michael Segal, *The Book of Jubilees: Rewritten Bible, Redaction, Ideology and Theology*, JSJSup 117 (Atlanta: Society of Biblical Literature, 2007), 21–46, 317–22; Kugel, *Walk through Jubilees*, 207–26. Werman rightly rejects this thesis (*Sefer ha-Yovelim*, 44–45).

29. Yadin, *Temple Scroll*, 1:73–76.

the harmonization in 11QT 11–29 of the two festival calendars of Lev 23 and Num 28–29.[30] At the same time, we have an intertextual relationship between the biblical material used here and the overall composition that has its own agenda, calling for a reform of the temple, purity law, the sacrificial system, and the Hasmonean government.[31]

Another form of intertextuality present in the scrolls is much subtler. Over and over, biblical terms and expressions are reused to create secondary texts. Some of these secondary texts might even be described as pastiches based on biblical expressions. I have argued that use of a book in this manner indicates the equivalent of what we usually term canonicity, perhaps better described as authority.[32] Examples of this phenomenon are rampant, since biblical language was so prominent in the Qumran compositions. Most scholars assume that because of the intensive study of the texts that we term biblical among the Qumran sectarians, a phenomenon described explicitly by the texts, members of this group would have well recognized many, if not most, of the biblical references.[33] It seems, however, that not all of such experiences should be deemed intertextual. Recognition of a term, for example, used in the Bible and appearing in the scrolls—that is, a lexical item that is common—should not be defined as intertextuality. It simply rises to too low a threshold. This is because it does not call up reference to a text, only to a vocabulary item or perhaps a grammatical form. What we intend to describe as intertextual is a group of words, sometimes only a two-word phrase but sometimes something more extensive, in which the reader or hearer would have immediately made such a connection.

An excellent example of this phenomenon is in the poem at the end of the Rule of the Community (1QS 10–11).[34] One has only to look at

---

30. On the festivals of the Temple Scroll, see Yadin, *Temple Scroll*, 1:89–136; and Schiffman, *Courtyards of the House of the Lord*, 99–122, which discusses the relationship of the festivals in the Temple Scroll to the Book of Jubilees.

31. See Schiffman, *Courtyards of the House of the Lord*, xvii–xxxvi.

32. Schiffman, *Reclaiming the Dead Sea Scrolls*, 162–69.

33. Schiffman, *Halakhah at Qumran*, 32–49, 54–60.

34. Elisha Qimron and James H. Charlesworth, "Rule of the Community," in *Rule of the Community and Related Documents*, vol. 1 of *The Dead Sea Scrolls: Hebrew, Aramaic, and Greek Texts with English Translations*, ed. James H. Charlesworth, PTSDSSP 1 (Tübingen: Mohr Siebeck; Louisville: Westminster John Knox, 1994), 1–52; Qimron, *Megillot Midbar Yehudah: ha-Ḥibburim ha-ʿIvriyim*, Between Bible and Mishnah (Jerusalem: Yad Ben-Zvi Press, 2010), 1:209–34.

the verbiage and expressions to realize that one of the passages (10:9–17) here describes the reading of the Shema ("Hear O Israel," Deut 6:4–9), apparently already an essential part of the Jewish liturgy for the Qumran sectarians.[35] In this example, we see the phrase "to sit down and to rise up" (line 14) that points explicitly to the Deuteronomic phrase, "when you sit in your house and when you go on your way; and when you lie down and when you get up."[36]

It is well known that the only book in our Hebrew Bible for which no manuscript fragment has been found among the Qumran scrolls is Esther. We note here, however, that there are certain passages in the scrolls that have an intertextual relationship with this book, raising the question of what its role may actually have been.[37] We raise this issue here only from the point of view of intertextuality to note that even a book that may have not been part of the library of the sect could have had intertextual relations with later sectarian compositions.

## Second Temple Period Texts as Intertexts

So far, we have been discussing intertextuality in terms of the relationship of Second Temple texts to earlier Hebrew biblical texts. A completely different intertextuality is the relationship of post-Hebrew biblical works one to another. On the surface, given the dependence of these authors on the biblical heritage, we would not have expected to find such a phenomenon. Indeed, I only know of one example in which two Dead Sea Scrolls texts seem to be quoting or directly alluding to a postbiblical text not in our possession.[38] Indeed, some scholars believe that this particular example is actually an allusion of both texts independently to the same biblical *Vorlage*.[39]

---

35. Qimron and Charlesworth, "Rule of the Community," 44–45; Qimron, *Megillot Midbar Yehudah*, 228.

36. Schiffman, *Reclaiming the Dead Sea Scrolls*, 293.

37. Shemaryahu Talmon, "Was the Book of Esther Known at Qumran?," *DSD* 2 (1995): 249–67; Sidnie A. White Crawford, "Has *Esther* Been Found at Qumran? 4QProto-Esther and the *Esther* Corpus," *RevQ* 17 (1996): 307–25.

38. See 1QS 6:27 and CD 9:9–10, which appear to be quoting the same earlier nonbiblical source.

39. Jacob Licht, *Megillat ha-Serakhim mi-Megillot Midbar Yehudah* (Jerusalem: Bialik Institute, 1965), 159–60.

More common, however, is the appearance of some of the same textual blocks of material in more than one composition. For the most part, in such examples, there will of course be differences. However, these differences will look no greater than those normally encountered in multiple manuscripts of the same text. One excellent example is a Code of Punishments for sectarian offenses. This material was known only in fragmentary form from the medieval manuscripts of the Zadokite Fragments (CD 14:17–22), but now, after the full publication of the Qumran corpus, we can speak of having an extensive version of this material from Cave 4.[40] It is closely parallel to, but not exactly the same as, a very similar code found in the Rule of the Community (1QS 7:7–16). A third version of this text is found in the Miscellaneous Rules text.[41] These codes list many of the same offenses and have the same types of punishments, even if at times there are differences between them.[42] What has happened here is that a literary unit—albeit in variant forms—has been placed in several distinct compositions. Trying to untangle the exact relationship of these versions is impossible, but ancient sectarian readers, encountering almost the same material in several texts, must certainly have experienced what we would see as a type of intertextuality.

One further phenomenon deserves to be mentioned, although some may argue that here I have overstepped even my maximalist definition of intertextuality. I refer here to varying recensions of the same work. This phenomenon was already observed in the two medieval manuscripts of the Zadokite Fragments, and so we should not be at all surprised to find it in the Rule of the Community.[43] Examination of the manuscripts of this latter text, only possible with the full release of the scrolls, has indicated

---

40. For a list of Cave 4 manuscripts of the Penal Code, see David Hamidović, *L'Ecrit de Damas: Le manifeste essénien*, CRÉJ 51 (Leuven: Peeters, 2011), 170. He restores the text from Cave 4 on pp. 170–79, although it is not necessary to agree that it extends so far but rather may be assumed to end at his line 24 on p. 174.

41. Joseph M. Baumgarten, "4Q Miscellaneous Rules," in *Qumran Cave 4.XXV: Halakhic Texts*, ed. Emmanuel Tov, DJD 35 (Oxford: Clarendon, 1999), 57–78.

42. Schiffman, *Sectarian Law in the Dead Sea Scrolls*, 155–90; Sarianna Metso, *The Textual Development of the Qumran Community Rule*, STDJ 21 (Leiden: Brill, 1997), 124–28; Metso, *The Serekh Texts*, LSTS 62, CQS 9 (London: T&T Clark, 2007), 12; Charlotte Hempel, *The Laws of the Damascus Document: Sources, Tradition and Redaction*, STDJ 29 (Leiden: Brill, 1998), 163–70.

43. Sidnie A. White Crawford, "A Comparison of the 'A' and 'B' Manuscripts of the *Damascus Document*," RQ 12 (1987): 537–53.

clearly that this text circulated in different recensions and that, as suspected by some earlier scholars, it had a complex literary history.[44] Another excellent example of this phenomenon is the existence of two recensions of the Scroll of the War of the Sons of Light against the Sons of Darkness.[45] Here we have two very clear recensions, without even mentioning the complex literary history of the text.[46]

What remains, however, is to explain this phenomenon as intertextuality. I make the assumption that the varying recensions of the text continued to circulate in the community and that the older recensions were not retired. This means that members of the group encountered at different times different versions of the same texts.[47] These texts were understood as relating to one another in some kind of dynamic manner, being at once the same and different. There is evidence from some marginal corrections in these manuscripts that efforts were even made to correct one text in light of the other.[48]

This summary has only scratched the surface regarding the phenomenon, or better phenomena, of intertextuality in the Dead Sea Scrolls. We have not even touched on the complex issues pertaining to copying and editing biblical and postbiblical texts, marginal glosses, and the comparison of manuscripts that apparently lies behind them. Indeed, one could say that the entire effort of the ancient Qumran sectarians was an effort of intertextuality. In seeking to modulate the biblical tradition into a Second Temple key, the authors of the various Dead Sea Scrolls remained tied to the Hebrew Bible even more closely than they may have been tied

---

44. Only a partial list of variants had previously been released. See, J. T. Milik, "Texte des variants des dix manuscrits de la Règle del Communauté trouvés dans la grotte 4," *RB* 67 (1960): 411–16. On its complex literary history, see Crawford, *Rewriting Scripture*, 69–155; Metso, *Serekh Texts*, 15–19.

45. Esther Eshel and Hanan Eshel, "Recensions and Editions of the War Scroll," in *The Dead Sea Scrolls: Fifty Years after Their Discovery; Proceedings of the Jerusalem Congress, July 20–25, 1997*, ed. Lawrence H. Schiffman, Emanuel Tov, and James C. VanderKam (Jerusalem: Israel Exploration Society, 2000), 351–63.

46. Philip R. Davies, *1QM, the War Scroll from Qumran: Its Structure and History*, BibOr 32 (Rome: Biblical Institute Press, 1977).

47. See Eugene Ulrich, *The Dead Sea Scrolls and the Origins of the Bible*, SDSS (Grand Rapids: Eerdmans; Leiden: Brill, 1999), 34–50, 99–120 for this phenomenon in the case of biblical books.

48. See Emanuel Tov, *Scribal Practices and Approaches Reflected in the Texts Found in the Judean Desert*, STDJ 54 (Leiden: Brill, 2004), 2–25.

to postbiblical compositions. The many ways in which biblical texts are reflected in the scrolls as well as the ways in which scrolls' compositions relate to one another can all be described as intertextual. Indeed, it is safe to say that Judaism as a whole could be chronicled as a history of texts and intertexts, extending from the earliest biblical materials down to the present. In such a chain of the tradition of intertextuality, the Qumran scrolls would constitute our earliest Hebrew documentation outside of Scripture. Indeed, the self-aware manner in which Qumran sectarians and other Second Temple period authors reworked and drew on biblical ideas and biblical phraseology raises one final question: Is it possible that intertextuality is simply a complex word for phenomena that were just second nature to ancient Jewish authors? Perhaps "there is nothing new under the sun" (Eccl 1:9).

# Intertextuality and Canonical Criticism: Lamentations 3:25–33 in an Intertextual Network

*Marianne Grohmann*

This paper addresses basic theoretical questions relating to the intersection between intertextuality and canonical criticism. As a case study for thinking about these general questions, a text from the book of Lamentations, Lam 3:25–33, will be read in intertextual relationship to other parts of the Hebrew Bible and its interpretation, including both the New Testament and rabbinic literature.

## Intertextuality and Canonical Criticism

About fifty years after Julia Kristeva and others initialized ongoing discussions about intertextuality, it is still relevant to ask about the remaining potential and problems of this concept in research on the Hebrew Bible. The endless discussions about intertextuality have two poles: a broad concept of intertextuality claiming that "all texts are a 'mosaic' of marked and unmarked citations from earlier texts" and a narrower understanding that describes citations, echoes, and allusions as more or less explicit references between texts.[1]

---

I am grateful to the participants in the Consultation Intertextuality and the Hebrew Bible at the Annual Meeting of the Society of Biblical Literature in Atlanta 2015, where a first version of this paper was presented and discussed. My thanks go to Eve Levavi Feinstein, Jeanine Lefèvre, and Karoline Rumpler for support in the editing process.

1. For the former, see Daniel Boyarin, *Intertextuality and the Reading of Midrash*, ISBL (Bloomington: Indiana University Press, 1994), 19; for the latter, see Richard B. Hays, *Echoes of Scripture in the Letters of Paul* (New Haven: Yale University Press, 1993).

Patricia K. Tull defines intertextuality as follows:

> Intertextuality is more an angle of vision on textual production and reception than an exegetical methodology, more an insight than an ideology. But by removing artificially imposed boundaries between texts and texts, between texts and readers, by attending to the dialogical nature of all speech, intertextual theory invites new ventures in cultural and literary perception that will certainly introduce shifts in the ways biblical scholarship is carried out for many years to come.[2]

Intertextuality has become a useful concept for describing innerbiblical interpretation. In contrast to redaction history, the concept of intertextuality hints at three characteristics of the relationship between texts:

1. Instead of asking about source and influence, the concept of intertextuality looks at the text as a process of production.
2. Every text is part of a network of references to other texts (intertexts).
3. The reader plays a prominent role in the interpretation of texts.[3]

Marvin A. Sweeney refers to three major types of intertextual work, which are currently used in the field of biblical studies:

1. the citation of biblical texts,
2. the sequential reading of biblical texts within a single work, and
3. the dialogical reading of texts in relation to other texts.

He tries to combine the concept of intertextuality with a diachronic reading.[4]

---

2. Patricia K. Tull, "Intertextuality and the Hebrew Scriptures," *CurBS* 8 (2000): 83; see also her contribution in this volume.

3. Willem S. Vorster, "Intertextuality and Redaktionsgeschichte," in *Intertextuality in Biblical Writings: Essays in Honour of Bas van Iersel*, ed. Sipke Draisma (Leuven: Peeters, 1989), 21; Steve Moyise, "Intertextuality and Biblical Studies: A Review," *VEcc* 23 (2002): 418–31.

4. Marvin A. Sweeney, "Synchronic and Diachronic Concerns in Reading the

In combination with the reconstruction of the historical and literary context of a text, intertextuality provides an additional angle of vision to the dialogical character of all texts. Every text of the Hebrew Bible opens a window to other biblical texts and to postbiblical interpretations. Intertextuality as a perspective on the relationship between texts in the Hebrew Bible and their ongoing interpretation shares some characteristics with canonical criticism but also differs from it in significant ways.

On the one hand, the concept of intertextuality enables the inclusion of the different Jewish and Christian contexts of reading and the perspectives of different canons. "All canonical texts have an intertextual disposition independent from their intratextually perceptible references to other texts. The canon itself establishes this hermeneutical possibility. The biblical canon sets the individual writings in new relationships, and it is precisely this intertextual connection that alters the meaning potential of the individual writings."[5] In addition to the historic analysis of echoes, allusions, and citations, an intertextual perspective adds the mutuality of the reading process. Different canons make different intertextual links possible. The concept of intertextuality includes the reader: In the interactive process of reading, readers link texts with each other and with their own world.

The rabbinic readers and the authors of New Testament writings combine texts from the Hebrew Bible with their own world and context. Canon is a result of dialogue: "a canon … presupposes the possibility of correlations among its parts, such that new texts may imbed, reuse, or otherwise allude to precursor materials—both as a strategy for meaning-making, and for establishing the authority of a given innovation."[6]

On the other hand, the concept of intertextuality, especially in its broader sense, stands in tension with the notion of a canon. By calling into question the borders between canonical texts and their interpretations, it undermines the idea of canonical boundaries and challenges the distinc-

---

Book of the Twelve Prophets," in *Perspectives on the Formation of the Book of the Twelve*, ed. Rainer Albertz, James Nogalski, and Jakob Wöhrle, BZAW 433 (Berlin: de Gruyter, 2012), 21–33. According to Moyise, we can classify five types of intertextuality: intertextual echo, narrative, and exegetical, dialogical, and postmodern intertextuality ("Intertextuality and Biblical Studies," 419–28).

5. Stefan Alkier, "Intertextuality and the Semiotics of Biblical Texts," in *Reading the Bible Intertextually*, ed. Richard B. Hays, Stefan Alkier, and Leroy A. Huizenga (Waco, TX: Baylor University Press, 2009), 11–12.

6. Michael Fishbane, "Types of Biblical Intertextuality," VT 80 (2000): 39.

tion between text and commentary.⁷ In addition, *canon* is a postbiblical Christian term.⁸ The special relationship between the Old Testament and the New Testament has no exact parallel in the relationship between the Hebrew Bible and rabbinic literature. Nevertheless, the concept of intertextuality allows seeing parallel processes on both sides. A combination of intertextuality and canonical criticism makes it possible to integrate the perspective of reading communities into exegesis. Nevertheless, the search for historic interpretation of a text in its original context remains the primary goal of exegesis.

Below, one text from the Hebrew Bible, Lam 3:25–33, will serve as an example for an intertextual approach. It will first be read in its own context, then in an intertextual network with other texts from the Hebrew Bible. Finally, it will be interpreted from a New Testament perspective and in context of rabbinic intertextuality.

## Lamentations 3:25–33

The parenetic text Lam 3:25–33 has its origin in the postexilic community. Lamentations 3 is usually dated later than Lam 1, 2, and 4. As a postexilic reaction to Lam 2, it may be the latest of the five poems. Arguments for this late dating are the elaboration of the acrostic style (three lines beginning with every letter of the Hebrew alphabet) and the familiarity with many traditions of the Hebrew Bible, mainly from the Prophets and Psalms.⁹ The "double-voicing" of different, sometimes contradictory approaches is a deliberate literary device to create a dialogic

---

7. Marianne Grohmann, "Psalm 113 and the Song of Hannah (1 Samuel 2:1–10): A Paradigm for Intertextual Reading?," in *Reading the Bible Intertextually*, ed. Richard B. Hays, Stefan Alkier, and Leroy A. Huizenga (Waco, TX: Baylor University Press, 2009), 119.

8. Stefan Alkier, "Reading the Canon Intertextually: The Decentralization of Meaning," in *Between Text and Text: The Hermeneutics of Intertextuality in Ancient Cultures and Their Afterlife in Medieval and Modern Times*, ed. Michaela Bauks, Wayne Horowitz, and Armin Lange, JAJSup 6 (Göttingen: Vandenhoeck & Ruprecht, 2013), 288.

9. Christian Frevel, *Die Klagelieder*, NSKAT 20.1 (Stuttgart: Katholisches Bibelwerk, 2017), 39, justifies this late dating with parallels in the style of argumentation in postexilic poetry such as Ps 77 and Isa 63:7–64:11; Ulrich Berges, *Klagelieder*, HThKAT (Freiburg im Breisgau: Herder, 2002), 43.

polyphony, especially in wisdom-like units.[10] The parenetic and didactic character of Lam 3:25–33 parallels Deuteronomistic concepts and elements of wisdom.[11] In Lam 3:25–33, we find an external voice talking about the "man" (גבר) who speaks in first-person in the first part of the poem (Lam 3:1–24).[12] The verses contain general statements about an anonymous גבר—representing the whole people of Israel, "the personified voice of the exile."[13]

The different voices in Lam 3 express a discourse that can be paralleled with the dialogic interaction of externally authoritative and internally persuasive discourse described by Mikhail M. Bakhtin.[14] The language in Lam 3:25–33 is impersonal, presented in proverbial formulations: "Reading as an internal dialogue, here the גבר recollects earlier aphorisms, relying on traditional explanations for the way things 'work' in the world."[15] Lamentations 3 combines descriptions of suffering with theological challenges to the suffering. The different voices are juxtaposed without being reconciled.[16] In this context, Lam 3:25–33 recommends a behavior of patience, humility, and forbearance in situations of violence:

25 טוב יהוה לקוו לנפש תדרשנו
26 טוב ויחיל ודומם לתשועת יהוה
27 טוב לגבר כי־ישא על בנעוריו:

---

10. Elizabeth Boase, *The Fulfilment of Doom? The Dialogic Interaction between the Book of Lamentations and the Pre-exilic/Early Exilic Prophetic Literature*, LHBOTS 437 (New York: T&T Clark, 2006), 207.

11. Claus Westermann, *Die Klagelieder: Forschungsgeschichte und Auslegung* (Neukirchen-Vluyn: Neukirchener Verlag, 1990), 187; Boase, *Fulfilment of Doom?*, 43.

12. Adele Berlin, *Lamentations: A Commentary*, OTL (Louisville: Westminster John Knox, 2002), 84, ascribes the whole of Lam 3 to the voice of "a lone male, speaking in the first person, about what he has seen and felt and what sense he can make of it."

13. For other theories concerning the identity of the גבר in Lam 3—for example, the identification with a historical person, either the prophet Jeremiah, King Jehoiakim, or King Zedekiah—see Kim Lan Nguyen, *Chorus in the Dark: The Voices of the Book of Lamentations*, HBM 54 (Sheffield: Sheffield Phoenix, 2013), 125–53; and Boase, *Fulfilment of Doom?*, 223–24; quotation from Berlin, *Lamentations*, 84.

14. Miriam J. Bier, "'We Have Sinned and Rebelled; You Have Not Forgiven': The Dialogic Interaction between Authoritative and Internally Persuasive Discourse in Lamentations 3," *BibInt* 22 (2014): 146–67.

15. Bier, "We Have Sinned and Rebelled," 158.

16. See Berlin, *Lamentations*, 86.

28 ישב בדד וידם כי נטל עליו:
29 יתן בעפר פיהו אולי יש תקוה:
30 יתן למכהו לחי ישבע בחרפה:
31 כי לא יזנח לעולם אדני:
32 כי אם־הוגה ורחם כרב (חסדו) [חסדיו]:
33 כי לא ענה מלבו ויגה בני־איש:

25 The LORD is good to those who wait for him, to the soul that seeks him.
26 It is good that one should wait quietly for the salvation of the LORD.
27 It is good for one to bear the yoke in youth,
28 to sit alone in silence when the Lord has imposed it,
29 to put one's mouth to the dust (there may yet be hope),
30 to give one's cheek to the smiter, and be filled with insults.[17]
31 For the Lord will not reject forever.
32 Although he causes grief, he will have compassion according to the abundance of his steadfast love;
33 for he does not willingly afflict or grieve anyone. (NRSV)

These verses urge endurance of suffering in the hope of a change of fate. The behaviors and images recommended here are negative signs of defeat in other contexts:

1. the yoke (Lam 1:14; Prov 20:23): The yoke usually has negative connotations, as a symbol for hard work in agriculture (Deut 21:3); the yoke of foreign rulers (Gen 27:40; Isa 9:3; 10:27); and the yoke of exile (Isa 47:6; Jer 28:4);
2. sitting alone (Lam 1:1);
3. putting one's mouth in the dust (Lam 3:16); and
4. the shame of having the cheek struck (Job 16:10).

These symbols assume some positive connotations in Lam 3:25–33, where they take on a meaning that is intensified in Jewish tradition, such as in the targum: "Jewish tradition views God's commandments as 'yoke,' and the phrase is interpreted this way in the Targum."[18]

---

17. My translation is: "He will give the cheek to the one smiting him, he will become sated/satisfied with insult/shame/reproach." The LXX translates this verse in the following way: δώσει τῷ παίοντι αὐτὸν σιαγόνα χορτασθήσεται ὀνειδισμῶν.

18. Berlin, *Lamentations*, 94.

In Lam 3:25–33, we find an admonition to accept the suffering that comes from YHWH. The text gives a perspective of hope for those who accept God's judgement.[19] Lamentations 3:30 leaves open to interpretation who the "smiter" is: humans (enemies) or God. While God is mentioned as the cause of the insults in the broader context—but not in verse 30—the targum introduces him to the verse itself: "Let him offer his cheek to him that smites him. Because of the fear of YHWH let him accept insult."[20]

The word לחי does not only mean "cheek" but includes "chin" and "lower jaw" as well.[21] "The paraphrase makes clear that the suffering consists of God's punishment; not acceptance of the persecutor's blows, but acceptance of God's punishment warrants the 'turning of the cheek.' This point was already made by the Targum in the preceding verses, with great specificity in v. 29 where 'his Master' is mentioned."[22]

The parallelism in Lam 3:30—giving one's cheek to the smiter and being filled/sated with insults/shame—stresses not the physical assault but the social and emotional consequence of it, the aspect of humiliation. A strike in the face is an expression of deep humiliation (Job 16:10) and public chastisement (Mic 4:14).[23]

## Intertextual Links to Other Texts in the Hebrew Bible

The book of Lamentations has manifold intertextual links to other books of the Hebrew Bible, including Psalms, Leviticus, and Ezekiel. In the field of Hebrew Bible, intertextuality is similar to inner-biblical interpretation, an area of study that has been developed by Michael Fishbane and others. While inner-biblical interpretation is a one-way concept, intertextuality considers the dialogue between texts as a communication in two directions.

Lamentations 3 combines many elements from other texts of the Hebrew Bible. For example, in Isa 50:6, a verse in the third song of the

---

19. Hans Jochen Boecker, *Klagelieder*, ZBK 21 (Zurich: TVZ, 1985), 67.
20. Etan Levine, *The Aramaic Version of Lamentations* (New York: Hermon, 1981), 70.
21. Klaus Koenen, *Klagelieder (Threni)*, BKAT 20.4 (Neukirchen-Vluyn: Neukirchener Verlag, 2015), 254.
22. Levine, *Aramaic Version of Lamentations*, 141.
23. Frevel, *Klagelieder*, 232.

servant in Second Isaiah (Isa 50:4–9), we find a parallel to the behavior of turning or giving one's cheek to smiters, in different words:[24]

גוי נתתי למכים ולחיי למרטים פני לא הסתרתי מכלמות ורק:
I gave my back to those who struck me, and my cheeks to those who pulled out[25] the beard; I did not hide my face from insult and spitting. (Isa 50:6 NRSV)
τὸν νῶτόν μου δέδωκα εἰς μάστιγας τὰς δὲ σιαγόνας μου εἰς ῥαπίσματα τὸ δὲ πρόσωπόν μου οὐκ ἀπέστρεψα ἀπὸ αἰσχύνης ἐμπτυσμάτων. (Isa 50:6 LXX)

While Lam 3:30 might include both human strikes and God as causes of suffering, in Isa 50:6 mainly human strikes (probably by enemies) are addressed—מכים meaning both smites and smiters.[26] Isaiah 50:6 and Lam 3:30 are the only places in the Hebrew Bible where we find a combination of נתן + ל + מכה.[27]

A Qumran text (1QIsaᵃ) has an interesting different reading here: מטלים, "those who bring to fall/let down" (from נטל or טול).[28] The LXX reads: μάστιγας ("whips/scourges/afflictions"). Approaches to exegesis that are informed by theories of intertextuality can highlight the value of permitting different textual witnesses (e.g., the MT, the LXX, and Qumran texts) to be read alongside one another and thereby set in dialogue.[29] It is useful to understand textual criticism as an intertextual dialogue of different versions more than a search for the earliest available form of the text, which is hard to reconstruct.

Regarding the intention of Lam 3:30 and the whole context, Prov 20:22 is another close parallel:

---

24. Hans-Jürgen Hermisson, *Deuterojesaja*, BKAT 11.13 (Neukirchen-Vluyn: Neukirchener Verlag, 2008), 113.
25. Another possible translation of מרטים is "those who make bare."
26. Boecker, *Klagelieder*, 67.
27. Koenen, *Klagelieder*, 254.
28. Edward Yechezkel Kutscher, *The Language and Linguistic Background of the Isaiah Scroll (1Q Isaᵃ)*, STDJ 6 (Leiden: Brill, 1974), 255–56; Johannes Hempel, "Zu Jes 50,6," *ZAW* 76 (1964): 327.
29. Ulrike Bail, "Psalm 110: Eine intertextuelle Lektüre aus alttestamentlicher Perspektive," in *Heiligkeit und Herrschaft*, ed. Dieter Sänger, BTSt 55 (Neukirchen-Vluyn: Neukirchener Verlag, 2003), 94–121.

אל־תאמר אשלמה־רע קוה ליהוה וישע לך:
Do not say, "I will repay evil"; wait for the LORD, and he will help you. (Prov 20:22 NRSV)

Lamentations 3:30 opens another intertextual relationship to Job 16:10:

פערו עלי בפיהם בחרפה הכו לחיי יחד עלי יתמלאון
They have gaped at me with their mouths; they have struck me insolently on the cheek; they mass themselves together against me. (Job 16:10 NRSV)[30]

These texts reflect the common view that striking the cheek is combined with shame and degradation (חרפה). The subject is צרי, "my enemy" (Job 16:9). While Job 16:10 states that striking someone's cheek comes with reproach (בחרפה), Lam 3:30 recommends a behavior in which the shame is swallowed: one should become sated/satisfied by reproach/insult/shame. The texts highlight a human behavior of accepting injury and humiliation.

Intertextual Links from Lam 3:25–33 to the New Testament

Although Isa 50:6 and Lam 3:30 describe nonresistance to an evildoer, this behavior is presented as an antithesis in the Sermon on the Mount in Matt 5:38–39:

38 Ἠκούσατε ὅτι ἐρρέθη· ὀφθαλμὸν ἀντὶ ὀφθαλμοῦ καὶ ὀδόντα ἀντὶ ὀδόντος. 39 ἐγὼ δὲ λέγω ὑμῖν μὴ ἀντιστῆναι τῷ πονηρῷ· ἀλλ' ὅστις σε ῥαπίζει εἰς τὴν δεξιὰν σιαγόνα [σου], στρέψον αὐτῷ καὶ τὴν ἄλλην·
38 You have heard that it was said, "An eye for an eye and a tooth for a tooth." 39 But I say to you, Do not resist an evildoer. But if anyone strikes you on the right cheek, turn the other also. (Matt 5:38–39 NRSV)

Verse 38 presents a citation from the LXX including an introduction formula. Verse 39a offers a general ethical principle—μὴ ἀντιστῆναι τῷ πονηρῷ ("do not resist an evildoer")—as Jesus-tradition.[31] Verse 39b gives a first

---

30. My translation is: "They opened their mouths widely against me, with reproach they struck my cheek, they mass themselves together against me."

31. Concerning the origin and background of this text, see, for example, Martin Ebner, "Feindesliebe—Ein Ratschlag zum Überleben? Sozial- und religionsgeschichtliche Überlegungen zu Mt 5,38–47 par Lk 6,27–35," in *From Quest to Q: Festschrift*

example for this maxim, which is followed by others in verses 40–42.³² Usually, this well-known text is not associated with Lam 3:30 but with other texts from the Hebrew Bible. By creating an intertextual link to the torah of retaliation עין תחת עין ("eye for eye"; Exod 21:24; Lev 24:20; Deut 19:21), it puts a verse that is well-known from the biblical background in the context of an opposition. We find one version of the *lex talionis* in Exod 21:22–27:

22 וכי־ינצו אנשים ונגפו אשה הרה ויצאו ילדיה ולא יהיה אסון ענוש יענש כאשר ישית עליו בעל האשה ונתן בפללים:
23 ואם־אסון יהיה ונתתה נפש תחת נפש:
24 עין תחת עין שן תחת שן יד תחת יד רגל תחת רגל:
25 כויה תחת כויה פצע תחת פצע חבורה תחת חבורה:
26 וכי־יכה איש את־עין עבדו או־את־עין אמתו ושחתה לחפשי ישלחנו תחת עינו:
27 ואם־שן עבדו או־שן אמתו יפיל לחפשי ישלחנו תחת שנו:

> 22 When people who are fighting injure a pregnant woman so that there is a miscarriage,³³ and yet no further harm follows, the one responsible shall be fined what the woman's husband demands, paying as much as the judges determine. 23 If any harm follows, then you shall give life for life, 24 eye for eye, tooth for tooth, hand for hand, foot for foot, 25 burn for burn, wound for wound, stripe for stripe. 26 When a slaveowner strikes the eye of a male or female slave, destroying it, the owner shall let the slave go, a free person, to compensate for the eye. 27 If the owner knocks out a tooth of a male or female slave, the slave shall be let go, a free person, to compensate for the tooth. (NRSV)

An intertextual approach to the Bible highlights that the citation of a few keywords in Matt 5:38 opens a window to the whole context in Exod 21:22–27. The textual context clarifies that עין תחת עין ("eye for eye") is not a general principle of the Old Testament, as it is often seen to be, but a "law" in the sense of תורה ("torah/teaching") in concrete cases of bodily

---

*James M. Robinson*, ed. Jon M. Asgeirsson, Kristin de Troyer, and Marvin W. Meyer, BETL 146 (Leuven: Peeters, 2000), 119–42; John P. Meier, *A Marginal Jew: Rethinking the Historical Jesus*, vol. 4 (New Haven: Yale University Press, 2009), 613–16, 622.

32. Ulrich Luz, *Das Evangelium nach Matthäus*, EKKNT 1.1 (Zurich: Benziger, 2002), 390–91.

33. The Hebrew word אסון can be interpreted as "miscarriage," but it refers to "damage/mischief/evil/harm" in a more general way as well. It is not clear whether the "harm" affects the child or the mother.

injury. This torah tries to find a solution for a forensic problem, namely special cases of bodily harm that lead to injury or death.[34] The *lex talionis* has parallels in the Code of Hammurabi (e.g., §§209–214; eighteenth century BCE), which lists different cases of physical injury requiring different punishments, including physical damage and financial compensation. In this context, the intention of the biblical *lex talionis* is a limitation of excessive violence.[35] The text in the Hebrew Bible is thus already open to being interpreted either literally or as referring to pecuniary compensation with the value of an eye, tooth, foot, and so on; ונתתה ("you shall give") in Exod 21:23 can be read as an allusion to pecuniary damage compensation. The preposition תחת ("for") can be translated as "instead of," thus highlighting the idea of substitution.[36]

The intention of Exod 21:22–27 is to interrupt the cycle of revenge and replace it with the concept of balanced compensation and responsibility; the bodily injury of different persons shall be settled by compensation for their value, not by the same physical assault.[37] The text aims at reduction of violence, compensation for damage, and reparation.[38]

Richard B. Hays's distinction between quotation, echo, and allusion has become standard in research on intertextuality.[39] The criteria for intertextual relationships between the Old Testament and New Testament—availability, volume, recurrence, thematic coherence, historical plausibility, history of interpretation, and satisfaction—are only useful for texts with close linguistic correspondences. In our example, they make sense for the citation at the beginning. The introduction in Matt 5:38, "You have heard that it was said," marks the following clause, "an eye for an eye and a tooth for a tooth," explicitly as a citation.

---

34. Frank Crüsemann, "'Auge um Auge…' (Ex 21,24f): Zum sozialgeschichtlichen Sinn des Talionsgesetzes im Bundesbuch," *EvT* 47 (1987): 411–26.

35. This line of interpretation has a long tradition: see, for example, Tertullian, *Marc.* 4.16.

36. Benno Jacob, *Das Buch Exodus* (Stuttgart: Calwer, 1997), 668; cf. the translation "Augersatz für Auge," in *Die fünf Bücher der Weisung*, trans. Martin Buber and Franz Rosenzweig, 10th ed. (Stuttgart: Deutsche Bibelgesellschaft, 1992), 209.

37. Manfred Oeming, "Vom Eigenwert des Alten Testaments als Wort Gottes," in *Gottes Wort im Menschenwort: Die eine Bibel als Fundament der Theologie*, ed. Karl Lehmann and Ralf Rothenbusch, QD 266 (Freiburg im Breisgau: Herder, 2014), 333.

38. Eckart Otto, *Das Gesetz des Mose* (Darmstadt: Wissenschaftliche Buchgesellschaft, 2007), 166–70.

39. Hays, *Echoes of Scripture*, 29–32.

The guidance that follows not to withstand evil and to turn one's cheek to the smiter is presented as the word of Jesus, in antithesis to the citation of Exod 21:24 (Lev 24:20; Deut 19:21). In Hays's classification, it could be an echo of texts from the Hebrew Bible: Lam 3:30; Isa 50:6; and Prov 20:22. The only word that is used both in Matt 5:39 and Lam 3:30 LXX is σιαγών ("cheek"). The behavior is described in different words but reflects the same idea. While Lam 3:30 speaks only of the לחי ("cheek"), Matt 5:39 specifies the right cheek, which means a strike with the back of the hand, an even harder attack. Considering this context, it is plausible to understand δέ at the beginning of Matt 5:39 more as an addition in the sense of "and" than as a marker of contrast ("but").

Matthew 5:38–39 presents Jesus as a teacher of the torah who refers to the legal principle of appropriate punishment, as formulated in the Hebrew Bible in Exod 21:24; Lev 24:20; and Lev 24:20, and outside the Bible in the Code of Hammurabi. Already inside the Bible, there are hints that this measure is thought of as a general principle and refers to monetary compensation (Exod 21:18–19; 22:30). The concept of intertextuality enables us to see the biblical background of Matt 5:38–39. The principle of not resisting an evildoer has precedent in the Hebrew Bible, as we have seen in Lam 3:30 and Isa 50:6. While Isa 50:6 deals with human strikes and Lam 3:30 suggests that God is the cause of human strikes, it is clear in Matt 5:38–39 that human strikes are the focus.

## Rabbinic Intertextuality

The question of whether *lex talionis* is to be interpreted literally or as referring to pecuniary compensation figures in early Jewish and rabbinic writings. Josephus is aware of both possibilities: a literal understanding and monetary compensation (*A.J.* 4.280). Targum Pseudo-Jonathan explains Exod 21:24 as follows: "the equivalent value [דמי] of an eye for an eye."

It is helpful to read the so-called antithesis in Matt 5:38–39 intertextually with rabbinic interpretations. The Mishnah gives clear regulations regarding remunerations: compensation for damage, compensation for pain and suffering, costs for curative treatment, and money for absenteeism and humiliation (m. B. Qam. 8:1). In the Gemara, the rabbis gather arguments in favor of monetary compensation and against the literal meaning of "an eye for an eye" (b. B. Qam. 83b–84a; cf. Midrash Sipra).

Yet the rabbinic literature also contains much detail about what sort of restitution, if any, one needed to make for having either injured and/or humiliated another. The literature also speaks of the many ways in which one can injure and/or humiliate another, but the main examples are injuring the eye (which for the Rabbis meant both damage as well as physical pain); slapping (which meant pained embarrassment); and garment-taking (which meant embarrassment).[40]

A look at rabbinic texts clarifies that עין תחת עין never was understood in a literal sense but always as referring to monetary compensation.[41]

The behavior recommended in Matt 5:39 is to relinquish this right in some cases, not to go to court against an evildoer who caused one damage. The concrete example mentioned is getting involved in a fight. In accordance with biblical and rabbinic tradition, the ability to relinquish the right to compensation has its root in trust in God (Prov 20:22; b. Shabb. 88b; b. Git. 36b).[42] The verse contains an ethical guideline, not a new legal ruling.[43] "Matt 5:39b–41 describes metaphorically the extent of nonretaliation. One who has suffered insult and harm is called upon not just to tolerate what the evil assailant did to him. Rather, by turning the other cheek … he should be willing to accept twice the amount of harm that was done to him."[44]

In the Babylonian Talmud, a similar behavior is recommended by the rabbis:

תנו רבנן הנעלבין ואינן עולבים שומעין חרפתן ואין משיבין עושין מאהבה ושמחין ביסורין עליהן הכתוב אומר (שופטים ה, לא) ואוהביו כצאת השמש בגבורתו
Our Rabbis taught: They who suffer insults but do not inflict them, who hear their disgrace and do not answer, who act from love and rejoice in chastisement, of such the Scripture says, "May your friends [lovers] be like the sun as it rises in its might" (Judg 5:31). (b. Git. 36b)

---

40. Herbert W. Basser, *The Gospel of Matthew and Judaic Traditions: A Relevance-Based Commentary*, BRLA 46 (Leiden: Brill, 2015), 156.

41. Luz, *Evangelium nach Matthäus*, 391.

42. Peter Fiedler, *Das Matthäusevangelium*, THKNT 1 (Stuttgart: Kohlhammer, 2006), 145–47.

43. Luz, *Evangelium nach Matthäus*, 391.

44. Reinhard Neudecker, *Moses Interpreted by the Pharisees and Jesus: Matthew's Antitheses in the Light of Early Rabbinic Literature*, SubBi 44 (Rome: Gregorian & Biblical, 2012), 105–6.

This rabbinic interpretation creates an intertextual link to Judg 5:31, where the friends are contrasted with the enemies mentioned at the beginning of the verse:

כן יאבדו כל־אויביך יהוה ואהביו כצאת השמש בגברתו ותשקט הארץ ארבעים שנה

"So perish all your enemies, O Lord! But may your friends be like the sun as it rises in its might." And the land had rest forty years. (Judg 5:31 NRSV)

The verse resembles חרפה in Job 16:10, cited above. Reading Lam 3:30 as an intertext for Matt 5:38–39 stresses the aspect of insult because it introduces the moral aspect of striking the cheek as an expression of emotional and social insult: "The parallel of cheek/insults drives home the point that Matthew's 'striking the cheek' is an expression of insult rather than physical damage."[45]

Intertextuality characterizes rabbinic exegesis (and perhaps much of Jewish exegesis) in general: rabbinic exegesis has a special interest in and sensitivity to the interconnectedness of texts. It uses texts from the Hebrew Bible in different senses and contexts without reducing their meaning to one aspect.[46] Rabbinic intertextuality finds a balance in the tension between canonical criticism and intertextuality. Having a special interest in and sensitivity to the interconnectedness of texts, the rabbis use texts from different parts of the Hebrew canon and bring them together in a new text.

This network of texts relativizes the antithesis in Matt 5:38–39 and shows that this New Testament text fits well in the framework of rabbinic exegesis. "It is sound to assume that at the time of the New Testament the biblical *lex talionis* was not practiced according to its literal meaning and that physical harm to a person was settled by pecuniary penalties."[47] It is reasonable to understand the New Testament discourse against the background of early Jewish and rabbinic interpretation of Scripture. Placing Matt 5:38–39 in a wider intertextual network than the cited text from the Old Testament shows that the "antithesis" is a rhetorical strategy. The recommended behavior is not as new as presented but has a firm basis in the Hebrew Bible (Isa 50:6; Lam 3:25–33; Job 16:10) and in rabbinic literature.

---

45. Basser, *Gospel of Matthew and Judaic Traditions*, 157.
46. Alexander Samely, "Art. Intertextualität IV. Judaistisch," *LB*, 303.
47. Neudecker, *Moses Interpreted by the Pharisees and Jesus*, 100.

Thus, the interpretation of Lam 3:25–33 above opens windows to different intertexts within the Hebrew Bible, the New Testament, and rabbinic literature. Reflecting different voices, the text is dialogic in itself. This dialogical character continues in later interpretations and is made visible via an intertextual approach.

## Intertextuality and Canonical Criticism: Conclusions

The concept of intertextuality sheds light on the network of texts in which every biblical text is situated. While it is often difficult to date texts exactly, against the background of intertextuality, the relationship between texts is seen as a mutual process. Intertextuality is a frame for describing innerbiblical interpretation. Still, a remaining problem of intertextuality is the arbitrariness of relationships between texts: It is hard to define the borders of interpretation, and everything is possible. Rabbinic intertextuality finds a balance of plurality without arbitrariness.

The concept of intertextuality, especially in its broad sense, has a tense relationship with the notion of a canon. *Canon* is a term with a Christian background, developed in postbiblical times. Combining intertextuality with canonical criticism is a contradiction in itself. Nevertheless, an intertextual approach increases awareness of the dialogue between voices within the Bible, first within the Hebrew Bible/Old Testament and within the New Testament separately. In a second step, the Hebrew Bible/Old Testament and the New Testament can be read together in their relatedness. The different voices relativize a contrasting relationship between the Old and New Testaments. Including the reader and reading communities, the concept of intertextuality makes visible the different possibilities for reading texts from the Hebrew Bible: "The canon serves as the frame for the production of meaning in the act of reading. It is a semiotic power that engages the reader in the manifold relations of the canon's different books."[48] Canonical criticism can be useful in the broad sense of the word—not when it is restricted to the Christian canon, but with regard to different canons. A combination of intertextuality and canonical criticism can serve as a background frame for the comparison between Jewish and Christian approaches to the Hebrew Bible.

---

48. Alkier, "Reading the Canon Intertextually," 289.

# Who Is Solomon? Intertextual Readings of King Solomon in Reception History

*Susanne Gillmayr-Bucher*

For centuries, biblical texts have inspired artists to create and shape their own works. Biblical stories and characters have been retold, depicted, and staged countless times in Christian, Jewish, and also Islamic traditions. This creative process modifies the biblical images, for example, by changing the features of the figures or adding new episodes to the narratives. Hence, the tradition develops and broadens the motives and facets attached to biblical stories and characters. Such transformations are well-known from legends, but the arts also continue this process. That is why the understanding of biblical stories and in particular the characteristics of biblical figures change over the centuries. This special literary environment also affects the question of an intertextual relecture as it is not limited to two, nor even to any limited number of specified texts. The possible pretexts are countless and often not even identifiable. In the same way, dependencies become gradually blurred as it is no longer possible to ascertain the source of information for a specific reading. Nonetheless, an intertextual reading of literary adaptations of biblical texts is still able to produce important insights and to point to mutual influences between reading biblical and literary texts.

In the following I present observations on how we may construct such an intertextual reading process and what impact it might have on the understanding and interpretation of the texts using the example of King Solomon. The reception history of Solomon shows a rich and diverse

---

This essay is part of the research project "Ruler, Lover, Sage and Sceptic: Receptions of King Solomon" funded by the Austrian Science Fund. I would like to thank Antonia Krainer from our project team for her suggestions and critical remarks on this paper.

picture, making this biblical figure a suitable object of study. The diversity of the images of King Solomon already starts in the biblical texts and grows rapidly in the tradition. As a consequence, it is barely possible to depict a distinctive portrait of Solomon. This figure is in constant danger to merge into the great imaginative space of images of kings and rulers. Hence, Solomon might appear as just another legendary king, whose mentioning generates some interest but does not determine the character of the literary figure. In order to analyze and describe the intertextual reading process and its impact on the interpretations of the various images of Solomon in biblical and literary texts, I will first focus on interfigurality as a special aspect of intertextual relations. Then I will turn to the history of the reception of biblical texts and outline this specific intertext. In a next step, I will suggest to (re)construct an intertextual reading with the aid of "blending theory" as developed by Gilles Fauconnier and Mark Turner. Finally, an exemplary analysis of three poems on Solomon will show how such an intertextual reading may be applied.

## Intertextuality and Interfigurality

Interrelations between figures are a special but quite important way to establish relations between different texts.[1] There are numerous ways and a wide range of elements that may establish relations between literary figures, whereby proper names are among the most obvious ones. Quite similar to a quotation, a name uses and repeats a segment taken from a pretext within a subsequent text.[2] Once a name triggers the memory of another text, the readers start looking for similarities between the figures. The more unique the proper name is, the stronger the reference will be and the more intensely the readers will be searching for similarities. Vice versa, a common name will only add a fleeting awareness of other literary figures bearing the same name. Furthermore, if a figure reappears in another text, it is not necessarily certain that it really is the same figure, nor is it always possible to reidentify the same figure in a different text.[3] Searching for criteria to establish the identity of reoccurring literary figures, Uri

---

1. Wolfgang Müller, "Interfigurality: A Study on the Interdependence of Literary Figures," in *Intertextuality*, ed. Heinrich F. Plett, RTT 15 (Berlin: de Gruyter, 1991), 101.

2. Müller, "Interfigurality," 103.

3. See Uri Margolin, "Introducing and Sustaining Characters in Literary Narrative: A Set of Conditions," *Sty* 21 (1987): 116.

Margolin lists five minimal constitutive conditions under which literary characters can be introduced and sustained: (1) the figure has to exist in a work of literature; (2) it needs some unique traits to form a recognizable identity; (3) it must be unique in the text-world; (4) the figure has to form a paradigmatic unity—thus, its different traits must be coherent; and (5) it must be presented as a syntagmatic continuity. As such, its depiction needs continuity throughout diverse episodes, sequels, different books, and so forth.[4] If (at least some of) these core features remain constant, a figure can be identified by the readers.

Nevertheless, the figures and their characteristics may still vary significantly if they appear in different works. Wolfgang Müller points out that if "an author takes over a figure from a work by another author into his own work, he absorbs it into the formal and ideological structure of his own product, putting it to his own uses, which may range from parody and satire to a fundamental revaluation or re-exploration of the figure concerned."[5] Figures thus might take on a quite vivid "afterlife," especially figures from well-known literature like the Bible (the same holds true, for example, for figures from Greek mythology or classical literature). Although they are recognizable throughout many transformations, these figures are not identical with their first appearances.

If we apply these criteria to the biblical figure of King Solomon, the existence of the literary figure and its uniqueness is well established in 1 Kings and the books of Chronicles. His characterization is elaborate, although not unambiguous. In 1 Kings, Solomon is introduced as son of David, king of Israel, and builder of the temple. He is further portrayed as wisdom's apprentice, a wise king and judge; he fears God but also is disloyal, building sanctuaries for foreign deities. As a king, he is portrayed as a benevolent ruler but also demands forced labor for his building projects. The appearance of this royal figure in other biblical books shows some variations. In the books of Chronicles, the figure of King Solomon is easily recognizable. Its portrait is very similar to 1 Kings, although this Solomon is less complex, as he lacks all the negative traits. Three other biblical books mention Solomon only briefly. The Song of Songs introduces Solomon as a figure of the text. The short references mention him as king; however, his role is reduced to a suitor in a love song. The book of Ecclesiastes also points to Solomon and suggests that he is the lyrical

---

4. Margolin, "Introducing and Sustaining Characters in Literary Narrative," 111–21.
5. Müller, "Interfigurality," 107.

speaker (Eccl 1:12–2:26). However, the identification of Qoheleth with Solomon is not beyond doubt. The so-called royal fiction rather implies that Qoheleth identifies himself with Solomon as a thought experiment. The book of Proverbs refers to Solomon three times. He is mentioned in the headings of collections of proverbs (Prov 1:1; 10:1; 25:1), indicating that Solomon is the author (or editor) of these sayings. Thus, Solomon appears as an authority behind the narrating voice, the parent's voice, or the voice of wisdom. However, the recognizability of Solomon as a literary figure is rather low, and it takes considerable efforts from the readers to find "Solomonic" traits or a Solomonic voice in these texts.[6]

The issue of the figure as a paradigmatic unity can be answered for 1 Kings and the books of Chronicles, while the other books provide only partial images of Solomon, adding or emphasizing some traits to the overall picture. The syntagmatic unity of the figure of King Solomon is also clearly recognizable in 1 Kings and the books of Chronicles. Despite some differences, Solomon's most important achievements are presented in a similar way. While these books depict Solomon's whole reign, the other references point to specific episodes (Song of Songs) or allude to Solomon's kingship (Ecclesiastes) or his wisdom (Proverbs) in general.

To summarize, it can be noted that King Solomon is developed as a unique literary figure in 1 Kings and the books of Chronicles. Most probably, the portrayal in Chronicles already is an adaptation of 1 Kings, reshaping the image of the king according to its purpose. The other occurrences refer to these portraits as one, without differentiation.[7] This points to a dynamic of a growing and expanding character. The figure of Solomon is not recognized in a specific realization of one book. King Solomon, rather, is a character that changes continuously as new traits and aspects are added or modified. The different images are not passed on separately but rather combined. In this way, a complex figure with, in some instances, contradictive characteristics arises from the various portraits of Solomon. For the vast majority of artistic works, Solomon thus is a unique figure which includes an accumulation of character traits and skills. He is a great king and a wise judge (1 Kings, 1–2 Chronicles), a wisdom teacher (Prov-

---

6. See Mathias Winkler, *Das Salomonische des Sprichwörterbuchs: Intertextuelle Verbindungen zwischen 1Kön 1–11 und dem Sprichwörterbuch*, HBS 87 (Freiburg im Breisgau: Herder, 2017), 117–67.

7. The only exception is Sir 47:19–20 (LXX). Solomon's devotion to his wives that brought him disgrace is only mentioned in 1 Kgs 11.

erbs), a philosopher and skeptic (Ecclesiastes), and allegedly wiser than all men but also a fool (Sirach). Solomon fears God but also builds sanctuaries for foreign deities; he is a benevolent king and an oppressor; furthermore, he is a lover (Song of Songs) and is drawn to women and also captivated by them (1 Kings, Sirach). In this way, Solomon's biblical portrait as a whole becomes the pretext for later relectures, and not the different images of the single books.[8]

When the biblical texts are completed, the development of Solomon's image does not stop. This becomes already obvious in the widespread legends in Christian, Jewish, and Islamic tradition.[9] These texts added many stories not known in the Bible and thus enhanced the image of the great king. Subsequently, these stories and images became an integral part of Solomon's image, just like the biblical stories. It is out of these traditions that artists attain the biblical knowledge they use, shape, and modify for their own works. The wide range of characteristics for the figure of Solomon the artists may draw from results in widely divergent images of the biblical king. So, it happens that Solomon is a romantic lover in one novel and a womanizer or even a misogynist in others. He can be portrayed as the exemplary good king, a brutal dictator, or just another incompetent sovereign. In the same way, Solomon sometimes is extremely wise, sometimes unworldly and naive.

## The Reception of the Texts

In the long history of interpretation and artistic adaptations, the biblical images of Solomon are constantly expanded and transformed.[10] Due to this ongoing change, defining a pretext in this process is a challenge. As all texts and all figures of Solomon leave their marks on the picture of

---

8. Later traditions explicitly try to combine the various aspects of Solomon into the image of one character by taking into account various changes in his life. So, for example, the differences in the books attributed to Solomon are explained by assigning them to different stages of Solomon's life. See August Wünsche, *Der Midrasch Schir Ha-Schirim*, BibRab 6 (Leipzig: Schulze, 1880), 1, 9.

9. See Joseph Verheyden, ed., *The Figure of Solomon in Jewish, Christian and Islamic Tradition*, TBN 16 (Leiden: Brill, 2013).

10. Brennan W. Breed further distinguishes between processes that expand and adapt the text in a creative way (he calls transmutations) and readings that express the capacities proper to the text. See his *Nomadic Text: A Theory of Biblical Reception History*, ISBL (Bloomington: Indiana University Press, 2014), 133–34.

Solomon within cultural memory, every new image and every reuse of the figure of Solomon draws on a wide variety of characteristics as it constructs its own version of this figure. The intertextual relations are not restricted to a text and specific pretext(s), but rather a given text relates to a cloud of pretexts. Furthermore, musical adaptations or paintings may also contribute to Solomon's image and thus function as a pretext. A new image of the figure of Solomon hence may be rooted in the biblical texts or a particular interpretation of these texts, but it may also emerge from a mere passing familiarity with the biblical figure and its manifold traditions.

Nonetheless, as Brennan W. Breed points out, every new image of Solomon is based on this tradition and starts with an—at least—partial perception of it. In doing so, selections take place, as the process of reading and perceiving always narrows the potentials of texts and also other works of art. Hence, every reading, seeing, or hearing reorganizes a text or an artwork and, as a consequence, each element of this pretext will embrace only a (very) limited range of its potentials.[11] With regard to the totality of the interpretations and artworks dedicated to Solomon, the reception history appears as the story of the text's capacities.[12]

Although the receptions of King Solomon only form a very small section of the intertext, as Julia Kristeva envisioned it, the large network of texts, artworks, and their relations mirror its complexity on a small scale.[13] Focusing on such an overview, Breed further points out that "by tracing readings from many diverse contexts, a reception historian can locate various semantic nodes through which clusters of readings converge."[14] This suggestion offers a very helpful schema to organize the multitude of images and interpretations arising from biblical texts throughout the centuries.[15]

---

11. Breed, *Nomadic Text*, 138.

12. Breed, *Nomadic Text*, 140–41.

13. Julia Kristeva, *Desire in Language: A Semiotic Approach to Language and Art*, ed. Leon S. Roudiez, trans. Thomas Gora, Alice Jardine, and Leon S. Roudiez (New York: Columbia University Press, 1980), 64–91; Kristeva applied Mikhail M. Bakhtin's concept of dialogism to a discourse between all texts. She defines intertextuality as a characteristic feature of every text as every text is a mosaic of other texts. Intertextuality, therefore, defines an open text; it is a through road and a semantic crossing of many texts. Consequently, numerous combinations, relations, overlappings, and multiple meanings characterize every text.

14. Breed, *Nomadic Text*, 140.

15. Caroline Vander Stichele suggests speaking of the impact of texts instead of their history, thus focusing on the "cultural impact of scriptures rather than on their

For Solomon, several such nodes can be established.[16] The most obvious node is Solomon the king. At all times, people were interested in the image of a ruler, and they used Solomon as a role model in their reflections. Depending on the perspective and interests of the interpreters, Solomon is portrayed as a benevolent and just ruler, a king of peace and thus a role model for other rulers, or as an inept sovereign and sometimes even a brutal dictator exploiting his people. A crucial part of Solomon's kingship includes his building projects, especially the construction of the temple. In retelling this event, Solomon's attitude toward his reign, his people, and, of course, God is reflected. Frequently, Solomon's religious conviction and performance are closely connected to the image of the king. Solomon might be depicted as a God-fearing, pious ruler but also as a skeptic; other stories tell of his apostasy and repentance. Another very active node is Solomon's wisdom. Starting with the summary in 1 Kgs 5:9–14, where Solomon's wisdom surpasses that of all other people, this image is vastly expanded in the tradition. Subsequently, Solomon is not only able to talk about every possible topic, to rule justly in difficult court cases, and to solve any riddle, but he is also able to talk to everyone, humans and animals alike. Furthermore, his knowledge might even exceed earthly wisdom and encompass magic, which in turn gives him power over the world of the demons. In addition, Solomon's relationship to women is of wide interest and forms another such node. He is commonly depicted as a passionate lover, a womanizer, but also a misogynist.

It is evident that the well-established nodes for the reception of Solomon comply with the most prominent activities of his biblical portrait: the image of the king who builds the temple, loves many women, and is wise beyond all measure forms the backbone of many artistic adaptations. Solomon's character traits, however, are not clearly defined. In continuation of the biblical diversity, later portraits freely modify his personality.

---

history." This proposal adds the aspect of interaction to Breed's nodes, as all (cultural) texts interact within the intertext. See Caroline Vander Stichele, "The Head of John and Its Reception, or How to Conceptualize 'Reception History,'" in *Reception History and Biblical Studies: Theory and Practice*, ed. Emma England and William J. Lyons, LHBOTS 615 (London: Bloomsbury, 2015), 80.

16. For a more elaborate presentation, see Elisabeth Birnbaum, "Salomo in Barock und Moderne: Ein interdisziplinäres Kaleidoskop," *BArts* 1 (2017): 1–25, especially 1–7.

Nonetheless, the constancy of some core elements guarantees the recognizability of the biblical figure.

## Reading between the Texts

When literary works recreate a biblical figure for the eyes of their contemporary readers, they offer them a new approach to traditional and biblical images. The intertextual reading that may be stimulated by such works bridges the chronological distance between their own time and earlier or biblical times, thus enabling the readers to see the biblical stories becoming transparent for their contemporary questions, and, vice versa, to interpret the artwork's time in the light of a biblical figure and its (long) history. In this way, the worlds of the biblical stories and the literary or artistic work interact. They blend in the reading process as the readers construct meaning between different texts. New reading possibilities arise from the interplay of the texts, exceeding the given text and the pretexts alluded to. Renate Lachmann calls the crossing point of the texts an *implicit text*. This implicit text is a space where the given text and the absent texts intersect; it is a place of interference of texts which have coded and conveyed cultural experiences as communicative experiences. This implicit text can only be defined approximately, as the space where a dynamic constitution of meaning occurs.[17]

If we want to take a closer look at how this dynamic space between the texts is constructed and how meaning is created, insights from cognitive science are helpful. Fauconnier and Turner, for example, describe the process of how meaning is created in their well-received book, *The Way We Think: Conceptual Blending and the Mind's Hidden Complexities*.[18] In biblical studies, their insights have been used for metaphorical studies in particular, but their approach is of course not restricted to figurative language. According to Fauconnier and Turner, "conceptual blending" is a "basic mental operation, highly imaginative but crucial to even the simplest kinds of thought."[19] Explaining the concept of blending, Fau-

---

17. Renate Lachmann, "Ebenen des Intertextualitätsbegriffs," in *Das Gespräch*, ed. Karlheinz Stierle and Rainer Warnig, PH 11 (München: Wilhelm Fink Verlag, 1984), 133–38.

18. Gilles Fauconnier and Mark Turner, *The Way We Think: Conceptual Blending and the Mind's Hidden Complexities* (New York: Basic Books, 2002).

19. Fauconnier and Turner, *Way We Think*, 18.

connier and Turner show how it is possible to parse complex figures of thought into single, less complex concepts and to describe their different interactions in order to explain the new meaning such figures of thought offer. This approach works with a concept of different "spaces": the starting point is the so-called mental spaces, "small conceptual packets that are constructed as we think and talk." These mental spaces, in turn, "are connected to long-term schematic knowledge called frames."[20] There are different kinds of mental spaces: the "generic space" contains the elements the input spaces have in common, and the "blended space" combines the input spaces and their frames and thus creates something new. Blended spaces may, in turn, serve as input spaces in another blending process which results in a network of blends referred to as "megablend."[21]

If blending theory is applied to intertextual reading processes, it may provide new insights into how the implicit text in an intertextual reading emerges. I want to demonstrate this approach using the example of the description of Solomon's wisdom in 1 Kgs 5:12–14 and Prov 1:1–5.

(1) The input space created in 1 Kgs 5:12–14 shows Solomon as a very wise man, a universal scholar, who is admired by all the kings of the earth. The corresponding frame is both the content and structure of knowledge and its display and reception. The second input space displayed in Prov 1:1–5 presents King Solomon as a teacher of wisdom, who passes his knowledge on in his proverbs to all those who want to listen and learn. The corresponding frame is the content and structure of knowledge and the relation between teacher and pupil.

(2) When Prov 1 names King Solomon as writer of the proverbs, it takes up the image of the wise king in 1 Kgs 5 and expands it. Nonetheless, both texts are quite similar as they share the concept of a wise man who has great knowledge, presents his knowledge, and is heard by others. These elements, common to both mental spaces, form the generic space.

There is yet another element the mental spaces of this example share, namely the figure of King Solomon. In this example from the biblical text, the figure of King Solomon is explicitly reintroduced in Prov 1:1 as Solomon, son of David, king of Israel. Without this introduction, the points of reference would be too few to decide with certainty whether Solomon is the outlined author. Like Margolin, Fauconnier and Turner reflect on

---

20. Fauconnier and Turner, *Way We Think*, 40.
21. Fauconnier and Turner, *Way We Think*, 151.

the recognizability of figures across different contexts and works. In principle, they come to a quite similar conclusion: namely, that characters remain recognizable across different contexts and works because of some unchanging traits. According to the schema of blending theory, these elements are part of the generic space for that person, forming a personal character.[22] Thus, "characters, like frames, are basic cognitive cultural instruments. We may dispute every aspect of their accuracy or legitimacy or invariance, or even their very existence, but cognitively we cannot do without them."[23]

(3) Combining the mental spaces does not reduce them to their common elements, but this process also creates something new, namely the blended space (the blend). The example of Prov 1:1–5 shows a compression of time, space, and identity as the writer of the proverbs is identified with King Solomon. Furthermore, the different concepts of presenting and sharing wisdom are blended as the emphasis shifts from having and presenting wisdom to teaching and learning wisdom. Also, the exclusive knowledge of 1 Kgs 5:13 makes way for proverbs and commonly shared wisdom. The blend thus modifies the image of Solomon: On the one hand, the authority of the wisdom teacher is strengthened by King Solomon's fame. On the other hand, Solomon's wisdom is also put into perspective; he is not only an instructor, but—as a typical wise man—he is also someone who is instructed.

## Solomon the King throughout the Centuries

Throughout the centuries, King Solomon has been used as a model for contemporary rulers. In doing so, Solomon's exemplary reign, wisdom, and power are praised but also criticized. In the following, I will present three selected examples in order to show how Solomon's intertextual portrait develops in reception history. The biblical texts portray Solomon as a successful king who stabilizes the kingdom, inwardly and outwardly, so that peace is secured (1 Kgs 5:4, 18; 1 Chr 22:9). An important element in the description of his reign is his descent from David. Solomon is the thriving successor. Nonetheless, the depictions within 1 Kings and the books of Chronicles show two different political interests. In 1 Kings, Solomon

---

22. Fauconnier and Turner, *Way We Think*, 249–50.
23. Fauconnier and Turner, *Way We Think*, 250.

has to prove himself as king, and although he achieves great things, he does not measure up to the image of his father. Unlike this portrayal, the books of Chronicles present a more static picture showing David and Solomon together as the idealized beginning of the Davidic dynasty.[24] As far as domestic policy is concerned, the organization of the land (1 Kgs 4) and the building of the temple, palaces, and cities (1 Kgs 9:17–19) have to be mentioned. Solomon is presented as a powerful king who is able to enforce his will and to implement his ideas. Regarding foreign policy, Solomon is portrayed as a well-known, respected, and admired king. In this way, the biblical portraits of 1 Kings and 2 Chronicles correspond to the image of a great king. However, despite all his glory, Solomon's image in 1 Kings also includes a darker side. Not only does Solomon consolidate his power by destroying his (potential) enemies (1 Kgs 2), he also has to deal with political adversaries (1 Kgs 11). His treaty with King Hiram of Tyre, the use of forced labor, and the construction of sanctuaries for foreign deities further add to an ambivalent portrayal. The self-critical references to Solomon in the book of Ecclesiastes and the open criticism in the book of Sirach continue this critical trend, thus laying an ambiguous basis for later receptions.

Solomon the Model King

From the Middle Ages to the Renaissance, the so-called mirrors for princes instructed kings in the important virtues of a ruler.[25] Therein, Solomon appears as a paragon for wisdom, the first of all royal virtues. Frequently, Solomon is also mentioned in homages to a king, which compare a contemporary king with the biblical King Solomon and praise him as a new Solomon. In these examples, the character of Solomon remains mostly unchanged. The input spaces share the frame of kingship, thus creating a "mirror network," a blend of spaces that have the same "organizing frame."[26] Time, space, and identity are compressed. The blend adds to the image of the contemporary king the aspects of excellence and distinctiveness. This,

---

24. See Mark A. Throntveit, "The Idealization of Solomon as the Glorification of God in the Chronicler's Royal Speeches and Royal Prayers," in *The Age of Solomon: Scholarship at the Turn of the Millennium*, ed. Lowell K. Handy, SHCANE 11 (Leiden: Brill, 1997), 411–27.

25. Such texts were often composed at the accession of a new king, when a young and inexperienced ruler was about to come to power.

26. Fauconnier and Turner, *Way We Think*, 122–23.

first of all, helps to justify the king's reign. Implicitly, it also might raise the readers' hopes or expectations that the king will prove to be a Solomonic king, providing peace and well-being for his people. For the king addressed in the text, it adds the request to satisfy this high requirement.

Not all works portraying Solomon as an exemplary king are related to one specific ruler. Many rather refer to a common or ideal image of rulership of their time. A good example is the poem, "King Solomon and the Ants," by John Greenleaf Whittier (1807–1892).[27] In this poem, he describes different ways to exercise a king's power. He combines biblical and legendary elements to present Solomon as a role model for sovereigns. The poem starts with a description of the king riding out of Jerusalem with his entourage and the queen of Sheba. When their path approaches an anthill, Solomon overhears the ants' worries, and he translates their words for the queen of Sheba (seventh stanza):

> "Here comes the king men greet
> As wise and good and just,
> To crush us in the dust
> Under his heedless feet."

The queen is quite surprised by these words, and this starts a dialogue with Solomon on the ideal behavior of a wise king (ninth to eleventh stanzas):

> "O king!" she whispered sweet,
> "Too happy fate have they
> Who perish in thy way
> Beneath thy gracious feet!
>
> "Thou of the God-lent crown,
> Shall these vile creatures dare
> Murmur against thee where
> The knees of kings kneel down!"
>
> "Nay," Solomon replied,
> "The wise and strong should seek
> The welfare of the weak,"
> And turned his horse aside.

---

27. John Greenleaf Whittier, *The Vision of Echard and Other Poems* (Boston: Houghton, Osgood & Co., 1878), 99.

Two totally different images of the relation between a king and his subjects are set side by side. While the queen of Sheba sets out an absolutist rule which is totally centered on the king, Solomon replies with the image of a king who cares for all creatures in his kingdom. Without further argument, the queen admits that Solomon's attitude characterizes a truly wise king (thirteenth and fourteenth stanzas):

> The jeweled head bent low;
> "O king!" she said, "henceforth
> The secret of thy worth
> And wisdom well I know."
>
> "Happy must be the State
> Whose ruler heedeth more
> The murmurs of the poor
> Than flatteries for the great."

This reaction of the queen of Sheba emphasizes Solomon's portrait as a benevolent sovereign. She even declares this trait as the core of Solomon's wisdom. The last stanza draws a general conclusion from the depicted events that once more highlights the central theme of a considerate ruler and, in this way, links a distant past and present times.

An intertextual reading of this poem has to consider two earlier pretexts. The most obvious reference is the biblical story of King Solomon as it is depicted in 1 Kings. The figures of King Solomon and the queen of Sheba and also the examination and approval of Solomon's wisdom by the queen are common elements and form a generic space. The biblical portrait of Solomon is complemented by legendary images of Solomon, which add more mental spaces to the intertextual reading of this poem. These legends expanded the image of King Solomon's wisdom. One widely known additional trait is his ability to understand the language of animals. This ability is a key feature of Solomon's portrait in the poem; it is, however, not explained, indicating that this information is a widely known skill attributed to Solomon. Another legend tells about Solomon's encounter with an ant queen. In this episode, Solomon, who is shown as a ruthless king, wants to demonstrate his superiority, but the ant teaches him a lesson in humility.[28]

---

28. Louis Ginzberg, *Bible Times and Characters form Joshua to Esther*, vol. 4 of *The Legends of the Jews* (Philadelphia: Jewish Publication Society of America, 1913), 163.

In the blended space, the different portraits from these mental spaces come together and initiate a dynamic portrait of Solomon. The poem's criticism of a ruthless king alludes to the critical voices on Solomon's reign in 1 Kings, and the legend even strengthens the critical perspective. The legend uses the biblical frame of the king's dispute with the queen of Sheba, blending the wise Solomon of 1 Kgs 10 with the traits of a despotic king. The image of the queen, Solomon's dialogue partner, remains the same. Like the queen of Sheba, the queen of ants is very wise. However, the schema of the dialogue—namely, the seemingly inferior queen of ants beating the arrogant king with her arguments—is a new development in the legend.

Whittier's poem, in turn, picks up the characters and the frames from the biblical story and the legend and presents Solomon in a very positive light. This twist could be read as a sequel or a response to the legend. The king of the poem is shown as a modest ruler, while the queen of Sheba, at first, is arrogant and heartless. She combines the image of the biblical queen and the legendary Solomon. What these two figures have in common is that they are powerful monarchs. The biblical queen of Sheba and the legendary Solomon are, however, input spaces governed by two different frames, one of which prevails in the blend.[29] Thus, in the critical encounter between Solomon and the queen of Sheba, the roles shift, and Solomon now speaks against an arrogant and ruthless royal stance. The poem also modifies the dispute; instead of a heated argument, the dialogue unfolds very politely in the form of thesis, antithesis, and approval. While the legend only tells that King Solomon left abashed, the queen of Sheba is not humiliated but explicitly evaluates Solomon's considerations for the weak and gives credit to his attitude. The relation between a benevolent and a ruthless ruler would be termed as "Disanalogy" by Fauconnier and Turner, a relation which "is often compressed into Change."[30] By changing her mind, the queen of Sheba proves to be a wise monarch who recognizes wisdom in others. In this way, her biblical portrait is confirmed, whereas Solomon's image is restored. The focus on his considerate behavior alludes to the biblical image of security and welfare all people could enjoy during Solomon's reign. Hence, King Solomon is again approved as a paragon for all rulers.

---

29. The queen's image in the poem is thus the type of blend referred to as a "single-scope network" (Fauconnier and Turner, *Way We Think*, 126).

30. Fauconnier and Turner, *Way We Think*, 99.

## Solomon the Despot

During the last two hundred years of Solomon's literary reception, however, emphasizing only the positive aspects of his reign is the exception rather than the norm. Instead of a flawless sovereign, Solomon can be shown as a despot oppressing his people; as a failing king, a guilt-ridden ruler; or, especially in modern times, as a self-critical sovereign who knows about his strengths and weaknesses. From the tradition of Solomon the despot, I will briefly discuss two poems by Heinrich Heine (1797–1856) and Matthias Hermann (born 1958). Both highlight the discrepancy between the king's reputation and his rather cruel reign. These texts pick up the biblical image of Solomon as it is presented in 1 Kings and emphasize the cruel aspects of the king already implied there.

Heine's critical poem, "König David," focuses on the royal succession.[31] The first two stanzas introduce the theme of the poem, namely, the unchanging relationship between a ruler and his people:

| | |
|---|---|
| Lächelnd scheidet der Despot, | Smiling still a despot dies, |
| Denn er weiß, nach seinem Tod | For he knows, on his demise, |
| Wechselt Willkür nur die Hände, | New hands wield the tyrant's power— |
| Und die Knechtschaft hat kein Ende. | It is not yet freedom's hour.[32] |

From the third stanza onwards, this common reflection is replaced by a biblical example, restaging the scene at the deathbed of King David. From the pieces of advice David gave his son Solomon, the one concerning Joab (1 Kgs 2:5–6) is chosen for this poem:

| | |
|---|---|
| Sterbend spricht zu Salomo | On his deathbed, David told |
| König David: Apropos, | His son Solomon: "Behold, |
| Daß ich Joab dir empfehle, | You must rid me, in all candor, |
| Einen meiner Generäle. | Of this Joab, my commander. |
| | |
| Dieser tapfre General | Captain Joab's brave and tough |
| Ist seit Jahren mir fatal, | But he's irked me long enough; |

---

31. Heinrich Heine, *Romanzero*, vol. 3.1 of *Historisch-kritische Gesamtausgabe der Werke*, ed. Manfred Windfuhr (Hamburg: Hoffmann und Campe, 1992), 40–41. The *Romanzero* was first published in 1851.

32. Hal Draper, *The Complete Poems of Heinrich Heine: A Modern English Version* (Boston: Suhrkamp, 1982), 586.

| | |
|---|---|
| Doch ich wagte den verhaßten | Yet, however I detest him, |
| Niemals ernstlich anzutasten. | I have never dared arrest him. |
| | |
| Du, mein Sohn, bist fromm und klug, | You, my son, are wise, devout, |
| Gottesfürchtig, stark genug, | Pious—and your arm is stout; |
| Und es wird dir leicht gelingen, | You should have no trouble sending |
| Jenen Joab umzubringen. | Joab to a sticky ending."[33] |

The biblical story presents David as a king who, at the end of his life, fears that some people might become a danger for the reign of his son. He thus explains to Solomon what causes his deep mistrust and asks him to watch these people closely, respectively, to eliminate them. David is characterized as a proactive and suspicious king, recognizing potential risks and removing them as a precautionary measure. He is further described as a ruler who tries to dictate his succession and to prevent struggles for the throne.

Heine's poem presents King David as a king who, despite his power, feels quite uneasy about Joab and thus asks Solomon to eliminate him. At first sight, the texts show a broad consensus in their characterization of the figures of David and Solomon. The generic space includes David, a powerful monarch, who urges his son to follow his example. However, an intertextual reading of the two texts also reveals the differences. The poem uses a different frame which prevails in the blend, thus creating a single-scope network. The biblical image of the king is modified in two ways: on the one hand, it enhances David's image as a ruthless despot, and on the other hand, it highlights the aspect that David is afraid of Joab. While the biblical frame points out a political necessity for the king's instruction, Heine's David does not recount Joab's actions and thus justify his mistrust. Rather, he only points out that he detests his captain but does not dare to confront him. In this way, the seemingly justified anxiety of David in the biblical text is exposed as a merciless struggle for power. Thus, Heine's criticism of rulers modifies the image of the biblical king by emphasizing hints already present in the biblical texts. In turn, presenting David with the attitude of a contemporary ruler suggests that such a behavior is nothing new but typical for monarchs, past and present. The blending of the biblical David with Heine's David thus reveals the true image of a despot. In this way, the generalization offers a disguise of Heine's criticism of contemporary rulers.

---

33. Draper, *The Complete Poems*, 586–87.

Besides David, both texts also introduce Solomon as David's successor on the throne. In 1 Kgs 2:1–9, David urges Solomon to prove himself a capable ruler by being strong and keeping God's commandments (vv. 2–3). Regarding special cases, he also asks him to act according to his wisdom—to find a just solution to the problems (vv. 6, 9). While the abilities David attributes to Solomon in the biblical text express David's hope that Solomon will live up to this image and fulfill the tasks, the poem lists almost the same attributes and skills as a description. David calls Solomon pious, God-fearing, clever, and strong, and he reckons this combination as a good condition for one specific task. In this way, the poem modifies the task Solomon is given. The focus is not on being a strong and wise ruler who knows how to remain in power but on the elimination of Joab. This depiction blurs the boundaries between actions that may be justifiable from a political perspective and an assassination. Again, Heine's poem exploits the critical hints of the biblical text from a contemporary perspective and presents a quite unfavorable image of Solomon. In the blend, Solomon, like King David, turns into the image of a typical despot.

Another example in this tradition is the poem "Salomo" by Hermann. Like Heine, Hermann's poem uses the biblical portrait of Solomon in 1 Kgs 1–3 as a disguise for his critique on a contemporary political situation, in this case on the political system of the former German Democratic Republic. In his poem, Hermann uses the stream of consciousness technique to present the readers an insight into Solomon's thoughts:

| | |
|---|---|
| Um sattelfest zu | In order to sit firmly |
| Sitzen auf dem Dawidberg, | on David's mountain, |
| Fällte ich 3 Todesurteile. | I passed three death sentences. |
| Die fabelhaften Richtersprüche | The fabulous judgements |
| Werden von meinem | are being praised |
| Schmeichlervölkchen gepriesen, | by my flattering people, |
| Um mich einzulullen, | in order to lull me, |
| Auf daß ich nicht | so that I will not |
| Weiter fälle | render any more |
| Salomonische Urteile.[34] | Solomonic verdicts.[35] |

---

34. Matthias Hermann, *72 Buchstaben: Gedichte* (Frankfurt: Suhrkamp, 1989).
35. Translated by Antonia Krainer.

Like Heine, Hermann uses the critical hints in Solomon's biblical portrait as a starting point for his image. However, he does not focus on one death sentence but more generally on Solomon's jurisdiction. The narration in 1 Kgs 2–3 presents quite different verdicts. Nonetheless, they are all presented as examples of Solomon's wisdom. He is the wise king who is able to maintain political and social stability by his just ruling. Although there are some nuances, Solomon's positive image dominates within the biblical context. The poem, however, presents Solomon's thoughts from the perspective of the late-twentieth century and thus from a time which condemns the radical elimination of political opponents. Furthermore, it combines the politically motivated death sentences (1 Kgs 2) with the people's reaction to Solomon's decision in the dispute between the two mothers over the living and the dead infant (1 Kgs 3:16–28). The death sentences are presented as "Solomonic verdicts," which the people fearfully praise. By skipping the narration of the two women, the poem represses positive allusions and instead strengthens Solomon's negative image. This tendency is further enhanced by the stream of consciousness technique. In this way, the poem creates the impression of a cynical and scheming ruler who has little regard for his people.

The generic space of these two texts includes a ruler who has absolute control of jurisdiction and who is praised and feared by his people. Furthermore, the outline of the royal behavior is similar, but there are great differences in the evaluation of these actions due to the different cultural contexts. Within the frame of the biblical text of 1 Kings, the absolute jurisdiction is not only an integral part of Solomon's reign but a main cause for his praise. In contrast, the frame presented by the poem emphasizes that absolute jurisdiction only leads to an abuse of power.

In the blended space, the poem's frame prevails. Its claim to reveal Solomon's thoughts modifies the perception of the biblical text. Thus, Solomon's positive biblical image is deconstructed, and, again, he appears as an example of a ruthless dictator. The compression of time gives the impression that the present is a mirror image of the past.

The tradition of such critical images of Solomon deprives this biblical figure of its positive exemplary function.[36] Such images emphasize the contrast between the official image of a glamorous and peaceful king as

---

36. The most well-known example of a biblically embellished critique on the political situation in the former German Democratic Republic is probably Stefan Heym's novel, *The King David Report* (London: Quartet Book, 1977).

presented in the biblical texts and the people's experience of oppression and abuse of power, suggesting that a critical look reveals the dark side of a totalitarian rule. In contrast to earlier critical images of Solomon, these poems do not deliver a warning or urge the king to avoid such behavior. They rather deconstruct any absolutistic power. In this way, Solomon's reign appears as unavoidable evil, but the only way to revolt is to gain insight, to recognize the true nature of the political power, and therewith to deny the rule its justification.

## Summary

The reception history of King Solomon includes a wide variety of royal images. Focusing on the aspect of Solomon the king, the biblical figure usually is clearly recognizable by its proper name and its role as a monarch. All other characteristics, however, may vary. This also applies to all other biblical figures related to Solomon. The literary texts develop these common elements freely and adapt the biblical figures and their actions to relevant political challenges of their own time. Although the figures are recognizable, their storyline unfolds in different frames.

An intertextual reading reveals not only the differences between the biblical pretext and a later literary text but pays close attention to the new images, developing from the combination of both texts. As a model to describe such an intertextual reading, the model of blending with its different stages as developed by Fauconnier and Turner proves to be helpful since it allows (re)constructing the reading process. In addition, it also recognizes the mutual modification of the reading of the biblical and the literary texts in this process. Furthermore, an intertextual reading considers not only the biblical pretext but also other texts in the reception history. It attaches great importance to these traditions and takes the memory of texts in their intertextual allusions seriously.

# Writing FanFic: Intertextuality in Isaiah and Christopher Columbus's *Libro de las Profecías*

*Steed Vernyl Davidson*

In the lead up to the quincentenary of Christopher Columbus's voyages in 1992, Columbian scholars discovered two aspects of Columbus's biography that received little attention over the centuries: Columbus as a writer and, secondly, a reader of biblical texts.[1] These two roles came into sharp focus among a limited range of scholars. Few biblical scholars explored Columbus's reliance upon biblical texts or his extensive compilation of biblical material intended to serve as the basis for an epic poem that, prior to his death, never materialized. The limited works that explored the connection between Columbus and the Bible analyzed Columbus as a reader and interpreter of biblical texts.[2] In his writings, Columbus exhibits moderate competence in the use of the available exegetical skills that leads John V. Fleming to refer to him as an "'amateur' exegete, a kind of hermeneutical auto-didact."[3] Despite the eccentric and millenarian aspects of Columbus's interpretations of the Bible, and what to the world has been characterized as a daring scientific mind, Alain Milhou views him as largely conservative

---

1. For a comprehensive treatment on Columbus's writings that pays attention to the full range of his concerns, see Margarita Zamora, *Reading Columbus*, LALC 9 (Berkeley: University of California Press, 1993).

2. See Hector Avalos, "Columbus as Biblical Exegete: A Study of the Libro de Las Profecías," in *Religion in the Age of Exploration: The Case of Spain and New Spain*, ed. Bryan F. Le Beau and Menahem Mor (Omaha, NE: Creighton University Press, 1996), 59–80; John V. Fleming, "Christopher Columbus as Scriptural Exegete," in *Biblical Hermeneutics in Historical Perspective: Studies in Honor of Karlfried Froehlich on His Sixtieth Birthday*, ed. Mark S. Burrows and Paul Rorem (Grand Rapids: Eerdmans, 1991), 173–83; and Jean-Pierre Ruiz, *Readings from the Edges: The Bible and People on the Move* (Maryknoll, NY: Orbis Books, 2011), 123–35.

3. Fleming, "Christopher Columbus as Scriptural Exegete," 179.

and mostly orthodox in his exegesis and actually not ranging that far afield from prevailing millenarian thought.[4] Writings attributed to Columbus indicate not so much the Renaissance man of the popular Western imagination but rather a deeply medieval thinker.

Popular treatments of Columbus's biography make it easy to underestimate the role the Bible and religion played in his pursuit of a marine route to Asia. Although his conservative brand of biblical exegesis is not pervasive in all of his writings, neither is it incidental to his formation as thinker, navigator, and resident of fifteenth-century Spain. At the same time, Milhou credits Columbus with providing a new combination of old elements to ensure the funding and support he needed for his nautical project. From all indications, Columbus's project was not only a navigational or scientific endeavor but also a sectarian religious venture.[5] His writings reveal how Columbus relied upon the Bible and interpretations of biblical texts as much as upon scientific insights to guide his navigation of sea routes. In this regard, Columbus represents the medieval trend to read both books of God the Bible and nature. That he saw no contradictions between these two sources but in fact used them seamlessly to articulate the purposes of his voyages and, arguably, his life makes Columbus a generative source not simply of biblical interpretation but biblical productivity. Although seen as separate functions, in this essay—with the help of intertextual studies—I think of Columbus as a writer and a reader of biblical texts as a single function to situate him in the generation of new meaning in biblical texts.

The Bible occupies an increasingly large space among the collection of Columbian writings over time. The trove of Columbian texts includes "letters, memoranda, annotations, and ship-board logs."[6] While his early

---

4. Alain Milhou, *Colon Y Su Mentalidad Mesianica: En El Ambiente Franciscanista Español* (Valladolid, Spain: Seminario Americanista de la Universidad de Valladolid, 1983), 8.

5. The journal of the first voyage largely contains several Christian pieties. However, its framing as a document in its prologue written for the Spanish crown to assert the evangelical purposes of the voyages means that at several turns in the text the possibilities of converting "those lands of India ... to our Holy Faith" appears. John Cummins, *The Voyage of Christopher Columbus: Columbus' Own Journal of Discovery, Newly Restored and Translated* (New York: St. Martin's, 1992), 81.

6. Millie Gimmel, "Christopher Columbus (1451–20 May 1506)," in *Sixteenth-Century Spanish Writers*, ed. Gregory B. Kaplan, DLB 318 (Detroit: Thomson Gale, 2006), 35. Delno C. West and August Kling detail the collection of writings to include:

writings prior to the voyages reveal at best a standard Christian piety that quotes sections of the Bible, his literary output beginning with the letter to the Spanish crown on the return from the first voyage in 1493 and reaching a high point after the third voyage reflects a strong millenarian, messianic, and missionary turn, particularly in the use of biblical texts.[7] His most notable literary output—notable for its size and scope rather than being an impactful original work—is his compilation of *Las Libro de las Profecías*. This work at best falls into the category of curation, yet careful and purposeful curation as an act of "meaning-making."[8] While Columbus may have intended a different genre outcome for the compilation of works in *Libro*—a rewrite of Seneca's *Tragedy of Medea*—the resulting work has a different relationship with its sources than that of citations, copies, or even imitation.[9] The extended collection of scriptural texts along with extracts from religious writings may resemble in its form an overly pious sacred text; however, *Libro* in its use of scriptural genres can also be described as fan fiction. The term fan fiction as used here is not overly preoccupied with the exact replication of genres—either ancient or modern, fictive or not. Though genre imitation and replication prove useful conceits for fan fiction to presume the readers' familiarity, the generation of new meaning from existing texts serves as one of its core goals. As a form of intertextuality, fan fiction aptly captures the ardor associated with the meaning in the various works used and the reproduction of new

---

"over eighty letters, memoranda, supply lists, and miscellaneous documents," extensive coverage of the third and fourth voyages, his will, marginal notes in his books along with *Libro de las Profecías* and the *Book of Privileges*. They also note several other pieces of nonextant works along with others of doubtful provenance. West and Kling, *The Libro de las Profecías of Christopher Columbus*, ColQuin 2 (Gainesville: University of Florida Press, 1991), 25.

7. Zamora notes the clear absence of any evangelical purpose in "Capitulaciones de Santa Fe," dated April 17, 1492, a text from the Spanish crown to Columbus that scholars describe as "an imperialistic text" (Zamora, *Reading Columbus*, 27). However, Columbus in his response to that letter does include an evangelical purpose for his voyage (Zamora, *Reading Columbus*, 33). Catherine Keller suggests that "Relación" of the third voyage marks an identifiable shift where the millennial impulses surpass the economic motives (Keller, "Columbus/Colon," *EMMM*, 99).

8. Davina Lopez, "Curational Reflections: On Rhetorics of Tradition and Innovation in Biblical Scholarship," in *Present and Future of Biblical Studies: Celebrating Twenty-Five Years of Brill's Biblical Interpretation*, ed. Tat-siong Benny Liew, BibInt 161 (Leiden: Brill, 2018), 74.

9. Avalos, "Columbus as Biblical Exegete," 73.

meaning from those works. In this essay, I use the term to illustrate how intertextuality represents the way readers actively engage literary works in order to construct meaning that results in new work. From my perspective, intertextuality is more than simply the use of another work but an engaged production of meaning. In this case, *Libro* sets out to communicate how the Bible describes the eschatological future of the conversion of the world and Spain's role in the recapture of Jerusalem.[10] To achieve this goal requires appropriating textual sources in order to utilize, extend, and emphasize their embedded meanings and ideologies in new works in the way fan fiction does.[11]

Fan fiction as a form of intertextuality offers possibilities to analyze the intertextual use of biblical material. In this regard, as an active engagement with source material such as the Bible, fan fiction as a contemporary genre illustrates the importance of authors as readers of texts and their interaction and productive work with the ideologies embedded in those texts. The study of fan fiction brings to intertextuality studies the removal of privilege from a source text as a "valued original."[12] Fan fiction does not view works that engage with that source as derivative and therefore of lesser value, but instead pays attention to how authors interact with previous works in order to generate new products. Although enjoying its own classification as a genre, my interest in fan fiction in this essay goes beyond matters of genre classification. Instead, I am more attuned to how fan fiction operates as curation and, therefore, how the "arrangements and emphases" of the new work provide more fruitful sites for exploration.[13] This exploration, though, requires as much attention to the producer as to the produced text. Investigating the dynamic work of collection, rearrangement, and generation of new meaning from previous works into new ones presumes a living author, contrary to the poststructuralist notion of the death of the author. Fan fiction studies recognizes how authorial agnosticism advantages authors already wielding social benefits and access to the production of literature—benefits and access that accrue from their race,

---

10. West and Kling, *Libro de las Profecías*, 81.

11. Kristina Busse, *Framing Fan Fiction: Literary and Social Practices in Fan Fiction Communities* (Iowa City: University of Iowa Press, 2017), 142.

12. Mireia Aragay, "Reflection to Refraction: Adaptation Studies Then and Now," in *Books in Motion: Adaptation, Intertextuality, Authorship*, ed. Mireia Aragay (Amsterdam: Rodopi, 2005), 12.

13. Lopez, "Curational Reflections," 76.

gender, sexuality, and so on—while disadvantaging marginalized authors. As such, fan fiction advocates for attention to the authors of texts. Splitting the difference between the tyranny of the author over the meaning of a text and the death of the author, Mireia Aragay and Gemma López offer the idea of the author "*in rememoriam*."[14] Similarly, Kristina Busse uses the notion of the "return of the author" not as a means to solve questions of intentionality but instead to shine light on the ethos of the author.[15] This modification of Roland Barthes's influential theory leaves sufficient room to observe the impact of the author's production of new texts without vesting that new text—and, in particular, its meaning—as exclusively that of the author. Further, while an authorial focus does not set out to prove intention, this focus requires ethical attention to the intertextual relationships between several works.

Like several biblical texts, establishing clear authorship of Columbian texts can prove complex. Despite my assertion of Columbus as an author, the extant textual corpus of *Libro* represents layers of editing that can be attributed to a range of persons such as Bartolomé de Las Casas, Father Gaspar Gorrico, Ferdinand Columbus at thirteen years old, as well as various editors and translators.[16] While Columbus as a historical person is not too far from the concerns of this essay, my ultimate goal rests with examining the intertextuality with biblical and Columbian texts for the generated new meanings and ideologies of those texts. Intertextuality between Isaiah and *Libro* forms the limits of this essay. I begin by situating intertextuality as a form of recycling of texts where meaning and ideology are fluid in ways that make for the unfinalizability of texts. This assertion leads next to an examination of *Libro* as fan fiction, with the attention to Columbus as an author. An outline of the intertexts between Isaiah and *Libro* follows next, focused on four major themes: global geography, the conversion of foreigners, the wealth of the nations, and the divine imperium. The essay ends by looking at how *Libro* produces new meaning for Isaiah as a Christian text in relation to prophecy, Christian imperialism, and acpocalypticism.

---

14. Mireia Aragay and Gemma López, "Inf(l)ecting Pride and Prejudice: Dialogism, Intertextuality and Adaptation," in *Books in Motion: Adaptation, Intertextuality, Authorship*, ed. Mireia Aragay (Amsterdam: Rodopi, 2005), 202, emphasis original.

15. Busse, *Framing Fan Fiction*, 27.

16. West and Kling, *Libro de las Profecías*, 81; Gimmel, "Christopher Columbus," 35.

## Intertextuality as Recycling

Recycling provides new use for old material. Intertextuality is a form of textual recycling not of discarded texts or texts deemed useless in one space that find new value in another. Rather, intertextuality as a form of recycling represents the use of textual material that generates some form of meaning in one work being deployed for similar or different meaning in another. As a form of reuse of previous material, intertextuality at best demonstrates the impact of that material, whether as a valid insight or one worthy of contestation. Aragay and López refer to intertextuality as a form of "cultural recycling" to indicate how meanings are sustained and transmitted across several works.[17] In their thinking, intertextuality makes authors into mediators of meaning, where texts are not situated into discrete moments of "before-after hierarchies." In other words, new works neither displace old works nor supplant the meanings of older works. Instead, intertextual works exist together in similar cultural spaces that disrupt the debates regarding synchrony and diachrony. The intertexts between Isaiah and *Libro* mean that rather than Isaiah exerting a towering influence and determining the meaning of what Columbus produced in *Libro*, Columbus freely deploys Isaiah for unique purposes, and Columbus's work in turn affects Isaiah. Aragay and López speak of this dual and dynamic relationship between texts as "inf(l)ection" since what can be regarded as the source text, in this case Isaiah, "is neither hermetic, nor self-sufficient, not a closed system."[18]

Thinking of intertextuality as recycling regards texts and their meanings as fluid. Since meaning is not fixed into texts requiring a single interpretation, or the monologism that Mikhail M. Bakhtin critiques, but instead texts participate in dialogism (Bakhtin) or ambivalence (Julia Kristeva) or exist as sirens and echo chambers (Harold Bloom), not only is meaning unstable but also unfinalized. Intertextuality as recycling recognizes that the fluid nature of texts gives them generative capacities. As poststructuralists such as Kristeva would have it, meaning does not merely inhere in texts since texts simply house unfinished ideas that require readers to generate meaning for these ideas and to, as Graham Allen puts it, "step into the production of meaning."[19] Readers equally as writers perform

---

17. Aragay and López, "Inf(l)ecting Pride and Prejudice," 202.
18. Aragay and López, "Inf(l)ecting Pride and Prejudice," 203.
19. Graham Allen, *Intertextuality*, NCI (London: Routledge, 2000), 34.

critical roles in the production and generation of texts. Capturing the idea of the "joint production" that occurs in communication—mostly spoken, but the same holds for written texts—Deborah Tannen draws attention to the active nature of both parties and uses the terms "interlocutors" and "interactants" rather than "speaker" or "listener."[20] The competence of the reader to function as a writer should not distract from the point of reading as an engaged activity that at times results in the generation of new writing. Fan fiction as intertextuality illustrates the interactive use of meaning among related works.

Fan fiction as a form of writing destabilizes the eighteenth-century, Western creation of the author. The creation of the author not only introduces copyright and other legal considerations but also heightens "the myth of originality."[21] In this social context, works are easily classified into those deserving of attention (high art, original works, innovative) and those seen as mere knock-offs. Intertextuality studies have shown that "all texts are necessarily criss-crossed by other texts."[22] This realization helps shift the critical inquiry away from the work and its author as tightly circumscribed products with limited and controlled interaction with broader social and cultural sources to a more expansive understanding of genealogies of texts. Bloom's sweeping view that a "text is a relational event" that Allen summarizes as "all texts are inter-texts," although not getting at the economics and politics of the modern publishing world, raises awareness of textual productions such as fan fiction that are overt about their relational nature.[23] The temptation to dismiss fan fiction easily as just imitative misses how authors actively engage texts as readers to the point of producing new works. André Carrington's analysis of how fan fiction serves as a developmental step for science fiction writers indicates the generative

---

20. Deborah Tannen, *Talking Voices: Repetition, Dialogue, and Imagery in Conversational Discourse*, 2nd ed, SIS 26 (Cambridge: Cambridge University Press, 2007), 9. Theorists such as Barthes temper such generous views in the distinction they make between readers and critics, where readers engage stable meanings while critics seek out the unstable meanings. Even further, Barthes distinguishes between texts that are capable of production by readers and those that are not. For more on "readerly" and "writerly" texts, see Allen, *Intertextuality*, 76–89.

21. Busse, *Framing Fan Fiction*, 21.

22. Judith Still and Michael Worton, "Introduction," in *Intertextuality: Theories and Practices*, ed. Judith Still and Michael Worton (Manchester: Manchester University Press, 1990), 30.

23. Allen, *Intertextuality*, 136.

capacities of texts and readers of various sorts of texts like the Bible: "every interpretive act is an act of authorship, and every act of authorship is an act of interpretation."[24]

For the writers of fan fiction, the focus is not so much on the creation of new texts but participating in the construction of meaning. Drawing out the ideologies in texts as well as engaging the ideological tools of popular works form key features of fan fiction.[25] Therefore, fan fiction represents conscious acts of interpretation and meaning-making that, unlike forms of imitative literature, do not seek to displace their original work. Judith Still and Michael Worton, in their articulation of the relationship between imitations and original works, point out how new works attempt to finish the original but also to substitute for the original as "the pre-text of the 'original.'"[26] Their idea of how closely related works exist in complementary relationships is useful for understanding how fan fiction operates, even though I do not view fan fiction as merely imitative art. At the same time, they also construe a restrictive sociocultural space that does not allow the coexistence of multiple works, particularly work that critically engages and builds new meaning from a presumed original. The assumption of sociocultural spaces where a single, perhaps normative or even canonical, text serves as the defining authority encourages the consideration of works like fan fiction or even alternative knowledge texts as marginalized texts. As a cultural production, fan fiction already exists outside normative social structures in part by the daring subversion of the role and privilege of the author. Therefore, in terms of production, circulation, and consumption, fan fiction thrives in communities familiar with the original text but, importantly, open to ongoing conversations and construction of meaning across multiple texts. As an act of cultural recycling, fan fiction demonstrates how multiple works—the canonical text transformed to an open source text, the insurgent text granted authoritative status—coexist in a culture, similar to how Carrington insists that the marginality and popularity of blackness "coincides as names for multiple facets of the same cultural phenomenon."[27]

---

24. André Carrington, *Speculative Blackness: The Future of Race in Science Fiction* (Minneapolis: University of Minnesota Press, 2016), 9.

25. Carrington, *Speculative Blackness*, 9; Busse, *Framing Fan Fiction*, 7.

26. Still and Worton, "Introduction," 7.

27. Carrington, *Speculative Blackness*, 14.

The recycling metaphor may conjure images of noncompetence and other socioeconomic presumptions associated with persons who thrive upon recycled material. However, thinking of recycling as a commonplace practice in an age of limited primary resources where almost anything needs to be built out of recycled material, then cultural recycling seems normative at all levels of cultural productions, given the type of constraints on originality that Bloom observes. Fan fiction provides a way for me to talk about Columbus as a writer of scriptural texts. My claim here is that *Libro* does more than simply use or reference Isaiah but that it reproduces Isaiah and other prophetic texts to function as a contemporary instantiation of prophetic literature. In this regard, *Libro* does more than imitate prophetic texts but stakes bold claims about Columbus and the voyages in relation to a grand divine plan. In other words, I view Columbus as a fan of prophetic texts, reproducing those texts in a way that today we can regard as fan fiction. Yet, Columbus hardly seems to be the stereotypical insurgent or marginalized voice that populates fan fiction spaces. Despite the numerous privileges that accrue to Columbus, both in his lifetime and afterwards, Columbus as the nonexpert, untrained amateur in the field of biblical exegesis comes close to the portrait of the modern fan fiction author. Calling attention to his limited skill with biblical exegesis does not reduce the ethical implications of the meaning and ideologies embedded in his works. The engagement with Isaiah and the resultant embedding of meanings and ideologies in *Libro* amounts to the overt intertextuality that characterizes fan fiction.

So far, I have argued for Columbus as a writer of specific works. My comments now may amount to killing the author. The death of Columbus as author responds to two important considerations. The question of Columbus as a writer is as fraught as the claim of Isaiah as a writer of the canonical book. The editorial work of Las Casas as well as others in the shaping and preservation of the trove of Columbian texts appears too clear to ignore. In the case of *Libro*, Columbus's guidance can be seen, but other writers explicitly declare their hands. Anxieties regarding a single identified author, current in much modern reading, take me to the second consideration: the ethos of the author. Busse proposes that since concerns about author identity tend to betray interests in establishing authorial intentionality, the return of the author should take the form of authorial ethos. Ethos broadens the scope of consideration beyond the author as a single individual and instead examines the world that produces the individual "as a historical, political, national, social, gendered, and sexed being who writes and is read within particular contexts and against specific historicopolitical and socioeconomic events."[28] Therefore, acknowledging the corporate nature of Columbian texts operating from the perspective of the author's ethos enables me to view these texts as representative of the broad worldview that was not unique to Columbus but also embraced by those who perpetuated his original ideas and expanded upon them with their own. In other words, while *Libro* may not be an entirely original work to Columbus, as a curation it reflects a strain of thought to which Columbus subscribed and helped to perpetuate in various forms. I use Columbus, therefore, as shorthand for the multiple hands that produced *Libro*.

## *Libro* as Fan Fiction

Making some of my argument work in this essay requires establishing Columbus as a writer in relation to a particular community. While I return to the notion of Columbus as writer in relation to the extant Columbian texts, I deal first here with the way his textual output participates in the literary and religious cultures of his day. My approximation of *Libro* as fan fiction rests upon the importance of the community as the site through which the type of cultural recycling or intertextuality occurs. Texts are communal in nature, whether in the actual face-to-face encounters they stimulate or the gatherings of flesh-and-blood readers who construct meaning out of their words or in the genealogies of conversations with past and future works. Even though most of the Columbian texts are directed to the small audience of two—the king and queen of Spain—the circulation of these works at the time of their writing and since then points to an even larger audience that requires attention.[29] As an overt form of intertextuality, fan fiction highlights how the audience's familiarity with ongoing conversations enables the generation of new material as well as the circulation of meaning. Delineating the precise audience for Columbus's writings poses challenges not only because these can be so defuse,

---

28. Busse, *Framing Fan Fiction*, 27.

29. Gimmel, "Christopher Columbus," 36. The document put in circulation as Columbus's letter to the Spanish crown reporting his first voyage at the early part of 1493 was first printed in Spanish in March, and by April it was translated into Latin with several other productions in various formats later that year. Elizabeth Moore Willingham, *The Mythical Indies and Columbus's Apocalyptic Letter: Imagining the Americas in the Late Middle Ages* (Brighton: Sussex Academic, 2016), 240.

but trying to categorize cultures and subcultures of the period can lead to distortions. At the risk of oversimplification, I focus on Columbus as a writer to an audience steeped in the thought forms of the medieval period attempting to conform new knowledge, particularly of the world outside of the western European experience, to these old ways of European thinking. Columbian scholars regard him as an early medieval thinker despite the intentionally, publicly crafted image of a man of learning.[30] Rather than being on the cutting edge of new learning—particularly as it relates to geography, the size of the earth, navigation, and other scientific theories—Columbus relied heavily upon cosmographies developed in the earlier medieval period using "the Bible [to] underwrite" his ideas.[31] His insistence on the small size of the earth against theories gaining traction, like those contained in the republished works of Ptolemy, along with his notable engagements with medieval literature and the Bible indicate his adherence to an older worldview.[32] That these ideas emerged from his participation in religious circles heavily influenced by Franciscanism, Joachimism, and the cosmography of Cardinal Pierre d'Ailly[33]—various players in the production and maintenance of Spanish millenarianism—may indicate a built-in readership competent with ideas in Columbus's writing. In other words, Columbus's fan fiction would find a home among Spanish millenarianists.

Millenarianism forms only one feature of Columbus's work. *Libro* fits well into fan fiction as intertextuality because it distills two broad movements at the time: the cartographic field that represented the world based upon empirical evidence, with room for biblical and mythical thinking; and the theological field that used empirical evidence as confirmation

---

30. Avalos, "Columbus as Biblical Exegete," 67. See also Zamora's discussion of Las Casas's role in the rehabilitation of Columbus's reputation (Zamora, *Reading Columbus*, 43).

31. Valerie I. J. Flint, *The Imaginative Landscape of Christopher Columbus* (Princeton: Princeton University Press, 1992), xii. Cummins describes the popular depiction that opposition to Columbus consisted largely of flat earthers, while Columbus stood as a lone voice willing to risk sailing beyond the horizon of a spherical globe, as largely "nonsense" (Cummins, *Voyage of Christopher Columbus*, 7).

32. Keller, "Columbus/Colon," 98; Gimmel, "Christopher Columbus," 36.

33. For Franciscanism, see Milhou, *Colon Y Su Mentalidad Mesianica*, 8; for Joachimism, see Fleming, "Christopher Columbus as Scriptural Exegete," 29; and West and Kling, *Libro de las Profecías*; for the cosmology, see Milhou, *Colon Y Su Mentalidad Mesianica*, 11.

for biblical teleologies. The fields of thought marked by theology and empirical evidence were not vastly distinct nor opposing fields since the church served as a facilitator of these ideas. Delno C. West and August Kling describe Columbus as engaging in "a geoeschatology to describe the relationship between geography and theology of the last times."[34] As a term, geoeschatology captures the millenarian disposition of Columbus as a reader of biblical texts as well as those in his circle of support. The uniqueness of Columbus's contributions, which may lead us to think of him creating a new mode of writing, comes from the firsthand experience of geographical encounter that he explains through biblical and theological sources. Encounters with peoples, lands, and new geographical features merely confirm Columbus's cosmology rather than expand his knowledge of the world. Therefore, as an eyewitness to experiences, he brings a powerful testimony to what he regards as the validity of biblical claims. He demonstrates what Ashley J. Barner in relation to fan fiction regards as "absorbed reading," the deep immersion into a text that results in strong associations with characters and settings. Barner indicates that absorbed readers "find themselves inside the world of the text, transported to foreign lands."[35] Although Columbus does not rewrite biblical texts and there may be legitimate concerns about the intentional choices of textual versions, his collation of biblical material indicates on one level the type of absorbed reading associated with reading the Bible as a book of faith.[36] However, Columbus goes further by insinuating himself, his work, and his age in his reconstructed biblical narrative as the recipient of the contemporary divine vocation.

An audience existed for Columbus's writings. The multilingual distribution and consumption of his letter to the Spanish crown, known as *Carta a Luis Santángel*, about his first voyage indicates this.[37] Whether that audience resonated entirely with his brand of geoeschatology and whether

---

34. West and Kling, *Libro de las Profecías*, 67. Ruiz describes his eschatology as constructed along the axis of time following millenarian thought and the axis of space in response to "biblical cosmology" (Ruiz, *Readings from the Edges*, 133).

35. Ashley J. Barner, *The Case for Fanfiction: Exploring the Pleasures and Practices of a Maligned Craft* (Jefferson, NC: McFarland, 2017), 7. Other scholars may refer to this as "insertion fantasy."

36. Avalos indicates that the compilation reflects limited knowledge of the underlying Hebrew text or use of the so-called *Hebraicum* ("Columbus as Biblical Exegete," 62).

37. Gimmel, "Christopher Columbus," 38.

he and his supporters were able to sustain it over the tumultuous course of his career remains immaterial to my concerns. That a readership existed, predisposed to interpreting Isaiah in messianic and millenarian terms, creates the ground within which Columbus can introduce his embedded work. Yet, what Columbus offers in his writings goes beyond simple interpretation of the Bible to support a supposedly sincere Christian evangelism but rather reflects a decidedly European Christian imperialist ideology, as seen in his insistence on the first voyage that no other religion be allowed to "do business or gain a foothold ... but only Catholic Christians" in what he believed to be the islands situated off the Asian continent.[38] Imperialistic elements already existed in Western Europe's entanglements in the Crusades and took on a greater fervor with the recent conquest of Granada in Spain. The novelty here comes from Columbus's geoeschatology. Columbus's geoeschatology enters into the discussions regarding the western sea route to Asia and consequently offers a real-time unfolding of various forms of writing—travelogues, Christian and other adventure tales, explorer journals—notably, for our purposes here, biblical writings that confirm self-important and national imperialist impulses. How Isaiah serves as one of his intertexts in the production of Columbus's writing forms my focus in the next section.

## Isaiah in *Libro de las Profecías*

In this section, I show the intertextual links between Isaiah and *Libro*, specifically how Columbus recasts Isaiah in *Libro* through his use of four/five major themes in Isaiah. Jean-Pierre Ruiz describes Isaiah as "the core of [Columbus's] innermost canon" that makes it a foundational biblical text in each of the four major sections of *Libro*—the preliminary material along with three sections of detailed prophetic argumentation.[39] Isaiah appears in the preliminary material, setting out the major theme of the collection via various citations from Augustine, Rabbi Samuel, Nicolas of Lyra, and d'Ailly. *Libro*'s general threefold structure conforms to a temporal organization of

---

38. The comments go on to deal with the fear that religious competition could doom the benefits of his voyages for the church and the crown: "That is the beginning and end of the whole enterprise; it should be for the growth and glory of the Christian faith and you should allow no one but good Christians to come here" (Cummins, *Voyage of Christopher Columbus*, 128).

39. Ruiz, *Readings from the Edges*, 129.

the past, present, and future. The second section, though, combines both present and future even though the third section looks at the future.

*Libro* uses a variety of biblical texts but relies upon prophetic texts not only for content but for meaning and the structure of the argument. Therefore, the compilation, at best, styles Columbus as a contemporary prophet without using this precise language. The strong appropriation of Isaiah betrays this characterization together with Columbus's claims to several religious titles for himself—explicitly and implicitly.[40] The summary statement of the Bible as: "simply the fulfillment of what Isaiah had prophesied" further indicates this deference for Isaiah.[41] In fact, *Libro* conforms other biblical texts to the prophetic standard of Isaiah. The designation of the psalmist in the citation of Ps 21:17 as "the prophet" and framing Isaiah as the source for Christian global supremacy cited from Matthew and Revelation underscore this trend.[42] To a certain extent, Columbus follows the typical Christian supercessionism around Isaiah available to him at the time. Sources such as Augustine and the converso Rabbi Samuel are enlisted in their use of Isaiah texts such as 60:1–3 and 62:12–15 as the evidence of Israel's exclusion. Consequently, he is disposed to see prophetic texts as predictors of the future, but he goes further to argue that the apostles were directed to write for the future—the future as experienced in his present. Therefore, readers of *Libro* should see themselves as participants in the fulfillment of these predictions of which Columbus has become the messenger through his first-hand account. The work sets out not so much to justify the validity of biblical prophecies but to prove "a particular prophecy, because it applies particularly to my experience."[43] Not surprisingly, despite Columbus's original title for the work, "Notebook of authorities, statements, opinions and prophecies on the subject of the recovery of God's holy city and mountain of Zion, and on the discovery and evangelization of the islands of the Indies and of all other peoples and nations," later library catalogers titled the work, *Libro de las Profecías*.[44]

---

40. From 1501, Columbus adopts the signet *Xpō ferens* in his writings, which Las Casas views as an indication of his claim of the title "Christ bearer" (West and Kling, *Libro de las Profecías*, 2).

41. West and Kling, *Libro de las Profecías*, 111.

42. West and Kling, *Libro de las Profecías*, 103.

43. West and Kling, *Libro de las Profecías*, 110.

44. West and Kling, *Libro de las Profecías*, 2.

Both the original and adopted title of the work betray its direct engagement with prophetic literature. That catalogers saw resemblances to prophetic books is not only evident in the profound use of prophetic texts. The appropriation of prophetic literature also appears in the framing of the collection. The first major portion of *Libro* consists of a letter to Isabella and Ferdinand, where Columbus sets out the evangelical purposes of his voyages. In doing so, he presents himself as a divinely chosen servant echoing the motif of self-effacement common in prophetic narratives: "the Lord opened my mind to the fact that it would be possible to sail from here to the Indies," and "I am unlearned in literature, a layman, a mariner, a common worldly man, etc."[45] These attempts at humility are underscored by the citation of Matt 11:25 to claim the title of one of Jesus's infants blessed to receive the knowledge hidden from the wise. The contrived battle with knowledge leads to appropriating Paul's stance of the receipt of an entirely divine vocation without human approval (see Gal 1:1). In this case, Columbus asserts an overreliance upon the Bible at the expense of scientific knowledge: "And I lay aside all the sciences and books that I indicated above. I hold only to the sacred Holy Scriptures, and to the interpretations of prophecy by certain devout persons who have spoken on this subject by divine illumination."[46] The seemingly generalist features of these appropriations notwithstanding, Isaiah serves as an authoritative voice for the supercessionist argument directed at the financing of the recapture of Jerusalem to effect a Christian global imperialism. Columbus approvingly cites Augustine's affinity for Isaiah "because [Isaiah] predicts more clearly than the others concerning the gospel and the calling of the Gentiles."[47] Even more, he credits Isaiah with what he sees as the success of

---

45. West and Kling, *Libro de las Profecías*, 105. Columbus also invokes the intensity and sense of inevitability of the divine vocation as seen in Jer 20:9 in these words: "This was the fire that burned within me.... Who can doubt that this fire / was not merely mine, but also of the Holy Spirit"; West and Kling, *Libro de las Profecías*, 107. Columbus also makes use of the trope of the misunderstood prophet who suffers social ostracism and humiliation: "All who found out about my project denounced it with laughter and ridiculed me," as seen in Jer 20:4, 8.

46. West and Kling, *Libro de las Profecías*, 107.

47. West and Kling, *Libro de las Profecías*, 143. Columbus also includes other theological sources in support of the primacy of Isaiah: "Isaiah is the one [i.e., prophet] that is appreciated and esteemed / more than all the others by Jerome, Augustine and the other theologians" (West and Kling, *Libro de las Profecías*, 109). Isaiah's place as a revered book of the Bible continued into the medieval period. It was viewed as pro-

his voyages and link between the voyages and the reconquest of Jerusalem: "the journey to the Indies ... was simply the fulfillment of what Isaiah had prophesied, and this is what I desire to write in this book."[48]

While a seemingly random collection of biblical texts, *Libro* pulls together a number of citations that effectively channel the prophetic persona of the one announcing judgment upon Israel onto Columbus. Unlike the prophetic texts that resolve with the restoration of Israel, in keeping with other supercessionist ideas, *Libro* envisions the restoration of Jerusalem as an entirely Christian benefit. *Libro* aims at a novel purpose to position maritime travel and discovery as integral elements in effecting this divine plan. Isaiah, in particular, assists this purpose because his geographical and theological outlook could be forced into Columbus's geoeschatology. I now outline how four/five features of this Isaianic geography and theology produce *Libro* as fan fiction.

Geography forms the first major intertextual connection between *Libro* and Isaiah. In the first section, entitled "Concerning What Has Already Taken Place," *Libro* adopts Isaiah's cosmogony. Isaiah's worldview that includes islands and other references to the sea provides a formative ground for Columbus's geoeschatology. Biblical texts like 2 Esd 6:42, read as indicating the size of the earth as well as the relation of land masses to oceans, and Gen 10, leading to conclusions of three continents—one for each of Noah's sons—informed contemporary geographic knowledge. However, Isaiah's geography of islands offshore of a continent is read as continental coasts. That their conversion becomes a platform for the divine glory convinces Columbus of the rightness of his voyages. His own notion of a series of islands that lie off the Asian continent, perhaps drawn in part from Martin Behaim's 1492 globe, are confirmed for him when he lands in the Caribbean on the first voyage and later on the third voyage when he presumes to have found the gateway to Eden when he sails around the mouth of the Orinoco River.[49] The belief that his geographical experience exactly mirrors Isaiah's geography raises his cause to a higher and nobler

---

viding a range of knowledge from the revelation of Christ to, in Jerome's estimation, "whatever the human tongue can express and the mind of mortals understand, is contained in that book" (John F. A. Sawyer, *The Fifth Gospel: Isaiah in the History of Christianity* [New York: Cambridge University Press, 1996], 2).

48. West and Kling, *Libro de las Profecías*, 111.

49. Cummins, *Voyage of Christopher Columbus*, 8.

purpose as articulated in Isaiah—the conversion of the islands as the prelude to the restoration of Jerusalem.[50]

Isaiah exhibits a unique geographical knowledge among prophetic texts. Deportations and the return to Judah prompt the representation of an expansive geographical scope in prophetic texts. Even though other prophetic texts reflect this expansion in the range of landed spaces, Isaiah offers a more heightened marine spatiality. Isaiah deploys the term *'î* seventeen times as compared with four in Jeremiah, nine in Ezekiel, and once in Zephaniah. Establishing Isaiah's precise geographic references for the term *'î* can prove difficult—whether coastlines or islands are in view.[51] Nonetheless, the Vulgate consistently translates *'îîm* as *insule* ("islands"), so that *Libro* picks up ten of the mentions from Isaiah. In addition, Isaiah contains twenty-four references to marine and maritime spaces with the word *yām* and a further eight mentions of *mayim* as a nautical entity. *Libro* uses seven and four of these occurrences, respectively. Closer analysis of the Isaiah texts in *Libro* reveals more than simply a random or even consistent attraction to particular words. Instead, the spatial knowledge of marine spaces dotted with islands that travel across seas or waters, along with a developed sense of the existence of distant geographic spaces, paints a compelling worldview that *Libro* imbibes. Therefore, verses such as Isa 24:14–16; 41:1–5; 42:4, 10, 12, 15 that offer a geography of divine control over vast spaces that include islands and distant lands as well as the vision of these spaces becoming part of the praise, justice, and purview of God are characteristic of the statement that *Libro* constructs in its use of Isaiah.

This geography of distance being brought near as a result of God's intervention complements a geography of foreignness reduced by conversion. Drawing upon texts that include invocations of islands and other distant places to praise God (Isa 24:14–16; 41:1) as well as the first poem featuring the commission of the divine servant to the nations and the

---

50. Although Columbus's son Ferdinand compiles the material in the second major section of *Libro* relating to geography, biblical citations from Columbus's journal reflect similar ideas.

51. The standard view that *'î* refers to islands or coastlands, in particular "the coasts of Asia Minor and Syria" as well as "the Mediterranean islands and coastlands," means that Isaiah's geography is largely unremarkable for most modern commentators. Klaus Baltzer, *Deutero-Isaiah*, trans. Margaret Kohl, Hermeneia (Minneapolis: Fortress, 2001), 139, 305. At times, the term is read as a specific island, such as Tyre in Isa 23:2, 6. J. J. M. Roberts, *First Isaiah*, Hermeneia (Minneapolis: Fortress, 2015), 301.

islands' expectation of justice from this servant (Isa 42:1–4) reflects the second major intertextual connection—conversion of foreigners. These selected texts appear to establish a history of successful conversion of foreigners for the benefit of Jerusalem. *Libro* accomplishes this by gathering up portions of Isaiah's geography that include known and unknown places. This already known geography, as given in the Vulgate, consists of places in parts of Africa (Egypt, Ethiopia, Saba as cited in Isa 43:1–7; 60:1–22, Africa as a whole and Libya as cited in 66:18–24), Europe (Italy and Greece as cited in 66:18–24), and Asia (Midian, Lebanon as cited in 60:1–22, Bosrah as cited in 63:1). These citations make for a compelling case of a lived reality of the successful conversion of foreigners. Particular Isaiah texts are useful to make this point. The Cyrus oracle complements the servant poem with a named historical figure described as having conquered other peoples as a called servant of God (Isa 45:1–6). The citation following Cyrus, in the Vulgate text used, refers to a righteous man from the east (*iustum et de terra longinqua* [Isa 46:11]) called by God from a distant country to carry out the divine will. The vocation of the unnamed individual fits the purposes of *Libro* since the nature of the vocation involves the challenge to the stubborn that are distant (perhaps to be read spatially) to recognize the nearness of God's justice and salvation (Isa 46:12–13). Interestingly, when *Libro* turns to another of the servant poems, it intentionally zooms in on the glorification of the servant rather than the humiliation (so Isa 52:15, not 52:14) along with the successful cowering of nations and their rulers.

Using Isa 66:18–24 to close out the Isaiah portion of the first section, *Libro* builds the picture of conversion to Christianity. However folk as distinct from Judeans represented in the term *gôy* being brought to the glory of God in Isaiah is interpreted—perhaps as religious conversion or acknowledgment of God's supremacy—the Vulgate's translation of *gentes* conjures the non-Christian, given the broad evangelical purposes announced at the start of the compilation.[52] A fuller development of the use of Isaiah to fill out *Libro*'s evangelical vision occurs in the second section that focuses on the present and the future. This section begins with Isa 2:2–3, which sets the stage for the anticipated inflow of the people from distant lands into Jerusalem. The Isaiah texts used here involve a combination of those

---

52. For a discussion on religious conversion in Isaiah, see Joel Kaminsky and Anne Stewart, "God of All the World: Universalism and Developing Monotheism in Isaiah 40–66," *HTR* 99 (2006): 139–63.

that envision the movement of people toward the global center of Jerusalem (Isa 5:26; 6:11–13; 8:9), international recognition of and praise for God's deeds (Isa 12:4–6; 26:1–3; 33:13–14a, 17, 20), as well as commands to declare these deeds and praise in distant places (Isa 12:4b–6; 18:1–7). As such, they help frame the broader evangelical purposes assigned to Columbus's voyages as well as the incorporation of new geographic spaces into a European sphere of influence.

The third major intertextual connection, the hidden wealth of foreign lands, appears largely in the first section. The Isaianic vision of the wealth of nations as a source for the reconstruction of Jerusalem features prominently in this section of the compilation. The inclusion of the vocation of Cyrus that mentions the acquisition of hidden treasures from unknown places (Isa 45:3) stands out for its modeling of an ancient role that Columbus assumes. While the exploitation of this wealth is presented as historical fact, the passages used here reflect the Zionism of Isaiah that undergirds much of Columbus's conflation of the voyages with the reconquest of Jerusalem. The extensive use of a hymn to Jerusalem (Isa 60:1–22) helps to emphasize this point. In this promise to the lethargic Jerusalem, the ingathering of the world not only ushers in the return of Jerusalem's deported children (60:4) but also the conversion of those nations (60:3) and the appropriation of their wealth (60:6–7). At first glance, the inflow of wealth appears voluntary, but on closer reading, it stands as enforced handover of wealth (see 60:12).[53] The legal or moral nuances of the acquisition of the wealth notwithstanding, *Libro* makes the point that treasures exist in the world for the expressed purpose of the rebuilding of Jerusalem. Even more to the point, that these treasures exist overseas and require marine voyages to access them (60:9) falls in line with *Libro*'s central argument. The weight of the central argument in *Libro* requires more than generic references to treasures and instead relies upon the mention of specific minerals: hence the inclusion of verses that detail in tangible ways these sources of wealth. The concretizing of the appeal is first made with the inclusion of references to historic images of richness—flocks of Kedar, rams of Nebaioth (60:7), and Lebanon's lumber resources (60:13). The inclusion of specific forms of mineral wealth, in this case minerals of superior value (60:17), provides the enticement needed to support the voyages. Here, these seemingly crass

---

53. Charles E. Cruise, "The 'Wealth of the Nations': A Study in the Intertextuality of Isaiah 60:5, 11," *JETS* 58 (2015): 287.

motives are tempered with the noble purpose of the possibility of a new dispensation. The Isaiah portion of this section is closed out with the two verses from Isaiah that deal with new heaven and new earth (65:17 and 66:22). Isaiah's vision of improved quality of life following the re-creation of Jerusalem (65:19–25) along with religious orthodoxy (66:23–24) deepens the economic motivations for the voyages even as it exposes some of the contradictory impulses.

In the third and final section of *Libro*, titled "Prophecies of the Future: The Last Days," the imperialist designs are laid bare. In this section, the fourth intertextual connection, the divine imperium, appears in the form of expanding that imperium to include islands. In Isaiah, Zion's centrality forms the basis for the divine imperium with the rest of the world in various ways coming to acknowledge the divine supremacy. This section of *Libro* curiously omits references to Zion and instead leans upon verses from Isaiah that reference the incorporation of islands in the praise and justice of God. The emphasis upon the islands indicates that up to this point, for Columbus and others around him, exploration consisted largely of finding new islands rather than continents. Their positions also confirm the durability of the three-continent view of the earth. Therefore, these new islands are the new territories to be subsumed into the divine imperium. Further, these islands, presumably located on the edge of Asia, prove to be propitious for establishing the necessary contact with the Grand Khan as a partner in the conversion of the world as well as the exploitation of the riches needed for the reconquest of Jerusalem.[54] In other places in *Libro*, Zion's centrality builds a philosophical case for Christian imperialism; in this section, its absence enables the use of Isaiah's geography to construct a new cartography of empire. Islands rather than already-known continents—namely, Africa and Asia—form the new frontier of Christian domination.

The use of Isaiah's geography in this section takes a curious path. Rather than starting with Isaiah as the other two sections, section three

---

54. The notion of the Grand Khan as open to the receipt and possible expansion of Christianity in China dates back to the thirteenth century reports of Marco Polo and a history of general cordial relationships between Christian missionaries and Chinese leaders. This history may have exerted a strong influence upon Columbus. Although the situation drastically changed in the sixteenth century, limited communication allowed medieval perceptions to persist (Cummins, *Voyage of Christopher Columbus*, 8–16).

begins with the somewhat generic citation of Jer 25:1a to keep with the prophetic theme but also to characterize the quotation from Joachim as a prophetic prediction of a Spanish monarch leading the reconquest of Jerusalem as cited in the letter of the Genoese Deputies to the Spanish crown in 1492. The ten pages following this declaration are missing, so it is not clear how the work develops from this assertion and if any biblical texts are used. Nonetheless the artifice of leading with Isaiah as in the other two sections gives way here to Gen 10:1, 3 (cf. 1 Chr 1:7) to introduce the discussion on Tarshish. In a marginal note, Columbus in his own hand concludes that Tarshish has three different referents: that of the name of a man, the city of Paul's origins, and the name of an island. Various biblical references to Tarshish (nine in total), such as 2 Chr 20:35–37; 1 Kgs 10:21–22; and Jer 10:9 are squeezed into an island that Columbus regards as Ophir. Solomon's naval exploits as recorded in 1 Kgs 9:26–28 along with a comment from Nicholas of Lyra on the verse helps equate Tarshish with Ophir. This equation proves important since, biblically, Orphir appears as a source for gold, a source available to Solomon in his construction of the temple as seen in several verses that *Libro* cites, such as 1 Kgs 9:25; 10:11; 22:49. These verses lay the foundation for discussing Tarshish and Ophir as islands. Here, Isaiah takes the lead in confirming the existence of the island that it refers to as Cethim (Isa 23:1–2, 12). From there, *Libro* proceeds to highlight the value of islands for the reconstitution of Zion. As before, Isaiah's island geography proves useful. Previous verses are deployed again, this time with the full background of the necessity of islands in general but the biblically crucial island of Tarshish as a necessity to the reconquest of Jerusalem. In this regard, verses such as Isa 49:1; 51:5; 60:9; 66:19 assume strong evangelical as well as imperialist valences. The islands wait in expectation of a divine power ready to take possession of them in order that they may serve the purpose of establishing divine supremacy over the earth.

## *Libro*'s Construction of New Meaning

The extensive use of biblical texts in *Libro* means that the intertextual connections there are broader and more complex than indicated in this work. This narrow look at Isaiah—one of the biblical books used in *Libro*—has the potential to distort this complexity and even to oversimplify intertextual connections with Isaiah as well as Isaiah's intertextuality with other biblical texts, particularly New Testament texts. Despite these limitations, the curation of noticeable amounts of material from Isaiah indicates the decided recycling of Isaiah—in concert with other biblical texts—to create a new meaning for Isaiah. The aims of *Libro* to connect the reconquest of Jerusalem with Columbus's voyages mean that whatever interpretation of Isaiah existed previously, *Libro* deploys Isaiah for a unique purpose. This meaning may not be novel in the broadest sense of the term *new*, yet *Libro* brings emphases to Isaiah that heightens easily overlooked aspects of the book in its historical settings.

The threefold structure of *Libro* establishes a temporal frame for reading biblical texts, where prophetic predictions are read as historical record. Titling the first section as "What Has Already Taken Place" forces these selected texts within past history. The concern as to whether or not these texts point to actual historical events gives way to the more pressing concern to prove that God previously established Zion's supremacy and the various elements involved in that former event. While arguments for the Crusades and other Christian Zionist positions may have drawn upon Isaiah texts for their motivation, *Libro* builds its case on the basis of a historical nautical enterprise that establishes Zion's supremacy. That the past as read through Isaiah has several clear connections with the present is a convenient artifice that *Libro* both constructs and exploits. Engineering Isaiah as a historical text adds another element to the prediction-fulfillment role of prophetic texts. Here *Libro* offers two interesting developments: first, to call readers to see Isaiah as more than a pointer to an unknown future but as a recorder of a dependable past upon which to build contemporary action; second, *Libro* situates readers as direct recipients of Isaiah's prophetic vision. The orthodox christological outcomes of Isaiah give way here to realizable possibilities for the contemporary reader. *Libro* reshapes Isaiah's temporality into a different past, present, and future than already given within the book. Taken together with the application of Isaiah's geography to fit into existing cartographic frames, this temporality makes Isaiah, as text, at once a witness to and participant in Christian imperialism. The components of ideology and geography necessary for this religious imperialism may already lie within Isaiah in the form of Zionism and the aspirations of a dislocated group to repopulate their city. However, as *Libro* coopts these elements, the Zionism of Isaiah underwrites the historical trends of European displacement of indigenous peoples from their lands. Allowing for the contention as to whether removing Muslims from Jerusalem counts as displacement of indigenous people, the animus present within *Libro*, reflective of long-held Christian antipathy toward Jews, indicates that Isaiah serves once again as the convenient polemic against Jews and subsequent gateway for antagonisms against other groups.[55]

Reading Isaiah within the frame of Christian supercessionism is not unique to *Libro*, particularly in this time period. *Libro*, however, replaces Jews as the special targets of Christian displacement with Muslims along with other religions and nonreligious peoples. In this regard, *Libro* makes a special claim for using Isaiah to justify the necessity of nautical Christian missions to assert territorial control over Jerusalem. Isaiah then becomes not simply a supercessionist text vis-à-vis Jews or even Muslims, to the extent that they are seen as original participants in the divine covenant, but an authenticator of all forms of religious intolerance. Situating the Isaiah texts within Columbus's evangelical ideology as seen not only in *Libro* but also in his various correspondences with the Spanish crown reveals the Christian imperialism that propelled his vision. In the *Carta a Luis Santángel*, Columbus marvels at the naïve inhabitants—"so guileless and so free"—of the islands whom he regards as devoid of "any cult or idolatry."[56] In the concluding statements of the letter, connections are drawn that indicate the potential for exploitation of the people and land for Christianity: "Christians ought to take joy … for the great glory that they will have in converting so many nations … for material riches, for which not only Spain but all Christian lands, henceforward will have consolation and profit."[57] These sentiments recur in other places, notably in the title of *Libro*, where the recapture of Jerusalem and the evangelization of "the islands of the Indies" are joined goals.

When compared with earlier use of Isaiah in the New Testament, *Libro*'s production of imperialist and missionary meaning in Isaiah seems new. In fact, *Libro* appears to press the ancient Christian claim of Isaiah as "more evangelist than prophet" into service.[58] Of the several times New Testament works use Isaiah, no one uses the passages that reference geography, wealth of nations, or the centrality of Zion with the intensity of

---

55. Among early church fathers, Isaiah's critique of Israelites provides the justification for the denunciation of Jews and those considered heretical, such as Gnostics, Arians, or Pelagians. See Robert Louis Wilken, Angela Russell Christman, and Michael J. Hollerich, eds., *Isaiah: Interpreted by Early Christian and Medieval Commentators*, CB (Grand Rapids: Eerdmans, 2007), xxv.

56. Willingham, *Mythical Indies*, 192; Willingham, *Mythical Indies*, 193.

57. Willingham, *Mythical Indies*, 195.

58. Sawyer, *Fifth Gospel*, 1.

*Libro*.⁵⁹ Admittedly, the New Testament produces themes such as the stubbornness of outsiders that require light to be shed upon their darkness (for example, Matt 12:15–21; cf. Isa 42:1–4; Matt 13:14; Luke 8:8–9; cf. Isa 6:9; Acts 13:46–47; cf. Isa 49:6) without the level of geographic specificity that *Libro* implies. Of course, there is no straight line that connects an interpretative genealogy from Isaiah to *Libro*. Yet, the intertextual lines reveal new emphases in the imperialist and missionary use of Isaiah. Modern Isaiah scholarship is yet to explore fully the imperialist contours of the book and therefore to situate the production of Isaiah within an imperialist context, not simply as victims of empire or offering a "counter rhetoric" to empire but as implicated within and replicating imperial structures.⁶⁰ The generation and sustaining of imperialist meaning in Isaiah in *Libro* and at the hand of Columbus—directly or indirectly does not matter—whose voyages opened the door to modern European imperialism and imperialist missions may not settle a chicken-and-egg debate, but these features certainly illustrate the imperialist potential within Isaiah that *Libro* effectively exploits.⁶¹ With Isaiah as the basis for his argumentation, Columbus indicates to the Spanish crown how Isaiah and the prophecies relate to Jerusalem, which he refers to in affectionate terms: "so that you may rejoice in the other things that I am going to tell you about *our* Jerusalem upon the basis of the *same authority*."⁶²

The temporal recast of Isaiah in *Libro* also has the effect of heightening Isaiah's apocalyptic content. Columbus outlines a historical schema he credits to Augustine that indicates the end of the world in "the seventh millennium."⁶³ By tracing this idea through biblical and theological writings, he estimates a further one hundred fifty years before the end of the world. Although the biblical sources require both prophetic and gospel texts as the basis for apocalyptic ideas, these are all subsumed into Isaiah in his characterization of Isaiah as a shape-shifting book: "They say that Isaiah is not merely a prophet, but is a gospel writer as well. He is the one who concentrated every effort upon describing future events and upon

---

59. See the tables in Sawyer, *Fifth Gospel*, 26–28.
60. Walter Brueggemann, "Patriotism for Citizen of the Penultimate Superpower," *Di* 42 (2003): 342.
61. See the influence of Isaiah upon Methodist and Baptist missionary movements (Sawyer, *Fifth Gospel*, 149, 153).
62. West and Kling, *Libro de las Profecías*, 111, emphasis added.
63. West and Kling, *Libro de las Profecías*, 109.

calling all peoples to the holy catholic faith."[64] In this case, Isaiah performs the apocalyptic role not simply in a generic sense but in service of his "particular prophecy." To work in this way, Isaiah must be apocalyptic regarding a future that outlines the end of the world after the accomplishment of global evangelism, with global evangelism serving as the heart of his project. Consequently, broader sections of Isaiah are placed in the service of describing the future in the categories of Christian ascendency over new territories as the mark of the end of the age. Even the book of Revelation in its use of Isaiah to construct apocalyptic material does not resort to the texts used in *Libro* or to the argument reliant upon the sequence of historical events that tie evangelical conversions to Christianity to eschatology.[65]

The prefatory section of *Libro* conforms the collection to an outline of history that draws its dating from the *Book of Harmony of True Astronomy and Record of History* constructed out of a mixture of biblical material, astronomy, and maps. This work presumably sponsored by King Alfonso X divides history into seven periods with eight critical events. These events invariably involve some form of desecration of Jerusalem (apostasy) and its control by undesirable forces (Ishmaelites, Saracens). That "the king of the Romans" reoccupying Jerusalem "for a week and a half of time, that is ten / years and one half" marks the eighth event opens the space for a series of Isaiah texts to confirm this schema.[66] The Isaiah verses consist of texts that deal with the return of deported Judeans to Jerusalem (Isa 11:26; 27:13; 30:18–19; 35:1–2, 9–10), the global recognition of Jerusalem's centrality (Isa 25: 6–7, 9–10; 27:13; 40:17) as well as a savior figure who would deliver Jerusalem (Isa 22:20–25; 55:3–5). The effect here and in the other places that *Libro* uses Isaiah is that the book—rather than single portions of the book—is seen apocalyptically. Whatever cataclysmic events Isaiah envisages are expanded beyond the historical frame of the book into the fifteenth and sixteenth centuries. This interpretative stretching of Isaiah is not that different from the christological interpretation that dates to earliest Christian interpretation of Isaiah. The point here is that Isaiah serves not simply as biblical authentication for the ideas of Christian imperialism

---

64. West and Kling, *Libro de las Profecías*, 109.

65. Sawyer locates Revelation's use of Isaiah around themes of "visionary experience and language ... christological titles and descriptions,... and eschatology" (Sawyer, *Fifth Gospel*, 29).

66. West and Kling, *Libro de las Profecías*, 165.

but that the current age needs to be seen in apocalyptic terms to situate the Columbus project as consonant with European imperialism. That is to say, *Libro* asserts a dramatic historical shift.

In making this claim, *Libro* both calls for action by the Spanish crown and consents to that action to initiate the recovery of Jerusalem and usher history to its fulfillment. The letter portion of *Libro* conveniently ends by citing Joachim's prophecy that "the restorer of the house of Mt. Zion would come out of Spain,"[67] presumably encouraging Ferdinand to see himself as the "new David."[68] Although framed within apocalyptic terms, where the final paragraph of the letter presents the urgency of the apocalyptic moment in Islamaphobic categories, the new David title participates in nationalist-imperialist ideas to position Spain ahead of its competitors. The use of apocalyptic in support of nationalist aspirations or to motivate political or military action is unsurprising at a time when texts like Tim LaHaye's *Left Behind* series proved crucial in manufacturing consent for US military action in Iraq at the start of the twenty-first century.[69] Yet, this use too may be commonplace for a medieval mindset. Interestingly, both *Libro* and *Left Behind* occupy the fan fiction space where biblical texts are recycled and where new meaning is inserted into those texts as they are presented in different forms. *Libro*'s lean to the apocalyptic and Isaiah becomes important to ensure that Columbus's work would be stalled by neither the controversies that followed his enchained return to Spain nor hesitance on the part of the Spanish crown to seize the moment. New meaning therefore occurs in the immediacy of Isaiah to the period, personalities, and program of the readers of *Libro*.

## Conclusion

Readers familiar with fan fiction will find *Libro* a far cry from its modern counterparts. Eccentric interpretations, special pleading, and absorbed readings along with other features common to fan fiction appear in *Libro* despite its medieval literary character. Repurposing Isaiah to ensure the continuation and success of evangelical imperialism that Columbus

---

67. West and Kling, *Libro de las Profecías*, 111.

68. West and Kling, *Libro de las Profecías*, 170; Milhou, *Colon Y Su Mentalidad Mesianica*.

69. Charles Marsh, "Wayward Christian Soldiers," *New York Times*, January 20, 2006.

articulates in *Libro* and other places results in a work that appeals to the millenarian mindset. The recycling of Isaiah in this regard may seem amateurish and therefore easily dismissed. For this reason, fan fiction offers to broaden the scope of intertextual use of biblical texts. Precisely the readers of the Bible willing to challenge, subvert, and even distort established meanings of biblical texts provide indications of engaged readings of these texts. These intertextual examples offer more than simple imitations and the pious reproductions of static confessional meanings. Of course, absorbed readers like Columbus illustrate how deep pieties can uncritically press authoritative biblical texts into service. This expanded field of inquiry connecting biblical intertextuality into arenas such as fan fiction illustrates that the Bible—either texts or purported authors—does not control its meaning. That the production of meaning occurs in various venues is no new revelation. However, the multiplicity of sites broadens the scope and nature of the history of interpretation, largely restricted to certain traditional locations. Such multiplicity enables not only greater diversity but also a more dynamic engagement with the production of biblical meaning. *Libro* indicates the existence of a thicker and deeper genealogy of interpretation of Isaiah, an interpretation that occurs at a crucial moment in history. While that history is not easily overlooked, the role that Isaiah and other biblical texts played not simply in that historical moment but in reaffirming that biblical texts can be selected, applied, and, in their authoritative role, be authenticated with the level of historical certainty that Columbus attempts to assert in *Libro* raises important ethical concerns regarding the generativity of biblical texts at various levels of the production and sustaining of meaning of these texts.

# Dietrich Bonhoeffer, Dongju Yun, and the Legacies of Jeremiah and the Suffering Servant

*Hyun Chul Paul Kim*

Reading the Bible in English provides clear nuances, but I also feel a degree of cultural and linguistic distance. Reading in Hebrew, the original language, yields new and deeper meanings, though I still feel like I am reading through several filters. Thus, when I read in Korean, my mother tongue (albeit another translation from the original language), I discover significantly different yet profound insights as intimate as a childhood memory and as illuminating as solving a riddle. It is like tasting my favorite comfort food from home or like the eureka moment from the animated film *Ratatouille*; it is an extraordinary feeling that seems almost impossible to describe. So, in the intertextual (and interlingual and intercultural) interactions, such unavoidable filters can function not only as obstacles to overcome or penetrate but also as lenses for a more lucid and authentic understanding.[1]

It is through the intertextual dialogues with my Korean heritage (such as culture, history, and literature) that I would like to (re)read and (re)interpret the select prophetic texts of Isaiah and Jeremiah. To do so, I will expound two great biblical figures—Jeremiah and the (suffering) servant—in intertextual comparisons with two modern heroic figures—Dietrich Bonhoeffer

---

1. "[The text] is a permutation of texts, an intertextuality: in the space of a given text, several utterances, taken from other texts, intersect and neutralize one another" (Julia Kristeva, *Desire in Language: A Semiotic Approach to Literature and Art*, ed. Leon S. Roudiez, trans. Thomas Gora, Alice Jardine, and Leon S. Roudiez [New York: Columbia University Press, 1980], 36). Consider also Michael Fishbane, *Biblical Interpretation in Ancient Israel* (Oxford: Clarendon, 1985), 7: "Inner-biblical exegesis starts with the received Scripture and moves forward to the interpretations based on it."

and Dongju Yun.² Admittedly, there is an enormous gap between the ancient texts/contexts and modern texts/contexts. At the same time, ironically, every reading is done by writing, and every interpretation is only possible by the interpreter's filtered reproduction.³ This reproduction is further filtered by language, be it English or Korean.⁴ There is no other way but to understand or interpret through language. Despite evident differences, I contend that interpretations and intertextual comparisons of Jeremiah and the servant can be enriched through dialogue with the lives, legacies, and literature of Bonhoeffer and Yun. First, we will briefly review the interrelated situations and impact of Jeremiah and the servant through literary links. Then we will analyze the common histories of Bonhoeffer and Yun by examining two select poems. Observations and delineations of both the commonalities and unique features of these modern figures offer the possibility of shedding new light on our understanding of the ancient texts, contexts, and theologies.

## Intertextuality between the Prophet Jeremiah and Deutero-Isaiah's Suffering Servant

Intertextuality on the literary connections between Isaiah and Jeremiah has been studied by numerous scholars. Among many, Shalom Paul's

---

2. For a study comparing Jeremiah and Bonhoeffer, see Ian Stockton, "Bonhoeffer's Wrestling with Jeremiah," *ModB* 40 (1999): 50: "For all their distance from each other and from us, Dietrich Bonhoeffer, the German Lutheran theologian and Jeremiah, the ancient Israelite prophet, are in my thinking inextricably linked ... because of certain parallels of circumstances, vocation and suffering." Note also the comparison chart on 53–54.

3. "One of the questions that arise when we are working with intertextuality is who decides which intertexts are *relevant* for the interpretation.... Is it the writer or the reader who decides? My immediate response is that it is the writer who through the use of markers indicates which intertexts the reader should include.... But what reader-response criticism reminds us is that texts can say both *more and less* than the writer's intention.... Poetical texts such as hymns can therefore say more than their writer originally intended" (Kirsten Nielsen, "The Holy Spirit as Dove and as Tongues of Fire: Reworking Biblical Metaphors in a Modern Danish Hymn," in *Enigmas and Images: Studies in Honor of Tryggve N. D. Mettinger*, ed. Göran Eidevall and Blaženka Scheuer [Winona Lake, IN: Eisenbrauns, 2011], 252–53, emphasis original).

4. "Each translation is, of course, a re-authoring.... Every reading is always a rewriting.... Readers, in any case, construct authors" (Daniel Chandler, "Intertextuality," in *Semiotics for Beginners* [London: Routledge, 2004], http://visual-memory.co.uk/daniel/Documents/S4B/sem09.html).

work is one of the most groundbreaking and meticulous.⁵ Concerning Jeremiah, Robert P. Carroll elucidated manifold features of intertextuality within Jeremiah, while William L. Holladay cogently constructed intertextual correlations of the two books in his commentaries.⁶ Ute Wendel, focusing primarily on the prophetic judgment of social and cultic corruption, presented cases of how Jeremiah adopted and reused many words, motives, and passages from Isaiah.⁷ Reinhard G. Kratz proposed a redactional reconstruction in which the *Grundschrift* of Isa 40:1–52:10, read closely from the literary horizon of Jer 25–51, quite possibly once existed as a follow-up, a next section, of the book of Jeremiah.⁸ In recent decades, Benjamin D. Sommer presented systematic analyses on Deutero-Isaiah's inner-biblical allusions on Proto-Isaiah and Jeremiah in light of various cases and patterns, just as Patricia Tull Willey provided an extensive study of Deutero-Isaiah's echoes of Jeremiah, Psalms, Lamentations, and more.⁹

In line with these pioneering works, we will examine select complaints of Jeremiah with the so-called servant passages in Isaiah with regard to the literary links alongside prophetic personas and legacies. The complaints

---

5. Shalom Paul, "Literary and Ideological Echoes of Jeremiah in Deutero-Isaiah," in vol. 1 of *Proceedings of the Fifth World Congress of Jewish Studies*, ed. Pinchas Peli (Jerusalem: World Union of Jewish Studies, 1969), 109–21. See also Umberto Cassuto, "On the Formal and Stylistic Relationships between Deutero-Isaiah and Other Biblical Writers," in vol. 1 of *Oriental and Other Studies*, ed. Umberto Cassuto (Jerusalem: Magnes, 1973), 143–60.

6. Robert P. Carroll, "Intertextuality and the Book of Jeremiah: Animadversions on Text and Theory," in *The New Literary Criticism and the Hebrew Bible*, ed. J. Cheryl Exum and David J. A. Clines, JSOTSup 143 (Sheffield: JSOT Press, 1993), 55–78; William L. Holladay, *Jeremiah 2*, Hermeneia (Minneapolis: Fortress, 1989).

7. Ute Wendel, *Jesaja und Jeremia: Worte, Motive und Einsichten Jesajas in der Verkündigung Jeremias*, BTSt 25 (Neukirchener-Vluyn: Neukirchener Verlag, 1995). See also Uwe Becker, "Jesaja, Jeremia und die Anfänge der Unheilsprophetie in Juda," *HBAI* 6 (2017): 79–100.

8. Reinhard G. Kratz, "Der Anfang des Zweiten Jesaja in Jes 40,1 f. und das Jeremiabuch," *ZAW* 106 (1994): 243–61.

9. Benjamin D. Sommer, *A Prophet Reads Scripture: Allusion in Isaiah 40–66*, Contra (Stanford, CA: Stanford University Press, 1998), 61–66; Patricia Tull Willey, *Remember the Former Things: The Recollection of Previous Texts in Second Isaiah*, SBLDS 161 (Atlanta: Scholars Press, 1997). See also Baruch Halpern, "The New Names of Isaiah 62:4: Jeremiah's Reception in the Restoration and the Politics of 'Third Isaiah,'" *JBL* 117 (1998): 623–43.

(also known as "confessions") of Jeremiah, like the lament psalms, share key phrases that recur in the depictions of the servant in Isaiah:

Jer 10:19, "Truly this is the sickness which I must carry"[10]
= Isa 53:4, "Truly it was our sickness that he carried";

Jer 10:21, "For the shepherds are stupid ... all their flock is scattered"
= Isa 53:6, "All of us like cattle have wandered away";

Jer 11:19a, "For I was like a docile lamb led to the slaughter"
= Isa 53:7, "He ... like a sheep being led to the slaughter";

Jer 11:19b, "against me, 'Let us cut him off from the land of the living'"
= Isa 53:8, "He was cut off from the land of the living"[11]

These literary links reveal strong inner-biblical exegeses and allusions. Reading these two books together, there are certain features we discover intertextually—in other words, if we read each book separately, we may not find the following observations. For example, we find consistent shifts from the first-person soliloquy of Jeremiah ("I" being Jeremiah) to the third-person reminiscence of the suffering servant in Isaiah ("he" being the servant). Jeremiah's personal agony is reflected in the servant's suffering, witnessed and recollected by others. Likewise, third-person plural enemies and shepherds who plot against Jeremiah ("they" being the shepherds) are now transferred to those who collectively acknowledge their waywardness and ignorance ("we" being the sheep). The sicknesses Jeremiah lamented to carry have been metamorphosed into the people's transgressions and iniquities, which the servant took upon himself. Therefore, whoever the

---

10. Unless otherwise noted, all biblical translations are my own.
11. Paul, "Literary and Ideological Echoes," 115–16. In addition to these citations, consider further possible indirect allusions: for example, Jer 10:20 // Isa 53:10, Jer 5:3–4 // Isa 50:5–6, Jer 11:20; 20:12 // Isa 50:8, and Jer 24:9; 25:9; 29:17–18; 42:18 // Isa 52:14–15. In many cases, intertextual connections are not necessarily one-directional: for example, Jer 10:25 = Ps 79:6–7 verbatim, Jer 20:15–18 // Job 3:3–11. Intertextual echoes and adaptations are thus a result of complicated and multidimensional processes.

servant may have been, in the intertextual connection, this servant's identity in the book of Isaiah embraces Jeremiah as one of its components.

Furthermore, these literary links—reading the correlated words, phrases, and motifs intertextually—can offer more than mere exegetical musings. The established intertextuality invites readers also to consider the persona of the main characters and their inevitable struggles within their respective contexts. That is to say, we are led beyond a discovery that the two texts are connected (and, most likely, that the servant text alludes to the Jeremiah text) to an implication to ask why these texts are interconnected.[12] To retrieve what may have caused these echoes, we need to compare the persona, struggles, and legacy of the prophet Jeremiah as well as those of the servant. The intertextual connections trigger the stories behind each character.

Who was the prophet Jeremiah? What events affected his prophetic ministry? How did he react to those life experiences? Jeremiah was, first and foremost, a prophet who lived during the turbulent times of war and exile. Jeremiah is "an artifact of terror" whose message "subverts long-held beliefs, dismantles trusted social structures, and exposes illusions and trivialities."[13] A resistant voice against the dominant political policy, this terrorized prophet was mocked and imprisoned; even so, he did not succumb to the constant threats but reacted with defiance. Yet, Jeremiah also struggled to find meaning both within his personal and the national crises, most profoundly captured in his outcry in Jer 20. Kathleen M. O'Connor elucidates that in the confessions, "Jeremiah's first-person speech concerns more than himself. His faltering faith in God brings to the foreground Judah's crisis of faith created by the Babylonian disaster."[14]

---

12. Katharine J. Dell posits that "indeed Jeremiah may have been the historical figure most likely to have been in mind, mainly because of his close historical proximity to the exile and as the one who tried very hard to warn the people of their fate, suffering as he did so." Katharine J. Dell, "The Suffering Servant of Deutero-Isaiah: Jeremiah Revisited," in *Genesis, Isaiah and Psalms: A Festschrift to Honour Professor John Emerton for His Eightieth Birthday*, ed. Katharine J. Dell, Graham Davies, and Yee Von Koh, VTSup 135 (Leiden: Brill, 2010), 133–34.

13. Louis Stulman and Hyun Chul Paul Kim, *You Are My People: An Introduction to Prophetic Literature* (Nashville: Abingdon, 2010), 110.

14. Kathleen M. O'Connor, *Jeremiah: Pain and Promise* (Minneapolis: Fortress, 2011), 87. "The prophet also emerges as a suffering servant who endures the pain of Judah's rejection and bears the brunt of the nation's scorn" (Louis Stulman, *Jeremiah*, AOTC [Nashville: Abingdon, 2005], 113).

The servant shares many common features of Jeremiah's prophetic life and legacy. The servant was conferred with divine commissioning:

> Before I formed you from the belly,
> before coming out of the womb I consecrated you;
> I have given you as a prophet to the nations; (Jer 1:5)
> YHWH called me from the belly,
> from my mother's insides he named me. (Isa 49:1; cf. 49:5)
> I will give you as a light to the nations. (Isa 49:6)

Interestingly, Jeremiah's divine call in the second-person form is picked up in the servant's recollection in the first-person speech. These royal and prophetic tasks place the servant on a pedestal. Like the Nazirites, both are called and set apart prior to birth to be a prophet or a light to the nations. Yet, at the same time, just like Jeremiah, this servant's actual life is replete with incessant opposition, taunt, and humiliation. Likewise, the war-torn cities and refugee camps of Jeremiah's environs reverberate in the exilic massacres and forced relocations of the servant. Jeremiah the "terror-encircled" (Jer 20:10) encounters the servant "disfigured [tortured] beyond recognition" (Isa 52:14). Both of these two heroic yet controversial prophets end up martyrs, despised and disregarded, "like a debilitated lamb led to the slaughter" (Jer 11:19; Isa 53:7).

Moreover, both figures share their laments from within excruciating agony. One of the most famous of Jeremiah's confessions starts with the unadulterated accusation against God: "YHWH, you have deceived me" (Jer 20:7), which O'Connor translates as "you have raped me."[15] The servant recalls a similar complaint: "I have toiled for nothing; I have exhausted my strength for fleeting chaos" (Isa 49:4; cf. 49:14; Lam 5:20, 22). In their social contexts of persecution and incapacity and their personal experiences of mockery and humiliation, these two figures are dishonored and made low. Paradoxically, the intertextual reading endows both figures with high esteem rather than shame, and they are depicted as larger-than-life heroes and servants of God (Jer 1:18–19; Isa 52:13).

Additionally, we should keep in mind the fact that the two books are placed right next to each other in the final canonical arrangement. Many literary features (such as key catchwords, phrases, motifs, episodes, depictions, and so forth) nicely conjoin the two books. Yet, at the same time,

---

15. O'Connor, *Jeremiah*, 87.

these two books are quite distinct, and often their themes and theologies seem to be in opposition (for example, Davidic tradition versus Mosaic tradition, pro-Zion ideology versus anti-Zion ideology, and the like). Fascinatingly, the two prophetic traditions that seem miles apart are placed right next to each other. It is as though we are invited to the hermeneutical dialogues or debates between the P source (Gen 1) and J source (Gen 2), between Jonah (LXX) and Nahum (LXX), between the Deuteronomist's history and the Chronicler's history, between Proverbs and Job/Qoheleth, and so on.[16] It is both the common features and motifs as well as the different and contrasting aspects of these two figures that invite us to engage in significant intertextual work. Jeremiah and the servant, therefore, come to us as complementary companions, both as uniquely contrary figures and as coherent figures.

Last but not least, it is noteworthy that, whereas the prophet's identity is evident in Jeremiah texts, the servant's identity is anonymous, ambiguous, and multivalent.[17] In this encounter between Jeremiah and the servant, readers are provided with more than linear or two-dimensional comparisons—comparing A with B and B with A—through the potentials of multidimensional comparisons—comparing A with B, C, and D and B with A, C, and D.[18] Hence, just as informed readers can compare Jeremiah with Moses as well as the servant, so we can also compare the servant not only with Jeremiah but also with many other suggested figures, such as a previous Davidic heir (for example, Jehoiachin or Zedekiah), a later Davidic descendant (for example, Zerubbabel or Jesus in the New Testament), Cyrus, an unknown prophet (a disciple of Isaiah), the community of Jacob-Israel as a collectivized entity, and so on. The open potential of such a hermeneutic allows us to take an interpretive leap to consider Jeremiah and the servant in light of comparable figures of the modern era. Before exploring these multidimensional hermeneutical encounters, a brief recap of the two modern figures—Bonhoeffer and Yun—is in order.

---

16. Hyun Chul Paul Kim, "Jonah Read Intertextually," *JBL* 126 (2007): 497–518.

17. Kim, *Ambiguity, Tension, and Multiplicity in Deutero-Isaiah*, StBibLit 52 (New York: Lang, 2003).

18. Key phrases or depictions of Jeremiah make him comparable to Moses and even some aspects of Job. Likewise, the servant has been compared to Jeremiah and Job in reception history.

## Intertextuality between Dietrich Bonhoeffer and Dongju Yun

Enter the two modern thinkers and poets, prophets and martyrs themselves, not unlike the two ancient prophets considered above. Bonhoeffer's life and legacy are well-known. Because numerous studies are published about Bonhoeffer in Western scholarship, only a brief recap of key episodes would suffice here. Bonhoeffer was born in Breslau, Germany, on February 4, 1906. Bonhoeffer had a sense of call to become a theologian at the age of fourteen. Having completed his doctoral dissertation, *Sanctorum Communio*, at the University of Berlin at the age of twenty-one, he completed his Habilitationsschrift, *Act and Being*, at the same institution at the age of twenty-four. An extraordinary theological thinker, Bonhoeffer additionally developed his values of Christian life together in a "this-worldliness" vocation, particularly through his pastorate and educational experiences abroad in places such as Rome and North Africa (1924), Barcelona (1924–1927), New York (1930–1931 and 1939), London (1933), and Anglican monasteries in Britain (1934–1935). While Bonhoeffer's theological undercurrents against social evil would trace back to his earlier years, it was in 1938 that he made formal contacts with the resistance leaders against Hitler.[19] He was arrested in April 1943 and killed by the Gestapo on April 9, 1945. During the years of his imprisonment, Bonhoeffer was engaged to his fiancée Maria von Wedemeyer and continued writing important works, primarily through correspondence with Eberhard Bethge (the husband of Bonhoeffer's niece, Renate).

Yun was born in Myongdong village of the Jiandao area (also called Pukkando, today's Yanbian) in the Manchurian province of China (northern area outside the border of North Korea) on December 30, 1917. Yun's grandfather moved to this area in 1900 due to economic deterioration and political turmoil toward the end of the Joseon dynasty (1392–1910) and became a Christian in 1910.[20] During middle school, Yun developed his poetic passion, winning first prize in the school's speech contest. On Christmas Eve of 1934, six days prior to his seventeenth birthday,

---

19. Geffrey B. Kelly, ed., *Life Together; Prayerbook of the Bible*, DBW 5 (Minneapolis: Fortress, 1996), 184.

20. David E. Shaffer, trans., *The Heavens, the Wind, the Stars and Poetry: The Works of Yun Tong-ju, Korean Patriot and Poet* (Seoul: Hakmun, 1999), 181.

Yun completed his first three poems, inaugurating his career as a poet.[21] Having written poems prolifically during his high school years, Yun entered Yonhee College (now Yonsei University) in 1938. Upon graduation on December 27, 1941, mere days after the Japanese attack on Pearl Harbor, Yun moved to Japan to further his study and writing amid cultural assimilation policies in Korea that enforced the sole use of the Japanese language and names and banned any publications in Korean. As a poet, Yun unleashed his literary force to preserve Korean heritage and inspire a spirit of resistance through the influence and inspiration of many teachers, sages, and friends, such as the poets Chiyong Jung, Sang Yi, Rainer Maria Rilke, the artist Vincent van Gogh, the existentialist philosopher Søren Kierkegaard, and Yagyeon Kim (his maternal uncle who, as a Chinese Confucian scholar, an independence activist, and later an ordained minister, had a significant influence upon Yun). On July 14, 1943, Yun was arrested, and then on March 31, 1944, he was sentenced to two years imprisonment in Fukuoka prison. Yun received a daily injection—presumably for Japan's biological warfare experimentation—and was pronounced dead on February 16, 1945.

Despite the differences (nationality, geography, no mutual interaction, etc.) between these two figures, we can consider some similarities (contemporary, World War II, resistance, incarceration, hardship, poets, thinkers, leaders, persecution, legacy, inspiration, impacts, etc.). Although they had no awareness of each other, readers can form a kind of intertextuality between them through their comparable contexts, lives, and legacies. To undertake such an intertextual dialogue, we will focus on two select poems, amid a plethora of other important works. It is my hope that these texts (miles apart in many ways) can build intertexts, triggering us to get some glimpses of their shared struggles and aspirations.

Dietrich Bonhoeffer's "Who Am I?"

> Who am I? They often say to me
> relaxed and cheerful and determined,
> like a lord from his castle.
>
> Who am I? They often say to me
> I talk with my guards,

---

21. Shaffer, *Heavens*, 183.

freely and friendly and clearly,
as though I were in charge.

Who am I? They also say to me
I bear the days of misfortune
placidly smiling and proud,
like one who is used to winning.

Am I really what others say about me?
Or am I only what I know about myself?
Anxious, yearning, ill, like a bird in a cage,
struggling for the breath of life, as though someone were strangling my throat,
hungering for colors, for flowers, for birdsong,
thirsting for gracious words, for human closeness,
shivering with anger toward capriciousness and pettiest offense,
worried from waiting for great things,
powerlessly trembling for friends in endless distance,
exhausted and empty for praying, thinking, working,
faint and ready to bid farewell to all?

Who am I? The one or the other?
Am I this today and tomorrow another?
Am I both simultaneously?
In front of people a hypocrite and before myself a scornfully whining wimp?
Or does what is still in me resemble the defeated army that chaotically retreats from victory already won?

Who am I? Lonesome questioning taunts me.
Whoever I am, You know me: I am Yours, O God! [June 1944][22]

Of numerous important works from prison, this poem powerfully portrays Bonhoeffer's agony over self-identity amid the tension between his noble vocation in the past and painful uncertainty in the future. His noble

---

22. My translation from the original German poem, "Wer bin ich?" (Dietrich Bonhoeffer, *Widerstand und Ergebung*, ed. Christian Gremmels, Eberhard Bethge, and Renate Bethge, DBW 8 [Gütersloh, Germany: Gütersloher, 1998], 513–14). Special thanks to Prof. Kang Na for sharing feedback on this translation. My selection of this poem by Bonhoeffer, in connection to Jeremiah, is inspired by Jack R. Lundbom, *Jeremiah 1–20*, AB 21A (New York: Doubleday, 1999), 863–64.

heritage, religious piety, and educational background shaped his vocation and were instrumental in earning him respect, even in prison ("relaxed and cheerful and determined ... as though I were in charge ... like one who is used to winning"): "It was not just the result of Christian discipline, but also the heritage of family tradition and upbringing. The Bonhoeffer family as a whole required certain conduct from its members and maintained it in severe suffering and voluntary sacrifice."[23]

However, despite his model background and reputation, Bonhoeffer struggles with his vocational identity during incarceration: "I often wonder who I really am: the one always cringing in disgust, going to pieces at these hideous experiences here, or the one who whips himself into shape, who on the outside (and even to himself) appears calm, cheerful, serene, superior, and lets himself be applauded for this charade—or is it real?"[24] In the midst of this extraordinary effort to preserve calmness and strength, Bonhoeffer is aware of his fragility as a human being. His restlessness bespeaks his vulnerability ("thirsting for gracious words, for human closeness"), which Bonhoeffer achingly laments in the unavoidable departures when each visitor would have to leave him alone in the prison: "For me, this confrontation with the past, this attempt to hold on to it and to get it back, and above all the fear of losing it, is almost the daily background music of my life here, which at times—especially after brief visits, which are always followed by long partings—becomes a theme with variations."[25]

Notably, this dispirited soul ("whining wimp") not only acknowledges the indescribable pain and overwhelming hardship but also trenchantly diagnoses the current hurting world with which Bonhoeffer fearfully yet uncompromisingly shares his solidarity. In this theology of here and now, Bonhoeffer discovers the meaning of faith—godliness within this-worldliness—even in the seeming defeat by tyrannical evil ("the defeated army"): "In the last few years I have come to know and understand more and more the profound this-worldliness of Christianity."[26] Bonhoeffer recalls his

---

23. Dietrich Bonhoeffer, *Prayers from Prison*, interp. Johann Christoph Hempe (Minneapolis: Fortress, 1978), 59.

24. Gruchy, *Letters*, 221 [December 15, 1943]. "Few prisoners in the building are as well known as he is. But he is a contradiction to himself" (Bonhoeffer, *Prayers from Prison*, 57).

25. Gruchy, *Letters*, 416.

26. Gruchy, *Letters*, 485 [July 21, 1944]. For Bonhoeffer's theology tied to Jeremiah's message (cf. Jer 32:15), see Gruchy, *Letters*, 55.

conversation about the goal of life with a young French pastor during his stay in the United States: "And he said, I want to become a saint (—and I think it's possible that he did become one.)... Nevertheless, I disagreed with him,... Later on I discovered, and am still discovering to this day, that one only learns to have faith by living in the full this-worldliness of life.... (Cf. Jer. 45!)."[27] Bonhoeffer's vocation is rooted in his uncompromising solidarity with fellow human beings, especially those who suffer in this world: "We are not Christ, but if we want to be Christians it means that we are to take part in Christ's greatness of heart ... and in the true sympathy that springs forth not from fear but from Christ's freeing and redeeming love for all who suffer."[28]

Bonhoeffer, the defenseless victim ("like a bird in a cage"), ends up martyred. Nevertheless, he leaves a lasting legacy, grounded in the visions and promises of God's truth and power: "These texts do not reveal a super-hero, a happy warrior blithely going to the grave.... Contrariwise, the letters and sermons, lectures, and essays reveal a human being who sought to live before God and with human beings with a mature sense of his own creatureliness as a reality of both limitation and promise."[29] Bonhoeffer's faithfulness and courage continue in the people who are inspired by his relentless struggle in pursuit of the vicarious cost of discipleship.

## Dongju Yun's "Confessions"

> In the rusty green copper-mirror
> still left over is my face,
> which like a treasure of the old dynasty
> brings utter shame.
>
> I'll compress my confession into a single line

---

27. Gruchy, *Letters*, 486. On Jer 32:15, from Tegel, August 12, 1943: "That requires faith, and may God grant us it daily. I don't mean the faith that flees the world, but the faith that endures in the world and loves and remains true to the world in spite of all the hardships it brings us" (Ian Stockton, "Bonhoeffer's Wrestling with Jeremiah," *Modern Believing* 40 [1999]: 50).

28. Gruchy, *Letters*, 49.

29. Mark W. Hamilton and Samjung Kang-Hamilton, "Dietrich Bonhoeffer: A Review Essay," *ResQ* 58 (2016): 245. "Who would we be if we really knew ourselves? The Christian has firm ground under his feet because God knows him" (Bonhoeffer, *Prayers from Prison*, 58).

—for twenty-four years plus one month,
for what joy have I lived?

Tomorrow, the day after, or on some joyous day,
I will have to write another single-line confession
—back then, at such a young age,
why did I make such a shameful acquiescence?

Night after night, let me wipe my own mirror
with the palms of my hands and the soles of my feet.

Then, walking alone under a shooting star,
the back of a sorrowful person
returns inside the mirror. [January 24, 1942][30]

Yun was not of noble lineage but was brought up in a well-educated and well-respected middle-class family. His uncle, Yag-yeon Kim, founded the Myongdong School in the early 1900s, and Yun's father was a teacher there. As the Myongdong village in the Manchurian province of China was also active in the independence movement, Yun grew up with an elite education and social awareness in diaspora. As will be discussed below, both Confucian values and Christian faith have made significant impacts on Yun's poems and personhood.

However, like Bonhoeffer, Yun agonizes over his identity in "Confessions" as someone imperfect, privileged, and powerless all at the same time. Both poets characterize such internal and external identity struggles, and both do so with a strong first-person focus. As a third-generation immigrant who was born in China outside Korea under Japanese colonization, Yun wrestles with the liminal and hybrid boundaries of his personal-religiohistorical locus and sociocultural-political circumstances.[31] Thus, the poem is embedded with three time frames—from the rusty green copper-mirror ("the old dynasty") in the first stanza, to the confession of the present ("twenty-four years plus one month") in the second stanza,

---

30. My translation from the original Korean. Special thanks to Prof. Paul Cho and Prof. Donald Kim for sharing feedback on the translations of the two Korean poems.

31. "Most of his poems are about himself.... But this does not mean that Yoon Dong-Ju was a narcissist or self-indulgent man. We should rather take this as evidence of his existential search" (Sung-il Lee, *The Wind and the Waves: Four Modern Korean Poets* [Berkeley: Asian Humanities Press, 1989], 9).

and then to the question for the future ("tomorrow, the day after, or on some joyous day") in the third stanza—depicting "the three stages of the Kierkegaardian search for self-fulfillment—the aesthetic, the ethical, and the religious stages."[32]

Such an identity struggle operates both internally (within himself) and externally (with the social contexts), through the motif of shame. Shame here, and in many other poems by him, unveils both Christian/religious essences and Confucian/philosophical traditions (especially Mencius, whose philosophy Yun attained from his uncle). On the one hand, via Christian/religious ethos, Yun identifies himself as a sinful, imperfect weakling, susceptible to succumb to the daunting colonial threat. This sense of guilt discloses the context when Imperial Japan forced Koreans to use Japanese names and language only.[33] In order to survive and for Yun to study in Japan, his family had to adopt this policy after sustained civil disobedience. Having adopted another name Tochu Hiranuma (on January 29, 1942), Yun wrote this poem of confessions—the last poem he composed in his motherland ("back then, at such a young age, / why did I make such a shameful acquiescence?"). At the same time, however, this guilt does not merely allude to the acquiescence of the colonized but also the very greed of the powerful and the injustice of the colonizers. Alas, the righteous are few and persecuted; shame on the wicked, including the old dynasty ("brings utter shame"). Shame associates with what is lost ("left over ... a treasure")—the glory, honor, and joy that seems difficult to regain.

On the other hand, via Confucian/philosophical traditions, Yun's shame paradoxically connotes that which is lofty and honorable:

> Mencius said: "The noble-minded have three great joys, and ruling all beneath Heaven is not one of them. To have parents alive and brothers [and sisters] well—that is the first joy. To face Heaven above and people below without any shame—that is the second joy. To attract the finest students in all beneath Heaven, and to teach and nurture them—that is the third joy."[34]

---

32. Shaffer, *Heavens*, 245.

33. Historians further inform that Imperial Japan changed not only the names of the Koreans but also the names of many cities and landmarks.

34. David Hinton, trans., *Mencius* (Berkeley: Counterpoint, 2015), 171; see also Eun-Young Jin and Kyung-Hee Kim, "A Study on Shame in Yun, Dong-Ju's Poetry from a Confucian Perspective," *KPS* 52 (2017): 304–5.

The well-being of family members (first joy) and the gathering of best students (third joy) are not within one's own control. On the contrary, to live out one's life with integrity (second joy) is something one can actively aspire to and achieve. One of the most beloved poems by Yun, titled "Prologue," opens with lines that echo Mencius's second joy: "May I look up to the heavens until the day I die / Without a bit of shame."[35] Accordingly, shame in the Confucian value is not passive but voluntary and active shame.[36] It is a willful shame, so to speak. It is assertive and courageous to acknowledge shame and disingenuous and cowardly to deny it. Put another way, it is honorable to feel shame, whereas one who is shameless is truly dishonorable: "Mencius said: It is impossible to be shameless. The shame of being shameless—that is shameless indeed."[37]

Consequently, shame in Yun's poem is a compassionate shame. To feel shame is to have compassion, aching with the current social problems and pains while also sharing solidarity with those who pursue good against staggering evil. In his compassionate shame, Yun is neither embarrassed nor shameful but a resolute prophet displaying indomitable resistance against cowardice and wrongdoing. Therefore, Yun's shame is also a righteous shame. Toward the end of 1930s, most poets in Korea resorted to write praises of the Japanization movement, quickly selling their souls. Their literary works were neither authentic nor creative but numb imitations of the puppeteers. Yun's shame connotes righteous indignation against so many fellow poets who succumbed to colonial pressure, while also feeling sorrow ("the back of a sorrowful person") at his powerlessness against it.[38]

In his shameful sorrows of having lost his name, "his life-long Korean identity,"[39] as well as his own country, Yun depicts his world as dark nights

---

35. Shaffer, *Heavens*, 12.

36. Jin and Kim, "Study on Shame," 306.

37. Hinton, trans., *The Four Chinese Classics: Tao Te Ching, Chuang Tzu, Analects, Mencius* (Berkeley: Counterpoint, 2013), 542. Consider also Timothy K. H. Chong, *Strategies in Church Discipline from 1 Corinthians: A Chinese Perspective* (Bloomington, IN: WestBow, 2016), 156: "[In Chinese/Asian culture] to call someone 'shameless' (*mei-yu lien*) is to invoke 'the most severe condemnation that can be made to a person.' It is to imply that people have 'laid aside all pretensions of being decent human beings'; an animal according to Mencius."

38. Mi-yeon Kim, "A Study on the Poetry of Yoon Dong-Joo," *KTC* 89 (2017): 136, 146.

39. Shaffer, *Heavens*, 248.

("night after night"), visible only via a dim mirror ("rusty green copper-mirror"). This portrays his shame in genuine solidarity with the colonized people in sorrow and oppression. Amid the endless dark nights of colonization, exile, and diasporic homelessness, Yun also yearns for home and hope. We should note that Yun's musical passion was influenced by the African American spirituals, especially the song "Carry Me Back to Old Virginny," the tune of which he would frequently whistle.[40] Thus, this search for hope swings between night/darkness and star/light, between sorrow and joy, between exile/colonization and homecoming/liberation.

This spirit of resistance and hope for liberation and homecoming often shines through the motif of stars ("walking alone under a shooting star"). Stars evoke lonely, nostalgic memories with the imagination of people across different, faraway continents observing the same and wishfully connecting loved ones together. Out in the sky, difficult to reach and touch, each star would remind Yun of the memories of each person and moment that have blessed his innocent yet troubled childhood.[41] In another poem titled "A Starry Night," Yun indulges in counting each of those countless stars:

...
One star as memory,
Another star as love,
Another star as dejection,
Another star as aspiration,
Another star as poetry,
Another star as mother, mother,

Mother, I try to name each star with each beautiful word.
Thus I count the names of those kids with whom we shared the table at my elementary school; Pei, Kyeong, Oak—such exotic names of foreign girls; names of the gals who already became moms; names of those neighbors in poverty; pigeon, puppy, bunny, donkey, deer;
Frances Jammes, Rainer Maria Rilke—these poets' names.

---

40. Ji-eun Yun, "A Study on Yun Dong-ju as a Marginal Man and a Place Where the Homeland Would Be in His Poetry," *JKML* 18 (2017): 171–72, 175–81.

41. In the following poem, the word *names* occurs repeatedly, reminiscing both the fond memories of loved ones in the distant past and the remorseful situations of Korean names lost and soon to be forgotten. See Eung-gyo Kim, "Forced Names: Somura Mukei and Hiranuma Tochu," *ChT* (November 2014): 197.

They are all so far away from me.
Just as stars are so faintly far away,

Mother,
and you are far away in Manchuria....[42]

Paradoxically, those distant, unreachable stars also signify the utopian hope that shines perennially.[43] Such a starry utopia, in Yun's poetic world, does not denote abstract escape from reality but rather concrete, contextual "this-worldliness." Yun's stars do not remain as mere imagination but rather symbolize peace and harmony in "this world" where each star, and each human being, does their best in the sacred tasks of restoring justice and righteousness. While yearning for a utopian dream or heaven, therefore, Yun's stars also equate with persistent resistance against the present reality of colonial policies and threats.[44] Stars shine more vividly and brightly in the night. Each glowing star would ignite a spark of dignity and honor within, nothing short of the miraculous hope for joy amid sorrow ("for what joy have I lived? … on some joyous day"). Ultimately, Yun's shame-filled, passionate confession was "a revolutionary attempt to overthrow the era's oppressors and resist their reality, who was conscious of the boundary between the imperial Japan, the colonial Joseon, and [Manchuria]."[45]

---

42. My translation from the original Korean. Consider the last letter (written on December 19, 1944) Bonhoeffer's fiancée Maria received: "You, the parents, all of you, the friends and students of mine at the front, all are constantly present to me. Your prayers and good thoughts, words from the Bible, discussions long past, pieces of music, and books—[all these] gain life and reality as never before" (André Dumas, *Dietrich Bonhoeffer: Theologian of Reality*, trans. R. M. Brown [New York: Macmillan, 1971], 171).

43. "Just as stars are distant yet assuredly existent, in Yun's poetic vision, salvation in the remotest future will certainly come" (Sung-hee Hong, "'Too Many Nights' and Poetry: Repetition in Yoon Dong Ju's Poetry," *JKML* 63 [2017]: 106).

44. Yun, "Study on Yun Dong-ju," 194–98.

45. Yun, "Study on Yun Dong-ju," 203. "From one perspective, the 'sorrowful man' is shamed by his wavering in his Christian faith, but foresees a 'joyful day' when the hope of salvation may be obtained. From another perspective, that same 'sorrowful man' is shamed by Japanese domination of his fatherland, Korea, and by having to change his Korean name to a Japanese one. The 'joyful day' that is hoped for is the day when Korea will again be free from Japanese control" (Shaffer, *Heavens*, 249).

## The Ancient Prophets/Martyrs Meet the Modern Prophets/Martyrs

What can be gained from these multifarious intertextual (and intercontextual and intercultural) comparisons of biblical themes and hermeneutical reading strategies? First, in light of the above analyses of the commonality between two ancient figures and two modern figures, we observe that they represent the minority voices of defiance against tyranny and oppression. Due to their fervent criticism against the dominant societal forces, they encountered threats, persecution, and an ultimately tragic demise, like "a docile lamb led to the slaughter" and "cut off from the land of the living" (Jer 11:19; Isa 53:7–8). They each, in turn, experienced a crisis of self-identity amidst social and political turmoil and ultimately persevered in their vocational convictions. Their weakness and vulnerability made them ostracized victims of the social evil: Jeremiah as "terror-encircled" (Jer 20:10), the servant as one "disfigured beyond recognition" (Isa 52:14), Bonhoeffer as "a scornfully whining wimp," and Yun as "a sorrowful person." And yet their scathing criticism against evil made them like "a fortified city, an iron pillar, and a bronze wall" (Jer 1:18) and the "exalted, honored ... righteous one" (Isa 52:13; 53:11).[46]

Furthermore, another prominent theme is the profoundly authentic "this-worldliness" of the prophetic traditions. Indeed, this down-to-earth hermeneutical orientation is an important contribution by the Hebrew Bible to biblical theology.[47] Both Jeremiah and the servant mutually echo many of the lament psalms that underscore the very tears, pains, and cries of the dejected and marginalized. They explicitly or subtly allude to the rhetoric and issues of Lamentations. Similarly, both Bonhoeffer and Yun were influenced and transformed by the moving tunes and messages of the African American spirituals. Bonhoeffer personally encountered these while visiting and preaching at African American churches in Harlem, while Yun was introduced to the spirituals by American mission-

---

46. "[Bonhoeffer at Finkenwalde seminary] and the incessant struggle against the church bureaucracy's dance between resistance to, and acceptance of, the National Socialist attempts to conform the church to its vision of German society all consumed the attention of the entire seminary and the congregations supporting it" (Hamilton and Kang-Hamilton, "Dietrich Bonhoeffer," 244).

47. "The source and force of Israel's spirituality is the presence and work of [YHWH] in its life and midst" (Rolf P. Knierim, *The Task of Old Testament Theology: Substance, Method, and Cases* [Grand Rapids: Eerdmans, 1995], 295).

aries.⁴⁸ The writings and concepts of both poets display the radical impact of human suffering and irresistible hope extant in the spirituals. Similar to Bonhoeffer's quintessential this-worldliness theology, Yun's poems are grounded in his courageous, compassionate shame, which displays not only human fragility but also righteous outrage against corrupt, recalcitrant shamelessness in the troubled world. All these prophets and martyrs share their sorrows and hopes firmly rooted in this world, and their utopian visions target their fellow sisters and brothers, especially those suffering in this world.⁴⁹

Moreover, these martyrs, even in their tragic ends, left lasting legacies which transformed them into larger-than-life figures. Notably, it is the perception of readers and interpreters that place them on pedestals worthy of their extraordinary vocational calls. Jeremiah, shunned by many as a false prophet, was reckoned a true prophet (Jer 25:11–12; 29:10; cf. Ezra 1:1; Dan 9:2). The servant, falsely accused and despised (Isa 53:3–4, 9), was rightfully recognized as the one who took on the transgressions and iniquities of many others (Isa 53:5, 12) and who will ultimately "make many righteous" (Isa 53:11). We do not have any archaeological information of the whereabouts of these two prophets. But, their personas and legacies through millennia have earned them the monumental titles respectively as "a prophet to the nations" (Jer 1:5) and "a light to the nations" (Isa 49:6; cf. 42:6).⁵⁰ Likewise, Bonhoeffer, who never got to

---

48. Reggie L. Williams expounds that Bonhoeffer's academic readings of Harlem Renaissance intellectuals, such as W. E. B. Du Bois; his experiences as a lay leader at Abyssinian Baptist Church; and his witnesses of the color line and racial fragmentation in American Christendom must have made a genuine impact on his theology: "It is the Christ 'hidden in suffering' that Bonhoeffer came to see within the hidden perspective of Harlem, by exposure to the latent critique of the problem of race during the Harlem Renaissance" (Reggie L. Williams, "Dietrich Bonhoeffer, the Harlem Renaissance, and the Black Christ," in *Interpreting Bonhoeffer: Historical Perspectives, Emerging Issues*, ed. Clifford J. Green and Guy C. Carter [Minneapolis: Fortress, 2013], 161).

49. "[Dongju Yun] generated his own meaning of life and death before 'salvation' which was ever-delayed but still believed to come, in order to greet the desperate life as it stands with hospitality" (Hong, "'Too Many Nights' and Poetry," 125).

50. "Like the God of Israel, Jeremiah has endured the pain of rejection and borne the sorrow of scorn and reproach.... This portrait of the prophet is a painful reminder of the cost of discipleship (Dietrich Bonhoeffer). It is also a sure testimony that words and witness outlive the nightmare of abuse" (Stulman, *Jeremiah*, 344–45).

see the end of evil but instead was unjustly executed just a few months before the end of World War II, is considered one of the most profound and influential theologians of the twentieth century. Yun, who also never got to see his poetry ever formally published but was brutally killed just six months before liberation, has himself become a beacon of light to later generations who continue to be inspired by so many of his achingly sad yet beautiful poems.[51]

Finally, while cultivating the very ancient contexts is essential to understanding the ancient texts, hermeneutical implications provide for equally enriching comprehension in comparisons with the pertinent contexts of today.[52] As explored in this study, considering the writings and legacies of Bonhoeffer and Yun can offer insightful perspectives in interpreting the texts and contexts of Jeremiah and Isaiah's servant. The world of the Hebrew Bible is remote and thus difficult to reconstruct or re-present. Through comparison with comparable modern texts and contexts, what seems disconnected in these ancient texts can become more real and intimate. Our detached reading of the ancient books can cause us to adopt clichéd viewpoints or even romanticize the pain, suffering, agony, injustice, sorrow, rage, prayer, yearning, and hope of each person in the real world. Rather than reading from a distance, the intertextual engagement with today's issues vis-à-vis the interpreter's milieu creates a more up-close and personal understanding. Jeremiah's incarceration and the servant's suffering were not mere emotionless episodes suitable for forensic lab research. Bonhoeffer's spirited words and Yun's shame-laden agony can take us into the likely situations and vivid pictures of the ancient prophets' personas and pathos. Modern stories and histories unearth the calamitous events and aftermath of colonization as well as the incessant threats and palpable abuses upon the colonized.

The intertextual dialogues between Jeremiah and Isaiah's servant provide insights far more complex than a simple arithmetic formula of "one plus one equals two." Instead, the compound result is bountiful: for example, Jeremiah alone, the servant alone, Jeremianic servant, servant-like Jeremiah, both Jeremiah and the servant merged together, and so on. When we then add Bonhoeffer and Yun, our hermeneutical horizons expand to multidimensional, almost infinitesimal encounters.[53] In such multifarious

---

51. Eun-Ae Lee, "From 'Self-Portrait' to "Confessions," *JKP* 16 (2005): 135.
52. Knierim, *Task of Old Testament Theology*, 69–71.
53. "A text is not a line of words releasing a single 'theological' meaning (the 'mes-

intertextual encounters, we have discovered many similar texts, contexts, stories, histories, messages, and so on.[54] For our understanding of Jeremiah and the servant, for example, we can enlist many other ancient and modern figures for such intertextual encounters (Gwan-sun Yu—a Korean "Jeanne d'Arc,"[55] Martin Luther King Jr., Nelson Mandela, Fannie Lou Hamer, Angela Davis, Elie Wiesel, and the like).[56] Bonhoeffer and Yun, through their poems, poetic personas, and poetic worlds, help us more forcefully read and interpret Jeremiah and the servant, as all four of them come to us as troubled yet faithful and larger-than-life servants of God.

---

sage' of the Author-God) but a multi-dimensional space in which a variety of writings, none of them original, blend and clash" (Roland Barthes, *Image, Music, Text*, trans. Stephen Heath [New York: Hill and Wang, 1977], 146).

54. Equally legitimately, we should also search for intertextual cases that project contending perspectives. In such contrasts as well as similarities—as in the hermeneutical yin-yang dynamics, our interpretive insights may be further deepened. See Hyun Chul Paul Kim, "Interpretative Modes of Yin-Yang Dynamics as an Asian Hermeneutics," *BibInt* 9 (2001): 287–308.

55. On Gwan-sun Yu, see Niraj Chokshi, "South Koreans in New York Celebrate a 100-Year-Old Independence Movement," *New York Times*, 1 March 2019, https://tinyurl.com/SBLPress03103a.

56. Willis Jenkins and Jennifer M. McBride, eds., *Bonhoeffer and King: Their Legacies and Import for Christian Social Thought* (Minneapolis: Fortress, 2010).

# Interpreting the Bible in the Age of #BlackLivesMatter: The Gideon Story and Scholarly Commitments

*Valerie Bridgeman*

For some years now, I have been reflecting on Judg 6:11–24 as a central theme for the Hebrew texts as we find them canonically. Located in the cycle of violent stories where the people are blamed repeatedly for their conditions, Gideon asks the question that might be the central one for all of the Hebrew Bible. In this story, Gideon resorts to hiding wheat in wine presses. While working subversively to feed his community, an "angel of the Lord" appears to him and declares that God is with him. The angel calls Gideon a strong warrior, a גבור החיל, and Gideon responds, not with the singular "if God is with me," but rather with a communal עמנו: "If God is with *us*, what is this finding us [מצאתנו]?" (Judg 6:13, my translation). This phrase often is translated "why then has all this happened to us," perhaps because translators find it difficult to imagine trouble finding a people. But in the early parts of the twenty-first century, black people in the United States of America, on the African continent, and in other parts of the African diaspora understand the concept of trouble and struggle finding a people, stalked by a death-dealing culture of white supremacist domination.

In the book of Judges, Gideon recounts the histories of deliverance as he has learned them, noting the necessity, strength, and problem with history in their current struggles for freedom. Gideon tells the story the ancestors told him (6:13) and acknowledges it, but he asks: where are all the wonderful deeds now? The book of Judges is, no doubt, redacted as

---

A version of this paper was presented in the Minoritized Criticism and Biblical Interpretation Section at the Annual Meeting of the Society of Biblical Literature under the title, "Writing Phone Numbers on My Arm: Activism and Scholarship in the Age of #BlackLivesMatter" (Boston, MA, November 18, 2017).

a propagandized call for a king, or as law-and-order propaganda. But Gideon, in the inception of this story, seems more concerned for his community, even as the story has been framed as the exploits of a singular man. He doubts his ability to make a difference: "How can I deliver Israel?" And as any soon-to-be hero does, he maintains that he is from the least family of the weakest clan in the smallest tribe (6:15 NRSV).

Gideon's story became, for me, a starting point for a way to answer the question of how minoritized biblical scholars could forge a dialogue with sociopolitical activists.[1] As both a biblical scholar and an activist, pondering the ways the Bible speaks into violent and volatile events in our times is important work, professionally and personally for me. This kind of intertextuality—where the lives before the text are its primary conversation partners and reflectors—is key to the texts continuing to be relevant in times of crisis. Or, as Gideon notes, to keep asking the question of how and where God is when violent realities irrupt. In recent years, some black activist-scholars in the United States have sought to bring the weight of their academic training to liberationist projects for black lives. I come to this work as a womanist biblical scholar and homiletician, as an ordained religious professional, and as an activist in the streets. We have role models for developing lenses that attend to reading texts not simply as historical documents but as texts that inform and ignite conversation in their reading contexts. Feminist and postcolonial approaches bridge interested readings and historical-critical methods (which also are interested). "These hermeneutical strategies have consistently led the way in raising the question of the ethics or politics of interpretation, an issue very near to the heart of postmodern hermeneutics."[2] Two notable examples—the liberating, biblical works of Cheryl B. Anderson and Musa W. Dube, both of whom work on HIV/AIDS issues in their activist work—have shown us a roadmap for how womanists and black feminists who read biblical texts from liberationist and postcolonial viewpoints can do this work.[3]

---

1. Note to me from an email I received from Gregory L. Cuéllar, January 23, 2017, when he invited me to present in the Minoritized Criticism and Biblical Interpretation Section of the Annual Meeting of the Society of Biblical Literature in 2017.

2. George Aichele, Peter D. Miscall, and Richard Walsh, "An Elephant in the Room: Historical-Critical and Postmodern Interpretations of the Bible," JBL 128 (2009): 386.

3. See Cheryl B. Anderson, "Biblical Interpretation as Violence: Genesis 19 and Judges 19 in the Context of HIV and AIDS," in *La Violencia and the Hebrew Bible: The*

Miguel A. De La Torre's work, among others, also helps to form how to read texts while reading communities and in community.[4] This type of intertextuality—reading texts and reading lives as texts—is paramount if our scholarship will be useful to the world. This essay, then, is not about Gideon or his story but about how his question sharpens mine: "If God is with us, why is trouble finding black people?" In such biblical scholarship, the audience is not the academy but the people gravely affected by social dystopia. Academy members, though curating and sometimes condemning such readings, are overhearing a conversation for freedom among and for people in particular communities.

There are also other activist-scholars from other disciplines to help with framing one's mindset for how to read texts. For this biblical work, I also turn to a historian and an ethicist to consider ways biblical scholars may lend their expertise and voice to freedom. I engage the late African American historian and activist Vincent Harding's essay, "The Vocation of the Black Scholar and the Struggles of the Black Community," and Vanderbilt University Divinity School Dean and E. Rhodes and Leona B. Carpenter Professor of Womanist Ethics and Society Emilie M. Townes's American Academy of Religion 2008 Presidential Address, "Walking on the Rim Bones of Nothingness; Scholarship and Activism."[5] Each provides insights, in conversation with scholars, activists, and artists before them, for the role of the (black) scholar in a protesting and activist life.

---

*Politics and Histories of Biblical Hermeneutics on the American Continent*, ed. Susanne Scholz and Pablo R. Andiñach, SemeiaSt 82 (Atlanta: SBL Press, 2016), 121–36; and Musa W. Dube, *The HIV and AIDS Bible: Selected Essays* (Scranton, PA: University of Scranton Press, 2008). Both scholars have grounded their research in current-day crises as hermeneutical lenses. For a reflection on Dube's work, see Emmanuel Katongole, "Embodied and Embodying Hermeneutics of Life in the Academy: Musa W. Dube's HIV/AIDS Work," in *Postcolonial Perspectives in African Biblical Interpretations*, ed. Musa W. Dube, Andrew M. Mbuvi, and Dora R. Mbuwayesango, GPBS 13 (Atlanta: Society of Biblical Literature, 2012), 407–16.

4. Miguel A. De La Torre, *Reading the Bible from the Margins* (Maryknoll, NY: Orbis Books), 2002.

5. Vincent Harding, "The Vocation of the Black Scholar and the Struggles of the Black Community," in *Education and Black Struggle: Notes from the Colonized World*, ed. Institute of the Black World (Cambridge: Harvard Educational Review, 1974), 3–30; Emilie M. Townes, "2008 Presidential Address: Walking on the Rim Bones of Nothingness; Scholarship and Activism," *JAAR* 77 (2009): 1–15.

On August 8–9, 2015, a team of self-described activist-scholars arrived in Ferguson, Missouri, to reflect on how Michael Brown Jr.'s death one year earlier had affected us and to determine how we now wanted his memory to impact our scholarship.[6] I served as one of nine people on the coordinating committee that designed and implemented the conference.[7] Each of us, as a part of our commitment, had elicited funds from our institutions to support the gathering and our travel. Besides presenting scholarly reflection, we also participated in local activist-led actions. We did not gather to critique the current movement; there has been more than enough of that without the distance of time. We did not gather to study the movement, though the Movement for Black Lives/Black Lives Matter Movement needs its chroniclers, historians, and theologians to be present, while it is happening, to study and learn from it. Since, as Cynthia Edenburg argues, intertextuality requires literary competence, a consciousness of the signifier and the signified, it was imperative that we not assume we knew the contours of the bodily texts on which violence had been poured in Ferguson. Edenburg argues that intertextuality requires literary, oral, and aural competency.[8] We arrived to learn from the stories that emerged in Ferguson and to look for the places where our memories were provoked. We did not show up to instruct activists or to give scholarly papers, though there were three plenaries to provoke our encounter.[9]

---

6. Unarmed black teenager Michael Brown Jr. was shot and killed by Darren Wilson, a white police officer in Ferguson, Missouri, a suburb of Saint Louis. His death set off a series of protests that lasted more than a year and, by some accounts, continue to this moment in 2017. See this article for an account of what happened: "What Happened in Ferguson?," *New York Times*, August 15, 2015, https://www.nytimes.com/interactive/2014/08/13/us/ferguson-missouri-town-under-siege-after-police-shooting.html?_r=0.

7. The other members of the committee were: Candice Benbow (Princeton Theological Seminary, doctoral student); Traci Blackmon (Pastor, Christ the King UCC, Florissant, MO); Leah Gunning Francis (Eden Theological Seminary); F. Willis Johnson (Pastor, Wellspring Church, Ferguson, MO); Pamela R. Lightsey (Boston University School of Theology); Eboni Marshall Turman (Duke University Divinity School); Herbert R. Marbury (Vanderbilt University Divinity School); and Stephen Ray (Garrett-Evangelical Theological Seminary).

8. Cynthia Edenburg, "Intertextuality, Literary Competence, and the Question of Readership: Some Preliminary Observations," *JSOT* 35 (2010): 135.

9. The plenary speakers were Brittney Cooper, J. Kameron Carter, and Blackmon.

We gathered, instead, to learn from the movement and its leaders and to critique our own complicity in attempts to destroy the movement in its infancy—by our silence, by our safe academic distance, or by our uninformed writings about it. We were not looking for some objective or uninterested truth but rather for a useful dialogical relationship with black experiences and how to foreground those experiences (including our own) as an interrogative process in our work. Pamela R. Lightsey, then Associate Dean for Community Life and Lifelong Learning and Clinical Assistant Professor of Contextual Theology and Practice at Boston University's School of Theology, and Brittney Cooper, Assistant Professor of Women's and Gender Studies and Africana Studies at Rutgers University, were among us as exemplars. Both women had put their scholarship on hold in 2014 in order to be present in and to document the movement at ground zero, as Ferguson became known. We arrived a year later at the flashpoint to think together about how to be in service to the movement. Many of us had been on the front lines both in Ferguson and in places throughout the country where black lives have been systematically destroyed. Some of us had been tear gassed, sound bombed, or shot at with rubber bullets. Those of us who met that criteria spoke, but only to bear witness. Each session was designed to help us reflect and to provoke those of us who are scholars to show up. If intertextuality includes "genre, motif, formulae, type-scenes and parallel accounts, allusion, quotation and hypertextual commentary,"[10] then our time in Ferguson quickly commended itself as an exercise in intertextuality. The stories were familiar; the police-encounter-ends-with-dead-black-man was too common; parallelisms abounded. We could identify our text.

We had decided before we arrived that we would have a panel discussion that biblical scholar Herbert R. Marbury would moderate, titled "Organic, Degree, Experience: The Necessity of a Multifaceted Black Scholarship for Such a Time as This." None of us claimed many or any answers. We did want to know what does (or ought) our work mean for black communities, as black scholars writing, researching, and teaching in the era of #BlackLivesMatter. In many ways, we simply reformulated Harding's 1970s Watergate-era questions: "What are the stakes for which we now struggle? What are the goals toward which we now move? What do liberation, independence, authentic black humanity, self-determination,

---

10. Edenburg, "Intertextuality," 137.

victory mean in the world of the 1970s and 1980s? What is the nature of the society we seek?"[11] Forty years later, these questions haunted us. We were and are in search of our living role in the current Movement for Black Lives.[12]

We sought to find our places in the symphony of voices and actions like those at the Movement for Black Lives website, a collective of organizations and persons dedicated to the freedom and soul force of black people in the United States, in Africa, and in the African diaspora.[13] Like them, we understood ourselves to be in the stream of the struggle for black freedom that was as old as any invasion into black space, from King Leopold II to the slave ship *Jesus* to the Jim Crow South to the current slow genocide of black people in the United States. We wanted to reclaim our center in black communities and our work as belonging to those communities. We are still in a "black and broken background," the soundtrack of which is bullets, police batons on black bodies, sound booms and bleeding ears, and the screams and moans of parents and friends in grief.[14] We have parallel accounts on which to draw, those stories that "share a common plotline and present *similar* (or parallel) accounts of events, even though they may differ in details such as characters, place and time" (emphasis original).[15] It includes the landscape of burning eyes from tear gas in a media world that comes for violence but not the truth of the movement.

As Black Lives Matter Movement members, we found ourselves trying to create a healing space for black scholars and black religious leaders to think outside of the confines of the (white) academy.[16] While several of us were women, we did not actively lift up the role of black women and queer people—women, men, gender-nonconforming, trans—in the movement. As I think back to the moment, this oversight seems odd since most everyone gathered identified as a feminist, womanist, and/or intersectional scholar in some particular way. We missed the moment to reflect during those days, but we acknowledged these gifts in the statement we later wrote and to which I will return in this essay. We know how colo-

---

11. Harding, "Vocation of the Black Scholar," 13.
12. Harding, "Vocation of the Black Scholar," 27.
13. "Platform," *Movement for Black Lives*, https://tinyurl.com/SBL03103b. See also the work of Black Lives Matter at https://blacklivesmatter.com/.
14. Harding, "Vocation of the Black Scholar," 6.
15. Edenburg, "Intertextuality," 142.
16. "Healing Justice," *Black Lives Matter*, https://tinyurl.com/SBL03103c.

nized we have been by the academy, and this pilgrimage to Ferguson was in homage to Brown and all the other black people who suffered death-by-state-sanctioned-violence.

But, of course, the academy was with us. Being among other activists reminded us that as scholars with appointments at seminaries and universities, all tenured or on tenure track, we have the privilege of the wall of respectability. I reflected on our time in Ferguson, first on Facebook, then in reflections published on *Patheos*.[17] I was aware that people who did not have our privileges were much more vulnerable than we were and that we were seen as outsiders using their pain, not only by police who resented us but also by the mostly young black people who protested nightly and defiantly, chanting, "we're young, we're strong, we're marching all night long."

Yet these traumatic times affect scholars as well. Whatever the optics, we are not safe; we could not choose nonaction. Like Dube, we were being called to interruption.[18] We arrived knowing nothing would be easy. We knew that healing trauma would be a part of the project we had to embrace and that it had to be done.[19] Harding had warned us that, as black scholars:

> We are constantly tempted by a strange and poignant set of yearnings to let white America's style become our own, repeatedly forgetful that the best hopes and interests of the masses of black people have always been out of style in America (save for a few visionary and deceptively halcyon years in the 1860s and 1960s when our cause preoccupied, even obsessed, a nation). It is a warning because we are tempted even now, in the midst of the stench of national corruption, to accept American definitions of wisdom, probity, and truth—or, worse, to accept America's claims that such things are not worth discussing.[20]

As a biblical scholar, the temptation to let white America's style become our own is overwhelming. As De La Torre has noted, "the challenge faced by those who read the Bible from the margins is that the dominant culture has the power to shape and legitimize the religious discourse."[21] Schooled

---

17. Valerie Bridgeman, "#Ferguson Reflections: Privilege, Protest, and Place," *Patheos*, August 14, 2015, https://tinyurl.com/SBL03103d.
18. Katongole, "Embodied and Embodying Hermeneutics of Life in the Academy," 409.
19. "Healing Justice."
20. Harding, "Vocation of the Black Scholar," 5.
21. De La Torre, *Reading the Bible*, 27.

in the historical-critical methods, biblical scholarship that situates itself in the midst of a modern-day movement seemed hardly like scholarship. It is the kind of hermeneutical work that often is sidelined as specialty or interested research. It often is not taken seriously in the guild. But Harding's words drove me to Ferguson as much as they drove theologians, ethicists, and cultural critics there. As a biblical scholar, I became aware of the need to think more clearly about how my work belongs to the public square, much like Richard D. Nelson argues that the book of Judges provides us a way to consider the Bible "as a theater of values directed toward the public square."[22] What that would mean in the day-to-day interrogating of texts remained to be seen, but it at least must have meant self-reflective awareness of how neither the movement to which I wanted to speak, the biblical text, nor I was without complexity. There would always be drama with "conflicting ideals or principles about shared public life."[23] There would be times when the call of the academy pulled us away from the activist-scholarship we believed we must live. Although it might be true that "an activist theology or advocacy [or biblical interpretation—my addition] can never be ambitious enough," we could not afford the alternative of retreating into the academy and classroom.[24]

Thus we arrived in Ferguson in hopes of reclaiming ourselves, in hopes of re-member-ing, and mostly, in hopes of not forgetting. As a result, after we returned to our various institutions, the coordinating committee collected and collated our learnings and wrote a manifesto. Titled "Learning from Black Lives Conversation: A Statement of Solidarity and Theological Testament," we called our time in Ferguson "a holy encounter." We deliberately chose the phrase *holy encounter*. It is our assertion that the lives of black people are holy texts that deserve our study as much as the biblical texts or theological concepts or cultural anthropological issues. Each of our disciplines provides an entrée into deeper understanding of black lives, which in turn provides insight into our disciplines. We would have what any intertextual reading provides: a surplus of meaning, a way to see worlds from many sides. These are our ideological commitments.[25]

---

22. Richard D. Nelson, "Judges: A Public Canon for Public Theology," *WW* 29 (2009): 399.

23. Nelson, "Judges," 400.

24. Katongole, "Embodied and Embodying Hermeneutics of Life in the Academy," 411.

25. See Timothy K. Beal's work on how challenging it is to stabilize meanings, or,

We sought to acknowledge the diverse gifts of the Movement for Black Lives. In effect, this commitment was intertextual in that it averred that there is no univocality in texts or contexts, but rather they are many-voiced.[26] We did not want to make what we saw as the mistake of another era, in which cisgender women, lesbians, gay men, bisexual people, and transgender, queer-identified, asexual, and other sexual minorities were ignored. We reflected this concern in the statement by declaring:

> We particularly celebrate the voices that started the movement and those who continue the resistance. We are grateful for the resilience and trailblazing work of those who have been silenced before—lesbian, gay, bisexual, trans* and queer. Personhood, then, is theologically connected to constitution. All Black life is, as a gift of its creation, made in the image of God. In lifting up Black Life, we will lift up all others who are left out and behind.[27]

We also were taking seriously a call Townes made in her American Academy of Religion address, in which she asserted that "our scholarship should *also* help map out strategies for creating a more just and free society and world."[28] If we were going to be useful scholars, then the questions we asked and the commitments we made had to matter. Whether reading Genesis or listening to Gideon, biblical scholars, too, had to ask every research question with the saving and thriving of black lives in mind. The statement the group conceived was our stab at articulating our way forward. We wrote:

> We came to affirm our commitment to types of scholarship and activism that prizes justice and works for transformation. We came prepared to lend our hands, heads, and hearts to catalyze a movement—to do

---

more directly, who gets to control meanings. Timothy K. Beal, "Ideology and Intertextuality: Surplus of Meaning and Controlling the Means of Production," in *Reading between Texts: Intertextuality and the Hebrew Bible*, ed. Danna Nolan Fewell (Louisville: Westminster John Knox, 1992), 31.

26. Beal, "Ideology and Intertextuality," 30.

27. "Learning from Black Lives Conversation: A Statement of Solidarity and Theological Testament," *KineticsLive*, September 22, 2015, https://tinyurl.com/SBL03103f.

28. Townes, "2008 Presidential Address," 2, emphasis original.

the work of transforming the death of Michael Brown, Jr. and so many others into new life. We knew that it had been done before.[29]

It was not just a statement of commitment, however. We also knew we needed to confess our failings and shortcomings and to call ourselves and others to action. To that end, we wrote that "we call ourselves and other people of goodwill to confess that we have been seduced by the false security of the politics of respectability, frequently leaving an entire generation of Black people to fend for themselves."[30] The call, then, was not only to black scholars but to scholars and people of goodwill to take up the mantle to research, write, and present with the liberation of black people in mind.

This territory, though new to us, was not new. Here, as Edenburg suggested, our memory was at play and the intertextual nature of encounter was pronounced. Though, unlike Edenburg, our competency was not based in memorization but memory alone—cultural, historical, and personal memory.[31] As we had written, we were aware that it had been done before. We were following in the footstep of scholars like those who inaugurated the Society for the Study of Black Religion in 1969, "the oldest scholarly society dedicated to the study and production of knowledge about the broad diaspora of Black religion."[32] As a new generation of scholars, we had to be about the work more urgently. As Townes noted, we also were aware that the academy "did not prepare [us] for the calls in the wide variety of communities that ask [us] to help them think through the issues they face and to translate [our] public lectures into the everydayness of their lives to develop survival strategies and to encourage them to trust the integrity of their own insights."[33]

The knowledge that we were not prepared for our new commitments did not stop us. Several black scholars created courses directly using the phrase, "#BlackLivesMatter." An example is Wil Gafney's course, "The Bible in the Public Square: Interpreting the Bible in the Age of #BlackLivesMatter," which she taught at Brite Divinity School during the 2017

---

29. "Learning from Black Lives Conversation."
30. "Learning from Black Lives Conversation."
31. Edenburg, "Intertextuality," 133.
32. Society for the Study of Black Religion Collection (Archives Research Center, Atlanta University Center Robert W. Woodruff Library).
33. Townes, "2008 Presidential Address," 3.

spring semester.³⁴ Changed by the movement as an activist-scholar, Gafney's commitment also appeared in her 2016 presentation in the Biblical Literature and the Hermeneutics of Trauma; Exile (Forced Migrations) in Biblical Literature section at the Annual Meeting of the Society of Biblical Literature. There, Gafney presented a paper using the #SayHerName hashtag in honor of Sandra Bland to reinterpret royal women in the Torah.³⁵ Her title, "Princess Propaganda: Forced Migration and Royal Women Hostages," was described with this abstract:

> One of the rallying cries of the #BlackLivesMatter movement is #SayHerName; saying her name refers to preserving the names and memories of black and brown trans- and cis-gendered women whose lives have been disposed of often along with their names and memory in public consciousness. This paper will explore the phenomenon of royal women offered, secured and held as hostages to facilitate forced migration in the Judean context, focusing primarily on the royal women of Jehoiachin (Jer 38:22), Zedekiah (Jer 38:23) and unidentified princesses (Jer 41:16; 43:6). The disposition of their bodies will be read through a womanist #SayHerName #BlackLivesMatter hermeneutic.³⁶

My own first and halting steps after the Ferguson gathering were to reframe an essay due for a Festschrift for my doctoral mentor, William H. Bellinger Jr. at Baylor University. In this essay, I practiced what we talked

---

34. Wil Gafney, "The Bible in the Public Square: Interpreting the Bible in the Age of #BlackLivesMatter," https://brite.edu/programs/black-church-studies/black-lives-matter/. See also Adelle M. Banks, "Seminaries across the Country Now Offering Black Lives Matter Courses," *Sojourners*, December 7, 2016. https://tinyurl.com/SBL03103g. For another example, see Mitzi Smith, *Womanist Sass and Talk Back: Social (In)Justice, Intersectionality, and Biblical Interpretation* (Eugene, OR: Cascade, 2018).

35. Sandra Bland died while in the Waller County, TX jail, after she had been jailed on July 10, 2015 and after the trooper accused her of assaulting him during a routine traffic stop. Her death was officially ruled a suicide. Family and friends never believed the official report, and protests persisted for some time. Of note was the fact that Waller County has a sad history of discrimination and lynching. See David A. Graham, "Sandra Bland and the Long History of Racism in Waller County, Texas," *Atlantic*, July 21, 2015, https://tinyurl.com/SBL03103e.

36. Wil Gafney, "Princess Propaganda: Forced Migration and Royal Women Hostages" (paper presented at the Annual Meeting of the Society of Biblical Literature, San Antonio, TX, November 20, 2016), https://www.sblcentral.org/conferencePaperDetails/40301.

about in August 2015. I first presented the essay, titled "'A Long Ways from Home': Displacement, Lament, and Singing Protest in Psalm 137," at the International Organization for the Study of the Old Testament in Stellenbosch, South Africa, in September 2016.[37] In that presentation, later an essay, I argued that the psalm was not a lament but a protest song. More specifically, I argued that:

> While other scholars have assumed that sitting by the river in Babylon was/is an act of despair, reading through 2016 eyes and taking seriously the whole of the text, it can be reasonably argued that sitting by the river and hanging their harps on willow trees was as much protest to the nation-state of Babylon as the 2014 and 2015 "die-ins" of the Ferguson protests are/were against the police-state of the United States. Because most scholars have labeled Ps 137 only as "communal lament," they have read the beginning of the psalm always as despondency. Sitting down, however, may be protest against the request. For example, in the 1960s, lunch counter sit-ins protested Jim Crow laws. During the height of the protests sparked by Michael Brown Jr.'s death, protestors conducted sit-downs, die-ins, and tied up traffic in protest. In 2016, a national football league player protested police brutality and violence against African Americans by sitting down on the national anthem and later by taking a knee. Similarly, hanging one's harps reflect the same defiant refusal to perform in a way that makes those who terrorize, oppress, or enslave others feel entertained. Remembering Zion is an act of cultural reintegration.[38]

Emboldened as I had been by the Movement for Black Lives/Black Lives Matter Movement, reading Ps 137 as protest seemed obvious now. The movement has changed me and radicalized me as a scholar. I was concerned about seeing something that was not there or imposing a possibility onto the text that was implausible. But I pressed into the challenge,

---

37. First presented on September 28 in the Psalms section at the International Organization for the Study of Old Testament (IOSOT) in Stellenbosch, South Africa; Valerie Bridgeman, "'A Long Ways from Home': Displacement, Lament, and Singing Protest in Psalm 137," *PRSt* 44 (2017): 213–23.

38. Bridgeman, "Long Ways from Home," 217. Rodney S. Sadler Jr. argued a similar protest and subversion without directly referencing #BlackLivesMatter. See Rodney S. Sadler Jr., "Singing a Subversive Song: Psalm 137 and 'Colored Pompey,'" in *The Oxford Handbook of the Psalms*, ed. William P. Brown (Oxford: Oxford University Press, 2015), 447–58.

knowing that the essay would be peer reviewed and edited by nonblack scholars. I continued to think about the lament portion of Ps 137, noting:

> The lament in verse 14 is filled with pathos, to be sure. Pain gives power to the protest. When Alicia Garza created the hashtag BlackLivesMatter with Patrisse Cullors and Opal Tometi after George Zimmerman was acquitted on July 13, 2013 of murdering Trayvon Martin in a gated community, no one could have known that her painful declaration, "our lives matter y'all," would become a movement and not just a tweet forwarded and liked many times over. What began as an ember with the Zimmerman verdict, however, burst into a fiery flame after Michael Brown Jr. was gunned down on August 9, 2014 by a sworn peace officer in the apartment complex where his grandmother lived. Over and over in Facebook postings, blogs, think pieces, Twitter feeds and more, the pain spilled over into protest. "By the rivers of Babylon, we sat down and we wept" could have been the rallying cry. The Hebrew might be aptly rendered, "we kept weeping" as we remembered.[39]

The call to reframe and refocus our hermeneutical lenses meant that we could not work in a silo or a vacuum. While we are trying out our new way of approaching our scholarship, each of us keeps showing up for protests and vigils in our respective cities. We write phone numbers on our arms in the event we are arrested. We alert our deans and presidents that we might end up in jail. We call and text one another to encourage each other. We are trying to live into Harding's call to live an embodied scholarship enthralled with activism. As Harding had asserted, "when we ask what it means as a black scholar to live the truth of black struggle and black hope, it is self-evident that words are not sufficient. Examples are far more to the point and many are available, some illuminating one aspect of the living, some another, a significant number illustrating an impressive integrity and wholeness."[40] We are deliberately out-of-bounds of the academy. We are convinced our words only matter if we live them.

We continue to imagine ways of doing this scholarly, communal work in a way that harnesses our gifts and those of the communities we made commitments to in August 2015. We wrote in the statement of solidarity that:

---

39. Bridgeman, "Long Ways from Home," 218.
40. Harding, "Vocation of the Black Scholar," 21.

We acknowledge our deep need for the gifts and abilities that God has placed in the streets, in prisons, in churches, in the academy, in places yet unrevealed, and in places that we in our privilege have ignored. We acknowledge and appreciate the broadness of this work. It is an intergenerational movement with people from diverse contexts "doing the work."[41]

The goal, then, is to avoid trending scholarship that does not endure and to engage in scholarship that is pertinent to our times. Harding and Townes warned us against merely engaging the next *it* methodologies. We seek to be "those black scholars who recognize their profound relationship to the ongoing life and struggles of the larger black community, all work is a pathway to the next stages of the struggle."[42] We are called, to use the language of vocation, to expand the way we do our work and to commit to not coloring inside the lines of our respective disciplines. None of us is deluded into believing that scholars bound to the dispassionate notion of objectivity—of which we roundly denounce—will take seriously our work. But we still must do it until there is an overwhelming volume of it, and it cannot be ignored.

I end where I began. Gideon's question: "If God is with us, what is this finding us?" is at the heart of a Black Lives Matter biblical activist hermeneutic. Such a hermeneutic is located in the story I have told you of Ferguson, an intertextuality that requires seeing and understanding parallelisms, allusions, memory, and remembering. It also is located in the reflections of Harding and Townes and in the harnessed gifts from people in the streets, prisons, churches, and beyond. It means hearing the poetry and songs of everyday people and taking their questions to our various disciplines. In biblical studies, it means centering those questions and stories. It means seeing the connection and hearing the allusions, where our black stories sound like and look like something we have seen in the Bible and, as their own holy selves, speak back to the text. The text must meet us at the intersection of its history and our questions. Such a hermeneutic means entering the work with the struggle for freedom in mind. It is an interested, ideologically invested work. People are at stake.

So, an intertextual activist hermeneutic is vocational, located in the scholar's study and in the streets' struggles. It is the quintessential reflec-

---

41. "Learning from Black Lives Conversation."
42. Harding, "Vocation of the Black Scholar," 17.

tion-praxis-reflection model of being useful to the people. It is consciously subversive. As activist-scholars, we keep Gideon's question in front of us, even if we must hide in a proverbial winepress to thresh the wheat of our insights. This is the work that has found us. Our conversion to activism hermeneutics means we must never be content with simple questions or easy answers. It means we must always be intersectional and intertextual. And we must also find a way to be present to the movement while we work, if indeed we have been found in trouble and in the struggle.

# Bibliography

Ackerman, Susan. "A Marzēaḥ in Ezekiel 8:7–13?" *HTR* 82 (1989): 267–81.
Ackroyd, Peter R. "Isaiah I–XII: Presentation of a Prophet." Pages 16–48 in *Congress Volume: Göttingen 1977*. Edited by John A. Emerton. VTSup 29. Leiden: Brill, 1978.
———. *Studies in the Religious Tradition of the Old Testament*. London: SCM, 1987.
Adams, Hazard, and Leroy Searle, eds. *Critical Theory since Plato*. 3rd ed. Belmont, CA: Wadsworth, 2004.
Adams, Jim W. *The Performative Nature and Function of Isaiah 40–55*. LHBOTS 448. New York: T&T Clark, 2006.
Aichele, George, Peter D. Miscall, and Richard Walsh. "An Elephant in the Room: Historical-Critical and Postmodern Interpretations of the Bible." *JBL* 128 (2009): 383–404.
Aichele, George, and Gary A. Phillips. "Introduction: Exegesis, Eisegesis, Intergesis." *Semeia* 69/70 (1995): 7–18.
Albeck, Chanoch. *Das Buch der Jubiläen und die Halacha*. BHWJ 47. Berlin: Hochschule für die Wissenschaft des Judentums, 1930.
———. *Shishah Sidre Mishnah*. 6 vols. Jerusalem: Bialik Institute; Tel Aviv: Dvir, 1952–1959.
Alkier, Stefan. "Intertextuality and the Semiotics of Biblical Texts." Pages 3–21 in *Reading the Bible Intertextually*. Edited by Richard B. Hays, Stefan Alkier, and Leroy A. Huizenga. Waco, TX: Baylor University Press, 2009.
———. "Reading the Canon Intertextually: The Decentralization of Meaning." Pages 288–302 in *Between Text and Text: The Hermeneutics of Intertextuality in Ancient Cultures and Their Afterlife in Medieval and Modern Times*. Edited by Michaela Bauks, Wayne Horowitz, and Armin Lange. JAJSup 6. Göttingen: Vandenhoeck & Ruprecht, 2013.
Allen, Graham. *Intertextuality*. NCI. London: Routledge, 2000.

Alston, William P. *Illocutionary Acts and Sentence Meaning*. Ithaca, NY: Cornell University Press, 2000.

Alter, Robert. *The Art of Biblical Narrative*. New York: Basic Books, 1981.

Andersen, Francis I., and A. Dean Forbes. *Biblical Hebrew Grammar Visualized*. LSAWS 6. Winona Lake, IN: Eisenbrauns, 2012.

Anderson, Cheryl B. "Biblical Interpretation as Violence: Genesis 19 and Judges 19 in the Context of HIV and AIDS." Pages 121–36 in *La Violencia and the Hebrew Bible: The Politics and Histories of Biblical Hermeneutics on the American Continent*. Edited by Susanne Scholz and Pablo R. Andiñach. SemeiaSt 82. Atlanta: SBL Press, 2016.

Aragay, Mireia. "Reflection to Refraction: Adaptation Studies Then and Now." Pages 11–34 in *Books in Motion: Adaptation, Intertextuality, Authorship*. Edited by Mireia Aragay. Amsterdam: Rodopi, 2005.

Aragay, Mireia, and Gemma López. "Inf(l)ecting Pride and Prejudice: Dialogism, Intertextuality and Adaptation." Pages 210–19 in *Books in Motion: Adaptation, Intertextuality, Authorship*. Edited by Mireia Aragay. Amsterdam: Rodopi, 2005.

Aschkenasy, Nehama. "Reading Ruth through a Bakhtinian Lens: The Carnivalesque in a Biblical Tale." *JBL* 126 (2007): 437–53.

Attridge, Harold, Torleif Elgvin, Jozef Milik, Saul Olyan, John Strugnell, Emanuel Tov, James C. VanderKam, and Sidnie A. White. *Qumran Cave 4.VIII: Parabiblical Texts, Part I*. Edited by Emanuel Tov. DJD 13. Oxford: Clarendon, 1994.

Auerbach, Erich. *Mimesis: Dargestellte Wirklichkeit in der Abendländischen Literatur*. SD 90. Bern: Francke, 1971.

Austin, John L. *How to Do Things with Words*. Cambridge: Harvard University Press, 1962.

Avalos, Hector. "Columbus as Biblical Exegete: A Study of the Libro de Las Profecías." Pages 59–80 in *Religion in the Age of Exploration: The Case of Spain and New Spain*. Edited by Bryan F. Le Beau and Menahem Mor. Omaha, NE: Creighton University Press, 1996.

Bail, Ulrike. "Psalm 110: Eine intertextuelle Lektüre aus alttestamentlicher Perspektive." Pages 94–121 in *Heiligkeit und Herrschaft*. Edited by Dieter Sänger. BTSt 55. Neukirchen-Vluyn: Neukirchener Verlag, 2003.

Bakhtin, Mikhail M. "Author and Hero in Aesthetic Activity." Pages 4–256 in *Art and Answerability: Early Philosophical Essays by M. M. Bakhtin*. Edited by Michael Holquist and Vadim Liapunov. Translated by Vadim Liapunov. Austin: University of Texas Press, 1990.

———. *The Dialogic Imagination*. Edited by Michael Holquist. Translated by Caryl Emerson and Michael Holquist. Austin: University of Texas Press, 1981.

———. "Discourse in the Novel." Pages 259–422 in *The Dialogic Imagination*. Edited by Michael Holquist. Translated by Caryl Emerson and Michael Holquist. Austin: University of Texas Press, 1981.

———. *Problems of Dostoevsky's Poetics*. Edited and translated by Caryl Emerson. Minneapolis: University of Minnesota Press, 1984.

———. *Speech Genres and Other Late Essays*. Edited by Caryl Emerson and Michael Holquist. Translated by Vern W. McGee. UTPSS 9. Austin: University of Texas Press, 1986.

———. "Toward a Methodology for the Human Sciences." Pages 159–72 in *Speech Genres and Other Late Essays*. Edited by Caryl Emerson and Michael Holquist. Translated by Vern W. McGee. UTPSS 9. Austin: University of Texas Press, 1986.

Bal, Mieke. "Introduction." Pages 11–24 in *Anti-Covenant: Counter-reading Women's Lives in the Hebrew Bible*. Edited by Mieke Bal. JSOTSup 81. BLS 22. Sheffield: Almond Press, 1989.

———. "The Laughing Mice; or, On Focalization." *PT* 2 (1981): 202–10.

Baltzer, Dieter. *Ezechiel und Deuterojesaja: Berührungen in der Heilserwartung der beiden großen Exilspropheten*. Berlin: de Gruyter, 1971.

Baltzer, Klaus. *Deutero-Isaiah*. Translated by Margaret Kohl. Hermeneia. Minneapolis: Fortress, 2001.

Bandstra, Barry L. "Concubinage." Pages 159–61 in *Dictionary of Scripture and Ethics*. Edited by Joel B. Green. Grand Rapids: Baker Academic, 2011.

Banks, Adelle M. "Seminaries across the Country Now Offering Black Lives Matter Courses." *Sojourners*. December 7, 2016. https://tinyurl.com/SBL03103g.

Barner, Ashley J. *The Case for Fanfiction: Exploring the Pleasures and Practices of a Maligned Craft*. Jefferson, NC: McFarland, 2017.

Bartelt, Andrew H. *The Book around Immanuel: Style and Structure in Isaiah 2–12*. BJSUCSD 4. Winona Lake, IN: Eisenbrauns, 1996.

Barthel, Jörg. *Prophetenwort und Geschichte: Die Jesajaüberlieferung in Jes 6–8 und 28–31*. FAT 19. Tübingen: Mohr Siebeck, 1997.

Barthes, Roland. *Image, Music, Text*. Translated by Stephen Heath. New York: Hill and Wang, 1977.

———. "The Death of the Author." Pages 142–48 in *Image, Music, Text*. Translated by Stephen Heath. New York: Hill and Wang, 1977.

———. *S/Z*. Translated by Richard Miller. New York: Hill & Wang, 1974.

———. "Theory of the Text." Pages 31–47 in *Untying the Text: A Post-Structuralist Reader*. Edited by Robert Young. Translated by Ian McLeod. London: Routledge, 1981.

———. *Writing Degree Zero*. Translated by Annette Lavers and Colin Smith. New York: Hill & Wang, 1977.

Barton, John. *Ethics in Ancient Israel*. Oxford: Oxford University Press, 2014.

———. *Reading the Old Testament: Method in Biblical Study*. 2nd ed. Louisville: Westminster John Knox, 1996.

———. *The Theology of the Book of Amos*. Cambridge: Cambridge University Press, 2012.

———. *Understanding Old Testament Ethics: Approaches and Explorations*. Louisville: Westminster John Knox, 2002.

Basser, Herbert W. *The Gospel of Matthew and Judaic Traditions: A Relevance-Based Commentary*. BRLA 46. Leiden: Brill, 2015.

Batto, Bernard F. *Slaying the Dragon: Mythmaking in the Biblical Tradition*. Louisville: Westminster John Knox, 1992.

Bauer, Dale M., and S. Jaret McKinstry. "Introduction." Pages 1–6 in *Feminism, Bakhtin, and the Dialogic*. Edited by Dale M. Bauer and S. Jaret McKinstry. Albany: State University of New York Press, 1991.

Bauks, Michaela. "Erkenntnis und Leben in Gen 2–3: Zum Wandel eines ursprünglich weisheitlich geprägten Lebensbegriffs." *ZAW* 127 (2015): 20–42.

Baumgarten, Joseph M. "4Q Miscellaneous Rules." Pages 57–78 in *Qumran Cave 4.XXV: Halakhic Texts*. Edited by Emanuel Tov. DJD 35. Oxford: Clarendon, 1999.

Bautch, Richard. "Intertextuality in the Persian Period." Pages 25–35 in *Approaching Yehud: New Approaches to the Study of the Persian Period*. Edited by Jon L. Berquist. SemeiaSt 50. Atlanta: Society of Biblical Literature, 2007.

Beal, Timothy K. "Ideology and Intertextuality: Surplus of Meaning and Controlling the Means of Production." Pages 27–39 in *Reading between Texts: Intertextuality and the Hebrew Bible*. Edited by Danna Nolan Fewell. Louisville: Westminster John Knox, 1992.

———. "The System and the Speaking Subject in the Hebrew Bible: Reading for Divine Abjection." *BibInt* 2 (1994): 171–89.

Becker, Uwe. "Jesaja, Jeremia und die Anfänge der Unheilsprophetie in Juda." *HBAI* 6 (2017): 79–100.

Beebee, Thomas O. *The Ideology of Genre: A Comparative Study of Generic Instability*. Toronto: University of Toronto Press, 2004.
Ben Zvi, Ehud. *Hosea*. FOTL 21A. Grand Rapids: Eerdmans, 2005.
———. "Is the Twelve Hypothesis Likely from an Ancient Reader's Perspective?" Pages 41–96 in *Two Sides of a Coin: Juxtaposing Views on the Book of the Twelve/The Twelve Prophetic Books*. Edited by Ehud Ben Zvi and James Nogalski. Piscataway, NJ: Gorgias, 2009.
———. "Isaiah, a Memorable Prophet: Why Was Isaiah So Memorable in the Late Persian/Early Hellenistic Periods? Some Observations." Pages 365–83 in *Remembering Biblical Figures in the Late Persian and Early Hellenistic Periods: Social Memory and Imagination*. Edited by Diana V. Edelman and Ehud Ben Zvi. Oxford: Oxford University Press, 2013.
———. *Micah*. FOTL 21B. Grand Rapids: Eerdmans, 2000.
Berges, Ulrich F. *The Book of Isaiah: Its Composition and Final Form*. Translated by Millard C. Lind. HBM 46. Sheffield: Sheffield Phoenix, 2012.
———. *Klagelieder*. HThKAT. Freiburg im Breisgau: Herder, 2002.
Bergmann, Claudia D. *Childbirth as a Metaphor for Crisis: Evidence from the Ancient Near East, the Hebrew Bible, and 1QH XI, 1–18*. BZAW 382. Berlin: de Gruyter, 2008.
Berlin, Adele. *Lamentations: A Commentary*. OTL. Louisville: Westminster John Knox, 2002.
Bernstein, Moshe J. "4Q452: From Rewritten Bible to Bible Commentary." *JJS* 45 (1994): 1–27.
———. "Introductory Formulas for Citation and Re-citation of Biblical Verses in the Qumran Pesharim." *DSD* 1 (1994): 30–70.
———. *Reading and Re-Reading Scripture at Qumran*. 2 vols. STDJ 107. Leiden: Brill, 2013.
———. "Rearrangement, Anticipation and Harmonization as Exegetical Features in the Genesis Apocryphon." *DSD* 3 (1996): 37–57.
———. "Rewritten Bible: A Generic Category Which Has Outlived Its Usefulness?" *Text* 22 (2005): 169–96.
Beuken, Willem A. M. "The Unity of the Book of Isaiah: Another Attempt at Bridging the Gorge between Its Two Main Parts." Pages 50–60 in *Reading from Right to Left: Essays on the Hebrew Bible in Honour of David J. A. Clines*. Edited by J. Cheryl Exum and H. G. M. Williamson. JSOTSup 373. London: Sheffield Academic, 2003.
Bier, Miriam J. "'We Have Sinned and Rebelled; You Have Not Forgiven': The Dialogic Interaction between Authoritative and Internally Persuasive Discourse in Lamentations 3." *BibInt* 22 (2014): 146–67.

Birdsong, Shelley L. *The Last King(s) of Judah: Zedekiah and Sedekias in the Hebrew and Old Greek Versions of Jeremiah 37(44):1–40(47):6*. FAT 2/89. Tübingen: Mohr Siebeck, 2017.

Birnbaum, Elisabeth. "Salomo in Barock und Moderne: Ein interdisziplinäres Kaleidoskop." *BArts* 1 (2017): 1–25.

Blanchot, Maurice. "Prophetic Speech." Pages 79–85 in *The Book to Come*. Translated by Charlotte Mandell. Stanford, CA: Stanford University Press, 2003.

Blenkinsopp, Joseph. *Creation, Un-Creation, Re-Creation: A Discursive Commentary on Genesis 1–11*. London: T&T Clark, 2011.

———. "The Judge of All the Earth: Theodicy in the Midrash on Genesis 18:22–33." *JJS* 41 (1990): 3–12.

Block, Daniel I. *The Book of Ezekiel: Chapters 1–24*. NICOT. Grand Rapids: Eerdmans, 1997.

———. "Echo Narrative Technique in Hebrew Literature: A Study in Judges 19." *WTJ* 52 (1990): 325–34.

———. *Judges, Ruth*. NAC 6. Nashville: Broadman & Holman, 1999.

Blum, Erhard. "Jesajas prophetisches Testament: Beobachtungen zu Jes 1–11." *ZAW* 108 (1996): 547–68; 109 (1997): 12–29.

Boase, Elizabeth. *The Fulfilment of Doom? The Dialogic Interaction between the Book of Lamentations and the Pre-Exilic/Early Exilic Prophetic Literature*. LHBOTS 437. New York: T&T Clark, 2006.

———. "Grounded in the Body: A Bakhtinian Reading of Lamentations 2 from Another Perspective." *BibInt* 22 (2014): 292–306.

Boda, Mark J., Carol J. Dempsey, and LeAnn Snow Flesher, eds. *Daughter Zion: Her Portrait, Her Response*. AIL 13. Atlanta: Society of Biblical Literature, 2012.

Boecker, Hans Jochen. *Klagelieder*. ZBK 21. Zürich: TVZ, 1985.

Bonhoeffer, Dietrich. *Prayers from Prison*. Interpreted by Johann Christoph Hempe. Minneapolis: Fortress, 1978.

Booth, Wayne C. *The Rhetoric of Fiction*. Chicago: University of Chicago Press, 1961.

Bovati, Pietro, and Roland Meynet. *Le Livre du Prophète Amos*. Paris: Cerf, 1994.

Bowen, Nancy R. "Ezekiel." *OEBB* 1:282–300.

Boyarin, Daniel. *Intertextuality and the Reading of Midrash*. ISBL. Bloomington: Indiana University Press, 1994.

Breed, Brennan W. *Nomadic Text: A Theory of Biblical Reception History*. ISBL. Bloomington: Indiana University Press, 2014.

Bridgeman, Valerie. "'A Long Ways from Home': Displacement, Lament, and Singing Protest in Psalm 137." *PRSt* 44 (2017): 213–23.

———. "Writing Phone Numbers on My Arm: Activism and Scholarship in the Age of #BlackLivesMatter." Paper presented at the Annual Meeting of the Society of Biblical Literature. Boston, MA, November 18, 2017.

Briggs, Richard S. *Words in Action: Speech Act Theory and Biblical Interpretation*. Edinburgh: T&T Clark, 2001.

Brooke, George J. "The Genre of 4Q252: From Poetry to Pesher." *DSD* 1 (1994): 160–79.

———. "Genre Theory, Rewritten Bible and Pesher." *DSD* 17 (2010): 361–86.

Brueggemann, Walter. "Patriotism for Citizens of the Penultimate Superpower." *Di* 42 (2003): 336–43.

———. *Theology of the Old Testament: Testimony, Dispute, Advocacy*. Minneapolis: Fortress, 1997.

Buber, Martin, and Franz Rosenzweig, trans. *Die fünf Bücher der Weisung*. 10th ed. Stuttgart: Deutsche Bibelgesellschaft, 1992.

Burgess, Jonathan S. "Intertextuality without Text in Early Greek Epic." Pages 168–83 in *Relative Chronology in Early Greek Epic Poetry*. Edited by Øivind Andersen and Dag T. T. Haug. Cambridge: Cambridge University Press, 2011.

Buss, Martin J. "Potential and Actual Interactions between Speech Act Theory and Biblical Studies." *Semeia* 41 (1987): 125–34.

Busse, Kristina. *Framing Fan Fiction: Literary and Social Practices in Fan Fiction Communities*. Iowa City, IA: University of Iowa Press, 2017.

Callaway, Mary C. "Black Fire on White Fire: Historical Context and Literary Subtext in Jeremiah 37–38." Pages 171–78 in *Troubling Jeremiah*. Edited by A. R. Pete Diamond, Kathleen M. O'Connor, and Louis Stulman. JSOTSup 260. Sheffield: Sheffield Academic, 1999.

Carr, David M. *The Formation of the Hebrew Bible: A New Reconstruction*. Oxford: Oxford University Press, 2011.

———. "The Many Uses of Intertextuality in Biblical Studies: Actual and Potential." Pages 505–35 in *Congress Volume: Helsinki 2010*. Edited by Martti Nissinen. VTSup 148. Leiden: Brill, 2012.

———. *Reading the Fractures of Genesis: Historical and Literary Approaches*. Louisville: Westminster John Knox, 1996.

Carrington, André. *Speculative Blackness: The Future of Race in Science Fiction*. Minneapolis: University of Minnesota Press, 2016.

Carroll, Robert P. "Intertextuality and the Book of Jeremiah: Animadversions on Text and Theory." Pages 55–78 in *The New Literary Criticism and the Hebrew Bible*. Edited by J. Cheryl Exum and David J. A. Clines. JSOTSup 143. Sheffield: JSOT Press, 1993.

Cartwright, Michael G. "The Uses of Scripture in Christian Ethics—After Bakhtin." *ASCE* (1992): 263–76.

Cassuto, Umberto. "On the Formal and Stylistic Relationships between Deutero-Isaiah and Other Biblical Writers." Pages 143–60 in vol. 1 of *Oriental and Other Studies*. Edited by Umberto Cassuto. Jerusalem: Magnes, 1973.

Chandler, Daniel. *Semiotics for Beginners*. London: Routledge, 2004. http://visual-memory.co.uk/daniel/Documents/S4B/.

Chatman, Seymour Benjamin. "On Defining 'Form.'" *NLH* 2 (1971): 217–28.

———. *Story and Discourse: Narrative Structure in Fiction and Film*. Ithaca, NY: Cornell University Press, 1978.

Cheon, Samuel. "Filling the Gap in the Story of Lot's Wife (Genesis 19:1–29)." *AsJT* 15 (2001): 14–23.

Childs, Brevard S. *Introduction to the Old Testament as Scripture*. Minneapolis: Fortress, 1979.

Chokshi, Niraj. "South Koreans in New York Celebrate a 100-Year-Old Independence Movement." *New York Times*, 1 March 2019. https://tinyurl.com/SBLPress03103a.

Chong, Timothy K. H. *Strategies in Church Discipline from 1 Corinthians: A Chinese Perspective*. Bloomington, IN: WestBow, 2016.

Claassens, L. Juliana M. "Biblical Theology as Dialogue: Continuing the Conversation on Mikhail Bakhtin and Biblical Theology." *JBL* 122 (2003): 127–44.

———. "Laughter and Tears: Carnivalistic Overtones in the Stories of Sarah and Hagar." *PRSt* 32 (2005): 295–308.

Clark, Katerina, and Michael Holquist. *Mikhail Bakhtin*. Cambridge: Harvard University Press, 1984.

Clayton, Jay, and Eric Rothstein. "Figures in the Corpus: Theories of Influence and Intertextuality." Pages 3–36 in *Influence and Intertextuality in Literary History*. Edited by Jay Clayton and Eric Rothstein. Madison, WI: University of Wisconsin Press, 1991.

Clements, Roland E. "A Light to the Nations: A Central Theme of the Book of Isaiah." Pages 57–69 in *Forming Prophetic Literature: Essays on Isaiah and the Twelve in Honor of John D. W. Watts.* Edited by James W. Watts and Paul R. House. JSOTSup 235. Sheffield: Sheffield Academic, 1996.

Coates, Ruth. *Christianity in Bakhtin: God and the Exiled Author.* CSRL. Cambridge: Cambridge University Press, 1998.

Coats, George W. *Exodus 1–18.* FOTL 2A. Grand Rapids: Eerdmans, 1999.

Coleridge, Samuel Taylor. *Biographia Literaria.* Edited by Nigel Leask. London: J. M. Dent, 1997.

Contino, Paul J., and Susan M. Felch. "Introduction: A Feeling for Faith." Pages 1–24 in *Bakhtin and Religion: A Feeling for Faith.* Edited by Susan M. Felch and Paul J. Contino. Evanston, IL: Northwestern University Press, 2001.

Cook, Stephen L., and Corrine L. Patton, eds. *Ezekiel's Hierarchical World: Wrestling with a Tiered Reality.* SymS 31. Atlanta: Society of Biblical Literature, 2004.

Cooper, Alan. "The Suffering Servant and Job: A View from the Sixteenth Century." Pages 189–200 in *"As Those Who Are Taught": The Interpretation of Isaiah from the LXX to the SBL.* Edited by Claire M. McGinnis and Patricia K. Tull. SymS 27. Atlanta: Society of Biblical Literature, 2006.

Craffert, Pieter F. "Alternate States of Consciousness and Biblical Research: The Contribution of John Pilch." *BTB* 47 (2017): 100–10.

———. "Shamanism and the Shamanic Complex." *BTB* 41 (2011): 151–61.

Crawford, Sidnie A. White. "4QDt$^n$: Biblical Manuscript or Excerpted Text?" Pages 13–20 in *Of Scribes and Scrolls: Studies on the Hebrew Bible, Intertestamental Judaism, and Christian Origins Presented to John Strugnell on the Occasion of His Sixtieth Birthday.* Edited by Harold W. Attridge, John J. Collins, and Thomas H. Tobin. Lanham, MD: University Press of America, 1990.

———. "The All Souls Deuteronomy and the Decalogue." *JBL* 109 (1990): 193–206.

———. "A Comparison of the 'A' and 'B' Manuscripts of the *Damascus Document*." *RQ* 12 (1987): 537–53.

———. "Has *Esther* Been Found at Qumran? 4QProto-Esther and the *Esther* Corpus." *RevQ* 17 (1996): 307–25.

———. *Rewriting Scripture in Second Temple Times.* SDSS 1. Grand Rapids: Eerdmans, 2008.

Crenshaw, James L. *Ecclesiastes: A Commentary.* OTL. Philadelphia: Westminster, 1987.

———. "The Influence of the Wise upon Amos: The 'Doxologies of Amos' and Job 5:9–16, 9:5–10." *ZAW* 79 (1967): 42–52.

———. "Method in Determining Wisdom Influence upon 'Historical' Literature." *JBL* 88 (1969): 129–42.

———. Review of *Die "Bindung Isaaks" im Kanon (Gen 22): Grundlagen und Programm einer kanonisch-intertextuellen Lektüre*, by G. Steins. *JBL* 121 (2002): 152–54.

———. *A Whirlpool of Torment: Israelite Traditions of God as an Oppressive Presence*. OBT 12. Philadelphia: Fortress, 1984.

Cross, Frank Moore. *The Ancient Library of Qumran*. 3rd ed. BibSem 30. Sheffield: Sheffield Academic, 1995.

Cruise, Charles E. "The 'Wealth of the Nations': A Study in the Intertextuality of Isaiah 60:5, 11." *JETS* 58 (2015): 283–97.

Crüsemann, Frank. "'Auge um Auge…' (Ex 21,24f): Zum sozialgeschichtlichen Sinn des Talionsgesetzes im Bundesbuch." *EvT* 47 (1987): 411–26.

Culler, Jonathan D. "Presupposition and Intertextuality." Pages 100–18 in *The Pursuit of Signs: Semiotics, Literature, Deconstruction*. Ithaca, NY: Cornell University Press, 1981.

———. *The Pursuit of Signs: Semiotics, Literature, Deconstruction*. Ithaca, NY: Cornell University Press, 1981.

Cummins, John. *The Voyage of Christopher Columbus: Columbus' Own Journal of Discovery, Newly Restored and Translated*. New York: St. Martin's, 1992.

Davies, Eryl W. "Ethics of the Hebrew Bible: The Problem of Methodology." *Semeia* 66 (1994): 43–53.

Davies, Philip R. *1QM, the War Scroll from Qumran: Its Structure and History*. BibOr 32. Rome: Biblical Institute Press, 1977.

Day, John. *From Creation to Babel: Studies in Genesis 1–11*. LHBOTS 592. Edinburgh: T&T Clark, 2013.

De La Torre, Miguel A. *Reading the Bible from the Margins*. Maryknoll, NY: Orbis Books, 2002.

deClaissé-Walford, Nancy L. *Introduction to the Psalms: A Song from Ancient Israel*. Saint Louis, MO: Chalice, 2004.

———, ed. *The Shape and Shaping of the Book of Psalms: The Current State of Scholarship*. AIL 20. Atlanta: SBL Press, 2014.

Dell, Katharine J. "The Suffering Servant of Deutero-Isaiah: Jeremiah Revisited." Pages 119–34 in *Genesis, Isaiah and Psalms: A Festschrift to Honour Professor John Emerton for His Eightieth Birthday*. Edited by Katharine J. Dell, Graham Davies, and Yee Von Koh. VTSup 135. Leiden: Brill, 2010.

Dell, Katharine J., and Will Kynes, eds. *Reading Job Intertextually*. LHBOTS 587. London: T&T Clark, 2013.

Dentith, Simon. *Bakhtinian Thought: An Introductory Reader*. CRTP. London: Routledge, 1995.

Derrida, Jacques. *Of Grammatology*. Translated by Gayatri Chakravorty Spivak. Baltimore: Johns Hopkins University Press, 1976.

Dewrell, Heath D. *Child Sacrifice in Ancient Israel*. EANEC 5. Winona Lake, IN: Eisenbrauns, 2017.

Dimant, Devorah. "Apocalyptic Texts at Qumran." Pages 175–91 in *The Community of the Renewed Covenant: The Notre Dame Symposium on the Dead Sea Scrolls*. Edited by Eugene Ulrich and James C. VanderKam. CJAS 10. Notre Dame, IN: University of Notre Dame Press, 1994.

———. "The Qumran Manuscripts: Contents and Significance." Pages 23–58 in *Time to Prepare the Way in the Wilderness: Papers on the Qumran Scrolls by Fellows of the Institute for Advanced Studies of the Hebrew University, Jerusalem, 1989–1990*. Edited by Devorah Dimant and Lawrence H. Schiffman. STDJ 16. Leiden: Brill, 1995.

Dobbs-Allsopp, F. W. *On Biblical Poetry*. Oxford: Oxford University Press, 2015.

Dozeman, Thomas B. *Exodus*. ECC. Grand Rapids: Eerdmans, 2009.

Dozeman, Thomas B., and Konrad Schmid, eds. *A Farewell to the Yahwist? The Composition of the Pentateuch in Recent European Interpretation*. SymS 34. Atlanta: Society of Biblical Literature, 2006.

Draper, Hal. *The Complete Poems of Heinrich Heine: A Modern English Version*. Boston: Suhrkamp, 1982.

Dube, Musa W. *The HIV and AIDS Bible: Selected Essays*. Scranton, PA: University of Scranton Press, 2008.

Dubrow, Heather. *Genre*. London: Methuen, 1982.

Dufault-Hunter, Erin. "Sex and Sexuality." Pages 718–20 in *Dictionary of Scripture and Ethics*. Edited by Joel B. Green. Grand Rapids: Baker Academic, 2011.

Duff, William. *An Essay on Original Genius*. London, 1767.

Dumas, André. *Dietrich Bonhoeffer: Theologian of Reality*. Translated by R. M. Brown. New York: Macmillan, 1971.

Ebner, Martin. "Feindesliebe—Ein Ratschlag zum Überleben? Sozial- und religionsgeschichtliche Überlegungen zu Mt 5,38–47 par Lk 6,27–35."

Pages 119–42 in *From Quest to Q: Festschrift James M. Robinson*. Edited by Jon M. Asgeirsson, Kristin de Troyer, and Marvin W. Meyer. BETL 146. Leuven: Peeters, 2000.

Edenburg, Cynthia. *Dismembering the Whole: Composition and Purpose of Judges 19–21*. AIL 24. Atlanta: SBL Press, 2016.

———. "Intertextuality, Literary Competence, and the Question of Readership: Some Preliminary Observations." *JSOT* 35 (2010): 131–48.

Eidevall, Göran. *Amos: A New Translation with Introduction and Commentary*. AYBRL. New Haven: Yale University Press, 2017.

Eissfeldt, Otto. *Der Maschal im Alten Testament: Eine wortgeschichtliche Untersuchung nebst einer literargeschichtlichen Untersuchung der* משל *genannten Gattungen "Volkssprichwort" und "Spottlied."* Giessen: Töpelmann, 1913.

Elliger, Karl. *Leviticus*. HAT 1/4. Tübingen: Mohr Siebeck, 1966.

Elliott-Binns, L. E. "Some Problems of the Holiness Code." *ZAW* 67 (1955): 26–40.

Emerson, Caryl. "Bakhtin at 100: Art, Ethics, and the Architectonic Self." *CR* 39 (1995): 397–418.

———. *The First Hundred Years of Mikhail Bakhtin*. Princeton: Princeton University Press, 1997.

Engelken, Karen. "*pîlegeš*." *TDOT* 11:549–51.

Eshel, Esther. "4QDeut$^n$: A Text That Has Undergone Harmonistic Editing." *HUCA* 62 (1991): 117–54.

Eshel, Esther, and Hanan Eshel. "Recensions and Editions of the War Scroll." Pages 351–63 in *The Dead Sea Scrolls: Fifty Years after Their Discovery; Proceedings of the Jerusalem Congress, July 20–25, 1997*. Edited by Lawrence H. Schiffman, Emanuel Tov, and James C. VanderKam. Jerusalem: Israel Exploration Society, 2000.

Eslinger, Lyle. "Inner-Biblical Exegesis and Inner-Biblical Allusion: The Question of Category." *VT* 42 (1992): 47–58.

Evans, Craig A., and Jeremiah J. Johnston, eds. *Searching the Scriptures: Studies in Context and Intertextuality*. LNTS 543; SSEJC 19. London: T&T Clark, 2015.

Evans, Craig A., and James A. Sanders. *Luke and Scripture: The Function of Sacred Tradition in Luke–Acts*. Minneapolis: Fortress, 1993.

———, eds. *Paul and the Scriptures of Israel*. JSNTSup 83. Sheffield: Sheffield Academic, 1993.

Evans, Donald D. *The Logic of Self-Involvement: A Philosophical Study of*

*Everyday Language with Special Reference to the Christian Use of Language about God as Creator*. LPT. London: SCM, 1963.

Evans, Paul S. "The Hezekiah-Sennacherib Narrative as Polyphonic Text." *JSOT* 33 (2009): 335–58.

Exum, J. Cheryl. "The Centre Cannot Hold: Thematic and Textual Instabilities in Judges." *CBQ* 52 (1990): 410–29.

———. *Fragmented Women: Feminist (Sub)Versions of Biblical Narratives*. Valley Forge, PA: Trinity Press International, 1993.

———. *Was sagt das Richterbuch den Frauen?* SBS 169. Suttgart: Katholisches Bibelwerk, 1997.

Fabry, H. J. "מַרְזֵחַ." *TDOT* 9:10–15.

Fauconnier, Gilles, and Mark Turner. *The Way We Think: Conceptual Blending and the Mind's Hidden Complexities*. New York: Basic Books, 2002.

Ferry, Joëlle. *Isaïe: "Comme les mots d'un livre scellé" (Is 29,11)*. LD 221. Paris: Cerf, 2008.

Fewell, Danna Nolan, ed. *Reading between Texts: Intertextuality and the Hebrew Bible*. Louisville: Westminster John Knox, 1992.

Fichtner, J. "Isaiah among the Wise." Pages 429–38 in *Studies in Ancient Israelite Wisdom*. Edited by James L. Crenshaw. New York: Ktav, 1976.

———. "Jesaja unter den Weisen." *TLZ* 74 (1949): 75–80.

Fiedler, Peter. *Das Matthäusevangelium*. THKNT 1. Stuttgart: Kohlhammer, 2006.

Fisch, Harold. "Ruth and the Structure of Covenant History." *VT* 32 (1982): 425–37.

Fishbane, Michael. *Biblical Interpretation in Ancient Israel*. Oxford: Clarendon, 1985.

———. "Types of Biblical Intertextuality." *VT* 80 (2000): 39–44.

Fitzmyer, Joseph A. *The Genesis Apocryphon of Qumran Cave 1: A Commentary*. BibOr 18A. Rome: Biblical Institute Press, 1971.

Fleming, John V. "Christopher Columbus as Scriptural Exegete." Pages 173–83 in *Biblical Hermeneutics in Historical Perspective: Studies in Honor of Karlfried Froehlich on His Sixtieth Birthday*. Edited by Mark S. Burrows and Paul Rorem. Grand Rapids: Eerdmans, 1991.

Flint, Valerie I. J. *The Imaginative Landscape of Christopher Columbus*. Princeton: Princeton University Press, 1992.

Fohrer, Georg. *Introduction to the Old Testament*. Translated by David E. Green. Nashville: Abingdon, 1968.

———. "Jesaja 1 als Zusammenfassung der Verkündigung Jesajas." *ZAW* 74 (1962): 251–68.

Fokkelman, Jan P. "Structural Remarks on Judges 9 and 19." Pages 33–45 in *"Sha'arei Talmon": Studies in the Bible, Qumran, and the Ancient Near East Presented to Shemaryahu Talmon*. Edited by Michael A. Fishbane, Emanuel Tov, and Weston W. Fields. Winona Lake, IN: Eisenbrauns, 1992.

Fontaine, Carole R. *Traditional Sayings in the Old Testament: A Contextual Study*. BLS 5. Sheffield: Almond Press, 1982.

Fowler, Alastair. *A History of English Literature: Forms and Kinds from the Middle Ages to the Present*. Oxford: Blackwell, 1987.

———. *Kinds of Literature: An Introduction to the Theory of Genres and Modes*. Cambridge: Harvard University Press, 1982.

———. "The Life and Death of Literary Forms." *NLH* 2 (1971): 199–216.

Fox, Michael V. *Proverbs 1–9: A New Translation with Introduction and Commentary*. AB 18A. New York: Doubleday, 2000.

———. *Proverbs 10–31: A New Translation with Introduction and Commentary*. AB 18B. New Haven: Yale University Press, 2000.

———. *Qohelet and His Contradictions*. JSOTSup 71. BLS 18. Sheffield: Sheffield Academic, 1989.

Freedman, David Noel. "The Broken Construct Chain." *Bib* 53 (1972): 534–36.

Frendo, Anthony. "The 'Broken Construct Chain' in Qoh 10,10b." *Bib* 62 (1981): 544–45.

Frevel, Christian. *Die Klagelieder*. NSKAT 20.1. Stuttgart: Katholisches Bibelwerk, 2017.

Friedman, Susan S. "Weavings: Intertextuality and the (Re)Birth of the Author." Pages 146–80 in *Influence and Intertextuality in Literary History*. Edited by Jay Clayton and Eric Rothstein. Madison, WI: University of Wisconsin Press, 1991.

Fuchs, Esther. "Structure, Ideology and Politics in the Biblical Betrothal Type-Scene." Pages 273–81 in *A Feminist Companion to Genesis*. Edited by Athalya Brenner. FCB 2. Sheffield: Sheffield Academic, 1993.

Gafney, Wil. "The Bible in the Public Square: Interpreting the Bible in the Age of #BlackLivesMatter." https://brite.edu/programs/black-church-studies/black-lives-matter/.

———. "Princess Propaganda: Forced Migration and Royal Women Hostages." Paper presented at the Annual Meeting of the Society of Biblical Literature. San Antonio, TX, November 20, 2016.

Gaon, Amram. *Seder Rav 'Amram Ga'on*. Edited by Daniel S. Goldschmidt. Jerusalem: Mosad Harav Kook, 1971.

Gardner, Kirsten H. "Reading Judges 19: A Study of Narrated Apostasy and Literary Representations of Violence." PhD diss., Fuller Theological Seminary, 2017.

Gauvin, Mitchell J. "Can Isaac Forgive Abraham?" *JRE* 45 (2017): 83–103.

Gench, Frances Taylor. Review of *After Exegesis: Feminist Biblical Theology*, ed. by Patricia K Tull and Carol A Newsom. *Int* 70 (2016): 347–48.

Genette, Gérard. *Palimpsests: Literature in the Second Degree*. Translated by Channa Newman and Claude Doubinsky. Lincoln: University of Nebraska Press, 1982.

Gerhart, Mary. "The Dilemma of the Text: How to 'Belong' to a Genre." *Poet* 18 (1989): 355–73.

Gerstenberger, Erhard S. *Theologies in the Old Testament*. Translated by John Bowden. London: T&T Clark, 2002.

Gertz, Jan C., Bernard M. Levinson, Dalit Rom-Shiloni, and Konrad Schmid, eds. *The Formation of the Pentateuch: Bridging the Academic Cultures of Europe, Israel, and North America*. FAT 111. Tübingen: Mohr Siebeck, 2016.

Giere, Samuel D. *A New Glimpse of Day One: Intertextuality, History of Interpretation, and Genesis 1.1–5*. BZNW 172. Berlin: de Gruyter, 2009.

Gillmayr-Bucher, Susanne. "Framework and Discourse in the Book of Judges." *JBL* 128 (2009): 687–702.

Gimmel, Millie. "Christopher Columbus (1451–20 May 1506)." Pages 35–43 in *Sixteenth-Century Spanish Writers*. Edited by Gregory B. Kaplan. DLB 318. Detroit: Thomson Gale, 2006.

Ginzberg, Louis. *Bible Times and Characters from Joshua to Esther*. Vol. 4 of *The Legends of the Jews*. Philadelphia: Jewish Publication Society of America, 1913.

Goldingay, John. "Isaiah I 1 and II 1." *VT* 48 (1998): 326–32.

Goody, Jack. *The Interface between the Written and the Oral*. Cambridge: Cambridge University Press, 1987.

Gordon, Robert P. "The Ethics of Eden: Truth-Telling in Genesis 2–3." Pages 11–33 in *Ethical and Unethical in the Old Testament: God and Humans in Dialogue*. Edited by Katharine J. Dell. LHBOTS 528. New York: T&T Clark, 2010.

Graf, Karl Heinrich. *Die geschichtlichen Bücher des Alten Testaments: Zwei historisch-kritische Untersuchungen*. Leipzig: Weigel, 1866.

Graham, David A. "Sandra Bland and the Long History of Racism in Waller County, Texas." *Atlantic*, July 21, 2015. https://tinyurl.com/SBL03103e.

Green, Barbara. "Bakhtin and the Bible: A Select Bibliography." *PRSt* 32 (2005): 339–45.

———. *Mikhail Bakhtin and Biblical Scholarship: An Introduction*. SemeiaSt 38. Atlanta: Society of Biblical Literature, 2000.

———. "Mikhail Bakhtin and Biblical Studies." *PRSt* 32 (2005): 241–48.

Grohmann, Marianne. "Psalm 113 and the Song of Hannah (1 Samuel 2:1–10): A Paradigm for Intertextual Reading?" Pages 119–35 in *Reading the Bible Intertextually*. Edited by Richard B. Hays, Stefan Alkier, and Leroy A. Huizenga. Waco, TX: Baylor University Press, 2009.

Gruber, Mayer. *Hosea: A Textual Commentary*. LHBOTS 653. London: Bloomsbury, 2017.

Gruchy, John W. de, ed. *Letters and Papers from Prison*. DBW 8. Minneapolis: Fortress, 2009.

Halpern, Baruch. "The New Names of Isaiah 62:4: Jeremiah's Reception in the Restoration and the Politics of 'Third Isaiah.'" *JBL* 117 (1998): 623–43.

Hamidović, David. *L'Ecrit de Damas: le manifeste essénien*. CRÉJ 51. Leuven: Peeters, 2011.

Hamilton, Mark W., and Samjung Kang-Hamilton. "Dietrich Bonhoeffer: A Review Essay." *ResQ* 58 (2016): 240–45.

Harding, Vincent. "The Vocation of the Black Scholar and the Struggles of the Black Community." Pages 3–30 in *Education and Black Struggle: Notes from the Colonized World*. Edited by Institute of the Black World. Cambridge: Harvard Educational Review, 1974.

Harper, William R. *A Critical and Exegetical Commentary on Amos and Hosea*. ICC. New York: Scribner's Sons, 1905.

Hartenstein, Friedhelm. *Das Archiv des verborgenen Gottes: Studien zur Unheilsprophetie Jesajas und zur Zionstheologie der Psalmen in assyrischer Zeit*. Neukirchen-Vluyn: Neukirchener Verlag, 2011.

Hatina, Thomas R. *In Search of a Context: The Function of Scripture in Mark's Narrative*. JSNTSup 232. SSEJC 8. London: Bloomsbury, 2002.

House, Paul R. *Zephaniah: A Prophetic Drama*. BLS 16. Sheffield: Sheffield Academic, 1989.

Hays, Richard B. *Conversion of the Imagination: Paul as Interpreter of Israel's Scripture*. Grand Rapids: Eerdmans, 2005.

———. *Echoes of Scripture in the Letters of Paul.* New Haven: Yale University Press, 1989.
Hays, Richard B., Stefan Alkier, and Leroy A. Huizenga, eds. *Reading the Bible Intertextually.* Waco, TX: Baylor University Press, 2009.
Hazony, Yoram. *The Philosophy of Hebrew Scripture.* Cambridge: Cambridge University Press, 2013.
"Healing Justice." *Black Lives Matter.* https://tinyurl.com/SBL03103c.
Heine, Heinrich. *Romanzero.* Vol. 3.1 of *Historisch-kritische Gesamtausgabe der Werke.* Edited by Manfred Windfuhr. Hamburg: Hoffmann und Campe, 1992.
Hempel, Charlotte. *The Laws of the Damascus Document: Sources, Tradition and Redaction.* STDJ 29. Leiden: Brill, 1998.
Hempel, Johannes. "Zu Jes 50,6." *ZAW* 76 (1964): 327.
Hendel, Ronald. *Remembering Abraham: Culture, Memory, and History in the Hebrew Bible.* New York: Oxford University Press, 2005.
Hermann, Matthias. *72 Buchstaben: Gedichte.* Frankfurt: Suhrkamp, 1989.
Hermisson, Hans-Jürgen. *Deuterojesaja.* BKAT 11.13. Neukirchen-Vluyn: Neukirchener Verlag, 2008.
Heym, Stefan. *The King David Report.* London: Quartet Book, 1977.
Hinton, David, trans. *The Four Chinese Classics: Tao Te Ching, Chuang Tzu, Analects, Mencius.* Berkeley: Counterpoint, 2013.
———, trans. *Mencius.* Berkeley: Counterpoint, 2015.
Holladay, William L. *Jeremiah 2.* Hermeneia. Minneapolis: Fortress, 1989.
Hölscher, Gustav. *Hesekiel: Der Dichter und das Buch; Eine literarische Untersuchung.* BZAW 39. Berlin: de Gruyter, 1924.
Holt, Else K. *Prophesying the Past: The Use of Israel's History in the Book of Hosea.* JSOTSup 194. Sheffield: Sheffield Academic, 1995.
Holt, Else K., and Carolyn J. Sharp, eds. *Jeremiah Invented: Constructions and Deconstructions of Jeremiah.* LHBOTS 595. London: T&T Clark, 2015.
Hong, Sung-hee. "'Too Many Nights' and Poetry: Repetition in Yoon Dong Ju's Poetry." *JKML* 63 (2017): 85–126.
Hooper-Greenhill, Eilean. *Museums and the Shaping of Knowledge.* New York: Routledge, 1992.
Horgan, Maurya P. *Pesharim: Qumran Interpretations of Biblical Books.* CBQMS 8. Washington, DC: Catholic Biblical Association of America, 1979.
Horovitz, H. S., and I. A. Rabin, eds. *Mekhilta' de-Rabbi Yishma'el.* 2nd ed. Jerusalem: Bamberger & Wahrman, 1960.

Hossfeld, Frank-Lothar. *Untersuchungen zu Komposition und Theologie des Ezechielbuches*. 2nd ed. FB 20. Würzburg: Echter, 1983.
Hudson, Don Michael. "Living in a Land of Epithets: Anonymity in Judges 19–21." *JSOT* 64 (1994): 49–66.
Irwin, William. "Against Intertextuality." *PL* 28 (2004): 227–42.
Iser, Wolfgang. *The Implied Reader: Patterns of Communication in Prose Fiction from Bunyan to Beckett*. Baltimore: Johns Hopkins University Press, 1974.
Jacob, Benno. *Das Buch Exodus*. Stuttgart: Calwer, 1997.
Jacobs, Mignon R. *The Conceptual Coherence of the Book of Micah*. JSOTSup 322. Sheffield: Sheffield Academic, 2001.
Jakobson, Roman. "Closing Statement: Linguistics and Poetics." Pages 350–77 in *Style in Language*. Edited by Thomas A. Sebeok. Cambridge: MIT Press, 1960.
Jarrett, Charles E. "Philosophy of Language in the Service of Religious Studies." *Semeia* 41 (1988): 143–59.
Jenkins, Willis, and Jennifer M. McBride, eds. *Bonhoeffer and King: Their Legacies and Import for Christian Social Thought*. Minneapolis: Fortress, 2010.
Jensen, Klaus Bruhn. "Text and Intertextuality." *IEC* 11 (2008): 5126–30.
Jin, Eun-Young, and Kyung-Hee Kim. "A Study on Shame in Yun, Dong-Ju's Poetry from a Confucian Perspective." *KPS* 52 (2017): 299–326.
Johnson, Benjamin J. M. "David Then and Now: Double-Voiced Discourse in 1 Samuel 16.14–23." *JSOT* 38 (2013): 201–15.
Jong, Matthijs J. de. *Isaiah among the Ancient Near East Prophets: A Comparative Study of the Earliest Stages of the Isaiah Tradition and Neo-Assyrian Prophets*. VTSup 117. Leiden: Brill, 2007.
Joosten, Jan. *People and Land in the Holiness Code: An Exegetical Study of the Ideational Framework of the Law in Leviticus 17–26*. VTSup 67. Leiden: Brill, 1996.
Kaminsky, Joel, and Anne Stewart. "God of All the World: Universalism and Developing Monotheism in Isaiah 40–66." *HTR* 99 (2006): 139–63.
Katongole, Emmanuel. "Embodied and Embodying Hermeneutics of Life in the Academy: Musa W. Dube's HIV/AIDS Work." Pages 407–16 in *Postcolonial Perspectives in African Biblical Interpretations*. Edited by Musa W. Dube, Andrew M. Mbuvi, and Dora R. Mbuwayesango. GPBS 13. Atlanta: Society of Biblical Literature, 2012.
Keller, Catherine. "Columbus/Colon." *EMMM*, 98–100.

Kelly, Geffrey B., ed. *Life Together: Prayerbook of the Bible*. DBW 5. Minneapolis: Fortress, 1996.
Kelly, Joseph Ryan. "Orders of Discourse and the Function of Obedience in the Hebrew Bible." *JTS* 64 (2013): 1–24.
Kim, Eung-gyo. "Forced Names: Somura Mukei and Hiranuma Tochu." *ChT* (2014): 196–208.
Kim, Hyun Chul Paul. *Ambiguity, Tension, and Multiplicity in Deutero-Isaiah*. StBibLit 52. New York: Lang, 2003.
———. "Interpretative Modes of Yin-Yang Dynamics as an Asian Hermeneutics." *BibInt* 9 (2001): 287–308.
———. "Jonah Read Intertextually." *JBL* 126 (2007): 497–518.
Kim, Hyun Chul Paul, and M. Fulgence Nyengele. "Murder S/He Wrote? A Cultural and Psychological Reading of 2 Samuel 11–12." Pages 95–116 in *Pregnant Passion: Gender, Sex, and Violence in the Bible*. Edited by Cheryl A. Kirk-Duggan. SemeiaSt 44. Atlanta: Society of Biblical Literature, 2003.
Kim, Mi-yeon. "A Study on the Poetry of Yoon Dong-Joo." *KTC* 89 (2017): 133–61.
Kindt, Tom, and Hans-Harald Müller. *Implied Author: Concepts and Controversy*. Translated by Alastair Matthews. Nar. 9. Berlin: de Gruyter, 2006.
Klaiber, Isabell. "Multiple Implied Authors: How Many Can a Single Text Have?" *Sty* 45 (2011): 138–52.
Klostermann, August. "Beiträge zur Entstehungsgeschichte des Pentateuchs." *ZLThK* 38 (1877): 401–45.
———. "Ezechiel und das Heiligtumsgesetz." Pages 368–418 in *Der Pentateuch: Beiträge zu seinem Verständnis und seiner Entstehungsgeschichte*. Edited by August Klostermann. Leipzig: Böhme, 1893.
Knierim, Rolf P. "Criticism of Literary Features, Form, Tradition, and Redaction." Pages 123–65 in *The Hebrew Bible and Its Modern Interpreters*. Edited by Douglas A. Knight and Gene M. Tucker. BMI 1. Chico, CA: Scholars Press, 1985.
———. "Old Testament Form Criticism Reconsidered." *Int* 27 (1973): 435–68.
———. *The Task of Old Testament Theology: Method and Cases*. Grand Rapids: Eerdmans, 1995.
Koch, Klaus. "Is There a Doctrine of Retribution in the Old Testament?" Pages 57–87 in *Theodicy in the Old Testament*. Edited by James L. Crenshaw. IRT 4. Philadelphia: Fortress, 1983.

Koenen, Klaus. *Klagelieder (Threni)*. BKAT 20.4. Neukirchen-Vluyn: Neukirchener Verlag, 2015.

Kövecses, Zoltán. *Where Metaphors Come From: Reconsidering Context in Metaphor*. New York: Oxford University Press, 2015.

Kratz, Reinhard G. "Der Anfang des Zweiten Jesaja in Jes 40,1 f. und das Jeremiabuch." *ZAW* 106 (1994): 243–61.

———. *The Prophets of Israel*. Translated by Anselm C. Hagedorn and Nathan MacDonald. CSHB 2. Winona Lake, IN: Eisenbrauns, 2015.

Kristeva, Julia. *Desire in Language: A Semiotic Approach to Literature and Art*. Edited by Leon S. Roudiez. Translated by Thomas Gora, Alice Jardine, and Leon S. Roudiez. New York: Columbia University Press, 1980.

———. *Powers of Horror: An Essay on Abjection*. Translated by Leon S. Roudiez. New York: Columbia University Press, 1982.

———. *Revolution in Poetic Language*. Translated by Margaret Waller. New York: Columbia University Press, 1984.

———. *Strangers to Ourselves*. Translated by Leon S. Roudiez. New York: Columbia University Press, 1991.

———. "Word, Dialog and Novel." Pages 34–61 in *The Kristeva Reader*. Edited by Toril Moi. New York: Columbia University Press, 1986.

———. "Word, Dialogue, and Novel." Pages 64–91 in *Desire in Language: A Semiotic Approach to Literature and Art*. Edited by Leon S. Roudiez. Translated by Thomas Gora, Alice Jardine, and Leon S. Roudiez. New York: Columbia University Press, 1980.

Kugel, James L. *The Great Shift: Encountering God in Biblical Times*. Boston: Houghton Mifflin Harcourt, 2017.

———. *The Idea of Biblical Poetry: Parallelism and Its History*. New Haven: Yale University Press, 1981.

———. *A Walk through Jubilees: Studies in the Book of Jubilees and the World of Its Creation*. JSJSup 156. Leiden: Brill, 2012.

———. "Wisdom and the Anthological Temper." *Proof* 17 (1997): 9–32.

Kutscher, Edward Yechezkel. *The Language and Linguistic Background of the Isaiah Scroll (1Q Isa$^a$)*. STDJ 6. Leiden: Brill, 1974.

Kwon, Jiseong James. *Scribal Culture and Intertextuality: Literary and Historical Relationships between Job and Deutero-Isaiah*. FAT 2/85. Tübingen: Mohr Siebeck, 2016.

Lachmann, Renate. "Ebenen des Intertextualitätsbegriffs." Pages 133–38 in *Das Gespräch*. Edited by Karlheinz Stierle and Rainer Warnig. PH 11. München: Wilhelm Fink Verlag, 1984.

Lakoff, George, and Mark Johnson. *Metaphors We Live By*. Chicago: Chicago University Press, 1980.

Landy, Francis. *Hosea*. 2nd ed. Readings. Sheffield: Sheffield Phoenix, 2011.

———. "Isaiah 2: Torah and Terror." Pages 259–71 in *Far from Minimal: Celebrating the Influence of Philip R. Davies*. Edited by Duncan Burns and John W. Rogerson. LHBOTS 484. New York: T&T Clark, 2012.

———. "Levinas on Prophecy." Pages 179–203 in *Making a Difference: Essays on the Bible and Judaism in Honor of Tamara Cohn Eskenazi*. Edited by David J. A. Clines, Kent H. Richards, and Jacob L. Wright. HBM 49. Sheffield: Sheffield Academic, 2012.

———. "Maurice Blanchot on Prophetic Speech." Pages 356–67 in *Welcome to the Cavalcade: A Festschrift in Honour of Rabbi Professor Jonathan Magonet*. Edited by Ellie Tikvah Sarah, Colin Eimer, and Howard Cooper. London: Kulmus, 2013.

———. "Shamanic Poetics: With Stammering Lips and Another Tongue Will He Speak to This People." Paper presented at the International Meeting of the Society of Biblical Literature/European Association of Biblical Studies. Berlin, Germany, August 11, 2017.

———. "Three Sides of a Coin: In Conversation with Ben Zvi and Nogalski, *Two Sides of a Coin*." *JHS* 10 (2010): 1–21.

Lang, Bernhard. "Three Philosophers in Paradise: Kant, Tillich, and Ricœur Interpret and Respond to Genesis 3." *SJOT* 28 (2014): 298–314.

Langer, Gerhard. *Midrasch*. JS 1; UTB 4675. Tübingen: Mohr Siebeck, 2016.

Lee, Archie C. C. "The Chinese Creation Myth of Nu Kua and the Biblical Narrative in Genesis 1–11." *BibInt* 2 (1994): 312–24.

Lee, Eun-Ae. "From 'Self-Portrait' to 'Confessions.'" *JKP* 16 (2005): 134–49.

Lee, Sung-il. *The Wind and the Waves: Four Modern Korean Poets*. Berkeley: Asian Humanities Press, 1989.

Lehman, Ilana Elkad. "Spinning a Tale: Intertextuality and Intertextual Aptitude." *ESLL* 5 (2005): 39–56.

Leuchter, Mark. *The Levites and the Boundaries of Israelite Identity*. Oxford: Oxford University Press, 2017.

Levenson, Jon D. *The Death and Resurrection of the Beloved Son: The Transformation of Child Sacrifice in Judaism and Christianity*. New Haven: Yale University Press, 1993.

Levinas, Emmanuel. *Otherwise Than Being or Beyond Essence*. Translated by Alphono Lingis. Pittsburgh: Duquesne University Press, 1981.

Levine, Etan. *The Aramaic Version of Lamentations*. New York: Hermon, 1981.

Lévi-Strauss, Claude. *Structural Anthropology*. New York: Basic Books, 1963.

Licht, Jacob. *Megillat ha-Serakhim mi-Megillot Midbar Yehudah*. Jerusalem: Bialik Institute, 1965.

Liew, Tat-siong Benny. *Politics of Parousia: Reading Mark Inter(con)textually*. BibInt 2. Leiden: Brill, 1999.

Linville, James R. *Amos and the Cosmic Imagination*. SOTSMS. Farnham, Surrey, UK: Ashgate, 2008.

Liss, Hanna. *Die unerhörte Prophetie: Kommunikative Strukturen prophetischer Rede im Buch Yesha'yahu*. Berlin: Evangelische Verlagsanstalt, 2003.

Longman, Tremper, III. *The Book of Ecclesiastes*. NICOT. Grand Rapids: Eerdmans, 1998.

Lopez, Davina. "Curational Reflections: On Rhetorics of Tradition and Innovation in Biblical Scholarship." Pages 68–92 in *Present and Future of Biblical Studies: Celebrating Twenty-Five Years of Brill's Biblical Interpretation*. Edited by Tat-siong Benny Liew. BibInt 161. Leiden: Brill, 2018.

Lundbom, Jack R. *Jeremiah 1–20*. AB 21A. New York: Doubleday, 1999.

Luz, Ulrich. *Das Evangelium nach Matthäus*. EKKNT 1.1. Zurich: Benziger, 2002.

Lyons, Michael A. *From Law to Prophecy: Ezekiel's Use of the Holiness Code*. LHBOTS 507. New York: T&T Clark, 2009.

Machacek, Gregory. "Allusion." *PMLA* 122 (2007): 522–36.

Machiela, Daniel A. *The Dead Sea Genesis Apocryphon: A New Text and Translation with Introduction and Special Treatment of Columns 13–17*. STDJ 79. Leiden: Brill, 2009.

Machinist, Peter. "Assyria and Its Image in First Isaiah." *JAOS* 103 (1983): 719–37.

Macintosh, A. A. *Hosea: A Critical and Exegetical Commentary*. ICC. London: Bloomsbury, 2014.

Mai, Hans-Peter. "Bypassing Intertextuality: Hermeneutics, Textual Practice, Hypertext." Pages 30–59 in *Intertextuality*. Edited by Heinrich F. Plett. RTT 15. Berlin: de Gruyter, 1991.

Mandolfo, Carleen. *Daughter Zion Talks Back to the Prophets*. SemeiaSt 58. Atlanta: Society of Biblical Literature, 2007.

Mann, Steven T. "Performative Prayers of a Prophet: Investigating the Prayers of Jonah as Speech Acts." *CBQ* 79 (2017): 20–40.

———. *Run, David, Run! An Investigation of the Theological Speech Acts of David's Departure and Return (2 Samuel 14–20)*. Siphrut 10. Winona Lake, IN: Eisenbrauns, 2013.

Margolin, Uri. "Introducing and Sustaining Characters in Literary Narrative: A Set of Conditions." *Sty* 21 (1987): 107–24.

Marsh, Charles. "Wayward Christian Soldiers." *New York Times*, January 20, 2006.

Martin, Elaine. "Intertextuality: An Introduction." *Compar* 35 (2011): 148–51.

Mathys, Hans-Peter. *Liebe deinen Nächsten wie dich selbst: Untersuchungen zum alttestamentlichen Gebot der Nächstenliebe (Lev 19,18)*. OBO 71. Göttingen: Vandenhoeck & Ruprecht, 1986.

McLaughlin, John L. "Is Amos (Still) among the Wise?" *JBL* 133 (2014): 281–303.

———. *The Marzēaḥ in the Prophetic Literature: References and Allusions in Light of the Extra-Biblical Evidence*. VTSup 86. Leiden: Brill, 2001.

Meek, Russell L. "Intertextuality, Inner-Biblical Exegesis, and Inner-Biblical Allusion: The Ethics of a Methodology." *Bib* 95 (2014): 280–91.

Meier, John P. *A Marginal Jew: Rethinking the Historical Jesus*. Vol. 4. New Haven: Yale University Press, 2009.

Mein, Andrew. "Ezekiel as a Priest in Exile." Pages 199–213 in *The Elusive Prophet: The Prophet as a Historical Person, Literary Character and Anonymous Artist*. OtSt 45. Edited by Johannes C. de Moor. Leiden: Brill 2001.

Mekhon ha-Midrash ha-Mevo'ar. *Qohelet Rabbah*. Vol. 15 of *Midrash Rabbah HaMevo'ar*. Jerusalem: Ḥavre ha-Makhon ha-Midrash ha-Mevo'ar, 1995.

Melugin, Roy F. "Isaiah 40–66 in Recent Research: The 'Unity' Movement." Pages 142–94 in *Recent Research on the Major Prophets*. Edited by Alan J. Hauser. RRBS 1. Sheffield: Sheffield Phoenix, 2008.

Metso, Sarianna. *The Serekh Texts*. LSTS 62. CQS 9. London: T&T Clark, 2007.

———. *The Textual Development of the Qumran Community Rule*. STDJ 21. Leiden: Brill, 1997.

Mettinger, Tryggve N. D. *The Eden Narrative: A Literary and Religio-historical Study of Genesis 2–3*. Winona Lake, IN: Eisenbrauns, 2007.

Meyers, Carol. *Rediscovering Eve: Ancient Israelite Women in Context*. Oxford: Oxford University Press, 2011.

Mihailovic, Alexander. *Corporeal Words: Mikhail Bakhtin's Theology of Discourse*. SRLT. Evanston, IL: Northwestern University Press, 1997.

Milgrom, Jacob. *Leviticus 1–16*. AB 3. New York: Doubleday, 1991.

———. *Leviticus 17–22*. AB 3A. New York: Doubleday, 2000.

Milhou, Alain. *Colon Y Su Mentalidad Mesianica: En El Ambiente Franciscanista Español*. Valladolid, Spain: Seminario Americanista de la Universidad de Valladolid, 1983.

Milik, J. T. "Texte des variants des dix manuscrits de la Règle del Communauté trouvés dans la grotte 4." *RB* 67 (1960): 411–16.

Miller, Charles William. "Reading Voices: Personification, Dialogism, and the Reader of Lamentations 1." *BibInt* 9 (2001): 393–408.

Miller, Geoffrey D. "Intertextuality in Old Testament Research." *CurBR* 9 (2010): 283–309.

Miller, Patrick D. "Deuteronomy and Psalms: Evoking a Biblical Conversation." *JBL* 118 (1999): 3–18.

Milstein, Sara J. *Tracking the Master Scribe: Revision through Introduction in Biblical and Mesopotamian Literature*. Oxford: Oxford University Press, 2016.

Mirenayat, Sayyed Ali, and Elaheh Soofastaei. "Gérard Genette and the Categorization of Textual Transcendence." *MJSS* 6 (2015): 533.

Miscall, Peter D. "Isaiah: The Labyrinth of Images." *Semeia* 54 (1991): 103–21.

Moberly, R. W. L. "Did the Interpreters Get It Right? Genesis 2–3 Reconsidered." *JTS* 59 (2008): 22–40.

———. *Old Testament Theology: Reading the Hebrew Bible as Christian Scripture*. Grand Rapids: Baker Academic, 2013.

Morgan, Robert. *Biblical Interpretation*. Oxford: Oxford University Press, 1988.

Morgenstern, J. "The Decalogue of the Holiness Code." *HUCA* 26 (1955): 1–27.

Moyise, Steve. "Intertextuality and Biblical Studies: A Review." *VEcc* 23 (2002): 418–31.

Moyise, Steve, and Maarten J. J. Menken, eds. *Isaiah in the New Testament*. NTSI. London: T&T Clark, 2005.

Möller, Karl. *A Prophet in Debate: The Rhetoric of Persuasion in the Book of Amos*. JSOTSup 372. Sheffield: Sheffield Academic, 2003.

Mroczek, Eva. *The Literary Imagination in Jewish Antiquity*. Oxford: Oxford University Press, 2016.

Muilenburg, James. "Form Criticism and Beyond." *JBL* 88 (1969): 1–18.

Müller, Wolfgang. "Interfigurality: A Study on the Interdependence of Literary Figures." Pages 101–21 in *Intertextuality*. Edited by Heinrich F. Plett. RTT 15. Berlin: de Gruyter, 1991.

Müllner, Ilse. "Tödliche Differenzen: Sexuelle Gewalt als Gewalt gegen Andere in Ri 19." Pages 81–100 in *Von der Wurzel getragen: Christlich-feministische Exegese in Auseinandersetzung mit Antijudaismus*. Edited by Luise Schottroff and Marie-Theres Wacker. BibInt 17. Leiden: Brill, 1996.

Nadella, Raj. *Dialogue Not Dogma: Many Voices in the Book of Luke*. LNTS 431. London: T&T Clark, 2011.

Nelson, Richard D. "Judges: A Public Canon for Public Theology." *WW* 29 (2009): 397–406.

Neudecker, Reinhard. *Moses Interpreted by the Pharisees and Jesus: Matthew's Antitheses in the Light of Early Rabbinic Literature*. SubBi 44. Rome: Gregorian & Biblical, 2012.

Neusner, Jacob. *What Is Midrash?* Philadelphia: Fortress, 1987.

Newsom, Carol A. "Bakhtin, the Bible, and Dialogic Truth." *JR* 76 (1996): 290–306.

———. *The Book of Job: A Contest of Moral Imaginations*. Oxford: Oxford University Press, 2003.

———. "The Book of Job as Polyphonic Text." *JSOT* 97 (2002): 87–108.

Nguyen, Kim Lan. *Chorus in the Dark: The Voices of the Book of Lamentations*. HBM 54. Sheffield: Sheffield Phoenix, 2013.

Niditch, Susan. "Genesis." Pages 27–45 in *Women's Bible Commentary*. Edited by Carol Newsom, Sharon H. Ringe, and Jacqueline E. Lapsley, 3rd ed. Louisville: Westminster John Knox, 2012.

———. "The 'Sodomite' Theme in Judges 19–20: Family, Community, and Social Disintegration." *CBQ* 44 (1982): 365–78.

Nielsen, Kirsten. "The Holy Spirit as Dove and as Tongues of Fire: Reworking Biblical Metaphors in a Modern Danish Hymn." Pages 239–56 in *Enigmas and Images: Studies in Honor of Tryggve N. D. Mettinger*. Edited by Göran Eidevall and Blaženka Scheuer. Winona Lake, IN: Eisenbrauns, 2011.

Nihan, Christophe. *From Priestly Torah to Pentateuch*. FAT 2/25. Tübingen: Mohr Siebeck, 2007.

Nitzan, B. *Megillat Pesher Ḥabakkuk: mi-Megillot Midbar Yehudah (1Qp Hab)*. Jerusalem: Bialik Institute, 1986.

Nogalski, James D. *Literary Precursors to the Book of the Twelve*. BZAW 217. Berlin: de Gruyter, 1993.

Noort, Edward, and Eibert J. C. Tigchelaar, eds. *The Sacrifice of Isaac: The Aqedah (Genesis 22) and Its Interpretations*. TBN 4. Leiden: Brill, 2002.

Noth, Martin. *A History of Pentateuchal Traditions*. Chico, CA: Scholars Press, 1981.

O'Brien, Julia M. *Micah*. WisC 37. Collegeville, MN: Liturgical Press, 2015.

O'Connor, Kathleen M. *Jeremiah: Pain and Promise*. Minneapolis: Fortress, 2011.

O'Day, Gail R. "Intertextuality." *DBI* 1:546–48.

Oderberg, David S. *Real Essentialism*. SCP 11. London: Routledge, 2008.

Oeming, Manfred. "Vom Eigenwert des Alten Testaments als Wort Gottes." Pages 305–36 in *Gottes Wort im Menschenwort: Die eine Bibel als Fundament der Theologie*. Edited by Karl Lehmann and Ralf Rothenbusch. QD 266. Freiburg im Breisgau: Herder, 2014.

Ogden, Graham. *Qoheleth*. Readings. Sheffield: Sheffield Academic, 1987.

Oliver, Kelly. *Reading Kristeva: Unraveling the Double-Bind*. Bloomington: Indiana University Press, 1993.

Ollenburger, Ben C. "What Krister Stendahl 'Meant': A Normative Critique of 'Descriptive Biblical Theology.'" *HBT* 8 (1986): 61–98.

Olson, Dennis T. "Biblical Theology as Provisional Monologization: A Dialogue with Childs, Brueggemann, and Bakhtin." *BibInt* 6 (1998): 162–80.

Oropeza, B. J. "Intertextuality." *OEBI*, 453–63.

Oropeza, B. J., and Steve Moyise, eds. *Exploring Intertextuality: Diverse Strategies for New Testament Interpretation of Texts*. Eugene, OR: Cascade, 2016.

Orr, Mary. *Intertextuality: Debates and Contexts*. Malden, MA: Blackwell, 2003.

Otto, Eckart. *Das Gesetz des Mose*. Darmstadt: Wissenschaftliche Buchgesellschaft, 2007.

———. "Das Heiligkeitsgesetz Leviticus 17–26 in der Pentateuchredaktion." Pages 65–80 in *Altes Testament: Forschung und Wirkung; Festschrift H. Reventlow*. Edited by Peter Mommer and Winfried Thiel. Frankfurt: Lang, 1994.

———. *Der Wandel der Rechtsbegründungen in der Gesellschaftsgeschichte des antiken Israel: Eine Rechtsgeschichte des "Bundesbuches," Exodus XX 22–XXIII 13*. StudBib 3. Leiden: Brill, 1988.
Paden, William E. *Religious Worlds: The Comparative Study of Religion*. Boston: Beacon, 1994.
Park-Taylor, Geoffrey H. *The Formation of the Book of Jeremiah: Doublets and Recurring Phrases*. SBLMS 51. Atlanta: Society of Biblical Literature, 2000.
Paton, L. B. "The Holiness-Code and Ezekiel." *PRR* 26 (1896): 98–115.
Paul, Shalom. "Literary and Ideological Echoes of Jeremiah in Deutero-Isaiah." Pages 109–21 in vol. 1 of *Proceedings of the Fifth World Congress of Jewish Studies*. Edited by Pinchas Peli. Jerusalem: World Union of Jewish Studies, 1969.
Peterson, Brian Neil. *Ezekiel's Message Understood in Its Historical Setting*. PTSMS 182. Princeton: Princeton University Press, 2012.
Pfister, Manfred. "How Postmodern Is Intertextuality?" Pages 207–24 in *Intertextuality*. Edited by Heinrich F. Plett. RTT 15. Berlin: de Gruyter, 1991.
Phillips, Gary A. "Sign/Text/Difference: The Contribution of Intertextual Theory to Biblical Criticism." Pages 78–97 in *Intertextuality*. Edited by Heinrich F. Plett. RTT 15. Berlin: de Gruyter, 1991.
Piirainen, Elisabeth. "Metaphors of an Endangered Low Saxon Basis Dialect: Exemplified by Idioms of Stupidity and Death." Pages 339–58 in *Engaged Metaphors*. Edited by Elisabeth Piirainen and Anna Idström. Amsterdam: John Benjamins Publishing Company, 2012.
"Platform." *Movement for Black Lives*. https://tinyurl.com/SBL03103b.
Pohlmann, Karl-Friedrich. *Ezechiel: Der Stand der theologischen Diskussion*. Darmstadt: Wissenschaftliche Buchgesellschaft, 2008.
———. *Der Prophet Hesekiel/Ezechiel Kapitel 20–48*. ATD 22. Göttingen: Vandenhoeck & Ruprecht, 2001.
Polk, Timothy. *The Prophetic Persona: Jeremiah and the Language of Self*. JSOTSup 32. Sheffield: JSOT Press, 1984.
Polzin, Robert. *Moses and the Deuteronomist: A Literary Study of the Deuteronomic History, Part One*. ISBL. Bloomington: Indiana University Press, 1980.
Propp, William H. C. *Exodus 1–18*. AB 3. New Haven: Yale University Press, 2010.
Qimron, Elisha. *Megillot Midbar Yehudah: ha-Ḥibburim ha-'Ivriyim. Between Bible and Mishnah*. Jerusalem: Yad Ben-Zvi Press, 2010.

———. *The Temple Scroll: A Critical Edition with Extensive Reconstructions.* JDS. Jerusalem: Israel Exploration Society, 1996.

Qimron, Elisha, and James H. Charlesworth. "Rule of the Community." Pages 1–52 *Rule of the Community and Related Documents.* Vol. 1 of *The Dead Sea Scrolls: Hebrew, Aramaic, and Greek Texts with English Translations.* Edited by James H. Charlesworth. PTSDSSP 1. Tübingen: Mohr Siebeck; Louisville: Westminster John Knox, 1994.

Quash, Ben. "Heavenly Semantics: Some Literary-Critical Approaches to Scriptural Reasoning." *MTh* 22 (2006): 403–20.

Raj, P. Prayer Elmo. "Text/Texts: Interrogating Julia Kristeva's Concept of Intertextuality." *ArsArt* 3 (2015): 77–80.

Richardson, Brian. "Singular Text, Multiple Implied Readers." *Sty* 41 (2007): 259–74.

Riegner, Irene E. *The Vanishing Hebrew Harlot: The Adventures of the Hebrew Stem ZNH.* StBibLit 73. New York: Lang, 2009.

Riffaterre, Michael. "Intertextual Representation: On Mimesis as Interpretive Discourse." *CI* 11 (1984): 141–62.

———. "The Intertextual Unconscious." *CI* 13 (1987): 371–85.

———. *Semiotics of Poetry.* Bloomington: Indiana University Press, 1978.

———. "Syllepsis." *CI* 6 (1980): 624–38.

Rimmon-Kenan, Shlomith. *Narrative Fiction: Contemporary Poetics.* London: Methuen, 2002.

Roberts, J. J. M. *First Isaiah.* Hermeneia. Minneapolis: Fortress, 2015.

Rogerson, John W. "Old Testament Ethics." Pages 116–37 in *Text in Context: Essays by Members of the Society for Old Testament Study.* Edited by A. D. H. Mayes. Oxford: Oxford University Press, 2000.

Rollston, Christopher A. *Writing and Literacy in the World of Ancient Israel: Epigraphic Evidence from the Iron Age.* ABS 11. Atlanta: Society of Biblical Literature, 2010.

Roudiez, Leon S. Introduction to *Desire in Language: A Semiotic Approach to Literature and Art,* by Julia Kristeva. Edited by Leon S. Roudiez. Translated by Thomas Gora, Alice Jardine, and Leon S. Roudiez. New York: Columbia University Press, 1980.

Ruiz, Jean-Pierre. *Readings from the Edges: The Bible and People on the Move.* Maryknoll, NY: Orbis Books, 2011.

Sadler, Rodney S., Jr. "Singing a Subversive Song: Psalm 137 and 'Colored Pompey.'" Pages 447–58 in *The Oxford Handbook of the Psalms.* Edited by William P. Brown. Oxford: Oxford University Press, 2015.

Samely, Alexander. "Art. Intertextualität IV. Judaistisch." *LB*, 303.

Samuel, Geoffrey. *Civilized Shamans: Buddhism in Tibetan Societies.* Washington, DC: Smithsonian Institution Press, 1993.
Sanders, James A. *From Sacred Story to Sacred Text: Canon as Paradigm.* Philadelphia: Fortress, 1987.
Sanders, Seth L. *The Invention of Hebrew.* Urbana: University of Illinois Press, 2009.
Sandoval, Timothy J. *The Discourse of Wealth and Poverty in the Book of Proverbs.* BibInt 77. Leiden: Brill, 2006.
Sandoval, Timothy J., and Dorothy B. E. A. Akoto. "A Note on Qohelet 10,10b." *ZAW* 122 (2010): 90–95.
Sawyer, John F. A. *The Fifth Gospel: Isaiah in the History of Christianity.* New York: Cambridge University Press, 1996.
Schaeffer, Jean-Marie. "Literary Genre and Textual Genericity." Pages 167–87 in *The Future of Literary Theory.* Edited by Ralph Cohen. New York: Routledge, 1989.
Schiffman, Lawrence H. *The Courtyards of the House of the Lord: Studies on the Temple Scroll.* Edited by Florentino García Martínez. STDJ 75. Leiden: Brill, 2008.
———. *The Halakhah at Qumran.* SJLA 16. Leiden: Brill, 1975.
———. *Reclaiming the Dead Sea Scrolls: The History of Judaism, the Background of Christianity, the Lost Library of Qumran.* Philadelphia: Jewish Publication Society of America, 1994.
———. *Sectarian Law in the Dead Sea Scrolls: Courts, Testimony and the Penal Code.* BJS 33. Chico, CA: Scholars Press, 1983.
Schiffman, Lawrence H., Andrew D. Gross, and Michael C. Rand. "Temple Scroll." Pages 1–173, 266–405 in *Temple Scroll and Related Documents.* Vol. 7 of *The Dead Sea Scrolls: Hebrew, Aramaic, and Greek Texts with English Translations.* Edited by James H. Charlesworth. PTSDSSP 7. Tübingen: Mohr Siebeck; Louisville: Westminster John Knox, 2011.
Schniedewind, William M. *How the Bible Became a Book.* Cambridge: Cambridge University Press, 2004.
———. *A Social History of Hebrew: Its Origins through the Rabbinic Period.* AYBRL. New Haven: Yale University Press, 2013.
Scholem, Gershom G. *On the Kabbalah and Its Symbolism.* Translated by Ralph Manheim. New York: Schocken Books, 1965.
Schorsch, Stefan. "Die Propheten und der Karneval: Marzeach—Maioumas—Maimuna." *VT* 53 (2003): 397–415.
Searle, John R. *Expression and Meaning: Studies in the Theory of Speech Acts.* Cambridge: Cambridge University Press, 1979.

———. *Speech Acts: An Essay in the Philosophy of Language.* Cambridge: Cambridge University Press, 1969.
Segal, Michael. *The Book of Jubilees: Rewritten Bible, Redaction, Ideology and Theology.* JSJSup 117. Atlanta: Society of Biblical Literature, 2007.
Sekine, Seizo. "Philosophical Interpretations of the Sacrifice of Isaac." Pages 339–66 in *Congress Volume: Ljubljana 2007.* Edited by André Lemaire. VTSup 133. Leiden: Brill, 2010.
Shaffer, David E., trans. *The Heavens, the Wind, the Stars and Poetry: The Works of Yun Tong-ju, Korean Patriot and Poet.* Seoul: Hakmun, 1999.
Sheppard, Gerald T. *Wisdom as a Hermeneutical Construct: A Study in the Sapientializing of the Old Testament.* BZAW 151. Berlin: de Gruyter, 1980.
Ska, Jean Louis. *The Exegesis of the Pentateuch: Exegetical Studies and Basic Questions.* FAT 66. Tübingen: Mohr Siebeck, 2010.
Slater, Peter. "Bakhtin on Hearing God's Voice." *MTh* 23 (2007): 1–25.
Smith, Duane E. "The Divining Snake: Reading Genesis 3 in the Context of Mesopotamian Ophiomancy." *JBL* 134 (2015): 31–49.
Smith, Mitzi. *Womanist Sass and Talk Back: Social (In)Justice, Intersectionality, and Biblical Interpretation.* Eugene, OR: Cascade, 2018.
Sneed, Mark R., ed. *Was There a Wisdom Tradition? New Prospects in Israelite Wisdom Studies.* AIL 23. Atlanta: SBL Press, 2015.
Snyman, Gerrie. "Who Is Speaking? Intertextuality and Textual Influence." *Neot* 30 (1996): 427–49.
Society for the Study of Black Religion Collection. Archives Research Center, Atlanta University Center Robert W. Woodruff Library.
Soggin, J. Alberto. "Amos and Wisdom." Pages 119–23 in *Wisdom in Ancient Israel: Essays in Honour of J. A. Emerton.* Edited by John Day, Robert P. Gordon, and H. G. M. Williamson. Cambridge: Cambridge University Press, 1995.
———. *Judges.* OTL. Philadelphia: Westminster, 1981.
Sommer, Benjamin D. "Exegesis, Allusion and Intertextuality in the Hebrew Bible: A Response to Lyle Eslinger." *VT* 46 (1996): 479–89.
———. *A Prophet Reads Scripture: Allusion in Isaiah 40–66.* Contra. Stanford, CA: Stanford University Press, 1998.
Sperber, Alexander, ed. *The Hagiographa: Transition from Translation to Midrash.* Vol. 4A of *The Bible in Aramaic: Based on Old Manuscripts and Printed Texts.* Edited by Alexander Sperber. Leiden: Brill, 1968.
Stackert, Jeffrey. "Holiness Code and Writings." *OEBL*, 389–96.

———. *Rewriting the Torah: Literary Revision in Deuteronomy and the Holiness Legislation*. FAT 52. Tübingen: Mohr Siebeck, 2007.
Stansell, Gary. "Isaiah 28–33: Blessed Be the Tie that Binds (Isaiah Together)." Pages 68–103 in *New Visions of Isaiah*. Edited by Marvin A. Sweeney and Roy F. Melugin. JSOTSup 214. Sheffield: Sheffield Academic, 1996.
Steck, Odil Hannes. *Studien zu Tritojesaja*. BZAW 203. Berlin: de Gruyter, 1991.
Steingrimsson, S. "זמם." *TDOT* 4:89–90.
Steins, Georg. *Die "Bindung Isaaks" im Kanon (Gen 22): Grundlagen und Programm einer kanonisch-intertextuellen Lektüre*. HBS 20. Freiburg im Breisgau: Herder, 1999.
———. *Kanonisch-intertextuelle Studien zum Alten Testament*. SBAB 48. Stuttgart: Katholisches Bibelwerk, 2009.
Stendahl, Krister. "Biblical Theology, Contemporary." *IDB* 1:418–32.
Sternberg, Meir. *The Poetics of Biblical Narrative: Ideological Literature and the Drama of Reading*. ISBL. Bloomington: Indiana University Press, 1985.
Stewart, Anne W. "Eve and Her Interpreters." Pages 46–50 in *Women's Bible Commentary*. Edited by Carol Newsom, Sharon H. Ringe, and Jacqueline E. Lapsley, 3rd ed. Louisville: Westminster John Knox, 2012.
Stewart, Susan. *On Longing: Narratives of the Miniature, the Gigantic, the Souvenir, the Collection*. Durham, NC: Duke University Press, 1993.
Stichele, Caroline Vander. "The Head of John and Its Reception, or How to Conceptualize 'Reception History.'" Pages 79–93 in *Reception History and Biblical Studies: Theory and Practice*. Edited by Emma England and William J. Lyons. LHBOTS 615. London: Bloomsbury, 2015.
Still, Judith, and Michael Worton. "Introduction." Pages 1–44 in *Intertextuality: Theories and Practices*. Edited by Judith Still and Michael Worton. Manchester: Manchester University Press, 1990.
Stipp, Hermann-Josef. "Richter 19: Ein frühes Beispiel schriftgestützter politischer Propaganda in Israel." Pages 127–64 in *Ein Herz so weit wie der Sand am Ufer des Meeres*. Edited by Susanne Gillmayer-Bucher and Annett Giercke. ETS 90. Würzburg: Echter, 2006.
Stockton, Ian. "Bonhoeffer's Wrestling with Jeremiah." *ModB* 40 (1999): 50–58.
Stone, Timothy J. *The Compilational History of the Megilloth*. FAT 2/59. Tübingen: Mohr Siebeck, 2013.

Stordalen, Terje. *Echoes of Eden: Genesis 2–3 and the Symbolism of the Eden Garden in Biblical Hebrew Literature.* CBET 25. Leuven: Peeters, 2000.
Strawson, P. F. "Austin and 'Locutionary Meaning.'" Pages 46–68 in *Essays on J. L. Austin.* Edited by Isaiah Berlin. Oxford: Clarendon, 1973.
Strollo, Magan Fullerton. "The Value of the Relationship: An Intertextual Reading of Song of Songs and Lamentations." *RevExp* 114 (2017): 190–202.
Stromberg, Jacob. *Isaiah after Exile: The Author of Third Isaiah as Reader and Redactor of the Book.* Oxford: Oxford University Press, 2011.
Strugnell, John, Daniel Harrington, and Torleif Elgvin. *Qumran Cave 4: XXIV Sapiential Texts, Part 2; 4QInstruction (Mûsār Lĕ Mēvîn): 4Q415 ff.* In consultation with Joseph A. Fitzmyer. Edited by Emanuel Tov. DJD 34. Oxford: Clarendon, 1999.
Stulman, Louis. *Jeremiah.* AOTC. Nashville: Abingdon, 2005.
———. *The Other Text of Jeremiah: A Reconstruction of the Hebrew Text Underlying the Greek Version of the Prose Sections of Jeremiah.* Lanham, MD: University Press of America, 1985.
Stulman, Louis, and Hyun Chul Paul Kim. *You Are My People: An Introduction to Prophetic Literature.* Nashville: Abingdon, 2010.
Stump, Eleonore. *Wandering in Darkness: Narrative and the Problem of Suffering.* Oxford: Oxford University Press, 2012.
Swanson, Dwight D. *The Temple Scroll and the Bible: The Methodology of 11QT.* STDJ 14. Leiden: Brill, 1995.
Sweeney, Marvin A. *1 and 2 Kings: A Commentary.* OTL. Louisville: Westminster John Knox, 2007.
———. "Davidic Polemics in the Book of Judges." *VT* 47 (1997): 517–29.
———. *Isaiah 1–39 with an Introduction to Prophetic Literature.* FOTL 16. Grand Rapids: Eerdmans, 1996.
———. "Isaiah 60–62 in Intertextual Perspective." Pages 131–42 in *Subtle Citation, Allusion, and Translation in the Hebrew Bible.* Edited by Ziony Zevit. Sheffield: Equinox, 2017.
———. *The Pentateuch.* CBS. Nashville: Abingdon, 2017.
———. *Reading the Hebrew Bible after the Shoah: Engaging Holocaust Theology.* Minneapolis: Fortress, 2008.
———. "Samuel's Institutional Identity in the Deuteronomistic History." Pages 165–74 in *Constructs of Prophets in the Former and Latter Prophets and Other Texts.* Edited by Lester L. Grabbe and Martti Nissinen. ANEM 4. Atlanta: Society of Biblical Literature, 2011.

———. "Synchronic and Diachronic Concerns in Reading the Book of the Twelve Prophets." Pages 21–33 in *Perspectives on the Formation of the Book of the Twelve*. Edited by Rainer Albertz, James Nogalski, and Jakob Wöhrle. BZAW 433. Berlin: de Gruyter, 2012.

———. *The Twelve Prophets*. 2 vols. BO. Collegeville, MN: Liturgical Press, 2000.

———. "The Wilderness Traditions of the Pentateuch: A Reassessment of Their Function and Intent in Relation to Exodus 32–34." *SBLSP* (1989): 291–99.

Talmon, Shemaryahu. "Was the Book of Esther Known at Qumran?" *DSD* 2 (1995): 249–67.

Tannen, Deborah. *Talking Voices: Repetition, Dialogue, and Imagery in Conversational Discourse*. 2nd ed. SIS 26. Cambridge: Cambridge University Press, 2007.

Terrien, Samuel. "Amos and Wisdom." Pages 108–15 in *Israel's Prophetic Heritage: Essays in Honor of James Muilenburg*. Edited by Bernhard W. Anderson and Walter J. Harrelson. New York: Harper & Brothers, 1962.

Throntveit, Mark A. "The Idealization of Solomon as the Glorification of God in the Chronicler's Royal Speeches and Royal Prayers." Pages 411–27 in *The Age of Solomon: Scholarship at the Turn of the Millennium*. Edited by Lowell K. Handy. SHCANE 11. Leiden: Brill, 1997.

Tov, Emanuel. "The Biblical Texts from the Judaean Desert: An Overview and Analysis." Pages 139–66 in *The Bible as Book: The Hebrew Bible and the Judaean Desert Discoveries*. Edited by Edward D. Herbert and Emanuel Tov. London: Oak Knoll Press, 2002.

———. "Groups of Biblical Texts Found at Qumran." Pages 85–102 in *Time to Prepare the Way in the Wilderness: Papers on the Qumran Scrolls by Fellows of the Institute for Advanced Studies of the Hebrew University, Jerusalem, 1989–1990*. Edited by Devorah Dimant and Lawrence H. Schiffman. STDJ 16. Leiden: Brill, 1995.

———. *Hebrew Bible, Greek Bible, and Qumran: Collected Essays*. TSAJ 121. Tübingen: Mohr Siebeck, 2008.

———. "Rewritten Bible Compositions and Biblical Manuscripts, with Special Attention to the Samaritan Pentateuch." *DSD* 5 (1998): 334–54.

———. *Scribal Practices and Approaches Reflected in the Texts Found in the Judean Desert*. STDJ 54. Leiden: Brill, 2004.

townes, emilie m. "2008 Presidential Address: Walking on the Rim Bones of Nothingness; Scholarship and Activism." *JAAR* 77 (2009): 1–15.

Trible, Phyllis. "Eve and Adam: Genesis 2–3 Reread." *ANQ* 13 (1973): 251–58.

———. *Texts of Terror: Literary-Feminist Readings of Biblical Narratives.* OBT 13. Philadelphia: Fortress, 1984.

Tull, Patricia K. "Bakhtin's Confessional Self-Accounting and Psalms of Lament." *BibInt* 13 (2005): 41–55.

———. "Intertextuality and the Hebrew Scriptures." *CurBS* 8 (2000): 59–83.

———. "Jobs and Benefits in Genesis 1 and 2." Pages 15–29 in *After Exegesis: Feminist Biblical Theology.* Edited by Patricia K. Tull and Jacqueline E. Lapsley. Waco, TX: Baylor University Press, 2015.

———. *Remember the Former Things: The Recollection of Previous Texts in Second Isaiah.* SBLDS 161. Atlanta: Scholars Press, 1997.

———. "Rhetorical Criticism and Intertextuality." Pages 156–80 in *To Each Its Own Meaning: An Introduction to Biblical Criticisms and Their Application.* Edited by Steven L. McKenzie and Stephen R. Haynes. Rev. ed. Louisville: Westminster John Knox, 1999.

Ulrich, Eugene. *The Dead Sea Scrolls and the Developmental Composition of the Bible.* VTSup 169. Leiden: Brill, 2015.

———. *The Dead Sea Scrolls and the Origins of the Bible.* SDSS. Grand Rapids: Eerdmans; Leiden: Brill, 1999.

Ulrich, Eugene, Frank Moore Cross, Sidnie A. White Crawford, Julie Ann Duncan, Patrick W. Skehan, Emanuel Tov, and Julio C. Trebolle Barrera, eds. *Qumran Cave 4.IX: Deuteronomy, Joshua, Judges, Kings.* DJD 14. Oxford: Clarendon, 1995.

Ulrich, Eugene, Frank Moore Cross, James R. Davila, Nathan Jastram, Judith E. Sanderson, Emanuel Tov, and John Strugnell, eds. *Qumran Cave 4.VII: Genesis to Numbers.* DJD 12. Oxford: Clarendon, 1994.

Van Seters, John. *A Law Book for the Diaspora: Revision in the Study of the Covenant Code.* Oxford: Oxford University Press, 2003.

VanderKam, James C., ed. *The Book of Jubilees.* 2 vols. CSCO 511. SAeth 88. Leuven: Peeters, 1989.

Verheyden, Joseph, ed. *The Figure of Solomon in Jewish, Christian and Islamic Tradition.* TBN 16. Leiden: Brill, 2013.

Vorster, Willem S. "Intertextuality and Redaktionsgeschichte." Pages 15–26 in *Intertextuality in Biblical Writings: Essays in Honour of Bas van Iersel.* Edited by Sipke Draisma. Leuven: Peeters, 1989.

Wellhausen, Julius. *Die Composition des Hexateuchs und der historischen Bücher des Alten Testaments.* Berlin: Georg Reimmer, 1889.

———. *Prolegomena to the History of Ancient Israel*. Translated by J. Sutherland Black and Allan Menzies. New York: Meridian Books, 1957.

Wendel, Ute. *Jesaja und Jeremia: Worte, Motive und Einsichten Jesajas in der Verkündigung Jeremias*. BTSt 25. Neukirchen-Vluyn: Neukirchener Verlag, 1995.

Wenham, Gordon J. "Sanctuary Symbolism in the Garden of Eden Story." Pages 19–25 in *Proceedings of the Ninth World Congress of Jewish Studies, Division A: The Period of the Bible*. Jerusalem: Magnes, 1985.

———. *Story as Torah: Reading Old Testament Narrative Ethically*. Edinburgh: T&T Clark, 2000.

Werman, C. *Sefer ha-Yovelim: Mavo', Targum u-Ferush*. Between Bible and Mishnah. Jerusalem: Yad Ben-Zvi Press, 2015.

West, Delno C., and August Kling. *The Libro de las Profecías of Christopher Columbus*. ColQuin 2. Gainesville, FL: University of Florida Press, 1991.

Westermann, Claus. *Genesis 12–36*. Translated by J. J. Scullion. CC. Minneapolis: Augsburg, 1985.

———. *Die Klagelieder: Forschungsgeschichte und Auslegung*. Neukirchen-Vluyn: Neukirchener Verlag, 1990.

———. *Praise and Lament in the Psalms*. Translated by K. R. Crim and R. N. Soulen. Atlanta: John Knox, 1981.

Weyde, Karl W. "Inner-Biblical Interpretation: Methodological Reflections on the Relationship between Texts in the Hebrew Bible." *SEÅ* 70 (2005): 287–300.

"What Happened in Ferguson?" *New York Times*. August 15, 2015. https://www.nytimes.com/interactive/2014/08/13/us/ferguson-missouri-town-under-siege-after-police-shooting.html?_r=0.

Whittier, John Greenleaf. *The Vision of Echard and Other Poems*. Boston: Houghton, Osgood & Co., 1878.

Whybray, R. Norman. *Wealth and Poverty in the Book of Proverbs*. JSOTSup 99. Sheffield: JSOT Press, 1990.

Wilken, Robert Louis, Angela Russell Christman, and Michael J. Hollerich, eds. *Isaiah: Interpreted by Early Christian and Medieval Commentators*. CB. Grand Rapids: Eerdmans, 2007.

Williams, Reggie L. "Dietrich Bonhoeffer, the Harlem Renaissance, and the Black Christ." Pages 155–68 in *Interpreting Bonhoeffer: Historical Perspectives, Emerging Issues*. Edited by Clifford J. Green and Guy C. Carter. Minneapolis: Fortress, 2013.

Williamson, H. G. M. *The Book Called Isaiah: Deutero-Isaiah's Role in Composition and Redaction.* Oxford: Clarendon, 1994.

———. *Isaiah 1–5.* ICC. London: T&T Clark, 2006.

Willingham, Elizabeth Moore. *The Mythical Indies and Columbus's Apocalyptic Letter: Imagining the Americas in the Late Middle Ages.* Brighton: Sussex Academic, 2016.

Wilson, Gerald H. *The Editing of the Hebrew Psalter.* SBLDS 76. Chico, CA: Scholars Press, 1985.

Wilson, Ian D. *Kingship and Memory in Ancient Judah.* Oxford: Oxford University Press, 2017.

Winkler, Mathias. *Das Salomonische des Sprichwörterbuchs: Intertextuelle Verbindungen zwischen 1Kön 1–11 und dem Sprichwörterbuch.* HBS 87. Freiburg im Breisgau: Herder, 2017.

Wolde, Ellen van. "Texts in Dialogue with Texts: Intertextuality in the Ruth and Tamar Narratives." *BibInt* 5 (1997): 1–28.

Wolff, Hans Walter. *Amos' Geistige Heimat.* WMANT 18. Neukirchen-Vluyn: Neukirchener Verlag, 1964.

———. *Amos the Prophet: The Man and His Background.* Edited by John Reumann. Translated by Foster R. McCurley. Philadelphia: Fortress, 1977.

———. *Hosea.* Translated by Gary Stansell. Hermeneia. Philadelphia: Fortress, 1974.

———. *Joel and Amos.* Translated by Waldemar Janzen, Sean D. McBride, and Charles A. Muenchow. Hermeneia. Philadelphia: Fortress, 1977.

Wong, Gregory T. K. *Compositional Strategy of the Book of Judges: An Inductive, Rhetorical Study.* VTSup 111. Leiden: Brill, 2006.

Wright, David P. *Inventing God's Law: How the Covenant Code of the Bible Used and Revised the Laws of Hammurabi.* Oxford: Oxford University Press, 2009.

Wünsche, August. *Der Midrasch Schir Ha-Schirim.* BibRab 6. Leipzig: Schulze, 1880.

Yadin, Yigael. *The Temple Scroll.* Rev. ed. 3 vols. Jerusalem: Israel Exploration Society, 1983.

Yamada, Frank M. *Configurations of Rape in the Hebrew Bible.* StBibLit 109. New York: Lang, 2008.

Yoder, Christine R. *Proverbs.* AOTC. Nashville: Abingdon, 2009.

Yoon, David I. "The Ideological Inception of Intertextuality and Its Dissonance in Current Biblical Studies." *CurBR* 12 (2012): 58–76.

Yoreh, Tzemach L. *The First Book of God*. BZAW 402. Berlin: de Gruyter, 2010.

Young, Edward. *Conjectures on Original Composition*. 1759.

Yun, Ji-eun. "A Study on Yun Dong-ju as a Marginal Man and a Place Where the Homeland Would Be in His Poetry." *JKML* 18 (2017): 169–204.

Zakovitch, Yair. "Inner-Biblical Interpretation." Pages 92–118 in *Reading Genesis: Ten Methods*. Edited by Ronald Hendel. New York: Cambridge University Press, 2010.

Zamora, Margarita. *Reading Columbus*. LALC 9. Berkeley: University of California Press, 1993.

Zapff, Burkard M. "Why Is Micah Similar to Isaiah?" *ZAW* 129 (2017): 536–54.

Zenger, Erich, ed. *Die Tora als Kanon für Juden und Christen*. HBS 10. Freiburg im Breisgau: Herder, 1996.

Zevit, Ziony, ed. *Subtle Citation, Allusion, and Translation in the Hebrew Bible*. Sheffield: Equinox, 2017.

———. *What Really Happened in the Garden of Eden?* New Haven: Yale University Press, 2013.

Zimmerli, Walther. *Ezekiel 1*. Translated by Ronald E. Clements. Hermeneia. Minneapolis: Fortress, 1979.

Žižek, Slavoj. *Violence: Six Sideways Reflections*. New York: Picador, 2008.

# Contributors

**Klaus-Peter Adam** is Associate Professor of Old Testament at the Lutheran School of Theology at Chicago, Chicago, Illinois.

**Valerie Bridgeman** is Academic Dean and Vice President of Academic Affairs and Associate Professor of Homiletics and Hebrew Bible at Methodist Theological School in Ohio, Delaware, Ohio.

**Steed Vernyl Davidson** is Associate Professor of Hebrew Bible/Old Testament and the Dean of the Faculty and Vice President for Academic Affairs at McCormick Theological Seminary, Chicago, Illinois.

**Hans Decker** is completing his DPhil at Oxford University, Oxford, United Kingdom.

**Tim Finlay** is Professor of Old Testament at Azusa Pacific University, Azusa, California.

**Kirsten H. Gardner** is an independent scholar. She holds a PhD in Old Testament Theology from Fuller Theological Seminary, Pasadena, California.

**Susanne Gillmayr-Bucher** is Professor of Old Testament at the Catholic Private University, Linz, Austria.

**Marianne Grohmann** is Professor of Old Testament at Universität Wien, Vienna, Austria.

**J. Todd Hibbard** is Associate Professor of Religious Studies and Chair of the Religious Studies Department at the University of Detroit Mercy, Detroit, Michigan.

**Hyun Chul Paul Kim** is Harold B. Williams Professor of Hebrew Bible at Methodist Theological School in Ohio, Delaware, Ohio.

**Soo J. Kim** is Academic Dean and Vice President of Academic Affairs and Professor of Old Testament at America Evangelical University, Los Angeles, California.

**Francis Landy** is Professor Emeritus of Religious Studies at the University of Alberta, Edmonton, Alberta, Canada.

**Timothy J. Sandoval** is Associate Professor of Hebrew Bible at Brite Divinity School at Texas Christian University, Fort Worth, Texas.

**Lawrence H. Schiffman** is the Judge Abraham Lieberman Professor of Hebrew and Judaic Studies and Director of the Global Network for Advanced Research in Jewish Studies at New York University, New York.

**Marvin A. Sweeney** is Professor of Hebrew Bible at the Claremont School of Theology, Claremont, California.

**Patricia K. Tull** is A. B. Rhodes Professor Emerita of Old Testament at Louisville Presbyterian Theological Seminary, Louisville, Kentucky.

# Index of Ancient Sources

Hebrew Bible/Old Testament

Genesis
| | |
|---|---|
| 1 | 10, 32, 186, 295 |
| 1–11 | 162 |
| 1:26–28 | 17, 186 |
| 1:26–31 | 71 |
| 1:27 | 33, 71 |
| 2 | 10, 28–29, 36, 186, 295 |
| 2:7 | 34 |
| 2:8 | 29 |
| 2:9 | 32 |
| 2:16–17 | 27 |
| 2:17 | 27–28 |
| 2:24 | 71 |
| 3 | 15, 23–31, 34–40 |
| 3:4–5 | 35 |
| 3:5 | 32, 35 |
| 3:6 | 32, 35 |
| 3:7 | 332–33, 71 |
| 3:14–19 | 28 |
| 3:16 | 35, 71 |
| 3:20 | 33 |
| 3:22 | 32 |
| 3:23 | 35 |
| 5:3 | 33 |
| 9:6 | 33, 106 |
| 10 | 276 |
| 10:1 | 281 |
| 10:3 | 281 |
| 12–24 | 162 |
| 12:2 | 36 |
| 12:10–13 | 218 |
| 13:10 | 59 |
| 13:14 | 59 |
| 13:16 | 36 |
| 15:5 | 36 |
| 16 | 59 |
| 16:8 | 56, 61–62 |
| 16:9 | 60 |
| 18 | 38, 60 |
| 18–19 | 56 |
| 18:2 | 59, 61 |
| 18:22–33 | 37 |
| 18:23 | 37 |
| 18:25 | 37 |
| 19 | 56, 63, 166–67 |
| 19:1 | 61–62 |
| 19:1–8 | 61 |
| 19:1–30 | 167 |
| 19:4 | 61 |
| 19:6 | 61 |
| 19:7 | 62 |
| 19:8 | 62 |
| 19:10 | 62 |
| 20:7 | 28 |
| 21 | 59 |
| 21:12 | 56, 61 |
| 22 | 15, 23–27, 29–31, 36–40, 56, 63 |
| 22:1 | 26 |
| 22:1–2 | 27 |
| 22:2 | 29, 39 |
| 22:4 | 59 |
| 22:6 | 38, 62 |
| 22:8 | 38 |
| 22:10 | 62 |
| 22:11 | 63 |
| 22:11–12 | 29 |
| 22:12 | 36, 38 |
| 22:13 | 59 |

*Genesis (cont.)*

| | | | |
|---|---|---|---|
| 22:15–19 | 36 | 29:15–19 | 168 |
| 22:16–18 | 36 | 29:20 | 168 |
| 22:19 | 38 | 29:22 | 168 |
| 24 | 62, 168–69 | 29:23–24 | 168 |
| 24:2 | 60 | 29:25–27 | 168 |
| 24:4 | 56 | 29:28–30 | 168 |
| 24:10 | 168 | 29:31–30:24 | 154 |
| 24:10–61 | 167–68 | 30 | 168 |
| 24:10–67 | 167–68 | 31:10 | 59 |
| 24:11 | 168 | 31:12 | 59 |
| 24:12–14 | 168 | 31:38–41 | 85 |
| 24:15 | 168 | 33:1 | 59 |
| 24:16–20 | 168 | 33:5 | 59 |
| 24:22–25 | 168 | 35:1–15 | 84 |
| 24:25 | 56, 61 | 37–50 | 162 |
| 24:28 | 168 | 37:25 | 59 |
| 24:29–31 | 168 | 38 | 166–67 |
| 24:32 | 61 | 43:29 | 59 |
| 24:34–51 | 168 | 50:21 | 59–60 |
| 24:47 | 60 | | |

*Exodus*

| | | | |
|---|---|---|---|
| 24:53 | 168 | 2 | 169 |
| 24:54 | 61–62, 168 | 2:15–21 | 167 |
| 24:55 | 168 | 3–4 | 156 |
| 24:56–59 | 168 | 11:1–10 | 46 |
| 24:62 | 39 | 12 | 219 |
| 24:62–67 | 168 | 12:1–28 | 46 |
| 24:63 | 59 | 12:43–49 | 46 |
| 24:64 | 59 | 12:43–50 | 46 |
| 25–36 | 162 | 12:50 | 46 |
| 25:9 | 39 | 12:51 | 46 |
| 25:11 | 39 | 13:1 | 36 47 |
| 25:22–23 | 84 | 13:1–2 | 46 |
| 27:40 | 230 | 13:1–16 | 15, 41, 46, 48, 51 |
| 28:10–22 | 84 | 13:2 | 47 |
| 29 | 169 | 13:2–5 | 47 |
| 29:1 | 168 | 13:2–16 | 47 |
| 29:1–20 | 167–68 | 13:3–16 | 46 |
| 29:1–30 | 167–68 | 13:6–8 | 47 |
| 29:2 | 168 | 13:9–10 | 47 |
| 29:8 | 168 | 13:11–15 | 47 |
| 29:10 | 168 | 13:13 | 50 |
| 29:11–12a | 168 | 13:16 | 47 |
| 29:12b | 168 | 13:17–22 | 46 |
| 29:13–14 | 168 | 15:25 | 26 |

| | | | |
|---|---|---|---|
| 16:4 | 26 | 10 | 91 |
| 20 | 96, 213 | 10:10–11 | 91 |
| 20:4–5 | 95 | 17–26 | 44, 91–92 |
| 20:6 | 95 | 18 | 96, 106 |
| 20:7 | 95 | 18–20 | 94, 107 |
| 20:8–11 | 95 | 18:1–5 | 107 |
| 20:11 | 213 | 18:6–23 | 107 |
| 20:13 | 95 | 18:17 | 107 |
| 20:14 | 95 | 18:22–24 | 65 |
| 20:16 | 95 | 18:24–30 | 107 |
| 20:17 | 95 | 18:26 | 107 |
| 20:20 | 26 | 19 | 16, 93–94, 96–97, 99, 106, 110 |
| 21–23 | 44 | 19:2 | 96–97, 110 |
| 21:2–23:19 | 96 | 19:2b | 95 |
| 21:18–19 | 236 | 19:3 | 95, 99 106 |
| 21:22 | 234 | 19:3–4 | 94–97, 106 |
| 21:22–27 | 234–35 | 19:4 | 95, 99, 106 |
| 21:23 | 234–35 | 19:5–8 | 96–97, 99 |
| 21:24 | 234, 236 | 19:9–10 | 96–97, 99 |
| 21:25 | 234 | 19:11 | 98 |
| 21:26 | 234 | 19:11–12 | 96, 98 |
| 21:27 | 234 | 19:11–18 | 16, 91, 93–99, 96, 98, 106–7, 109–10 |
| 22 | 56 | | |
| 22:28b | 36 | 19:12 | 99 |
| 22:28–29 | 15, 42, 47–51 | 19:13 | 98 |
| 22:29 | 36 | 19:13–14 | 96, 98 |
| 22:30 | 236 | 19:14 | 99 |
| 23:14–19 | 15, 47–48, 51 | 19:15 | 95, 98 |
| 23:16 | 170 | 19:15–16 | 96, 98 |
| 29:17 | 65 | 19:16 | 95, 98 |
| 29:22–28 | 50 | 19:17 | 98, 217 |
| 34:1–28 | 47–48 | 19:17–18 | 95, 96, 98, 110, 218 |
| 34:10–16 | 47 | 19:18 | 98, 217 |
| 34:10–27 | 15, 47–48 | 19:19 | 96–97 |
| 34:17 | 47 | 19:20–22 | 96–97 |
| 34:18–26 | 47, 51 | 19:23–24 | 96 |
| 34:19–20 | 41, 47 | 19:23–25 | 97, 99, 110 |
| 34:20 | 50 | 19:26–32 | 97–98 |
| | | 19:29 | 95, 107 |
| Leviticus | | 19:30 | 95 |
| 1:6 | 65 | 19:31 | 95 |
| 1:12 | 65 | 19:33–34 | 97 |
| 7:28–34 | 50 | 19:35–36a | 97 |
| 8:20 | 65 | 19:37 | 97 |
| 8:22–29 | 50 | 20 | 96, 102, 106 |

*Leviticus (cont.)*

| | | | |
|---|---|---|---|
| 20:13 | 107 | 5:18 | 95 |
| 20:14 | 107 | 5:20 | 95 |
| 23 | 220 | 5:21 | 95 |
| 23:3 | 110 | 6:4–9 | 221 |
| 23:14 | 110 | 7:1–7 | 47 |
| 23:17 | 110 | 7:7–16 | 18 |
| 23:21 | 110 | 8 | 213 |
| 23:31 | 110 | 8:2 | 26 |
| 24:20 | 234, 236 | 8:16 | 26 |
| 25:25–55 | 110 | 12–26 | 44, 96 |
| 26 | 93, 110 | 13:2–6 | 216 |
| | | 13:3 | 26 |
| | | 13:4 | 26 |
| Numbers | | 13:14 | 56, 61 |
| 1:1–10:10 | 49 | 19:1–12 | 109 |
| 3:1–4 | 49 | 19:5 | 119 |
| 3:5–10 | 49–50 | 19:10 | 109 |
| 3:11–13 | 15, 42, 48–51 | 19:21 | 234, 236 |
| 3:14–39 | 49 | 21:3 | 230 |
| 3:30–43 | 50 | 21:7 | 109 |
| 3:40–43 | 15, 42, 48–51 | 22:6–7 | 215 |
| 3:44–51 | 15, 42, 48–51 | 22:13–21 | 56, 61 |
| 8:5–22 | 50 | 23:4–7 | 170 |
| 8:13–19 | 15, 42, 48, 50–51 | 29:8 | 32 |
| 20:13b | 213 | 29:9 | 26 |
| 20:14 | 213 | 33:8 | 26 |
| 24:2 | 59 | | |
| 25:1–9 | 170 | Joshua | |
| 28–29 | 220 | 5:13 | 59 |
| 33:52 | 33 | | |
| 35:33 | 109 | Judges | |
| | | 2:22 | 26 |
| Deuteronomy | | 3 | 53 |
| 2:2–6 | 213 | 3:1 | 26 |
| 3:24–28 | 213 | 3:4 | 26 |
| 3:27 | 59 | 3:11 | 159 |
| 4:19 | 59 | 3:30 | 159 |
| 5 | 96, 213 | 4–5 | 53 |
| 5:7–9 | 95 | 5:31 | 159, 237–38 |
| 5:11 | 95, 213 | 6 | 156 |
| 5:12 | 215 | 6:11–24 | 311 |
| 5:12–15 | 95 | 6:13 | 311 |
| 5:15 | 213 | 6:15 | 312 |
| 5:16 | 95 | 8:28 | 159 |
| 5:17 | 95 | 8:31 | 59 |

# Index of Ancient Sources

371

| | | | |
|---|---|---|---|
| 9 | 53, 57 | 1 Samuel | |
| 9:5 | 57 | 1–3 | 15, 42, 51 |
| 9:19 | 56, 61, 64 | 1:1 | 51 |
| 9:27 | 56, 61 | 1:16 | 56, 61 |
| 9:53 | 57 | 3 | 51 |
| 11 | 53 | 6:13 | 59 |
| 14:14 | 61 | 11:7 | 56 |
| 17–21 | 169 | 14:44 | 28 |
| 17:8 | 169 | 22:16 | 28 |
| 17:9 | 169 | | |
| 19 | 16, 53–60, 62–64, 66–68, 70–72 | 2 Samuel | |
| 19:1 | 58–59, 63–64, 169 | 3:16 | 60 |
| 19:1–2 | 64 | 11:7 | 62 |
| 19:1–3 | 63 | 13 | 56, 63 |
| 19:2 | 64–65, 169 | 13:11–17 | 56 |
| 19:3 | 59, 64–65 | 13:12 | 62 |
| 19:4 | 62 | 13:14 | 62 |
| 19:5–9 | 57–58, 67–68 | 13:15 | 62 |
| 19:6 | 107 | 13:28–32 | 57 |
| 19:10 | 64-65 | 13:34 | 59 |
| 19:11 | 64–65 | 15:16 | 56, 60 |
| 19:12 | 64–65 | 16:1 | 56, 61 |
| 19:13 | 64–65 | 16:22 | 60 |
| 19:14 | 64–65 | 18:9 | 57 |
| 19:15 | 62, 64–65 | 18:14–15 | 57 |
| 19:15–24 | 61 | 18:24 | 59 |
| 19:16 | 63–65 | 20:3 | 56, 60 |
| 19:17 | 59, 62 | | |
| 19:18 | 64, 169 | 1 Kings | |
| 19:19 | 57, 62, 64–65 | 1–3 | 257 |
| 19:20 | 64 | 2 | 251, 258 |
| 19:21 | 65 | 2–3 | 258 |
| 19:22 | 65 | 2:1–9 | 257 |
| 19:23 | 65 | 2:2–3 | 257 |
| 19:24 | 65 | 2:5–6 | 255 |
| 19:25 | 62–63, 65 | 2:6 | 257 |
| 19:26 | 65 | 2:9 | 257 |
| 19:27 | 60, 62 | 2:37 | 28 |
| 19:27–29 | 64 | 2:42 | 28 |
| 19:29 | 63, 65 | 3:16–28 | 258 |
| 19:30 | 65 | 4 | 251 |
| 20 | 72 | 5 | 249 |
| 20:47 | 60 | 5:4 | 250 |
| 21 | 72 | 5:9–14 | 247 |
| 21:23 | 169 | 5:12–14 | 249 |

## Index of Ancient Sources

| 1 Kings (cont.) | | 8:9 | 279 |
|---|---|---|---|
| 5:13 | 250 | 8:16 | 79 |
| 5:18 | 250 | 9:3 | 230 |
| 9:17–19 | 251 | 10:27 | 230 |
| 9:25 | 281 | 11:26 | 285 |
| 9:26–28 | 281 | 12:4–6 | 279 |
| 10 | 254 | 18:1–7 | 279 |
| 10:11 | 281 | 22:20–25 | 285 |
| 10:21–22 | 281 | 23:1–2 | 281 |
| 11 | 244, 251 | 23:2 | 277 |
| 12:25–33 | 51 | 23:6 | 277 |
| 13 | 51 | 23:12 | 281 |
| 14 | 206 | 24:14–16 | 277 |
| 18 | 51 | 25:6–7 | 285 |
| 22:49 | 281 | 25:9–10 | 285 |
| | | 26:1–3 | 279 |
| 2 Kings | | 26:10 | 145 |
| 1:4 | 28 | 27:13 | 285 |
| 1:6 | 28 | 28–33 | 75 |
| 1:16 | 28 | 30:10 | 145 |
| 3 | 51 | 30:18–19 | 285 |
| 11:18 | 33 | 32:7 | 107 |
| 18–19 | 181 | 33:13–14a | 279 |
| 21:16 | 109 | 33:17 | 279 |
| | | 33:20 | 279 |
| Isaiah | | 34:16 | 80 |
| 1 | 87 | 35:1–2 | 285 |
| 1–12 | 75 | 35:5 | 32 |
| 1:2 | 90 | 35:9–10 | 285 |
| 1:20 | 90 | 36–37 | 181 |
| 1:26–31 | 87 | 40–66 | 200 |
| 2 | 90 | 40:1–52:10 | 291 |
| 2–33 | 87 | 40:2 | 59, 61 |
| 2:1 | 87 | 40:12–31 | 17, 186 |
| 2:2–3 | 278 | 40:17 | 285 |
| 2:2–4 | 86–87 | 40:26 | 59 |
| 2:3 | 88 | 41:1 | 277 |
| 2:5 | 88 | 41:1–5 | 277 |
| 2:5–6a | 88 | 42:1–4 | 278, 284 |
| 2:6–22 | 87, 89–90 | 42:4 | 277 |
| 2:7–8 | 86–87, 89 | 42:6 | 307 |
| 5:26 | 279 | 42:7 | 32 |
| 6 | 156 | 42:10 | 277 |
| 6:9 | 74, 284 | 42:12 | 277 |
| 6:11–13 | 279 | 42:15 | 277 |

| | | | |
|---|---|---|---|
| 43:1–7 | 278 | 59:14 | 145 |
| 45:1–6 | 278 | 60:1–3 | 274 |
| 45:3 | 279 | 60:1–22 | 278–79 |
| 46:11 | 278 | 60:3 | 279 |
| 46:12–13 | 278 | 60:4 | 59, 279 |
| 47:6 | 230 | 60:6–7 | 279 |
| 49:1 | 281, 294 | 60:7 | 279 |
| 49:4 | 294 | 60:9 | 279, 281 |
| 49:5 | 294 | 60:12 | 279 |
| 49:6 | 284, 294, 307 | 60:13 | 279 |
| 49:14 | 294 | 60:17 | 279 |
| 49:18 | 59 | 62:12–15 | 274 |
| 50:4–9 | 232 | 63:1 | 278 |
| 50:5–6 | 291 | 63:7–64:11 | 228 |
| 50:6 | 231–33, 236, 238 | 65:17 | 280 |
| 50:8 | 291 | 65:19–25 | 280 |
| 51–52 | 189 | 66 | 87 |
| 51:5 | 281 | 66:1–22 | 278 |
| 52:13 | 294, 306 | 66:18–24 | 278 |
| 52:14 | 278, 294, 306 | 66:19 | 281 |
| 52:14–15 | 291 | 66:22 | 280 |
| 52:15 | 278 | 66:23–24 | 280 |
| 53 | 207 | | |
| 53:3–4 | 307 | Jeremiah | |
| 53:4 | 291 | 1 | 156 |
| 53:5 | 307 | 1:5 | 294, 307 |
| 53:6 | 291 | 1:18 | 306 |
| 53:7 | 291, 294 | 1:18–19 | 294 |
| 53:7–8 | 306 | 3:2 | 59 |
| 53:8 | 291 | 5:3–4 | 291 |
| 53:9 | 307 | 5:7–9 | 102 |
| 53:10 | 291 | 7:6 | 107 |
| 53:11 | 306–7 | 9:1 | 102 |
| 53:12 | 307 | 10:9 | 281 |
| 55:3–5 | 285 | 10:19 | 291 |
| 56:1–8 | 170 | 10:20 | 291 |
| 57:2 | 145 | 10:21 | 291 |
| 58:13 | 216 | 10:25 | 291 |
| 59:1–7 | 108 | 11:19 | 291, 294, 306 |
| 59:3 | 108 | 11:20 | 291 |
| 59:3–7 | 108 | 13:20 | 59 |
| 59:4 | 108 | 13:27 | 107 |
| 59:5–6 | 108 | 18:18b | 91 |
| 59:6b | 108 | 20 | 292 |
| 59:7 | 108 | 20:4 | 275 |

| Jeremiah (cont.) | | 18:10 | 109 |
|---|---|---|---|
| 20:7 | 23, 294 | 20:4–5 | 100 |
| 20:8 | 275 | 20:25 | 30 |
| 20:9 | 275 | 21:19 | 101 |
| 20:10 | 294, 306 | 21:22 | 101 |
| 20:12 | 291 | 22 | 16, 93–94, 99, 104–7, 109–10 |
| 20:15–18 | 291 | 22:1 | 99, 102 |
| 22:3 | 108 | 22:1–2 | 100, 102 |
| 22:17 | 108 | 22:1–5 | 100–101 |
| 23:10 | 102 | 22:1–12 | 100–101 |
| 23:14 | 102 | 22:1–16 | 99, 101, 104 |
| 24:9 | 291 | 22:2 | 102 |
| 25–51 | 291 | 22:3 | 102, 107 |
| 25:1 | 281 | 22:3–5 | 100, 102 |
| 25:9 | 291 | 22:4 | 102, 107 |
| 25:11–12 | 307 | 22:5 | 102 |
| 28:4 | 230 | 22:6 | 95, 100–102, 104–7 |
| 29:17–18 | 291 | 22:6–7 | 100, 104–6 |
| 32:15 | 300 | 22:6–8 | 104 |
| 36 | 79 | 22:6–12 | 16, 91, 93–95, 99–102, 106–7, 109–10 |
| 37–38 | 205 | | |
| 38 | 204–6, 208–9 | 22:7 | 102–5, 106 |
| 38:22 | 321 | 22:8 | 102–3, 105–7 |
| 38:23 | 321 | 22:9 | 95, 100–106 |
| 38:28 | 18, 206 | 22:9b–11 | 105–6 |
| 39:1 | 206 | 22:10 | 102–5, 106 |
| 41:16 | 321 | 22:11 | 102–7 |
| 42:18 | 291 | 22:12 | 95, 100–107 |
| 43:6 | 321 | 22:13 | 95, 100, 102–4, 107 |
| 45 | 79, 300 | 22:13–14 | 100–101 |
| 45:28 | 206 | 22:13–16 | 100–103 |
| | | 22:14 | 101, 103 |
| Ezekiel | | 22:15 | 103 |
| 1–3 | 156 | 22:15–16 | 101 |
| 3:18 | 28 | 22:16 | 101, 103 |
| 7:26 | 91 | 22:17 | 99 |
| 7:20 | 33 | 22:17–22 | 99, 101, 103 |
| 8:5 | 59 | 22:23 | 99 |
| 9:9 | 109 | 22:23–29 | 99–101, 103 |
| 16:17 | 33 | 22:23–31 | 99 |
| 16:27 | 107 | 22:24 | 101 |
| 16:38 | 108 | 22:25 | 101, 103 |
| 16:43 | 107 | 22:25–29 | 91 |
| 16:58 | 107 | 22:26 | 101, 103, 107 |
| 18:5–18 | 109 | 22:27 | 101, 103 |

| | | | |
|---|---|---|---|
| 22:28 | 101, 103 | 1:9 | 147 |
| 22:29 | 101, 103 | 1:10 | 150 |
| 22:30–31 | 103 | 1:11 | 147 |
| 23:14 | 33 | 1:12 | 150 |
| 23:36 | 100 | 1:13 | 147 |
| 23:45 | 108 | 1:14–15 | 150 |
| 24:6–8 | 109 | 2:1 | 147 |
| 33:8 | 28 | 2:2–3 | 150 |
| 33:14 | 28 | 2:4 | 147 |
| 33:25 | 108 | 2:5 | 150 |
| 36:18 | 108 | 2:6 | 143, 146–47 |
| 43:18–19 | 197 | 2:6–16 | 48, 147 |
| 44:8–16 | 197 | 2:7 | 143, 148 |
| | | 2:8 | 143 |
| Hosea | | 2:9 | 150 |
| 1–3 | 75 | 2:12 | 148 |
| 2 | 75 | 2:13–16 | 150 |
| 2:16 | 59, 61 | 3:3–8 | 82 |
| 4–11 | 75 | 3:4 | 82 |
| 6:5 | 85 | 3:6 | 83 |
| 6:9 | 107 | 3:8 | 82, 90, 150 |
| 10:7 | 86 | 3:9–10 | 148 |
| 10:15 | 86 | 3:10 | 145 |
| 12 | 44, 83 | 3:11 | 150 |
| 12:3–6 | 83–84 | 3:14 | 147 |
| 12:10 | 85 | 3:14–15 | 150 |
| 12:11 | 85 | 4:1 | 143, 148 |
| 12:12 | 85 | 4:2 | 150 |
| 12:13–14 | 85 | 4:4 | 147 |
| 12:14 | 85 | 4:4–5 | 148 |
| 12:16 | 85 | 4:6–12 | 150 |
| 12–14 | 75, 85 | 4:13 | 83 |
| 14 | 75 | 5:4–6 | 148 |
| | | 5:7 | 142 |
| Joel | | 5:10 | 148 |
| 4:19 | 108 | 5:11 | 143, 148 |
| | | 5:12 | 143, 146–47 |
| Amos | | 5:14–15 | 148 |
| 1:1 | 81 | 5:15 | 142 |
| 1:2 | 81–82 | 5:16–17 | 150 |
| 1:3 | 147 | 5:18–20 | 150 |
| 1:3–2:3 | 148 | 5:21–22 | 142 |
| 1:5 | 150 | 5:21–25 | 148 |
| 1:6 | 147 | 5:24 | 142 |
| 1:7–8 | 150 | 5:26 | 33 |

| | | | |
|---|---|---|---|
| *Amos (cont.)* | | Zechariah | |
| 6:1 | 82, 148, 150 | 2:1 | 59 |
| 6:3 | 148, 150 | 5:1 | 59 |
| 6:6 | 143 | 5:9 | 59 |
| 6:7 | 150 | 6:1 | 59 |
| 6:9–11 | 150 | | |
| 6:12 | 142 | Malachi | |
| 6:14 | 150 | 3:16 | 80 |
| 7:1–9 | 147 | | |
| 7:12 | 147 | Psalms | |
| 7:17 | 151 | 2:10 | 32 |
| 8:1–3 | 147 | 7:15 | 116 |
| 8:3 | 151 | 9:15 | 116 |
| 8:4 | 143, 148 | 14:2 | 32 |
| 8:5 | 142, 148 | 21:17 | 274 |
| 8:6 | 143, 148 | 26:2 | 26 |
| 8:8 | 151 | 26:10 | 107 |
| 9:1–4 | 147, 151 | 32:8 | 32 |
| 9:3 | 82 | 35:7–8 | 116 |
| | | 36:3 | 32 |
| Micah | | 36:4 | 32 |
| 1–3 | 89 | 53:2 | 32 |
| 3:10 | 100 | 53:3 | 32 |
| 3:12 | 87 | 57:6 | 116 |
| 4:1–3 | 86–87, 89 | 62 | 189 |
| 4:4 | 90 | 77 | 228 |
| 4:4–5 | 88 | 79:3 | 108 |
| 4:5 | 89 | 79:6–7 | 291 |
| 4:14 | 231 | 94:8 | 32 |
| 5:6–7 | 90 | 104 | 17, 186 |
| 5:8–9 | 89 | 106:38 | 109 |
| 5:9–14 | 86–87, 89–90 | 119:99 | 32 |
| 5:15 | 89 | 119:150 | 107 |
| 6:7 | 36 | 137 | 19 |
| | | 137 | 322–23 |
| Nahum | | 137:14 | 323 |
| 1:2 | 217–18 | | |
| | | Job | |
| Habakkuk | | 1:1 | 36 |
| 1:5 | 216 | 1:8 | 36 |
| 2:12 | 100 | 2:3 | 36 |
| | | 3:3–11 | 291 |
| Zephaniah | | 4:2 | 26 |
| 1:17 | 109 | 16:9 | 233 |
| 3:3–4 | 91 | 16:10 | 230–31, 233, 238 |

| | | | |
|---|---|---|---|
| 17:11 | 107 | 11:31 | 151 |
| 38–42 | 186 | 12:2 | 151 |
| | | 12:5 | 145–46 |
| Proverbs | | 12:6 | 146 |
| 1 | 249 | 12:7 | 151 |
| 1:1 | 244, 249 | 12:10 | 145–46 |
| 1:1–5 | 249–50 | 12:12 | 146 |
| 1:3 | 32, 142 | 12:21 | 151 |
| 1:8 | 146 | 12:26 | 146 |
| 1:8–17 | 109 | 13:5 | 145 |
| 1:18–19 | 151 | 13:7 | 146 |
| 1:33 | 150–51 | 14:13 | 127, 143 |
| 2:9 | 142 | 14:32 | 146, 151 |
| 2:22 | 151 | 14:35 | 32 |
| 3:5 | 149 | 15:6 | 151 |
| 3:19–20 | 146 | 15:8 | 143 |
| 3:23 | 149 | 15:8–9 | 146 |
| 5:22 | 146 | 15:10 | 151 |
| 6:17 | 109 | 15:24 | 32, 146 |
| 8:9 | 145 | 15:28 | 145 |
| 8:20 | 142 | 15:29 | 145–46 |
| 8:22–31 | 146 | 16:4 | 151 |
| 9:7 | 146 | 16:8 | 142 |
| 9:9 | 145 | 16:11 | 142 |
| 10–29 | 134 | 16:20 | 32 |
| 10:1 | 244 | 16:23 | 32 |
| 10:5 | 32 | 17:2 | 32 |
| 10:6 | 146 | 17:8 | 32 |
| 10:9 | 149 | 17:23 | 146 |
| 10:11 | 145–46 | 17:26 | 146 |
| 10:15b | 149 | 18:5 | 142, 146 |
| 10:19 | 32 | 18:10 | 150 |
| 10:20 | 145–46 | 18:11 | 149 |
| 10:21 | 145 | 18:12 | 151 |
| 10:23 | 107 | 18:19 | 147 |
| 10:30 | 151 | 18:26 | 149 |
| 10:31 | 145 | 19:12a | 150 |
| 10:32 | 145–46 | 19:14 | 32 |
| 11:1 | 142 | 19:23 | 151 |
| 11:5 | 149 | 19:28 | 146 |
| 11:9 | 145 | 20:2a | 150 |
| 11:11 | 146 | 20:7 | 145 |
| 11:21 | 151 | 20:13 | 32 |
| 11:23 | 145–46 | 20:22 | 232–33, 236–37 |
| 11:28 | 145, 149 | 20:23 | 142, 230 |

## Proverbs (cont.)

| | | | |
|---|---|---|---|
| 21:3 | 142–43 | Ruth | |
| 21:4 | 146 | 1 | 165, 168 |
| 21:7 | 146, 151 | 1:1 | 169 |
| 21:10 | 146 | 1:2 | 169 |
| 21:11 | 32 | 1:4 | 169 |
| 21:12 | 32 | 1:8–9 | 165 |
| 21:15 | 142, 145 | 1:9 | 165 |
| 21:16 | 32 | 1:11–13 | 165 |
| 21:17 | 143, 149 | 1:15 | 165 |
| 21:27 | 107, 143, 146 | 1:16–17 | 165, 170 |
| 22:1 | 123 | 1:19 | 169 |
| 22:7 | 149 | 1:22 | 170 |
| 22:22 | 143 | 2 | 167 |
| 23:29–35 | 143 | 2:1 | 168 |
| 24:9 | 107 | 2:9 | 168 |
| 24:21–22 | 150 | 2:10 | 170 |
| 24:26 | 145 | 2:10–11 | 168 |
| 25:1 | 244 | 2:15–16 | 168 |
| 25:26 | 146 | 2:19 | 168 |
| 26:6–7 | 116 | 2:23 | 170 |
| 26:27 | 116 | 3:7 | 168, 170 |
| 28:1 | 146 | 3:10–11 | 170 |
| 28:2 | 147 | 3:10–12 | 168 |
| 28:11 | 149 | 4 | 165 |
| 28:20 | 149 | 4:1–2 | 170 |
| 28:22 | 149 | 4:1–12 | 168 |
| 28:25 | 149 | 4:5 | 166 |
| 28:26 | 116, 149 | 4:10 | 166 |
| 29:1 | 151 | 4:12 | 166–67 |
| 29:7 | 145–46 | 4:13 | 167–68 |
| 29:16 | 147 | 4:14–15 | 169 |
| 29:18 | 147 | 4:17 | 166, 169 |
| 29:25 | 149 | 4:18–22 | 166 |
| 29:27 | 145 | Ecclesiastes | |
| 30:1 | 147 | 1:1 | 113 |
| 30:14 | 143 | 1:9 | 7, 224 |
| 31:4 | 143 | 1:12–2:26 | 244 |
| 31:8 | 143 | 1:18 | 126 |
| 31:9 | 142 | 6 | 123–24 |
| 31:19 | 60 | 6:3 | 125 |
| 31:20 | 60, 62 | 6:12 | 123 |
| 31:23 | 170 | 7 | 123 |
| 31:31 | 60 | 7:1 | 123–26 |
| | | 7:1–3 | 16, 123 |

| | | | |
|---|---|---|---|
| 7:2 | 125–26 | Daniel | |
| 7:2–3 | 128 | 8:3 | 59 |
| 7:3 | 126 | 9:2 | 307 |
| 7:26 | 60 | 9:13 | 32 |
| 8:16–17 | 126 | 10:5 | 59 |
| 10:5 | 116, 119 | | |
| 10:5–7 | 115, 118 | Ezra | |
| 10:5–11 | 16, 116 | 1 | 197 |
| 10:6 | 116 | 1:1 | 307 |
| 10:6–7 | 116–17, 121 | 7–10 | 181 |
| 10:7 | 116 | | |
| 10:8 | 116–21 | 1 Chronicles | |
| 10:8–9 | 119 | 1:7 | 281 |
| 10:9 | 117–18 | 1:32 | 59 |
| 10:10 | 119–20 | 7:14 | 59 |
| 10:11 | 121 | 21:16 | 59 |
| 10:12–14 | 121 | 22:9 | 250 |
| 12:10 | 113 | | |
| 12:11 | 113 | 2 Chronicles | |
| | | 3:1 | 29 |
| Lamentations | | 13:23 | 159 |
| 1 | 180, 228 | 20:35–37 | 281 |
| 1:1 | 230 | 23:17 | 33 |
| 1:14 | 230 | | |
| 2 | 228 | Ancient Near Eastern Texts | |
| 3 | 228–29, 231 | | |
| 3:1–24 | 229 | Code of Hammurabi | |
| 3:16 | 230 | 209–214 | 235 |
| 3:25 | 229–30 | | |
| 3:25–33 | 18, 225, 228–31, 233, 238–39 | Deuterocanonical Books | |
| 3:26 | 229–30 | | |
| 3:27 | 229–30 | Sirach | |
| 3:28 | 230 | 11:19 | 145 |
| 3:29 | 230–31 | 11:21 | 145 |
| 3:30 | 230–34, 236, 238 | 11:28 | 124 |
| 3:31 | 230 | 12:13 | 122 |
| 3:32 | 230 | 47:19–20 | 244 |
| 3:33 | 230 | | |
| 4 | 228 | 2 Esdras | |
| 4:13 | 109 | 6:42 | 276 |
| 5:20 | 294 | | |
| 5:22 | 294 | 4 Maccabees | |
| | | 16 | 36 |
| Esther | | | |
| 6:7–11 | 116 | | |

## Pseudepigrapha

Book of Jubilees
17     36

## Dead Sea Scrolls

1QapGen ar (Genesis Apocryphon)
19:14–20     18, 218

1QIsa$^a$     232

1QpHab
1:16–2:5     216

1QS
6:27     221
7:7–16     18, 222
10–11     18, 220
10:9–17     221
10:14     18
7:7–16     18

4QNum$^b$     18, 213

4QDeut$^n$     18, 213

4Q417
2 I, 10–12     127

4Q418     127–28

11QT
11–29     18, 220
54:8–18     216
65:2–5     18, 215

CD (Cairo Genizah Copy of the Damascus Document)
9:2–8     18, 217
9:9–10     221
10:14–17     18, 215
10:17–19     18, 216
14:17–22     18, 222

## Ancient Jewish Writers

Josephus, *Jewish Antiquities*
4.280     236

## New Testament

Matthew
5:38     233–35
5:38–39     233, 236, 238
5:39     233, 236–37
5:39b–41     237
5:40–42     234
11:25     275
12:15–21     284
13:14     284

Mark
15:39     207

Luke
8:8–9     284

Acts
2     170
13:46–47     284

Galatians
1:1     275

Hebrews
11     36

James
2     36

## Early Christian Writers

Tertullian, *Adversus Marcionem*
4.16     235

## Rabbinic Works

b. Gittin
36b     237

b. Shabbat
    88b                        237

m. Baba Qamma
    8:1                         236

# Index of Modern Authors

| | | | |
|---|---|---|---|
| Ackerman, Susan | 58 | Batto, Bernard F. | 29 |
| Ackroyd, Peter R. | 86 | Bauer, Dale M. | 188 |
| Adam, Klaus-Peter | 16, 91 | Bauks, Michaela | 28 |
| Adams, Jim W. | 161 | Baumgarten, Joseph M. | 222 |
| Adorno, Theodor W. | 2 | Bautch, Richard | 191 |
| Aichele, George | 6, 201, 312 | Beal, Timothy K. | 178, 318–19 |
| Akoto, Dorothy B. E. A. | 119 | Beebee, Thomas O. | 153 |
| Albeck, Chanoch | 219 | Ben Zvi, Ehud | 74–75, 84, 86, 88–89 |
| Alkier, Stefan | 55, 227–28, 239 | Berges, Ulrich F. | 87, 228 |
| Allen, Graham | 266–67 | Bergmann, Claudia D. | 196 |
| Alston, William P. | 158–61, 165 | Berlin, Adele | 229–30 |
| Alter, Robert | 167–68 | Bernstein, Moshe J. | 214–15, 218 |
| Andersen, Francis I. | 164 | Beuken, Willem A. M. | 9 |
| Anderson, Cheryl B. | 312 | Birdsong, Shelley L. | 197 |
| Aragay, Mireia | 264–66 | Bier, Miriam J. | 182, 229 |
| Aschkenasy, Nehama | 182 | Birnbaum, Elisabeth | 247 |
| Auerbach, Erich | 129 | Blanchot, Maurice | 81 |
| Austin, John L. | 157–61 | Blenkinsopp, Joseph | 32, 37 |
| Avalos, Hector | 261, 263, 271–72 | Block, Daniel I. | 56, 93–94 |
| Bail, Ulrike | 232 | Bloom, Harold | 266–67, 269 |
| Bakhtin, Mikhail M. | 2–3, 7, 9, 17, 45, 76, 132, 137, 139–41, 144, 150, 151, 175–84, 186–89, 229, 246, 266 | Blum, Erhard | 75 |
| | | Boase, Elizabeth | 181, 229 |
| | | Boecker, Hans Jochen | 231–32 |
| Bal, Mieke | 194, 203 | Bonhoeffer, Dietrich | 19, 289–90, 295–301, 305–9 |
| Baltzer, Dieter | 110 | | |
| Baltzer, Klaus | 277 | Booth, Wayne C. | 194 |
| Bandstra, Barry L. | 59 | Bovati, Pietro | 82 |
| Banks, Adelle M. | 321 | Boyarin, Daniel | 8, 225 |
| Barner, Ashley J. | 272 | Breed, Brennan W. | 245–47 |
| Bartelt, Andrew H. | 75 | Bridgeman, Valerie | 19, 311, 317, 322–23 |
| Barthel, Jörg | 75 | Briggs, Richard S. | 161 |
| Barthes, Roland | 2, 4–5, 137–38, 175, 195–96, 198, 200, 265, 267, 309 | Brooke, George J. | 214 |
| | | Brueggemann, Walter | 14, 188, 284 |
| Barton, John | 23, 29–30, 44, 82, 118 | Buber, Martin | 7, 178, 235 |
| Basser, Herbert W. | 237–38 | Burgess, Jonathan S. | 201 |

# Index of Modern Authors

Buss, Martin J. 160
Busse, Kristina 264–65, 267–70
Callaway, Mary C. 205
Carr, David M. 6, 74, 200
Carrington, André 267–68
Carroll, Robert P. 291
Cartwright, Michael G. 186
Chandler, Daniel 5, 14, 290
Charlesworth, James H. 220–21
Chatman, Seymour Benjamin 153, 194
Cheon, Samuel 12
Childs, Brevard S. 8, 170, 188
Chokshi, Niraj 309
Chong, Timothy K. H. 303
Claassens, L. Juliana M. 181, 188
Clark, Katerina 178–80
Clayton, Jay 135, 138–39, 175–77, 182
Clements, Roland E. 9
Coates, Ruth 178
Coats, George W. 46
Coleridge, Samuel Taylor 203–4
Contino, Paul J. 176, 178
Cooper, Alan 10
Craffert, Pieter F. 79–80
Crawford, Sidnie A. White 213–14, 221–23
Crenshaw, James L. 39, 93, 124, 126, 131, 134
Cross, Frank Moore 212
Cruise, Charles E. 279
Crüsemann, Frank 235
Culler, Jonathan D. 2–6, 139, 175, 202
Cummins, John 262, 271, 273, 276, 280
Davidson, Steed Vernyl 18–19, 261
Davies, Eryl W. 24
Davies, Philip R. 223
Day, John 27–28, 33
De La Torre, Miguel A. 313, 317
Decker, Hans 16–17, 113
deClaissé-Walford, Nancy L. 11
Dell, Katharine J. 293
Dentith, Simon 137, 139–41, 144
Derrida, Jacques 2, 77, 137–38, 176
Dewrell, Heath D. 36
Dimant, Devorah 212
Dobbs-Allsopp, F. W. 79
Dostoevsky, Fyodor 176, 179–80
Dozeman, Thomas B. 46
Draper, Hal 255–56
Dube, Musa W. 312–13, 317
Dubrow, Heather 153
Dufault-Hunter, Erin 71
Duff, William 182
Dumas, André 305
Ebner, Martin 233
Edenburg, Cynthia 56, 68, 314–16, 320
Eidevall, Göran 82
Eissfeldt, Otto 124, 164
Elgvin, Torleif 127
Elliger, Karl 96
Elliott-Binns, L. E. 93
Emerson, Caryl 178–79
Engelken, Karen 58–59
Eshel, Esther 213, 223
Eshel, Hanan 223
Eslinger, Lyle 6, 138, 199
Evans, Craig A. 11
Evans, Donald D. 161
Evans, Paul S. 181
Exum, J. Cheryl 53, 67–68, 72
Fauconnier, Gilles 18, 201, 242, 248–51, 254, 259
Felch, Susan M. 176, 178
Ferry, Joëlle 87
Fichtner, J. 131
Fiedler, Peter 237
Finlay, Tim 17, 153
Fisch, Harold 166–67
Fish, Stanley 2
Fishbane, Michael 7–8, 16, 68, 86, 227, 231, 289
Fitzmyer, Joseph A. 127, 218
Fleming, John V. 261, 271
Flint, Valerie I. J. 271
Fohrer, Georg 87, 92
Fokkelman, Jan P. 68
Fontaine, Carole R. 124
Forbes, A. Dean 164
Foucault, Michel 2
Fowler, Alastair 153

| | | | |
|---|---|---|---|
| Fox, Michael V. | 118, 122, 134, 149, 151 | Hegel, G. W. F. | 2 |
| Freedman, David Noel | 121 | Heine, Heinrich | 18, 255–58 |
| Frendo, Anthony | 120–21 | Hempel, Charlotte | 222 |
| Frevel, Christian | 228, 231 | Hendel, Ronald | 37 |
| Friedman, Susan S. | 199 | Hermisson, Hans-Jürgen | 232 |
| Fuchs, Esther | 168–69 | Hermann, Matthias | 18, 255, 257–58 |
| Gabler, Johann Philipp | 14 | Heym, Stefan | 258 |
| Gadamer, Hans-Georg | 2 | Hibbard, J. Todd | 15, 23 |
| Gafney, Wil | 320–21 | Holladay, William L. | 291 |
| Galambush, Julie | 189 | Holquist, Michael | 178–80 |
| Gaon, Amram | 214 | Hölscher, Gustav | 94 |
| Gardner, Kirsten H. | 16, 53 | Holt, Else K. | 84, 205 |
| Gauvin, Mitchell J. | 38 | Hong, Sung-hee | 305, 307 |
| Gench, Frances Taylor | 189 | Hooper-Greenhill, Eilean | 203 |
| Genette, Gérard | 175, 196–97, 201 | Horgan, Maurya P. | 216 |
| Gerhart, Mary | 153 | Hossfeld, Frank-Lothar | 100–101 |
| Gerstenberger, Erhard S. | 14 | House, Paul R. | 194 |
| Giere, Samuel D. | 202 | Howard, Cameron | 189 |
| Gillmayr-Bucher, Susanne | 18, 181, 241 | Hudson, Don Michael | 63 |
| Gimmel, Millie | 262, 265, 270–72 | Irwin, William | 3 |
| Ginzberg, Louis | 253 | Iser, Wolfgang | 2, 198 |
| Goldingay, John | 87 | Jacob, Benno | 235 |
| Gordon, Robert P. | 27, 32–33 | Jacobs, Mignon R. | 87, 89 |
| Graf, Karl Heinrich | 92 | Jakobson, Roman | 2, 77 |
| Graham, David A. | 321 | Jarrett, Charles E. | 161 |
| Green, Barbara | 9, 45, 176–80, 183 | Jensen, Klaus Bruhn | 201 |
| Grohmann, Marianne | 1, 18, 225, 228 | Jin, Eun-Young | 302–3 |
| Gross, Andrew D. | 215 | Johnson, Benjamin J. M. | 181 |
| Gruber, Mayer | 84 | Johnson, Mark | 201 |
| Grünwaldt, Klaus | 92 | Jong, Matthijs J. de | 74 |
| Gunkel, Hermann | 158 | Joosten, Jan | 110 |
| Habermas, Jürgen | 2 | Kaminsky, Joel | 278 |
| Halpern, Baruch | 291 | Kang-Hamilton, Samjung | 300, 306 |
| Hamidović, David | 222 | Kant, Immanuel | 2, 25 |
| Hamilton, Mark W. | 300, 306 | Katongole, Emmanuel | 313, 317–18 |
| Harding, Vincent | 313, 315–18, 323–24 | Keller, Catherine | 263, 271 |
| Harper, William R. | 133 | Kelly, Joseph Ryan | 30–31 |
| Harrington, Daniel | 127 | Kim, Eung-gyo | 304 |
| Hartenstein, Friedhelm | 74 | Kim, Hyun Chul Paul | 1, 12, 19, 59, 289, 293, 295, 309 |
| Hatina, Thomas R. | 193 | | |
| Hays, Christopher B. | 181 | Kim, Kyung-Hee | 302–3 |
| Hays, Richard B. | 13, 55, 57, 225, 235–36 | Kim, Mi-yeon | 303 |
| | | Kim, Soo J. | 17–18, 191 |
| Hazony, Yoram | 30 | Kindt, Tom | 194 |
| Heffelfinger, Katie | 189 | Klaiber, Isabell | 193 |

Kling, August  262–65, 271–72, 274–76, 284–86
Klostermann, August  92
Knierim, Rolf P.  8, 14, 153–54, 306, 308
Koch, Klaus  117–18
Koenen, Klaus  231–32
Kövecses, Zoltán  206
Kratz, Reinhard G.  10, 74, 291
Kristeva, Julia  1–3, 5–7, 16, 54, 76–78, 80–81, 83, 137–39, 175–78, 184–85, 195–96, 201, 204, 208–9, 225, 246, 266, 289
Kugel, James L.  80, 114, 124–26, 219
Kutscher, Edward Yechezkel  232
Kwon, Jiseong James  10
Lacan, Jacques  2, 76, 176
Lachmann, Renate  248
Lakoff, George  201
Landy, Francis  16, 73, 75, 80–81, 83–84, 88, 90
Lang, Bernhard  25
Langer, Gerhard  7
Lapsley, Jacqueline E.  188–89
Lee, Archie C. C.  12
Lee, Eun-Ae  308
Lee, Sung-Il  301
Lehman, Ilana Elkad  201
Leuchter, Mark  74
Levenson, John D.  36
Levinas, Emmanuel  81
Levine, Etan  231
Lévi-Strauss, Claude  2, 166–67
Licht, Jacob  221
Liew, Tat-siong Benny  12
Linville, James R.  82
Liss, Hannah  74
Longman, Tremper, III  118, 126, 128
Lopez, Davina  263–64
López, Gemma  265–66
Lundbom, Jack R.  298
Luz, Ulrich  234, 237
Lyons, Michael A.  92–94
Machiela, Daniel A.  218
Machinist, Peter  74
Macintosh, A. A.  85
Mai, Hans-Peter  201
Mandolfo, Carleen  10, 43, 189
Mann, Steve T.  161, 164–65
Margolin, Uri  242–43, 249
Marsh, Charles  286
Martin, Elaine  25
Marx, Karl  2
Mathys, Hans-Peter  98
McKinstry, S. Jaret  188
McLaughlin, John L.  17, 58, 131–36, 143–44, 149, 151
Meek, Russell L.  6
Meier, John P.  234
Mein, Andrew  91
Mekhon ha-Midrash ha-Mevo'ar  124–25
Melugin, Roy F.  9
Metso, Sarianna  222–23
Mettinger, Tryggve N. D.  23, 26–28
Meyers, Carol  33–34
Meynet, Roland  82
Mihailovic, Alexander  178
Milgrom, Jacob  91, 96
Milhou, Alain  261–62, 271, 286
Milik, J. T.  223
Miller, Charles William  180
Miller, Geoffrey D.  6, 191, 199
Miller, Patrick D.  10
Milstein, Sara J.  82
Mirenayat, Sayyed Ali  201
Miscall, Peter D.  205, 312
Moberly, R. W. L.  28, 31, 192
Möller, Karl  82
Morgan, Robert  44
Morgenstern, J.  96
Mowinckel, Sigmund  164
Moyise, Steve  226–27
Mroczek, Eva  75
Muilenburg, James  8
Müller, Hans-Harald  194
Müller, Wolfgang  242–43
Müllner, Ilse  68
Nadella, Raj  180
Nashim  219
Neudecker, Reinhard  237–38
Neusner, Jacob  7, 19

| | | | |
|---|---|---|---|
| Newsom, Carol A. | 43, 180, 186–88, 191 | Rogerson, John W. | 24 |
| Nguyen, Kim Lan | 229 | Rollston, Christopher A. | 73 |
| Niditch, Susan | 34, 56 | Rothstein, Eric | 135, 138–39, 175–77, 182 |
| Nielsen, Kirsten | 290 | | |
| Nihan, Cristophe | 92, 98 | Roudiez, Leon S. | 175–76 |
| Nitzan, B. | 216 | Ruiz, Jean-Pierre | 261, 272–73 |
| Nogalski, James D. | 10, 75 | Sadler, Rodney S., Jr. | 322 |
| Noth, Martin | 42, 46 | Samely, Alexander | 238 |
| Nyengele, M. Fulgence | 12 | Samuel, Geoffrey | 80 |
| O'Brien, Julia M. | 89 | Sanders, James A. | 8, 11 |
| O'Connor, Kathleen M. | 293–94 | Sanders, Seth L. | 74 |
| O'Day, Gail R. | 199 | Sandoval, Timothy J. | 17, 119, 131, 148 |
| Oderberg, David S. | 161 | Sarna, Nahum M. | 7 |
| Oeming, Manfred | 235 | Saussure, Ferdinand de | 2, 137 |
| Ogden, Graham | 127 | Sawyer, John F. A. | 276, 283–85 |
| Oliver, Kelly | 76, 81 | Schaeffer, Jean-Marie | 153 |
| Ollenburger, Ben C. | 14 | Schiffman, Lawrence H. | 18, 211–12, 214–17, 220–23 |
| Olson, Dennis T. | 188 | | |
| Oropeza, B. J. | 91 | Schniedewind, William M. | 74 |
| Orr, Mary | 3–4, 6 | Scholem, Gershon G. | 214 |
| Otto, Eckart | 91–92, 97, 235 | Schorsch, Stefan | 58 |
| Qimron, Elisha | 215, 220–21 | Searle, John R. | 158–60 |
| Quash, Ben | 188 | Segal, Michael | 219 |
| Paden, William E. | 44 | Sekine, Seizo | 30 |
| Park-Taylor, Geoffrey H. | 205 | Sharp, Carolyn J. | 205 |
| Paton, L. B. | 93 | Sheppard, Gerald T. | 131–32 |
| Paul, Shalom | 290–92 | Ska, Jean Louis | 27, 36 |
| Peterson, Brian Neil | 110 | Slater, Peter | 187 |
| Pfister, Manfred | 206 | Smith, Duane E. | 28 |
| Phillips, Gary A. | 6, 191, 201 | Smith, Mitzi | 321 |
| Piirainen, Elisabeth | 206 | Snyman, Gerrie | 200 |
| Pohlmann, Karl-Friedrich | 92, 99 | Soggin, J. Alberto | 64, 131, 135 |
| Polk, Timothy | 161 | Sommer, Benjamin D. | 6, 10, 13, 19, 43, 78, 138, 191, 199–200, 291 |
| Polzin, Robert | 67 | | |
| Raj, P. Prayer Elmo | 3 | Soofastaei, Elaheh | 201 |
| Rand, Michael C. | 215 | Stackert, Jeffrey | 43, 92 |
| Rendtorff, Rolf | 170 | Stansell, Gary | 75 |
| Richards, I.A. | 2 | Steck, Odil Hannes | 8–9 |
| Richardson, Brian | 209 | Steingrimsson, S. | 107 |
| Ricœur, Paul | 2 | Steins, Georg | 8, 93 |
| Riegner, Irene E. | 64 | Stendahl, Krister | 14 |
| Riffaterre, Michael | 2, 4–6, 16, 77–78, 175 | Sternberg, Meir | 54, 157 |
| | | Stewart, Anne W. | 34, 278 |
| Rimmon-Kenan, Shlomith | 194 | Stewart, Susan | 114, 130 |
| Roberts, J. J. M. | 277 | Stichele, Caroline Vander | 246–47 |

| | | | |
|---|---|---|---|
| Still, Judith | 267–68 | Wilson, Gerald H. | 11 |
| Stipp, Hermann-Josef | 68 | Wilson, Ian D. | 78 |
| Stockton, Ian | 290, 300 | Winkler, Mathias | 244 |
| Stone, Timothy J. | 169–70 | Wolde, Ellen van | 54 |
| Stordalen, Terje | 26 | Wolff, Hans Walter | 17, 82, 85, 131–36, 140–45, 147–51 |
| Strawson, P. F. | 159 | | |
| Strollo, Magan Fullerton | 199 | Wong, Gregory T. K. | 57, 64 |
| Stromberg, Jacob | 9 | Worton, Michael | 267–68 |
| Strugnell, John | 127 | Wright, David P. | 48, 91 |
| Stulman, Louis | 10, 293, 307 | Wünsche, August | 245 |
| Stump, Eleonore | 30 | Yadin, Yigael | 215–16, 219–20 |
| Susswein, Sara | 204 | Yamada, Frank M. | 68 |
| Swanson, Dwight D. | 215 | Yee, Gale A. | 56 |
| Sweeney, Marvin A. | 10, 14–15, 41, 47–48, 51, 87, 158, 169, 199, 226 | Yoder, Christine R. | 151 |
| | | Yoon, David I. | 3–4, 6, 177 |
| Talmon, Shemaryahu | 221 | Yoreh, Tzemach L. | 48 |
| Tannen, Deborah | 267 | Young, Edward | 182 |
| Terrien, Samuel | 17, 131–36, 140 | Yun, Dongju | 19, 289–90, 295–97, 300–309 |
| Throntveit, Mark A. | 251 | | |
| Tov, Emanuel | 214, 223 | Yun, Ji-eun | 304–5 |
| Townes, Emilie M. | 313, 319–20, 324 | Zakovitch, Yair | 6 |
| Trible, Phyllis | 34, 54, 56, 68 | Zamora, Margarita | 261, 263, 271 |
| Tull, Patricia K. | 6, 10, 17, 43, 54, 175, 181, 187, 189, 191, 226 | Zapff, Burkard M. | 87 |
| | | Zevit, Ziony | 27–28 |
| Turner, Mark | 18, 201, 242, 248–51, 254, 259 | Zimmerli, Walther | 92–93, 102 |
| | | Žižek, Slavoj | 53 |
| Ulrich, Eugene | 212, 223 | | |
| Van Seters, John | 48 | | |
| Vorster, Willem S. | 226 | | |
| Walsh, Richard | 312 | | |
| Wellhausen, Julius | 43–45, 92 | | |
| Wendel, Ute | 291 | | |
| Wenham, Gordon J. | 24, 29 | | |
| Werman, C. | 219 | | |
| West, Delno C. | 262–65, 271–72, 274–76, 284–86 | | |
| Westermann, Claus | 11, 36, 229 | | |
| Weyde, Karl W. | 6 | | |
| Whittier, John Greenleaf | 18, 252, 254 | | |
| Whybray, R. Norman | 149 | | |
| Willey, Patricia Tull | 10, 183, 291 | | |
| Williams, Reggie L. | 307 | | |
| Williamson, H. G. M. | 9, 87 | | |
| Willingham, Elizabeth Moore | 270, 283 | | |
| Willis, Amy Merrill | 189 | | |

www.ingramcontent.com/pod-product-compliance
Lightning Source LLC
Chambersburg PA
CBHW051204300426
44116CB00006B/435